Mary E. Elliot, Sarah E. Fuller, Sarah E. Fuller

History of the Department of Massachusetts

Woman's Relief Corps

Mary E. Elliot, Sarah E. Fuller, Sarah E. Fuller

History of the Department of Massachusetts
Woman's Relief Corps

ISBN/EAN: 9783743410633

Manufactured in Europe, USA, Canada, Australia, Japa

Cover: Foto ©ninafisch / pixelio.de

Manufactured and distributed by brebook publishing software (www.brebook.com)

Mary E. Elliot, Sarah E. Fuller, Sarah E. Fuller

History of the Department of Massachusetts

SARAH E. FULLER

First Department President 1879 — 1882
Third Department Secretary 1882 — 1885
First National Secretary 1883, 1884
Third National President 1885, 1886

HISTORY

OF THE

DEPARTMENT OF MASSACHUSETTS

WOMAN'S RELIEF CORPS,

Auxiliary to the
GRAND ARMY OF THE REPUBLIC.

FROM DATE OF ORGANIZATION, FEBRUARY 12, 1879, TO
JANUARY 1, 1895.

WITH APPENDIXES.

PUBLISHED BY ORDER OF THE DEPARTMENT CONVENTION.

BOSTON, MASS.:
E. B. STILLINGS & CO., PRINTERS
55 SUDBURY STREET.
1895.

TABLE OF CONTENTS.

	PAGE
PREFACE	v
INTRODUCTORY	vii
CHAPTER I.— Formation of the Department	9
CHAPTER II.— Outline of the Work and its Early Progress,	23
CHAPTER III.— Memorial Day — Its observance by the Corps — General Orders of Department Presidents	37
CHAPTER IV.— Special Work for the Soldiers' Home	61
CHAPTER V.— Formation of the National Woman's Relief Corps — The trip to Denver and its results — Interest of the Department of Massachusetts in the National Organization	81
CHAPTER VI.— National Encampment Week in Boston, Aug. 11–16, 1890 — Part taken by the Woman's Relief Corps of Massachusetts	111
CHAPTER VII.— Relief and Pensions for Army Nurses — Department Relief Work — Memorial Fund — Aid Extended National W.R.C. Home	141
CHAPTER VIII.— Sketches of the Corps in Massachusetts — A Record of their Work	155
CHAPTER IX.— Biographical Sketches	283
CHAPTER X.— Relations of the Department of Massachusetts Woman's Relief Corps to the Grand Army of the Republic	327
In Memoriam	345
APPENDIX A — Administration of 1895 — Mrs. Eva T. Cook, Department President	353
APPENDIX B — Miscellaneous Information	361
APPENDIX C — Messages	379
APPENDIX D — Receptions and Camp-fires	385
APPENDIX E — Summary of the National Work	391

ILLUSTRATIONS.

Sarah E. Fuller	Frontispiece
E. Florence Barker	facing page 30
M. Susie Goodale	" " 36
Soldiers' Home	" " 60
S. Agnes Parker	" " 68
Emma B. Lowd	" " 110
Mary E. Knowles	" " 116
Augusta A. Wales	" 136
Mary G. Deane	" " 148
Emily L. Clark	" 154
Memorial Building (Milford, Mass.)	" " 218
Clare H. Burleigh	" " 226
Kathrina L. Beedle	" " 316
Pamelia F. Sprague	" 318
Lizabeth A. Turner	" " 320
James F. Meech	" " 326
Eva T. Cook	" " 352
Mary E. Elliot	378

PREFACE.

REALIZING that the Woman's Relief Corps is an organization whose work as an *Auxiliary* to the Grand Army of the Republic will cease when all the comrades are "mustered out," this record has been written for permanent preservation.

At the Fourteenth Annual Convention of the Department of Massachusetts in 1893, a vote was passed that a history of this, the Pioneer Department, be prepared, and the undersigned were subsequently appointed a committee to have charge of the work. The gathering of statistics, compilation from records, correspondence, etc., have required much time and labor, but we trust that the results will show that our efforts have not been useless.

We hope that in the years of the future, some historian may glean from these pages many evidences that the Woman's Relief Corps of Massachusetts honored the brave men of the Grand Army of the Republic.

MARY E. ELLIOT,
SARAH E. FULLER,
E. FLORENCE BARKER,
MARY G. DEANE,
EMILY L. CLARK,
Committee.

INTRODUCTORY.

During the four years of civil war services were rendered by loyal women that were recognized as invaluable to the Union cause. They cared for the sick and wounded on the battle-fields, in camps and hospitals and were active for the soldiers' welfare in all the cities, towns and villages of the North, while the loyal women of the South rendered self-sacrificing service. In several States women were appointed by Governors or Legislatures to officially represent this work in Washington.

The management of large fairs and plans for the distribution of field supplies were intrusted to them, and from 1861 to 1865 millions of dollars were raised by their efforts. In all this varied work the women of Massachusetts nobly bore their part, willing to perform any duty for the brave volunteers.

Though the battle-fields are silent and ambulances have ceased their solemn rounds, though the battle-flags, stained with the blood of the wounded, are folded away and the mighty armies disbanded, the suffering caused by the civil war remains. There are invalid and crippled veterans in thousands of homes. There are many who sigh for loved ones,

> " Who came not with the rest,"

and the protecting care of husband, father, son or brother will never again shield them from want.

When the Grand Army of the Republic was organized, patriotic women again responded to the call of duty. Ladies' Aid Societies, Sewing Circles, Relief Corps, etc., were formed to co-operate with Posts in their beneficent work.

The only recognized auxiliary to the Grand Army of the Republic is the Woman's Relief Corps, the first Department of which was organized in Massachusetts, and the record of its work forms a story that is worthy of permanent preservation.

CHAPTER I.

FORMATION OF THE DEPARTMENT.

ALTHOUGH the various societies co-operating with Posts conducted their work without a uniform plan or system, they were recognized at Department Headquarters of the Grand Army of the Republic, as efficient aids to the several Posts with which they were associated.

Gen. Horace Binney Sargent, during his official visits throughout the State, as Department Commander of the Grand Army of the Republic, in 1878, met on several occasions members of the Ladies' Aid organizations, and became interested in their work. During the latter part of his administration he attended a public gathering under the auspices of E. V. Sumner Post No. 19, of Fitchburg, which the Auxiliary Corps attended. He referred to the badges worn by the members, and inquired why all the women's societies did not adopt a *uniform* badge.

Capt. James F. Meech, Assistant Adjutant-General, was also present at this gathering, and immediately suggested to Mrs. Susie E. Goodrich, President of the Corps in Fitchburg, that a convention of all the societies connected with Posts in Massachusetts be called, and a State organization formed.

As a result of this conversation the following circular was subsequently prepared : —

E. V. SUMNER RELIEF CORPS,
POST 19, G.A.R.,
FITCHBURG, MASS., January, 1879.

It having been suggested that the several Ladies' Aid or Relief Societies connected with Posts of the Grand Army of the Republic of Massachusetts, could be more effective in their works of charity if directed by a similar form of government, and believing it to be the desire of such societies to form a State organization, the members of E. V. Sumner Relief Corps of Fitchburg have voted that a Convention of delegates from each Ladies' Relief organization connected with the Grand Army of the Republic throughout the State, be called to meet in this city for the purpose of forming a State organization.

The Convention will assemble at the hall of Post 19, G.A.R., on Wednesday, Feb. 12, 1879, at 10 o'clock A.M.

Each organization is entitled to three delegates besides the presiding officer, who, by virtue of her office, will be entitled to a seat in the Convention.

A list of delegates from each society should be sent to Mrs. E. H. B. Cummings, Secretary, on or before February 10, that proper arrangements may be made for the comfort of all.

Delegates will be entertained during their stay in the city by the members of E. V. Sumner Relief Corps.

Mrs. GEO. E. GOODRICH,
President.

Mrs. E. H. B. CUMMINGS,
Secretary.

This circular was endorsed by Horace Binney Sargent, Department Commander, and James F. Meech, Assistant Adjutant-General, who obtained through Post Commanders a list of presidents of local societies to whom the circular was issued.

Some of the societies invited did not respond to the call of the circular, but a sufficient number sent representatives to carry out the plan suggested.

Mrs. Susie E. Goodrich of Fitchburg was chosen presiding officer, and Mrs. Kathrina L. Beedle of Cambridge, secretary of the convention, which was held on the date and at the place designated.

Credentials' were presented by delegates from Fitchburg, Cambridge, East Boston, Spencer, Berlin, Leominster, Rockland, Orange, Shelburne Falls, Marlboro, Sterling, Abington, Quincy and Taunton.

The question of forming a State organization was one upon which all the delegates were unanimous in approving, but varied opinions were expressed in regard to the method of organizing.

The plan of holding open meetings was favored by some, while others advocated the adoption of a ritual.

After a lengthy but interesting discussion, it was voted that the new organization should be a secret one with ritualistic forms.

A committee was chosen to submit "a constitution and by-laws for the government of the State organization," viz.: —

Mrs. Mary L. Eastman of Orange, Mrs. Sarah A. Torrey of Cambridge, Mrs. Sarah J. Merchant of Fitchburg, Mrs. Sarah E. Fuller of East Boston and Mrs. Luanna R. Gillett of Shelburne Falls.

After several hours' deliberation, the committee presented a report that formed the basis upon which the Department of Massachusetts Woman's Relief Corps began its work.

Many of the delegates did not feel authorized to sign the constitution, not having received full instructions from the organizations they represented. Twenty-three members enrolled their names, however, and the Woman's State Relief Corps entered upon its mission with this small membership.

But it had a cause that appealed to the sympathy and patriotism of the women of Massachusetts, and with a leader whose heart was consecrated to the work, success was assured.

The election of officers resulted as follows: —

President: Mrs. Sarah E. Fuller, East Boston.

Vice-Presidents: Mrs. Mary L. Eastman, Orange; Mrs. Clara Wheeler, Rockland; Mrs. S. M. Weale, East Boston; Mrs. Ida Wales, Abington; Mrs. Harden, Quincy.

Secretary: Mrs. Kathrina L. Beedle, Cambridge.
Treasurer: Mrs. Sarah J. Merchant, Fitchburg.
Chaplain: Mrs. W. W. Webb, Cambridge.
Conductor: Mrs. Sidney Sibley, Fitchburg.
Guard: Mrs. Pamelia F. Sprague, East Boston.
Board of Directors: Mrs. Hopkins, Rockland; Mrs. Gillett, Shelburne Falls; Mrs. Hemmenway, Shelburne Falls; Mrs. Lackey, Spencer; Mrs. Miles, Cambridge; Mrs. Wheeler, Rockland; Mrs. Winn, Sterling; Mrs. Webb, Cambridge; Mrs. Goodrich, Fitchburg.

The Convention adjourned at midnight, Feb. 12, 1879, having inaugurated on that date, a work in aid of the Grand Army of the Republic, similar to that which loyal women performed for these comrades from 1861 to 1865.

A special meeting of the Department Convention was held at Cambridge, March 13 (1879), and continued in session the following day. Fourteen members were present. The plan outlined at Fitchburg had been endorsed by the Fitchburg, Cambridge, East Boston and Taunton Societies, and they soon after applied for charters.

The Department President and Department Secretary were authorized to institute subordinate Corps, and a ritual service, presented by Mrs. Susie E. Goodrich, was adopted.

It was voted, That uniform badges be issued, which shall be accepted by all subordinate Corps.

A Board of Trustees was elected, viz.: Mrs. Susie E. Goodrich, Fitchburg; Mrs. Sarah A. Torrey, Cambridge; Mrs. Pamelia F. Sprague, East Boston.

The constitution presented at Fitchburg was revised at this Convention, that finally adopted being the following Rules and Regulations, which was the first printed document issued by the Order.

RULES AND REGULATIONS

FOR THE GOVERNMENT OF THE

WOMAN'S STATE RELIEF CORPS,

DEPARTMENT OF MASSACHUSETTS,

GRAND ARMY OF THE REPUBLIC.

As Revised and Adopted by the Department Convention, Held at Cambridge, Mass., March 13 and 14, 1879.

PREAMBLE.

We, the undersigned, Mothers, Wives, Daughters and Sisters of the Soldiers, Sailors and Marines of the late Rebellion, and loyal women interested, do unite to establish a permanent State Association for the purposes and objects herein set forth, with such amendments as we shall from time to time think proper to make.

CHAPTER I.

DEPARTMENT CORPS.

ARTICLE I.
NAME.

This Association shall be known as the Woman's State Relief Corps, Department of Massachusetts, Grand Army of the Republic.

ARTICLE II.
OBJECTS.

To assist members and their families in sickness and distress, and all needy and sick soldiers, sailors and marines, or the widows and orphans of deceased soldiers, sailors and marines; to do all in our power to alleviate their distress, to further the interests of all subordinate Corps, and institute new Corps throughout the State.

ARTICLE III.
OFFICERS.

The officers of the Department Corps shall consist of a President, — Vice-Presidents, a Secretary, Treasurer, Chaplain, Conductor, Guard, and a Board of Directors that shall consist of the above-named officers, and —— members by election,—also a Board of Trustees, consisting of three members.

ARTICLE IV.
MEMBERSHIP.

All members of good standing in subordinate Corps shall be eligible for membership in Department Corps.

ARTICLE V.
MEETINGS.

The regular meeting of the Department Corps shall be held the fourth Wednesday in January.

ARTICLE VI.
ELECTIONS.

The officers shall be elected by written ballot at each annual meeting. A majority of all votes cast shall be requisite for an election.

Any vacancy occurring in the Executive Board shall be filled at a special meeting called for that purpose.

ARTICLE VII.
DUTIES OF OFFICERS.

SECTION 1. It shall be the duty of the President to preside at all meetings of the Department, and exact a strict observance of the Rules and Regulations, appoint all Committees not otherwise provided for, approve all orders drawn on the Treasurer, and attested by the Secretary, give the casting vote in case of a tie, except in case of written or ball ballot, announce the result of all voting; shall have power to call special meetings when necessary, or upon written request of five members; communicate the password to members; and perform such other duties pertaining to her office as are enjoined by the Rules and Regulations of the Order.

SECT. 2. The Vice-Presidents, in the order of their election, shall, in the absence of the President, discharge all duties appertaining to the office of President.

SECT. 3. The Secretary shall keep a true record of all proceedings of the Department Corps, attend to all matters of correspondence and notifications; draw all orders on the Treasurer, approved by the President; shall keep an order book, in which shall be recorded all orders drawn on the Treasurer; a Letter Book; a Black Book, in which shall be recorded the names of all rejected candidates; shall render at the end of each year, a report that shall embrace: the number of applications received, accepted and initiated; number rejected, expelled, or withdrawn; number of deaths; number of members in good standing at the end of the term, and all other statistical items of interest, furnished by the returns of subordinate Corps; and all other duties required for an efficient discharge of the duty of the Secretary, and shall deliver to her successor all properties of the Order in her possession.

SECT. 4. The Treasurer shall keep correct account between the Department and subordinate Corps, receive all moneys, and pay all orders regularly drawn on her signed by the President and attested by the Secretary. She shall make a report, at each meeting, of all receipts and expenditures, and also a report that shall embrace all moneys received on account of Charter fees, *per capita* tax, and other sources, and a statement of how the funds are invested, and deliver to her successor all moneys, books and other property belonging to her office.

SECT. 5. The Chaplain shall conduct the exercises pertaining to her office, and perform such other duties as are enjoined by the Rules and Regulations.

SECT. 6. The Conductor shall see that all persons present are members of the Order, and perform such other duties as may be required of her by the President.

SECT. 7. The Guard shall attend the door and admit none without password unless otherwise ordered by the President.

ARTICLE VIII.
FINANCE COMMITTEE.

SECTION 1. The President shall, immediately on her installation, appoint a Finance Committee, consisting of three members.

SECT. 2. It shall be their duty to inspect and audit the accounts of the Secretary and Treasurer, and other officers or committees charged with the receipt or expenditure of moneys, and report as speedily as possible on all matters committed to them.

ARTICLE IX.
QUORUM.

A majority of the number of members of Department shall constitute a quorum.

ARTICLE X.
PER CAPITA TAX.

SECTION 1. The Department Corps shall assess each subordinate Corps, at the Annual Meeting, a *per capita* tax, returnable quarterly, for every member in good standing.

SECT. 2. Any Corps in arrears for dues or returns shall be excluded from all representation in the Convention of the Department Corps until the same are forwarded.

ARTICLE XI.
UNIFORM.

The Department Corps shall issue uniform badges which shall be adopted by all subordinate Corps.

CHAPTER II.
SUBORDINATE CORPS.
ARTICLE I.
FORMATION.

SECTION 1. Subordinate Corps may be instituted by the authority of the Department President, on the application of not less than ten persons eligible to membership in the Woman's State Relief Corps.

No Corps shall be recognized by the Department Corps unless acting under a legal and unforfeited charter.

SECT. 2. No charter shall be surrendered as long as ten members demand its continuance, nor unless a proposition to surrender charter shall have been made, at a stated meeting, at least four weeks before the time of action, and due notice given to every member of the Corps.

SECT. 3. In case of the surrender or forfeiture of a charter the property of the Department, including Books of Record, Corps Papers and Rituals, shall be immediately turned over to the Department Secretary.

SECT. 4. Subordinate Corps shall be known as ——* Relief Corps No.——† Woman's State Relief Corps, Department of Massachusetts, Grand Army of the Republic.

ARTICLE II.
ELIGIBILITY.

SECTION 1. All loyal ladies interested in the good work shall be eligible to membership in the Woman's State Relief Corps.

ARTICLE III.
MEMBERSHIP.

SECTION 1. Every application for membership shall be made in writing, and vouched for by two members, and shall be referred to a committee of three, neither of whom shall be one of the vouchers, for investigation and report.

SECT. 2. The investigating committee shall render their report at next meeting of corps, after which the President shall give opportunity to any member having objections to the election of the applicant, to state

---
* State name of Post with which connected.
† Next consecutive number in order of application.

the same, after which a ballot with ball ballot shall be had. If, on a count of the balls deposited, more than three black balls are cast, the candidate shall be declared rejected; if three or less black balls are cast, the candidate shall be declared elected.

Sect. 3. Each application for membership shall be accompanied by the initiation fee; the amount of said initiation fee to be determined and controlled by each subordinate Corps.

Sect. 4. Applicants for membership shall be women of good moral character, and at least sixteen years old.

ARTICLE IV.
TRANSFER AND DISCHARGES.

Section 1. Any member having paid all dues, shall receive, upon application to the President, at a meeting of the Corps, a transfer card attested by the Secretary.

By presentation of said transfer card, to any Corps, within one year of date of issue, she may be admitted by a two-thirds vote of said Corps.

Sect. 2. Any member who has paid all dues shall, upon application to the President, at a meeting of the Corps, receive an honorable discharge signed by the President and attested by the Secretary.

ARTICLE V.
MEETINGS.

Section 1. The stated meetings of each Corps shall be held at least once a month, during nine months of the year.

Sect. 2. Special meetings may be convened by order of the President, or whenever request is made in writing by three members of the Corps.

Sect. 3. Seven members in good standing shall constitute a quorum.

ARTICLE VI.
OFFICERS.

Section 1. The officers of each Corps shall be a President, Vice-President, Secretary, Treasurer, Chaplain, Conductor and Guard.

Sect. 2. All members in good standing shall be eligible to office in the Corps.

ARTICLE VII.
ELECTION OF OFFICERS.

Section 1. The Corps officers shall be elected annually, at the last regular meeting in December, by ballot, unless ballot be dispensed with by unanimous consent. A majority of all votes cast shall be requisite to an election.

SECT. 2. Each Corps shall also elect delegates to the Department Convention, in the ratio of one for every — members in good standing, and one additional delegate for a final fraction of more than one-half that number. But each Corps shall be entitled to elect one delegate, whatever its number.

The President shall be entitled to a seat in Department Convention by virtue of her office (for whom no proxy or substitute can act).

ARTICLE VIII.
DUTIES OF OFFICERS.

SECTION 1. It shall be the duty of the President to preside at all meetings of the Corps, and to enforce a strict observance of the Rules and Regulations of the Department, and the By-Laws of the Corps, and all orders from proper authority.

To approve all orders drawn by the Secretary on the Treasurer for payment of moneys.

To forward all returns required by the Rules and Regulations, and perform such other duties as may appertain to her office.

SECT. 2. The Vice-President shall perform all duties required of her by the Ritual, and in the absence of the President shall discharge all duties appertaining to the office of the President.

SECT. 3. The Secretary shall keep in books, properly prepared, the Rules and Regulations of the Department and the By-Laws of the Corps, to be signed by every member of the Corps.

A journal of the proceedings of the Corps, after the same have been approved.

An order book, in which shall be recorded all orders drawn on the Treasurer.

A black-book, in which shall be recorded the names of all rejected candidates, and shall prepare all returns required by Rules and Regulations, and perform such other duties as appertain to her office; and transfer to her successor, without delay, all books, papers and other property in her possession.

SECT. 4. The Treasurer shall hold all funds and other property of the Corps, give receipts for all moneys received, and shall render to the Corps, monthly, a report specifying the amount of money received, for what purpose, and the date of the receipt, also the amount expended, and for what purpose.

She shall keep a strict account with each member, and notify all members in arrears.

She shall fill all orders drawn by the Secretary and approved by the President.

She shall make and deliver to the Corps President all reports and returns required by the Rules and Regulations; and shall deliver to her successor in office all moneys, books, and other property of the Corps in her possession.

SECT. 5. The Chaplain shall assist in conducting the ceremonies prescribed in the secret work of the Corps, and perform such other duties as are required by the Rules and Regulations and By-Laws of the Corps.

SECT. 6. The Conductor shall see that all present are members of the Order, prepare members for initiation, and perform such other work as may be required of her by the President.

SECT. 7. The Guard shall attend the door, and admit none without the password, unless otherwise ordered by the President.

ARTICLE IX.
RELIEF FUND.

SECTION 1. Each Corps may hold a Relief Fund, to which shall be credited all moneys acquired in the name of the Relief Fund of the Grand Army of the Republic.

ARTICLE X.
BY-LAWS.

SECTION 1. Corps may adopt by-laws not inconsistent with these Rules and Regulations, and may provide for the amendment of said by-laws.

CHAPTER III.
GENERAL RULES.
ARTICLE I.
CHARTERS.

SECTION 1. Charters shall be signed by the President and countersigned by the Secretary. The application for a charter shall be signed by at least ten persons, eligible to membership in the Woman's State Relief Corps, and shall in all cases be accompanied by the charter fee of five dollars.

SECT. 2. The President and Secretary, upon receipt of such application, shall admit the applicants into the Order, superintend the election of Corps officers for the remainder of the current year, and complete the organization by thoroughly instructing the newly made members in the work of the Order.

ARTICLE II.
INSTALLATION.

SECTION 1. Installing Officers shall be appointed by the Department, subject to special request for any person.

In the absence of the regularly appointed Installing Officer, the Senior Past Officer present shall act as Installing Officer.

ARTICLE III.
REPORTS AND RETURNS.

SECTION 1. Each Corps President shall make quarterly returns to the Secretary of the Department on the first days of January, April, July and October. Said report shall embody the whole number of members in good standing, number gained since last report, whether by initiation or transfer, number lost by withdrawal, expulsion or death, and names of rejected candidates, amount of money turned over to Post, or dispensed for relief, amount of Relief Fund on hand; and shall forward *per capita* tax assessed by the Department.

SECT. 2. Each Corps President shall also make quarterly reports to the Commander of the Post with which they are connected, on the first days of January, April, July and October, of the amount of money expended in relief during the preceding quarter.

SECT. 3. The Department at its Annual Convention, may revoke the charter of a Corps which for three-quarters of a year has failed to forward its reports or returns.

ARTICLE IV.
DUES AND REVENUES.

SECTION 1. Each Corps, by vote of Corps, or by by-laws, shall establish an initiation fee, also a yearly assessment, to be paid in equal quarterly instalments on the first days of January, April, July and October.

ARTICLE V.
SECRECY.

SECTION 1. The Ritual, and all works of the Woman's State Relief Corps, the names of persons causing the rejection of candidates for membership, or any information as to the cause or means of such rejection, shall be kept secret.

SECT. 2. Any member convicted of divulging the private affairs of the Woman's State Relief Corps, or of violating any of the provisions of this Article, shall be subject to suspension or dishonorable discharge.

ARTICLE VI.
AMENDMENTS.

SECTION 1. These Rules and Regulations shall not be altered, amended or suspended by any subordinate Corps.

SECT. 2. The Department Corps may, at any meeting of Department, alter or amend any of these Rules and Regulations, by a two-thirds vote.

The foregoing are the Rules and Regulations as revised and adopted at the meeting of Department, in session at Cambridge, March 13 and 14, 1879.

SARAH E. FULLER,
President.

KATHRINA L. BEEDLE,
Secretary.

The first public gathering under the auspices of the Department of Massachusetts was held in the hall of Charles Beck Post No. 56, Cambridge, on the evening of March 13, 1879, and was a pleasant feature of the Convention.

Mrs. Sarah E. Fuller conducted the exercises as President of the Department, and explained the objects of the new State organization.

After a piano solo by Mrs. Alexander and a song by Miss Clara Miles, Rev. J. P. Bland, pastor of Lee Street Unitarian church, addressed the audience. He thought that "the supreme duty of the citizens was to be present at this meeting," and expressing his interest in its object, said : —

"We should stand by those who were ready to give their lives in the hour of danger to their country, and by those mothers, wives and children who belonged to them. We should keep the pledge made to the brave men that they and their families should be cared. for. There is work to be done for the relief of suffering which men cannot find time to attend to, and it is proper and necessary that woman should interest herself. I am in sympathy with the good cause in which these ladies are engaged."

After a song by Miss Edith Torrey with piano accompaniment by Mrs. Robert Torrey, Past Department Senior Vice-Commander George S. Evans of Post 30 of Cambridgeport, was introduced. He assured the members of the Relief Corps that the Grand Army comrades would appreciate their work. A poem written by Mrs. Blodgett entitled "The Relief Corps Committee" was read by Mrs. Susie E. Goodrich.

Mrs. Kathrina L. Beedle, Secretary of the Department, upon responding to an introduction, said: "The great object of this society is charity, so wide and strong that it knows neither creed, color nor nationality, and is intended to aid soldiers, sailors, marines, and the mothers, wives and daughters of such as have either been killed in the war or have died since."

Miss Miles and Miss Alexander gave a duet.

Mr. F. L. Chapman, prominently known in Cambridge as "the soldiers' friend," spoke of his interest in the Relief Corps, and Commander Miles of Post 56 followed, expressing his approval of the work undertaken by the ladies, and assuring them that Post 56 would cordially aid them in their work. Mr. Davlin, Senior Vice-Commander of Post 57 of East Cambridge, was glad to extend a welcome to the new organization.

Mrs. Fuller, Department President, thanked the ladies associated with Post 56 for their hospitality, and read for the information of those present the preamble to the Rules and Regulations of the Order.

She announced that Mrs. Beedle, State Secretary, would be at Department Headquarters of the Grand Army of the Republic, at No. 53 Tremont Street, Boston, every Wednesday, from 12 o'clock M. to 1 o'clock P.M., to give information relative to the Relief Corps Work.

After a song by Miss Torrey, remarks were made by Past Commander W. W. Webb of Post 56, Mrs. Webb, one of the charter members of the State Relief Corps, Past Commander M. C. Beedle of Post 56, Mr. Lunt of Post 57 and Colonel Whitman of the Board of Assessors of Cambridge.

The meeting closed with a piano solo by Miss Alexander.

This gathering was not given the pretentious name that has since designated some of the public meetings of the Department, for a "Woman's Campfire" was unknown in those early days of the Order.

But a spirit of earnestness prevailed, and a key-note was struck that echoed through the land, bearing a message that touched the hearts of loyal men and women.

CHAPTER II.

OUTLINE OF THE WORK AND ITS EARLY PROGRESS.

NOT DISCOURAGED by the fact that only four Corps adopted the plan outlined at Fitchburg and Cambridge, the founders of the Department with faith in their cause felt sure of its ultimate success. Its platform, welcoming to membership all loyal women who were willing to work for the veterans, was surely a broad one. The impressive ritualistic service and thorough methods of organizing, indicated that the Order had been formed upon a permanent basis.

To win the approval of the Grand Army of the Republic was the next step taken in the line of progress, for Corps could only be instituted by request of Posts.

Capt. John G. B. Adams succeeded General Sargent as Department Commander, and Capt. James F. Meech continued to hold the office of Assistant Adjutant-General.

These officials tendered the officers of the State Relief Corps the use of Grand Army Headquarters every Wednesday, from 12 o'clock M. to 2 o'clock P.M., and valuable aid was thereby received.

Here they consulted the Department Commander and his Adjutant, conferred with Post Commanders, explained the objects of Relief Corps work to numerous inquirers, and conducted a plan of missionary work that proved of great value.

One of the first comrades to take an interest in the new movement was Commander George L. Goodale of S. C. Lawrence Post 66 of Medford. A large and enthusiastic meeting was held under the auspices of the Post early in April and addressed by Mrs. Sarah E. Fuller, Department President, and Mrs. Kathrina L. Beedle, Department Secretary. As a result, Corps No. 5 was instituted May 27.

Gen. H. G. Berry Post 40 of Malden held a public meeting in May, in which Commander Sturgeon, Col. Thomas E. Barker and other members were actively interested, and on May 29 Corps No. 6 was organized. Mrs. Fuller, who instituted the Corps, was entertained at the home of Colonel Barker and met for the first time Mrs. E. Florence Barker, who was one of the charter members.

Through the influence of Commander Alfred C. Monroe of Fletcher Webster Post 13 of Brockton, Mrs. Fuller was invited to address a public meeting under its auspices, and October 29, Corps No. 7 was added to the roster.

Mrs. Fuller visited Haverhill and instituted Major How Corps No. 8 in October. Maj. George L. Stearns Corps No. 9, Charlestown, Theodore Winthrop Corps No. 10, Chelsea (through the efforts of Commander William H. Hart of Post 35), and General Wadsworth Corps No. 11, Natick (since disbanded), were organized the same month. Paul Revere Corps No. 12 (number of which is now 103) of Quincy and A. St. John Chambre Corps No. 13 of Stoughton were organized in December.

Thus, when the First Annual Convention was held in East Boston, Jan. 28, 1880, there were thirteen Corps on the roster, the first twelve of which were represented at the Convention by fifty-two delegates.

The Department Secretary, Mrs. Beedle, reported an increase from twenty-three members at time of organization, to four hundred and fifty-three December 31. A relief fund had been established by eight Corps and the sum of $2,000 turned over to Posts. The reports of Corps Presidents were very encouraging.

A new installation service prepared by Mrs. Beedle was adopted, and a committee appointed to revise the ritual.

A vote of thanks was extended Past Department Commander Sargent, Department Commander Adams and Assistant Adjutant-General Meech for their courtesy and assistance during the past year.

Fraternal greetings were sent by telegram to the Department Encampment, Grand Army of the Republic, then in session at Lynn.

The clause in the Rules and Regulations relating to the election of trustees was annulled, and a Board of Directors established to consist of the Department officers and a director from each Corps not represented by a Department officer.

Mrs. E. Florence Barker of Malden and Mrs. S. Agnes Parker of Brockton, whose work for the veterans has given them a national reputation, were active participants in this Convention and served on important committees.

The second public meeting of the Department was held on the evening of the first day's session, in East Boston. Mrs. Sarah E. Fuller, Department President, conducted the exercises.

Addresses were made by Mrs. Kathrina L. Beedle, Department Secretary, George S. Evans, Department Senior Vice-Commander G.A.R., Mrs. Sophia M. Parker of Fitchburg, Miss Mary E. Elliot, President of the Independent Corps of Somerville, Commander William H. Ryan of Post 56, Cambridge, Charles B. Merchant, Past Commander Post 19, Fitchburg, Col. Thomas E. Barker of Post 40, Malden, Commander Henry Skilton of Post 35, Chelsea, Edmund Miles and M. C. Beedle, Past Commanders Post 56, Cambridge, and others. Mr. Beeching of E. Boston sang several patriotic songs. Letters of regret at their inability to be present, in response to an invitation, were received from Governor Long, Department Commander Adams, Assistant Adjutant-General Meech, Collector Beard and Commander Monroe of Post 7, Brockton.

The First Annual Convention closed on the afternoon of January 29, having elected and installed the following-named officers: —

President: Sarah E. Fuller of East Boston.
Senior Vice-President: E. Florence Barker of Malden.
Junior Vice-President: Sophia M. Parker of Fitchburg.
Secretary: Kathrina L. Beedle of Cambridge.
Treasurer: Amanda M. Thayer of Chelsea.
Chaplain: Francelia F. Boynton of East Boston.
Conductor: Ellen R. Barrows of Medford.
Guard: Sarah M. Scates of Haverhill.

Important measures were considered by the Board of Directors in 1880.

At a meeting held May 12, Mrs. Sarah E. Fuller, Mrs. E. Florence Barker, Mrs. Kathrina L. Beedle, Mrs. Francelia F. Boynton and Mrs. Amanda M. Thayer were appointed a committee to confer with the Department Council of Administration, G.A.R., regarding the relative position of the Woman's Relief Corps to the Grand Army of the Republic.

Department Commander John A. Hawes and Council met the committee June 3, and advised that the Woman's Relief Corps add to its title, the term "Auxiliary to the Grand Army of the Republic."

Commander Hawes pledged his support to the auxiliary, and assured the committee that a resolution of endorsement would be presented at the next Annual Encampment.

Mrs. Fuller and Mrs. Barker secured the interest of prominent comrades in New Hampshire and a General Order was issued September 11, by Department Commander George Bowers, who was authorized by the Council of Administration to call a Convention with a view of forming a State Relief Corps in

New Hampshire. It was announced in the General Order that the Convention would be held at Laconia, October 21, and that "Mrs. Sarah E. Fuller and Mrs. E. Florence Barker of the Massachusetts State Association and other ladies are expected to be present."

A meeting of the Board of Directors of Massachusetts was held in Boston, November 6, when the President, Mrs. Fuller, stated that "correspondence with and personal attendance at the Department Convention of New Hampshire Woman's State Relief Corps, had resulted in a vote of that body to adopt the work of the Woman's State Relief Corps of Massachusetts, if they may be permitted to do so."

Mrs. Barker, Department Senior Vice-President, expressed a deep interest in the progress of the work in the Granite State.

Mrs. Beedle, Department Secretary, suggested that the Corps in New Hampshire "have liberty to use our Ritual for the institution of Corps in New Hampshire only, and that they make no copies of the Ritual, written or printed, and that they accept the Rules and Regulations as they stand."

This suggestion of Mrs. Beedle was unanimously adopted, on motion of Mrs. Barker.

It was then voted on motion of Mrs. Barker, "That we invite the New Hampshire ladies, after organization as a Department, to form, in connection with us, a *mutual* Board of Directors, consisting of the officers of each Department."

An invitation extended by Mrs. Barker to hold the third meeting of the Board of Directors at her residence in Malden, was accepted, and the same held December 8.

The delegates from New Hampshire were present and signed the following agreement: —

MALDEN, MASS., Dec. 8, 1880.

We, the undersigned, officers of the New Hampshire Woman's State Relief Corps, have this day taken upon us the work of the Massachusetts Woman's State Relief Corps, subject to the conditions that we make no copies of the Ritual, written or printed, but shall make requisition on the Department Secretary of Massachusetts for the same, as we may need them; also, that we accept the Rules and Regulations as they stand.

   (Signed) MARY A. LULL, *Dept. Senior Vice-President.*
         MATTIE B. MOULTON, *Dept. Secretary.*
         LOUISE A. DEERING, *Dept. Chaplain.*
         FANNY M. KEYES, *Dept. Conductor.*
         FRANCES E. JOHNSON, *Dept. Guard.*

 The formal ceremony of admitting the New Hampshire delegates to the Order occurred at Grand Army Hall, Malden, in the evening, when they were duly initiated by the Department officers of Massachusetts.

 Gen. H. G. Berry Corps No. 6, Mrs. Barker, President, hospitably entertained the visitors, and the occasion was one of social interest.

 Mrs. Fuller read the report of Chaplain-in-Chief Joseph F. Lovering of the Grand Army of the Republic, in which he supported and recommended the Woman's State Relief Corps as the National organization; also, a report of the proceedings wherein that portion of the Chaplain's Report was referred to a special committee, of which Mr. Lovering was made chairman, for future report.

 The Union Board was formed and officers elected, viz. : —

President: Mrs. E. Florence Barker of Malden.

Secretary: Mrs. Kathrina L. Beedle of Cambridge.

Treasurer: Miss Fanny M. Keyes of New Hampshire.

 At the Second Annual Convention of the Department of Massachusetts, held in Boston Feb. 3, 1881, seventy delegates and alternates were present. Sixteen Corps and a membership of five hundred and eighty were reported.

 Corps instituted during the year, viz.: E. K. Wilcox No. 14 of Springfield, Col. Prescott No. 15 of Ashland and U. S. Grant No. 16 of Melrose.

A resolution adopted by the Department Encampment Jan. 27, 1881, was read, viz. : —

Resolved, That the Department of Massachusetts, G.A.R., recognizing in the Woman's State Relief Corps an invaluable ally in its mission of charity and loyalty, hails them as a noble band of Christian women, who, while not of the Grand Army of the Republic, are auxiliary to it.

That portion of the Rules and Regulations referring to the title of the organization, was amended by adding the words "auxiliary to."

At the closing session of the Convention (February 4) Mrs. Mattie B. Moulton, Department Secretary of New Hampshire, installed the following-named officers : —

President: Sarah E. Fuller of East Boston.
Senior Vice-President: E. Florence Barker of Malden.
Junior Vice-President: Hattie M. Mason of Haverhill.
Secretary: Pamelia F. Sprague of East Boston.
Treasurer: S. Agnes Parker of Brockton.
Chaplain: Francelia F. Boynton of East Boston.
Conductor: Ellen R. Barrows of Medford.
Guard: Martha A. Simonds of Natick.
Inspector: Kathrina L. Beedle of Cambridge.
Board of Directors: K. J. Libby of Fitchburg, Rebecca Brewer of Taunton, Ellen Johnson of Charlestown, Amanda M. Thayer of Chelsea, Julia M. Mills of Stoughton, Alice I. Wheelock of Springfield, Maria E. Ball of Ashland, Laura H. Baldwin of Melrose.

A meeting of the Board of Directors was held February 18, when the Printing Committee was instructed to prepare new charters and other printed matter to conform with the change in title.

Work for the Soldiers' Home in Massachusetts was planned; and several meetings of the Board were held during the year to arrange for tables in the proposed Soldiers' Home Bazaar.

At the Third Annual Convention, held in Boston Jan. 31, 1882, Mrs. Beedle, Department Secretary, reported a membership of seven hundred and fourteen, and an expenditure in relief of $1,117.97 to January 1. Three Corps were instituted during the year, viz.: P. T. Wyman, No. 17, Holliston; Burnside, No. 18, Saxonville (since disbanded); E. P. Wallace, No. 19, Amesbury.

A discussion upon the question of limiting the membership to relatives of soldiers, resulted in a vote to retain the clause in the Rules and Regulations referring to the eligibility of loyal women.

The following changes in the Rules and Regulations were adopted: —

The officers of the Department shall consist of one Director from each Corps not represented by a Department officer.

All members in good standing shall be eligible to any Department office.

The addition of Inspector to the list of Department officers, the defining of her duties and the adoption of a form of Inspection.

That the age of applicants for membership shall be eighteen years.

Mrs. Barker, Department Senior Vice-President, announced that she had received a communication from the Grand Army Encampment conveying the greetings to the Convention of the newly-elected Department Commander, George H. Patch, who wished the Woman's Relief Corps "long life and prosperity."

The question of forming a National Woman's Relief Corps was discussed, and action regarding the same indefinitely postponed.

Officers were elected, viz.: —

President: E. Florence Barker of Malden.
Senior Vice-President: Hattie M. Mason of Haverhill.
Junior Vice-President: Pamelia F. Sprague of East Boston.

E. FLORENCE BARKER

Second Department President 1882, 1883
First National President 1883, 1884

Secretary: Sarah E. Fuller of East Boston.
Treasurer: Matilda E. Lawton of South Boston.
Chaplain: Francelia F. Boynton of East Boston.
Inspector: S. Agnes Parker of Brockton.
Conductor: M. Susie Goodale of Medford.
Guard: Amanda M. Thayer of Chelsea.
Directors: Sophia M. Parker of Fitchburg, Rebecca Brewer of Taunton, Ellen Johnson of Charlestown, Cynthia Kimball of Stoughton, Sarah Brown of Springfield, Maria E. Ball of Ashland, Hannah Rowell of Melrose, Georgia F. French of Holliston, Ellen N. Winch of Saxonville, Mary L. Tucker of Amesbury, Mary E. Elliot of Somerville.

A copy of the first circular letter issued to the Corps is herewith given.

WOMAN'S STATE RELIEF CORPS,
AUXILIARY TO THE GRAND ARMY OF THE REPUBLIC,
DEPARTMENT OF MASSACHUSETTS.
BOSTON, May 1, 1882.

TO THE LOYAL PATRIOTIC WOMEN OF MASSACHUSETTS,

Greeting:

On the 12th of February, 1879, in compliance with a request from prominent comrades of the G.A.R., Department of Massachusetts, a convention was held at the Headquarters of Post 19, in the city of Fitchburg, to consider the advisability of forming a State organization of women to work in the interest of the G.A.R., and to assist the comrades in doing their noble work of relieving the wants of suffering comrades, or their families. More than sixty ladies, representing sixteen different aid societies connected with the G.A.R., responded to the call, and the organization now known as the "Woman's State Relief Corps" was formed. Plans and methods for future government and work were adopted, and its members pledged themselves to work in every possible way to advance the interests of the G.A.R., not only in this Department, but wherever and whenever we could be of service. At the Department Encampment held in Boston, January, 1881, the following resolution was unanimously adopted:—

"*Resolved*, That the Department of Massachusetts, G.A.R., recognizing in the 'Woman's State Relief Corps' an invaluable ally in its mission of charity and loyalty, hails them as a noble band of Christian women, who, while not of the Grand Army of the Republic are auxiliary to it."

At a meeting of the National Encampment, held at Indianapolis in June, 1881, a resolution was also unanimously adopted by that body recognizing and endorsing a "Woman's National Relief Corps." (See page 793, Report of National Encampment.) Such hearty and cordial endorsements as these, emanating as they have from those high in authority, has forever settled any doubts as to the support and sympathy we, as women, are to receive from the comrades of the G.A.R., and has inspired the hearts of loyal women all over our land to renewed interest and zeal in doing the work of relief among the families of those who "so bravely fought to defend their country's honor, and to preserve to us an unsullied flag."

When this organization was formed it numbered twenty-three members; at the present time it has a membership of more than nine hundred, connected with nineteen subordinate Corps, in various parts of the State, and we desire to call attention to some of the practical results of our work and labors as an organization during the past year.

At the Bazaar held in Boston in December, 1881, in aid of the Massachusetts Soldiers' Home in Chelsea, we were represented by four tables, viz.: Malden Corps, No. 6, Union (supported by nine different Corps), Brockton, No. 7, Haverhill, No. 8, making a total return of $4,189. The quarterly reports for the year 1881 showed the total amount expended in relief among the families of soldiers and sailors of the late rebellion to be over $1,100. In all our labors of love and loyalty during the short period of our existence as an organization, our reward has been the knowledge that desolate homes have been made happy, aching hearts have been made glad, soldiers' orphan children tenderly cared for, and some have been laid in their last resting-places by gentle, loving hands, that otherwise must have found a pauper's grave. More than twenty years have passed since the "brave boys who wore the blue" marched away from home, and all they held so dear, to defend their country's honor. Thousands of lonely graves, far from the homes they loved so well, tell of widows and orphan children needing the care and support thus taken from them. Men who returned to enjoy the peace and honor so richly earned, today need our care. The seeds of disease sown on Southern soil have ripened fast; painful wounds too plainly tell the story of heroic suffering, which now is so rapidly filling all our cemeteries with soldiers' graves. Women of Massachusetts, we cordially invite you to unite with us in the sacred duty of caring for the helpless and needy ones left by them, and to this end we would call your attention to the following from our Rules and Regulations, and hope you will enroll your names with ours, and assist in carrying on such a noble work.

PREAMBLE.

We, the mothers, wives, daughters and sisters of soldiers, sailors and marines who took part in the late rebellion, and other loyal women, do unite to establish a permanent State Association for the purposes and objects herein set forth, with such amendments as we shall from time to time think proper to make.

OBJECTS.

To assist members and their families in sickness and distress, and all needy and sick soldiers, sailors and marines, or the widows and orphans of deceased soldiers, sailors and marines; to do all in our power to alleviate their distress; to further the interests of all subordinate Corps, and institute new Corps throughout the State.

CHARTERS.

Charters shall be signed by the President and countersigned by the Secretary. The application for a charter shall be signed by at least ten persons eligible to membership in the Woman's State Relief Corps, and shall in all cases be accompanied by the charter fee of five dollars.

ELIGIBILITY.

Loyal women of good moral character, interested in the good work, shall be eligible to membership in the Woman's State Relief Corps.

For any additional information regarding the work of this Order, address the Secretary, Mrs. Sarah E. Fuller, East Boston, Mass.

Yours fraternally,

MRS. E. FLORENCE BARKER,
President.

Mrs. SARAH E. FULLER,
Secretary.

The success of the work having been assured in Massachusetts and New Hampshire, a correspondence was opened with officials of the Grand Army of the Republic in Connecticut, with what result is shown by the following communication : —

HEADQUARTERS DEPARTMENT OF CONNECTICUT,
GRAND ARMY OF THE REPUBLIC,
HARTFORD, CONN., Sept. 23, 1882.

Mrs. SARAH E. FULLER,
Secretary W.R.C., Auxiliary to the G.A.R.,
East Boston, Mass.

Dear Madam: Our Department Commander has taken action as shown in General Order which I enclose If this meets the response anticipated, we shall be very glad to accept your assistance and make the arrangements stated in yours of the 3d of July last.

If, however, there should be any delay, or such a want of interest among our ladies as to render it inadvisable to organize a Department of Connecticut *at once*, can your Department not furnish the work to such subordinate Corps as may be formed here, and then let them affiliate with your Department and be under your guidance, until such time as we can assume the dignity of a Department?

I am much interested in the Order and believe we can start it here in good shape.

I can see certain objections to organizing a single Corps in the way I suggest; but believe they could all be met.

I desire to see a *National* organization and for that reason am desirous that whatever is done here, shall be thoroughly in harmony with what is being done in Massachusetts and New Hampshire; hence, my desire to organize under your Rules and Regulations; and if we cannot do any better, should like to see one or more subordinate Corps working under your Ritual.

Awaiting your reply, I remain,

Very truly yours,

HENRY E. TAINTER,
Assistant Adjutant-General.

Mrs. Barker, Department President and Mrs. Fuller, Department Secretary, instituted Wadhams Corps No. 1, at Waterbury, Conn., November 16, and soon after instituted Nathaniel Lyon Corps No. 2, at Hartford, Conn.

At the Fourth Annual Convention held in Boston January 30 and 31, 1883, all the Department officers, sixty-four delegates, and many visiting members, were present.

Mrs. Fuller, Department Secretary, reported a membership of 993, and a gain of six Corps, viz.: Dahlgren No. 20, South Boston; Willard C. Kinsley No. 21, Somerville; Lyon No. 22, Westfield; E. J. Griggs No. 23, Belchertown; Col. C. R. Mudge No. 24, Merrimac; F. P. H. Rogers No. 25, Waltham.

A message from the Annual Encampment of the Grand Army of the Republic, stating that George S. Evans had been elected Department Commander, was received with applause.

Mrs. Mattie B. Moulton, Department President of New Hampshire, was present and installed the following officers elected for the ensuing year: —

President: E. Florence Barker of Malden.
Senior Vice-President: M. Susie Goodale of Medford.
Junior Vice-President: S. Agnes Parker of Brockton.
Secretary: Sarah E. Fuller of East Boston.
Treasurer: Matilda E. Lawton of South Boston.
Inspector: Hattie M. Mason of Haverhill.
Chaplain: Francelia F. Boynton of East Boston.
Conductor: Lizabeth B. Turner of Boston.
Guard: Mary J. Peck of Fitchburg.
Directors: Kathrina L. Beedle of Cambridge, Helen F. Johnson of Charlestown, Josie W. Connor of Chelsea, Mary E. Glover of Springfield, Maria E. Ball of Ashland, Hannah Rowell of Melrose, Eliza F. Talbot of Holliston, Ellen N. Winch of Saxonville, Mary L. Tucker of Amesbury, Mary E. Elliot of Somerville, Celestia E. Barton of Belchertown, Cinderella E. Clement of Merrimac, Mary E. Chipman of Waltham, Sarah B. Creasey of Newburyport, Maria A. Lull of Cambridgeport.

Delegates were chosen to the Union Board, viz.: Kathrina L. Beedle of Cambridge, Ellen Johnson of Charlestown, Amanda M. Thayer of Chelsea, Mary E. Glover of Springfield, Maria E. Ball of Ashland, Laura E. Baldwin of Melrose, Eliza F. Talbot of Holliston, Ellen M. Winch of Saxonville, Mary L. Tucker of Amesbury, Mary E. Elliot of Somerville.

This Convention was honored by a visit from Paul Van Der Voort, Commander-in-Chief, I. S. Bangs, Junior Vice-Commander-in-Chief, F. E. Brown, Adjutant-General, Rev. J. F. Lovering, Chaplain-in-Chief, George L. Goodale, Assistant Quartermaster-General, Col. Thomas E. Barker and Comrade E. B. Stillings of the Grand Army of the Republic, who were cordially welcomed by Mrs. E. Florence Barker, Department President. Their visit was a memorable one in the history of our work, for through its influence a National Woman's Relief Corps was organized during the year.

M. SUSIE GOODALE

Third Department President 1894-1895

CHAPTER III.

MEMORIAL DAY—ITS OBSERVANCE BY THE CORPS. GENERAL ORDERS OF DEPARTMENT PRESIDENTS.

WHILE with love and sympathy the members of our Order care for the living veterans of the Union, they also pay homage to the memory of the heroic dead, and this sacred duty was the first service rendered aside from their work of relief.

On each Memorial Day the Corps of this Department have twined laurel wreaths for monuments and cemeteries, and have garlanded the graves of the martyred dead with their choicest floral offerings.

They have united with and aided Posts of the Grand Army of the Republic in observing the day, and by invitation of the comrades have attended in a body the memorial exercises in churches and halls.

In response to an appeal from Richmond, Virginia, and from other sections of the South, contributions of money and barrels of evergreen were sent in 1888, for use of Southern Posts in decorating the graves in the National cemeteries. This custom has annually been continued, and donations from Corps, with thousands of flags sent from Department Headquarters, have shown to the loyal people of the South that we appreciate their interest in caring for the graves of the martyred dead.

Several Posts have secured the services of our members as Memorial Day orators and this custom is gaining in favor.

The first Department officer thus recognized was Mrs. Francelia P. Boynton of East Boston, who was invited by S. C. Lawrence Post 66 of Medford to give the address under its auspices, May 30, 1883.

Mrs. Boynton was Department Chaplain from 1879 until her removal to the west in the fall of 1883.

Her successor in office, Mrs. Elizabeth C. Lovering of Worcester, prepared a blank which was issued to Corps Chaplains, and so highly recommended by the National Chaplain, Mrs. Annie Wittenmyer, that it was adopted by the National Convention held that year in Portland, Maine.

This blank systematizes the work of Corps Chaplains who are required to fill out and forward the same to the Department Chaplain not later than June 10. Following is the original copy prepared by Mrs. Lovering : —

WOMAN'S RELIEF CORPS, DEPARTMENT OF

MEMORIAL DAY BLANK.

To be filled out and promptly returned to Department Chaplain.

1. Membership of Corps.
2. Members taking part in Memorial Day Services.
3. Give the title of Committees, and number of ladies on each one.
4. Did the Corps as a body attend Memorial services?
5. Did the children take part, and what number?
6. What expense was incurred?
7. Were refreshments provided for Post?
8. Were flowers furnished Post, by purchase (to what amount) or by contribution?
9. Did they prepare a Memorial for the Unknown Dead, and those who sleep on Southern battle-fields.
10. Any other facts that may be suggested.

The third question is omitted in the blank now in use and two questions have been added, namely : —

How many soldiers' graves were decorated?
What assistance was rendered for the observance of Memorial Day in the National cemeteries?

Extracts from the annual reports of Department Chaplains are herewith given. From the report of Mrs. Elizabeth C. Lovering, referring to the work of May 30, 1885 : —

"Reports were received from forty-seven out of fifty Corps, the former representing a membership of two thousand six hundred and sixty-one. Of the whole number of Corps on the Roster of the Department, but nine took little or no part in Memorial Day services. For several of these there were extenuating circumstances. Thirty-three Corps worked by committees; eight as committees of the whole; the remainder by a union of both. Refreshments were served by eighteen Corps to their Posts and Sons of Veterans as well, where such an organization existed. In some instances very fine collations were provided for large numbers of Veterans and Sons; $413.70 were expended in various directions. A large proportion of the fifty Corps attended memorial services, some on successive Sundays; and in three instances the church or hall was appropriately and beautifully trimmed. 'The unknown dead' were not forgotten; and mounds covered with flowers, stone urns, or vases placed permanently in soldiers' lots or before the monuments, were filled with growing plants; while elaborate sets of wreaths, Maltese crosses, stars, anchors and shields, made beautiful offerings to the Nation's dead heroes. Large numbers of women worked many hours in the preparation of evergreens, one Corps making three hundred wreaths, another two hundred and nineteen, besides arranging all loose flowers brought in, and furnishing ample collations. A pleasant feature in many of the Corps was the sympathetic interest and desire to help, shown by children.

"It gives me pleasure to state, that in a large number of instances, Corps manifested a most praiseworthy spirit in offering assistance to their Posts in every possible direction, some accompanying them to the cemeteries and aiding in the decoration of the graves and monuments, while the last resting places of their own deceased members were not forgotten. One Corps, No. 3, East Boston, placed beautiful tributes on the grave of an army nurse, Miss Helen F. Gilson."

From the report of Mrs. Mary E. Knowles (May 30, 1886) : —

"Reports have been received from seventy of the seventy-two Corps in the Department. Sixty-seven Corps participated in memorial services, a large number attending Divine service on Sunday and also taking part on Memorial Day.

"Forty-five Corps provided collations, not alone for their Posts, but in some instances for large numbers of Veterans and Sons. $640.51 were expended in various ways appertaining to the observance of the day.

"Nearly every Corps worked by committees, and in preparing the wreaths and memorials, a number of them worked two and three days in succession, the interest in the work being very marked. One Corps, No. 68 of Dorchester, prepared 867 bouquets, 6 large wreaths, 59 small ones, crosses, etc., and beautiful emblems for the ritualistic service of the Post; Corps No. 53 of New Bedford, 380 wreaths, 337 baskets, besides making a number of other tributes and arranging large quantities of loose flowers; Corps No. 37 of Pittsfield, 180 wreaths, 158 baskets, crosses, stars, and a shaft eight feet in height, covered with white flowers, and dedicated to the 'unknown dead.' Would time and space permit, I could cite many others, showing the *great* interest in this beautiful work.

"Corps No. 7 of Brockton, assisted by its Post, dedicated a monument to the 'unknown dead,' with this inscription : —

A TRIBUTE TO THOSE NOBLE WOMEN,
THE ARMY NURSES,
AND
TO THE MEN ON WHOSE UNKNOWN GRAVES
NO MOTHERS' TEARS SHALL FALL, OR DAUGHTERS' HANDS
PLANT SWEET FORGET-ME-NOTS.

"Corps No. 3 of East Boston held a very impressive service at the grave of Miss Helen F. Gilson, an army nurse; and the Post united with the Corps, all forming a hollow square around the grave; and after an appropriate address by the Corps President, a beautiful floral offering was placed thereon.

"Corps No. 40 of Everett placed memorials over the graves of army nurses, Helen F. Gilson and Rebecca Pomeroy. Corps No. 69 of Wakefield dedicated a beautiful cross seven feet in height, with a large wreath across it to the 'unknown dead.'"

From the report of Mrs. Mary E. Knowles (May 30, 1887) : —

"Complete reports were received from every Corps, ninety in number, showing that the women of the old 'Bay State' are as earnest and zealous in honoring the memory of our dead heroes as they were in the care of the living ones during the war.

"Eighty out of the ninety Corps attended memorial services in a body.

"Forty-one Corps placed *special* memorials for Gen. John A. Logan, and several honored the memory of Gen. U. S. Grant with appropriate floral tributes. The graves of Helen Gilson, Rebecca Pomeroy and Mrs. Merrick (army nurses) were specially decorated.

"In many places a large number of the Corps members worked two and three days in succession preparing memorials, assisting their respective Posts in making bouquets, wreaths, filling baskets, etc. In addition to this, bountiful collations were served to large numbers.

"Expenses incurred for refreshments, flowers, etc., $1,291.64.

"Corps 82 of Athol held a special service in memory of General Logan.

"Corps 25 of Waltham prepared and placed in the soldiers' lot in that city, a tribute in the form of a sarcophagus. It was completely covered with rare and beautiful flowers and evergreens; through the center of the front on a white ground bordered with beautiful violets was this inscription: —

IN MEMORY
OF THOSE WHO SLEEP ON SOUTHERN BATTLE-FIELDS, IN PRISON PENS, OR 'NEATH THE OCEAN WAVE.

"On the top were placed floral designs — a soldier's cap, two crossed swords and a large cross; on the sides a shield and anchor.

"This magnificent memorial was designed by the President, and she was assisted in its construction by members of the Corps. A letter from the Post was received by the Corps expressing gratitude and appreciation for the beautiful tribute."

From report of Mrs. Emily L. Clark (May 30, 1888) : —

"Complete reports were received from one hundred Corps, each showing commendable zeal in thus honoring our fallen heroes. Eighty-six of the one hundred Corps attended memorial services in a body, and placed memorials for the 'unknown dead' and for army nurses. Several Corps also placed special memorials to John A. Logan, Abraham Lincoln, George H. Patch and Gen. A. B. Underwood.

"The graves of Flora A. Haskell, Catherine Kimball, Helen Gilson, Eliza G. and Eliza A. Wood, Ruth Russell and Mrs. Merrick, army nurses, were specially decorated; also the grave of Mrs. Abby Curtin, who, for her bravery on the battle-field, was commissioned Lieutenant by Abraham Lincoln.

"Refreshments were served to seventy-five Posts, and in many places to Sons of Veterans, drum corps and children. The expenses incurred for refreshments, flowers, etc., amounted to $1,486.66. Large numbers of Corps members worked two and three, and one Corps reports six days' labor in preparation for the day."

From report of Mrs. Emily L. Clark (May 30, 1889) : —

"Every Corps, one hundred and twenty-one in number, reported, representing a membership of eight thousand five hundred and fifty-seven. The number taking part in the preparations for the day was five thousand two hundred and twenty-four.

"One hundred and two Corps attended service in a body. Four hundred and forty-eight members acted as Committee on Decoration, five hundred and ninety-four on Entertainment.

"Memorials were prepared for those who sleep in unknown graves, for army nurses, and also in honor of General Logan.

"Eighty-seven Corps provided refreshments for Posts, Sons of Veterans and children. Expenses incurred for flowers $610.74; other expenses $404.90.

"Reports and letters from Corps Chaplains, also letters from many Corps Presidents, were deeply interesting, and have tended to strengthen my love for this beautiful work, as well as increase my interest in all the work of our Order.

"Too well we realize the rapid falling off of our country's brave defenders, and *know* that in the coming years there will be more and more of this labor of love to perform."

From report of Mrs. Emily L. Clark (May 30, 1890) : —

"Every Corps reported, one hundred and thirty in number. Nearly every Corps attended memorial service in a body.

"Fourteen thousand nine hundred and forty-five of the turf-bound homes were decorated with evergreens and choice flowers. Several Corps placed memorials to the 'unknown dead.' Special services for these were performed by the Corps, and some of the floral tributes were very beautiful and elaborate. Memorials were also placed for General Logan, General Grant and army nurses by many of the Corps.

"$1,038.88 were expended for flowers, refreshments, etc. One hundred and one Corps furnished refreshments for Posts, Sons of Veterans, Cadets and Drum Corps.

"It is a gratifying proof of the growth and extent of patriotic spirit, that the observance of Memorial Day is every year becoming more general and marked by deeper, popular sympathy."

From report of Mrs. Sarah C. Walkley (May 30, 1891) : —

"Of the one hundred and forty-two Corps in the Department, one hundred and thirty-nine reported.

"Of these Corps, one hundred and twenty-four attended Memorial Day services, and many also attended divine service Memorial Sunday.

"Devotion was manifested in the preparation of elaborate and beautiful decorations for the graves of 16,324 of the nation's dead; soldiers' monuments were decorated, and many of the living heroes wore a choice memento of the day. One hundred and twenty Corps prepared memorials in honor of the 'unknown dead' and those who rest in the sunny southland.

"Many Corps also prepared memorials to General Sherman, Admiral Porter and army nurses. $1,961.70 were expended for decorations and refreshments. One hundred and fourteen Corps served refreshments to Posts, Sons of Veterans and invited guests.

"No additional words are necessary to show the increasing interest of the Woman's Relief Corps of this Department in Memorial Day, so helpful in promoting the best and truest patriotism.

"So much as in us lies, let us see that each soldier, living or dead, has his meed of honor, and that the glorious deeds of these men be perpetuated in the memory of their countrymen."

From report of Mrs. Sarah C. Walkley (May 30, 1892) : —

"The entire number of Corps in the Department (152) reported. Of these Corps 134 attended Sabbath Memorial services. 19,911 soldiers' graves were decorated. 141 Corps contributed flowers, 114 furnished refreshments, and 116 prepared memorials to the 'unknown dead' and those who lie on southern battle-fields. The amount of expense incurred by the Corps was $1,851.69.

"The above statistics clearly show the growing interest of the Woman's Relief Corps of this Department in Memorial Day — 'a day from which come inspiring voices, telling the youth from generation to generation how great is their country's worth and cost and how noble and beautiful it was to die for it.'"

From the report of Mrs. Hattie A. Ralph (May 30, 1893):—

"The consolidated report which I had the honor of forwarding to the National Chaplain contained a summary of the Memorial Day work in this Department, showing that all Corps (one hundred and fifty-eight in number) performed some service in recognition of the day.

"Flowers were furnished Posts by one hundred and thirty-four Corps, and over 21,000 soldiers' graves were decorated.

"Mounds, anchors, wreaths and other floral offerings were prepared by one hundred and twenty-nine Corps in memory of the 'unknown dead.' The army nurses, whose names are enrolled among the martyrs of the Union, were remembered by special tributes.

"Several Corps conducted services in the cemeteries.

"The expenses incurred by Corps in all their arrangements for Memorial Day amounted to nearly two thousand dollars.

"In accordance with the usual custom, Posts throughout the State invited their auxiliaries to attend the special church services on Memorial Sunday, and in some places our members participated in the special exercises in the public schools.

"Memorial Day addresses were delivered under the auspices of Posts by several members of this Department.

"It being the custom of many Corps to annually contribute for decorations in the National cemeteries of the South, said contributions should be reported on the blank designed to show the distinctive work of our Order for Memorial Day.

"I therefore *recommend* for action by the next National Convention, That the following question be added to this blank: What assistance was rendered for the observance of Memorial Day in the National cemeteries?

"The flowers and flags we place above the graves of the fallen, and the wreaths we twine around their monuments, are expressions of our regard for the living and our reverence for the memory of the dead.

"May these emblems bear with them *a spirit of love and gratitude* as an inspiration for truer service in all our work for the Grand Army of the Republic."

The following statistics from the report of Mrs. Hattie A. Ralph forwarded the National Chaplain in June, 1894, give a summary of the work on last Memorial Day: —

"All the Corps, one hundred and sixty-two in number, assisted in the sacred duties pertaining to Memorial Day. One hundred and twenty-one Corps erected memorials to the 'unknown dead'; 19,661 soldiers' graves were decorated. The graves of Maj. George L. Stearns and Col. J. P. Gould were decorated by the Corps of Charlestown and Stoneham, whose honored names they respectively bear and the graves of Union leaders and of army nurses were remembered. Fifty-nine Corps sent contributions to the South. The sum of $2,080.84 was expended."

During the past ten years about $14,000 have been expended by our Corps, for the observance of May 30.

On account of the limited financial resources of the Department in its early days, but few General Orders were issued; and the custom of printing a special Memorial Day Order was not established until 1886.

The First Department Presidents, however, impressed upon the Corps the importance of memorial work, and the lessons thus taught by Mrs. Sarah E. Fuller, Mrs. E. Florence Barker and Mrs. M. Susie Goodale, exerted an influence that has been permanent.

MEMORIAL DAY ORDERS

OF

DEPARTMENT PRESIDENTS.

HEADQUARTERS DEPT. OF MASS. WOMAN'S RELIEF CORPS,
AUXILIARY TO THE GRAND ARMY OF THE REPUBLIC,
NO. 1 PEMBERTON SQ.,
BOSTON, May 10, 1886.

GENERAL ORDERS,
No. 3.

1. The Department President earnestly desires that every Corps in the State should make special effort to assist their respective Posts in performing the sacred duties pertaining to Memorial Day. See to it, that flowers in abundance are gathered and arranged into bouquets and other designs, to decorate all our "brave defenders' graves," who died for their country's cause. With gentle, loving hands strew flowers o'er the mound erected in memory of the "Unknown Dead," our sleeping army nurses, and all who died for their country and flag, leaving nothing undone that woman's hand can do to make Memorial Day of 1886 a day which it is intended to be; showing to the G.A.R. that we are in deed, as well as name, an auxiliary, willing and anxious to be a helper to them on this sacred day.

By command of

S. AGNES PARKER,
Department President.

MARY E. ELLIOT,
Department Secretary.

HEADQUARTERS DEPT. OF MASS. WOMAN'S RELIEF CORPS,
AUXILIARY TO THE GRAND ARMY OF THE REPUBLIC,
NO. 1 PEMBERTON SQ., ROOM 14,
BOSTON, May 4, 1887.

GENERAL ORDERS,
No. 2.

I. Again Memorial Day is near at hand, and we are called with loving hearts to bring flowers and strew them upon the graves of our fallen heroes, the brave soldiers of our Nation, who have gone to their reward and whose bodies are so quietly sleeping in Mother Earth's bosom. Let us consecrate ourselves anew to the work of our Order, and assist the comrades of the Grand Army of the Republic in every way possible, in making Memorial Day the sacred day it was intended to be; see that no grave is passed by where sleeps a veteran. Let mounds be erected and decorated in memory of the "Unknown Dead," our army nurses and all who died for their country; let us remember the brave

Gen. John A. Logan who sent out the first "Memorial Order" calling upon the comrades of the G.A.R. to decorate the graves of the heroic dead; place to *his memory* some tribute in flowers, wherever a Woman's Relief Corps exists.

This day should be to all Americans a sacred day set apart that we might as a nation keep ever fresh in our minds the memory of our loved and honored dead, who gave their lives that we might enjoy the blessings of a free country, and live under the dear old flag they saved from dishonor.

II. The National Memorial Order is hereby promulgated.

By command of

S. AGNES PARKER,
Department President.

MARY E. ELLIOT,
Department Secretary.

HEADQUARTERS DEPT. OF MASS. WOMAN'S RELIEF CORPS,
AUXILIARY TO THE GRAND ARMY OF THE REPUBLIC,
NO. 1 PEMBERTON SQ., ROOM 12,
BOSTON, May 5, 1888.

GENERAL ORDERS,
No. 3.

I. Winter with its tempests and gloom and death-sleep of Nature has passed; spring with its bright hopes of the resurrection in the swelling bud and sweet early flowers is passing, and just at the threshold of summer we come to our Memorial Day.

Ours, because the heritage of every loyal heart, whether it beats in the breast of the veteran who pays tribute to his comrade-in-arms, or throbs in the breast of the woman who mourns her dearest.

So let us gather about "the low, green tents, whose curtain never outward swings," beneath whose shelter rests all that was mortal of our heroes.

Once more is ours the duty to gather with faithful hands the flowers of spring, and bring them as our tribute to our comrades of the Grand Army of the Republic, that they may perform that sacred duty they love so well.

My sisters, make all needful preparations for this holy work. Provide flowers, wreaths, special offerings to the "Unknown Dead," for the various services of the Posts to which you are auxiliary; thus testifying that you are in the Corps, as in the home, an helpmeet for man.

Do not let this day pass without special tribute from all Corps to those of your number who have passed on to the higher life. Strew their resting-places with flowers and cheer the dear ones they have left desolate.

Do not forget the army nurses; for in honoring their memory you are paying tribute to some of the grandest souls that ever wore the form of woman. Unpaid, many of them almost unrecognized and unthanked, save by the blessings breathed from the lips of the wounded or the dying they ministered unto, or by the lonely and aching hearts to whom they sent the last message. Most of them had no tie of blood in husband, son, father or brother to urge their self-sacrifice; only the divine instinct of humanity and their undying loyalty to principle and country, that knows no sex or race. For all they were to yours and mine, and for all they missed of those sweeter, tenderer ties we prize so much, "remember them today."

II. Attention of Corps is called to the action of National Convention regarding the donation of money or flowers to be used in decorating the graves of the "Unknown Dead" near Richmond, Va. All corps desiring to contribute can send donations to Mrs. Hattie A. Ralph, Department Treasurer, and the gifts will *be acknowledged by Department* in next General Order.

III. The General Order of National President is forwarded herewith.

By command of

EMMA B. LOWD,
Department President.

MARY E. ELLIOT,
Department Secretary.

HEADQUARTERS DEPT. OF MASS. WOMAN'S RELIEF CORPS,
AUXILIARY TO THE GRAND ARMY OF THE REPUBLIC,
657 WASHINGTON ST., ROOM 17,
BOSTON, April 27, 1889.

GENERAL ORDERS,
No. 3.

I. Again the reveille of the Spring-time calls us to one of the holiest duties devolving upon the Woman's Relief Corps as the Auxiliary of the Grand Army of the Republic. Nature, with fairest sunshine and gentle showers, is making ready the laurel and the flowers to bear as our tribute to the comrades for their Memorial offering to their comrades-in-arms. See to it that no mound that shelters the dust of the veteran is left without its token of grateful remembrance; its record made in flowers of our undying love for our nation's defenders who have answered to the last roll-call.

Let us be filled with the spirit of the hour. Serve in deed and truth our country. Strive to lighten the labor which presses, year by year more heavily upon those who hold this sacred charge. Aid them in teaching the new generation the story of patriotism and self-sacrifice, and arouse to renewed life in the hearts of the people, a realization of the price paid for their heritage.

And when the story is told and the day is done, let it have been to us as a communion with the saints, consecrating us anew to honor the immortal host who have crossed the river, by our devotion to those whom they have left us and our faith to the "boys" who yet remain.

Through the silence their voices, tender and earnest, remind us to go on with the work they have laid down. We hear them saying: —

> "We seek the comrades whom we left to thee;
> The weak who were thy strength, the poor who had
> Thy pride; the faint and few who gave to the
> One supreme hour from out the day of life,
> One deed majestic to their century.
> These were thy trust. How fare they at thy hands?
> Thy saviors then, are they thy heroes now?
> Our comrades still; we keep the step with them.
> Behold! As thou unto the least of them
> Shalt do, so dost thou unto us. Amen."

II. The Corps of this Department are reminded of the act of the Sixth National Convention, W.R.C., which again endorsed the appeal of Past Junior Vice-Commander-in-Chief Edgar Allan of Richmond, Va., for contributions of money or flowers to be used in decorating the graves about Richmond. The Post which he represents proposes to enlarge its work this year, and hopes to leave no mound that marks the last resting place of a Union soldier or sailor without its memorial message, sent through its hands from some loving heart for somebody's dear one, if not our own.

All donations for this purpose should be sent to Mrs. Harriette L. Reed, Department Treasurer, 251 Columbia Street, Dorchester, Mass.

IV. Blanks for Corps Chaplains' Memorial Day reports are forwarded with this Order. They will be properly filled out and forwarded, through Corps President, with her signature of approval, within ten days after Memorial Day, to Mrs. Emily L. Clark, Department Chaplain, Northampton, Mass.

By command of

EMMA B. LOWD,
Department President.

MARY E. ELLIOT,
Department Secretary.

HEADQUARTERS DEPT. OF MASS. WOMAN'S RELIEF CORPS,
AUXILIARY TO THE GRAND ARMY OF THE REPUBLIC,
657 WASHINGTON ST., ROOM 17,
BOSTON, May 3, 1890.

GENERAL ORDERS,
No. 3.

Time has rounded out another year, and once more as co-workers with the Grand Army of the Republic, we are privileged to do our part in assisting them to canonize their heroic dead in the services of Memorial Day. How fitting it is that this beautiful commemoration should take place in the month of May! The earth has awakened from its long sleep, and every leaf and bud is bursting into life and beauty, ready for the busy and loving hands that will form them into fragrant tributes to be laid upon the green mounds that mark the resting places of our honored dead. And let us ever remember that this grand and solemn service is not a personal tribute, but our offering as a nation the praise and thanksgiving of a grateful people, who realize that through the patriotism and self-sacrifice of these, "Our Heroes," they are living today in a country whose flag is unstained, and where all men are free and equal.

> "Between the living and the dead
> We stand today, but not with tears;
> For time the healing oil has poured
> And memory's sanctified by years.
> Yet misty eyes and throbbing hearts
> Are ours as back we glances cast,
> And through the present glory read
> The story of the past."

Let us not forget those, who, when the "God of Battles" blotted out their lives, left no trace, no living word, no message. Offer to their memory a fragrant tribute, for we know —

> "When at the last grand roll-call,
> The nation's honor roll is read,
> Not far from the top will be found a list
> Of the 'Unknown Soldier Dead.'"

Remember the deeds of those noble women who rendered loving service to our nation's defenders. Give a tender thought to those of your own number, who have laid down their life-work at the call of the Master, and twine for all a garland of the choicest flowers.

Any Corps of this Department who desires to assist Phil. Kearney Post No. 10 of Richmond, Va., in decorating the graves of the Union soldiers and sailors in that vicinity, should send all donations to Mrs. Harriette L. Reed, Department Treasurer, 251 Columbia Street, Dorchester, Mass.

Blanks for Corps Chaplains' Memorial Day reports are forwarded with order. Corps Presidents must attest by their signatures that they are correct, and forward them to Mrs. Emily L. Clark, Department Chaplain, Northampton, Mass., within ten days after Memorial Day.

By command of

MARY E. KNOWLES,
Department President.

MARY E. ELLIOT,
Department Secretary.

HEADQUARTERS DEPT. OF MASS. WOMAN'S RELIEF CORPS,
AUXILIARY TO THE GRAND ARMY OF THE REPUBLIC,
BOYLSTON BUILDING, ROOM 17, 657 WASHINGTON ST.,
BOSTON, May 5, 1891.

GENERAL ORDERS,
No. 4.

With the buds and flowers of Spring, comes the day sacred and precious to us — the Sabbath of the Grand Army, Memorial Day. It is proper for us to halt one day in the hurried march of the year and with sad, yet grateful hearts, pay homage to those, who in an hour of need heeded a Nation's cry and laid their all at her feet.

We are sad when we think of the brave, true-hearted boys who wore the blue, who came not back to the home they loved so well; yet grateful that America's sons were loyal to her flag and willing to defend it.

Not only while one veteran remains to honor the memory of his fallen comrade will this anniversary be a sacred, holy day, but on through the years some loving hand will offer sweet tokens of remembrance " for what he was and all he dared." This, in part, is the mission of the Woman's Relief Corps, for it is our privilege and duty to instil into the minds of those who shall come after us, lessons of patriotism and reverence for those who fought that our country, undivided, might be preserved.

The brain which planned, and the hand which penned the first Memorial Day Order is at rest, but the spirit of the noble man lives today in the hearts of thousands of his comrades of the Grand Army of the Republic, and the loyal women who are pledged to assist them.

"If other eyes grow dull, and other hands slack, and other hearts cold in this solemn trust, ours shall keep it as long as the light and warmth of life shall remain in us."

This was the solemn pledge of the Grand Army of the Republic twenty-three years ago, and faithfully has it been kept.

What more sacred promise can we, the Woman's Relief Corps, make than this?

Then let us assemble on Memorial Day and re-consecrate ourselves to the work for which we are organized, and

> "Bring flowers — sweet flowers, o'er the grave to shed,
> A crown, for the brow of the noble dead;
> For this, through its leaves hath the wild rose burst,
> For this, in the wood was the violet nursed;
> Tho' they smile in vain for what once was ours,
> They are love's last gift; bring flowers — sweet flowers."

Let us in some quiet spot strew these blossoms which shall be our tribute of love and honor to those whose low, white headstones in our National cemeteries give no tidings save that "somebody's darling slumbers here," and for the thousands who lie where they fell, in prison, hospital or in the ocean deep, in defense of their country and ours.

We honor, too, the loyal woman who, on the field, or by the cot of the wounded and dying, tenderly nursed the one to life, or bore to the watching, waiting mother, wife or loved one, some message from him whose last hours had been soothed and comforted by her presence.

Our hearts turn to many of our own members who have fallen by the wayside, and while our numbers may increase we miss *their* faces, their kind words and deeds, and we will place the wreath of immortelles above their resting places that we may not forget the tie which binds us still to them.

Encourage the children to take some part that they may learn to respect the day and to understand its meaning, and let one and all together unite in this sweet, solemn service, and in honoring the dead may we be fitted to go forth with purer, nobler hearts to do for the living while we may.

> "The shortest life is longest if 'tis best,
> 'Tis ours to work — to God belongs the rest.
> Our lives are measured by the deeds we do,
> The thoughts we think, the objects we pursue."

So with Fraternity of heart, with Charity for all and Loyalty of purpose, let us prove that we are worthy of being auxiliary to the Grand Army of the Republic.

National Orders, No. 8, are herewith transmitted.

By command of

AUGUSTA A. WALES,
Department President.

MARY E. ELLIOT,
Department Secretary.

HEADQUARTERS DEPT. OF MASS. WOMAN'S RELIEF CORPS,
AUXILIARY TO THE GRAND ARMY OF THE REPUBLIC,
657 WASHINGTON ST., ROOM 17,
BOSTON, May 6, 1892.

GENERAL ORDERS,
NO. 4.

I. Among the sacred legacies bequeathed to us by the Civil War is Memorial Day with its treasured memories. It reminds us of the time when loyal hearts responded to the battle-call, and when ties of home and companionship were severed forever. It recalls the sad messages of suffering and death that came from battle-field and hospital, from camp and prison, and the sublime courage of the men who were the saviors of the nation.

In the years that have intervened, no more inspiring thought has been crystalized into action than that which prompted an annual memorial to the patriot dead. This day, the "choicest in the calendar of the Grand Army," should be faithfully observed by the Woman's Relief Corps. It is a duty we owe to the living, on the muster-roll of whose hearts are inscribed the names of martyred thousands.

The flowers we may offer for the graves of the fallen will tenderly express our gratitude for their services. The wreaths we may weave for tablet or monument will be emblematical of the Union their lives preserved. The floral mounds in honor of those buried in National cemeteries or on fields unknown, will become historic with every century, though they fade from view with the passing days. Our tributes to the women martyrs of the rebellion, and to those who have worn our badge but whose work is finished, should be worthy the spirit of loyal womanhood: then

> "Let the flags float out above them —
> Let the music fill the air;
> In the hearts of those who love them
> It shall echo like a prayer."

When the Memorial Day reports are returned to the Department Chaplain, may they contain a record worthy of this commemorative service and of the Relief Corps of Massachusetts.

May they show that our members throughout the State honor the memory of the heroes who, after stormy battles, have encamped on peaceful fields.

II. Attention is called to the paragraph in General Orders, No. 6, of the National President, reminding us of "the thousands of graves that come under the care of isolated Posts, whose members are unable to give them the recognition demanded."

Let the Corps respond, wherever possible, to the eloquent appeal that comes from distant sections of the land. Your offering of plants, of evergreens or flags, however small, will be a memorial of your love which will meet with appreciation.

> "O birds! to other climes that wing,
> Repeat the story as ye sing!
> That ye have found no brighter green,
> No softer shade, no rarer sheen,
> Than that which fair Columbia spread
> Above her honored patriot dead."

III. Corps Chaplains are requested to forward to the Department Chaplain, on or before June 10, a report of the day's observance, blanks for which are forwarded with this order.

IV. National Orders, Nos. 6 and 7 are herewith transmitted.

By command of
MARY G. DEANE,
Department President.

Mary E. Elliot,
    Department Secretary.

Headquarters Dept. of Mass. Woman's Relief Corps,
Auxiliary to the Grand Army of the Republic,
657 Washington St., Room 17,
Boston, May 3, 1893.

General Orders,
No. 3.

Again we are called upon to arrange for the proper observance of May 30; but no General Order is needed to remind the members of the Order in this Department of their duties and privileges on Memorial Day.

With the real purpose of the day in view, Corps will render all needful aid in its observance to the Posts of the Grand Army of the Republic, to which they are auxiliary.

Let all be made to realize the value of the inheritance received from this silent Army, whose "green tents" we decorate that day; and let us consecrate ourselves anew to the work of our Order and assist the Grand Army of the Republic in making it the *holy day* it was intended to be. While we reverence the dead, let us comfort the living and be grandly loyal to all.

Since the last Memorial Day, many of the comrades have lain them down to sleep "the sleep that knows no waking" on this side of life, and we have many new graves to decorate.

> Steadily marches the Army, with painful steps and slow,
> Down into the shadowy valley where the mystic waters flow.
> They tarry not, nor falter, this Army of Soldiers true,
> When they hear from the Great Commander, "Forward, the Boys in Blue!"
> They close their ranks in order, down into the shadows they go,
> Following the voice of their Leader with the faith of years ago.
> So twine the evergreen wreath and bring the sweet Spring flowers,
> For those who lie beneath these sacred mounds of ours.

Remember with tender regard the graves of our members who have passed on to "the better land," during the year that has closed.

Attention is called to the appeal of the National President in behalf of Posts in the South.

Corps Chaplains will forward their Memorial Day Reports as early as June 10, to Mrs. Hattie A. Ralph, Department Chaplain, Somerville, Mass.

National General Orders, No. 7, is herewith transmitted.

By command of

EMILY L. CLARK,
Department President.

MARY E. ELLIOT,
Department Secretary.

HEADQUARTERS DEPT. OF MASS. WOMAN'S RELIEF CORPS,
AUXILIARY TO THE GRAND ARMY OF THE REPUBLIC,
657 WASHINGTON ST., ROOM 17,
BOSTON, May 1, 1894.

GENERAL ORDERS,
NO. 4.

General Orders, No. 6, of National President Mrs. Sarah C. Mink, is herewith transmitted, an eloquent reminder to the Woman's Relief Corps of duties pertaining to Memorial Day.

Attention is called to Decision No. 55 of Eleventh National Convention, which provides that all contributions to Memorial work in the South shall "be sent through the regular channel to the National Treasurer."

Funds for that purpose *must* be forwarded to the Department Treasurer, thence remitted to the National Treasurer, who will transfer the same "to the Quartermaster-General of the Grand Army, for distribution among the most needy and worthy Posts."

By valuable assistance rendered to the Grand Army of the Republic, by prompt and accurate reports of Corps Chaplains, by lessons in patriotism to the youth of this Department, Corps members are urged hereby to renewed devotion.

"May we join so reverently in these exercises, that what we call Memorial Day may be to our dead their day of coronation!"

MEMORIAL DAY.

The morning dawns, and lo! in light,
Up spring, from sea to sea,
"Columbia's passion flowers" bright,
The bloom of Liberty!

The tiny flags that lightly wave,
How eloquent they are!
We read, beside a soldier's grave,
A lesson in each star.

What messages of Hope they bear
For those bereft, who weep!
A Nation's benediction, where
Its leal defenders sleep.

Roses and lilies will we bring,
The evergreen and bay,
And all the jewels of the Spring,
Shall crown Memorial Day.

In every sacred, mournful rite,
To faithful souls so dear,
Will Loyalty and Love unite
To consecrate the year;

By requiem, by grateful meed,
The garland, and the throng
Who celebrate the valiant deed
In poesy and song.

But where the triune colors shine
Above the sleeping brave,
Celestial beauty doth enshrine
The patriot soldier's grave!

O *blessed* Standard of the world!
They gave their lives for *thee*!
That, stainless, thou should'st be unfurled,
The Banner of the Free!

By command of

CLARE H. BURLEIGH,
Department President.

MARY E. ELLIOT,
Department Secretary.

Be assured, and please assure the other ladies of your Corps, that loyalty to God and to the dear motherland shall govern the " Soldiers' Home" which you and they have so tenderly regarded and so greatly honored by your love. — General HORACE BINNEY SARGENT, in a letter to Mrs. Sarah E. Fuller, Department President, June 9, 1881.

SOLDIERS' HOME, CHELSEA, MASS.

CHAPTER IV.

SPECIAL WORK FOR THE SOLDIERS' HOME.

AMONG the many philanthropic enterprises that reflect credit upon the Old Bay State, none illustrates more clearly the principles of gratitude and justice than the Soldiers' Home.

Men, crippled, paralyzed and penniless, as a result of their war service, are tenderly cared for under the roof of this home which shelters 330 veterans of the Union Army.

Early in 1881 rumors of a bazaar in aid of a Soldiers' Home in Massachusetts, were found to be a reality. Then the little band of women who had pledged allegiance to the Grand Army of the Republic as its auxiliary promptly saw an opportunity to prove the sincerity of its professions.

A meeting of the Board of Directors of the State Relief Corps was held April 14, 1881, and an invitation to co-operate with the Trustees of the Soldiers' Home in their plans for a bazaar was favorably considered.

A committee was chosen for this purpose, consisting of Mrs. Sarah E. Fuller, Mrs. E. Florence Barker, Mrs. Pamelia F. Sprague, Mrs. Francelia P. Boynton, Mrs. S. Agnes Parker and Mrs. M. Susie Goodale.

A suggestion offered by Mrs. Fuller that a Bible, Burgee and Flag be presented the Home, was adopted on motion of Mrs.

Barker, and Mrs. Fuller, Mrs. Barker, Mrs. Boynton and Mrs. Goodale were chosen a committee to procure the gifts.

Contributions for the same were received from the Corps in Fitchburg, Cambridge, Taunton, Medford, Malden, Brockton, Haverhill, Charlestown, Chelsea, Natick, Stoughton, Springfield, Ashland and Melrose.

The Highland Park Hotel on Powderhorn Hill in Chelsea, was dedicated as a Soldiers' Home June 8, 1881, under the auspices of the Board of Trustees, viz. :

Horace Binney Sargent, Alexander H. Rice, William Gaston, Charles Devens, George S. Evans, George H. Patch, James F. Meech, Edward T. Raymond, Samuel Dalton, Andrew J. Bailey, Henry Wilson, Jr., William S. Brown, Joseph F. Lovering, Cyrus C. Emery, John McKay, Jr., John G. B. Adams, E. G. W. Cartwright and Charles W. Wilcox.

Theodore Winthrop Post No. 35 of Chelsea and its auxiliary, Corps No. 10, assumed the expense of the dedicatory ceremonies.

Department Officers of the State Relief Corps were among the invited guests on this occasion, and when the flag was unfurled, Mrs. Fuller, as chairman of the committee, gave the following address :

"When the message went forth that Massachusetts was to have a Soldiers' Home, thousands of hearts gave glad response, and today we gather from city and town, hilltop and valley, to unite in dedicating this beautiful spot as a hospital home for sick and disabled soldiers in this Commonwealth.

.   .   .

"I come before you as the representative of an organized body of women — women who, with willing hands and warm hearts, have banded ourselves together and pledged ourselves to work in every possible way properly within the sphere of woman's labor, to assist these men, their families and their loved ones.

"We bring to this work our best endeavors, for in memory's closet there is a shelf upon which the dust has never gathered. We cannot forget the day when with banner and drum-beat proudly they marched away. Think you the women can ever forget those terrible years? Those who were left to keep the hearthstone, the little ones or the aged ones, they were fraught with an anguish and an anxiety that only God and the women can ever know. And so I come to you today to ask you to accept, in behalf of the Woman's State Relief Corps, an auxiliary to the Department of Massachusetts, Grand Army of the Republic, our free-will offerings, the first fruits of what we hope may be an abundant harvest.

"We bring you first, God's holy Word, the sacred Scriptures of Divine truth, for upon its pages we find written the grand and true principles of loyalty and patriotism. May its precious truths ever bring peace and comfort to the hearts of every future inmate of this hospital home. May the heroes of war here learn to revere the name of Him who vouchsafed to bless our armies, and who gave to them such signal victories over those who would have brought a stain upon their country's flag and dishonor upon the best government this world ever knew.

"And then we bring you what must ever be so dear to every American heart — the beautiful tri-color — our flag. Long, long may it wave! Under its folds the precious boon of liberty is ours to enjoy. To the undaunted courage, bravery and self-sacrifices of the noble men who took their lives in their hands and marched away from home and loved ones, to protect them and their country from the hands of traitors, and to the blood of thousands so freely shed, we can today look upon this flag — our flag as unsullied! Not one star less upon its clear, azure field, than when the first rebel gun was fired in 1861; and while there remains one sick or disabled soldier in this dear old Commonwealth who needs the privileges of this hospital home, may each rising sun see this flag unfurled from its staff on this, the Massachusetts Soldiers' Home."

There is hanging upon the walls of Department Headquarters a beautifully engrossed testimonial presented by the Board of Trustees, the text of which reads as follows: —

BOSTON, July 7, 1881.
SARAH E. FULLER,
    President Woman's State Relief Corps.
  Madam: By a vote of the Board of Trustees of the Soldiers' Home in Massachusetts, I have the honor to transmit to the Woman's State Relief Corps the most respectful and grateful thanks of the Board for the elegant generosity of the eighth of June. It was indeed graceful and munificent.
  To the preciousness of the beautiful gifts — the Bible and the Flag — was added the charm of their delivery.
  Though it is impossible not to be moved by your kindness on Dedication Day, it is difficult to express our sense of obligation. Perhaps I could not more adequately fulfil my duty to the Trustees than by saying, on behalf of all of them, to the Ladies of the Woman's State Relief Corps, that you gave more pleasure than even your generous hearts intended.
  That you should so generously welcome our effort to make some provision for the destitute men whom the war has left unhappy, excites a respectful gratitude that we shall never forget.
  I have the honor to be

    Very respectfully yours,
      HORACE BINNEY SARGENT,
    President of the Board of Trustees of the Soldiers' Home.

Mrs. Fuller addressed several public gatherings and Corps meetings in behalf of the proposed bazaar, and also helped to awaken an interest by personal appeals and official correspondence.

Encouraging reports were received from Corps Presidents at a meeting of the Board of Directors held October 14, and at a subsequent meeting of the Board (November 18), it was announced that eleven Corps would be represented when the bazaar opened in Mechanics Building, Boston, on the evening of December 7.

Gen. H. G. Berry Corps No. 6 of Malden furnished a table, which was in charge of Mrs. E. Florence Barker, who was a member of the Executive Committee of the bazaar and one of the most active workers for its success.

An annex to the Malden table attracted widespread interest. It was in charge of Mrs. Lizabeth A. Turner, who for several months had been busy in collecting autographs of distinguished persons.

Her album, containing signatures of Washington and other Presidents, of leading generals, statesmen, authors and scientists, a thousand in number, was scanned with eager interest.

The album, which netted five hundred dollars to the bazaar treasury, came into possession of Mr. J. E. Sherman of Boston, who felt that an article of such historic value should be placed in some public library.

He gave Mrs. Turner the privilege of naming its future custodian, and the archives of the Loyal Legion secured this coveted treasure.

The Malden Corps table netted the sum of $2,800.

Other tables were furnished by Fletcher Webster Corps No. 7 of Brockton, Mrs. S. Agnes Parker, President, and Major How Corps No. 8 of Haverhill, Miss Hattie M. Mason, President.

There was also a Union table furnished by S. C. Lawrence Corps No. 5 of Medford, Maj. George L. Stearns Corps No. 9 of Charlestown, Theodore Winthrop Corps No. 10 of Chelsea, Gen. Wadsworth Corps No. 11 of Natick, A. St. John Chambre Corps No. 13 of Stoughton, U. S. Grant Corps No. 16 of Melrose, and Willard C. Kinsley (Independent) Corps of Somerville.

Officers of the Union table were: President, Mrs. Amanda M. Thayer, Chelsea; Vice-Presidents, Mrs. M. Susie Goodale, Medford, Miss Laura Baldwin, Melrose, Miss Mary E. Elliot, Somerville, Mrs. Ellen Johnson, Charlestown, Mrs. Maria A. Symonds, Natick, and Mrs. Julia Mills, Stoughton; Secretary, Mrs. Josie W. Connor, Chelsea.

One of the attractions at this table was a beautiful pen sketch (neatly framed) of Lincoln's famous speech at the dedication of the Gettysburg National Cemetery. It was penned by the late Alfred C. Monroe, who for several years was Assistant Adjutant-General of the Department of Massachusetts, G.A.R., and given by him to this table. It was purchased by friends of the Home and placed in its public parlor.

A marquee tent, loaned by Mr. R. M. Yale of Boston, was elaborately decorated, and served as Headquarters of the State Relief Corps. Receptions were here given by the Department Officers, and many pleasant greetings exchanged during the ten days of the bazaar.

The Relief Corps tables netted the sum of $4,189.25 to the treasury of the bazaar.

Frequent visits to Powder Horn Hill were made by our Corps after the home was first opened, July 22, 1882. Entertainments were arranged by Corps members, delicacies distributed to the inmates in the hospital and rooms furnished with substantial and ornamental articles.

These visits increased the interest of our members in the home, and when in January, 1885, Department Commander John D. Billings, members of his Staff and other comrades visited our State Convention and solicited interest in a Soldiers' Home Carnival to be held in April, the suggestion was greeted with applause.

It was voted that the subscription cards issued by the Carnival Committee be sent to every Corps.

Mrs. M. Susie Goodale, Department President, in her first General Order after Convention, referred to this carnival as follows : —

" By a vote of Convention, our organization pledged its assistance to the Carnival to be held in April, for the benefit of the Soldiers' Home. The work already accomplished by our members in this Department for this beloved object is most commendable, and is appreciated ; but, my sisters, we must not be weary in well doing. Remember the necessity that calls for this Carnival. We must not let the boys who fought for us, at life's dear peril wrought for us — suffer for hospital accommodations. We trust every heart will beat responsive to this appeal, and that every Corps in the Department will be in some manner represented.

"In every case where the Post has decided to furnish a table, it is expected the Corps connected with it will assist, feeling it not only their duty but a pleasure to do so. To Corps not interested in this manner, we ask for assistance, that the Department table may be a credit to our organization, and contribute largely to the success of the Carnival.

"Corps are requested to take immediate action in this matter, and report to the Department Secretary at once the decision. Contributions of money or goods are equally desirable."

That this appeal was heeded is shown by the following list of tables which was printed in the Carnival Souvenir, distributed at the opening in Mechanics' Building, April 7, 1885.

Merrimac Valley, represented by the Corps of Newburyport, Merrimac and Amesbury. President, Mrs. Abbie L. Wilson, Newburyport; Vice-Presidents, Mrs. D. E. Gale, Amesbury, Mrs. Cinderella E. Clement, Merrimac; Treasurer, Mrs. Mary L. Tucker, Amesbury.

Union table, representing Salem, Danvers, Peabody, Ipswich and Marblehead. President, Mrs. Emma B. Lowd, Salem; Vice-Presidents, Miss Florence Wentworth, Danvers, Miss Sarah F. Kittredge, Peabody. Secretary, Dr. Samuel Worcester, Salem; Treasurer, Capt. Benjamin Pitman, Marblehead.

Department of Massachusetts Woman's Relief Corps. President, Mrs. M. Susie Goodale, Medford; Vice-Presidents, Mrs. Mary A. B. Fellows, Chelsea, Mrs. S. Agnes Parker, Brockton, Mrs. E. Florence Barker, Malden, Mrs. Mary M. Perry, Springfield, Mrs. Helen F. Johnson, Somerville; Secretary, Mrs.

Kathrina L. Beedle, Cambridge; Treasurer, Mrs. Lizabeth A. Turner, Boston; Assistant Treasurers, Miss Alfrina J. Whittredge; Mrs. Annie Currier, Malden, Mrs. Eleanor B. Wheeler, South Boston; Quartermasters, Capt. James F. Meech, Col. Thomas E. Barker, Maj. F. E. Beebe, Capt. Geo. L. Goodale, Capt. John S. Beck, Mr. J. P. Litch.

General Lander Corps, Lynn. President, Mrs. Mary A. Bailey; Vice-Presidents, Mrs. Hattie A. Bray, Mrs. M. Mansfield, Mrs. M. E. Martin; Secretaries, Mrs. Eliza F. Stiles, Mrs. H. Latimer; Treasurers, Mrs. G. F. Batchelder, Mrs. H. A. Sawyer; Marshal, Myron H. Whittredge; Aides, A. J. Hoitt, L. S. Johnson; Quartermasters, A. A. Davis, Philip Smith.

Medford Section Woman's Relief Corps. President, Mrs. Laura Beck; Vice-Presidents, Mrs. Ellen M. Gill, Mrs. Hannah J. Dinsmore; Treasurer, Miss Jessie Dinsmore.

Cambridge Section Woman's Relief Corps. President, Mrs. Kathrina L. Beedle.

Brockton Section Woman's Relief Corps. President, Mrs. Sarah W. Murdoch.

Charlestown Section Woman's Relief Corps. President, Mrs. Helen F. Johnson.

Cake and Fruit Table and Ice Cream Room, John A. Hawes Corps No. 3, East Boston; President, Mrs. Sarah E. Fuller. Maj.-Gen. H. G. Berry Corps No. 6, Malden, Mrs. Lizabeth A. Turner, President.

Among the officers of other tables were the following-named members of Relief Corps: Mrs. Hattie A. Ralph and Mrs. Lizzie I. Fielding, Somerville; Mrs. Elizabeth C. Bickmore, Mrs. Elizabeth V. Lang, Hyde Park; Mrs. W. A. Wetherbee, Newton; Mrs. Eva T. Cook, Mrs. Georgie A. Center, Gloucester; Mrs. Sarah B. Creasey (present matron of the Home), Newburyport; Mrs. W. L. Wright, South Boston; Mrs. Angela H. Scranton, Mrs. Nannie Martin, Mrs. Sarah A. Torrey and Mrs. P. F. Kennear, Cambridgeport; Mrs. Abbie D. Danforth, Plymouth;

S. AGNES PARKER

Fourth Department President 1896, 1897
National Chaplain 1894, 1895

Miss M. Alice Carey, Malden; Mrs. Matilda E. Lawton, Mrs. Maria A. Brown, Mrs S. C. Wright, Mrs. Eleanor B. Wheeler, Mrs. Mary H. Vaughn, Mrs. J. L. Spooner, South Boston; Mrs. Ellen A. Gowell, Boston; Mrs. Augusta A. Wales, Mrs. Sarah D. Stiles, Dorchester.

In a General Order issued to the Corps May 14, 1885, Mrs. Goodale said: —

"It may be interesting to the members of our Order to know the result of our efforts as an organization in aid of the Soldiers' Home during the late Carnival. The Department Table, which was represented by ten Corps, with contributions from several others, will return about four thousand dollars. In addition to this, eleven other Corps assisted their respective Posts at various tables, all doing good, faithful work and thereby proving their loyalty to the interests of the Grand Army of the Republic, to which we are auxiliary.

"For the prompt, earnest manner in which the Corps throughout the Department responded to this call for work, the President desires to return her most sincere and grateful thanks."

Mrs. Sarah E. Fuller and Miss Mary E. Elliot were assistants to Capt. George W. Creasey, Secretary of the Executive Committee, and were on duty at the headquarters of the Committee in Pemberton Square several weeks previous to the opening of the Carnival.

Past Department Commander Adams, when visiting our Annual Convention in January, 1886, referred to the work of this Department for the Soldiers' Home, which he had acknowledged in his report as President of the Board of Trustees.

Mrs. S. Agnes Parker, in her address as Department President at the Annual Convention in 1887, referred to her acceptance of the invitation to assist in the exercises of dedication of the new hospital connected with the Soldiers' Home. In acknowledging an invitation from the Ladies' Aid Association to be present at the dedication of its soldiers' lot at Malden, she said: "I accepted the invitation, feeling we were one in purpose and resolve, working for the interests of the soldier."

The Ladies' Aid Association which was formed soon after the bazaar, is auxiliary to the Board of Trustees of the Home, and included in its active membership are many Relief Corps members, some of whom helped to form the association, and have served continuously as officers and on committees.

At this Convention (1887), Past Department Commander Evans made a pathetic appeal in behalf of a sick and needy veteran who was unable to be taken to the Home. This resulted in the establishing of an Invalid Veterans' Fund, the following motion offered by Miss M. Alice Carey of Malden having been adopted : —

"That the Department Secretary be empowered to write every Corps President, soliciting whatever funds they can afford, to be used for such cases as the hospital at the Soldiers' Home cannot accommodate, and that the money be forwarded to the Department Treasurer, as a Department Relief Fund, subject to the call of Comrade Evans, Secretary Board of Trustees of the Soldiers' Home."

The Department Secretary was instructed to notify Comrade Evans, Secretary Board of Trustees of the Soldiers' Home, of the vote just passed.

Mrs. Hattie A. Ralph, Department Treasurer, reported at the next annual Convention that : " The responses to the call for the Invalid Veterans' Fund were prompt and generous, Corps 5 of Medford leading, by presenting the sum of $20.00 before the official communication had time to reach them. Corps 62 of West Acton donated the largest amount, $50.00."

Total amount received	$674 85
Expended . .	57 00
Balance to new account	$617 85

In recognition of this fund the trustees sent the following letter : —

BOSTON, Jan. 22, 1888.

MRS. S. AGNES PARKER,
    President Department of Massachusetts, W.R.C.

Dear Madam : At a meeting of the Board of Trustees of the Soldiers' Home in Massachusetts, it was unanimously voted, That the thanks of the Board be tendered to the Woman's Relief Corps of Massachusetts for the thoughtful action which prompted the raising of a fund for the purpose of taking care of sick and destitute veterans who are applicants for admission to the Soldiers' Home, but who cannot be admitted for want of room. I can assure you, dear Madam, that it affords me great pleasure to thus convey to you, and through you to the members of your organization throughout the Commonwealth, the thanks of the Board of Trustees for your timely and generous action at your last Department Convention, and to assure you that we highly appreciate all that has been done by the Woman's Relief Corps of Massachusetts for our Soldiers' Home and for its inmates.

To the subordinate Corps that have contributed so liberally to the fund named, we desire to express our sincere thanks, and assure them that the money thus expended will make glad the hearts of many a deserving veteran.

The Trustees also desire to express their thanks to the Corps that have furnished rooms and otherwise contributed to the comfort and happiness of the men at the Home, and of every individual member of your organization who has been the means of making happy the hearts of its inmates.

The Trustees regret that the request of many Corps that rooms be assigned them to furnish and take care of, cannot be complied with as all are now assigned; but hope that the day is not far distant when the accommodations will be increased, more rooms added, and more of our comrades provided for.

Sincerely thanking *all* for the interest manifested in our beautiful Soldiers' Home, and yourself personally for your many acts of kindness, your kind words and cheerful endorsement at all times, and hoping that your future may be most happy and prosperous,

    I am yours sincerely and fraternally,

        GEORGE S. EVANS,
        Secretary Board of Trustees.

Capt. Adams in his annual report as President of the Board of Trustees in 1889, said: "The Woman's Relief Corps are waiting for more rooms to furnish, and with interest unabated, are willing to perform any duty assigned them."

Secretary Evans of the Board said: "I have been enabled during the past year to take care of a few through the kindness of the Department of Massachusetts Woman's Relief Corps, which has paid the board of some of the applicants in very extreme cases that could not be admitted to the home."

A General Order issued by Mrs. Emma B. Lowd, Department President, Nov. 20, 1889, contained the following: —

"Attention is called to the circular issued by the Trustees of the Soldiers' Home which accompanies this Order. The new plan adopted by them for covering the expense of furnishing the rooms assigned to Corps must necessarily tax our resources to a greater extent than before. It is hoped that no Corps that has already applied for a room will be discouraged because the sum named seems large, as terms of gradual payment may be made with the Treasurer of the Board. Remember that the needs of this grand charity were never so pressing as now. The enlargement of the Home involves largely increased expense in its maintenance; about one hundred and forty more veterans will be sheltered beneath its roof. The coming of the National Encampment to Boston next year absorbs to a great extent the energy and funds of many friends of the Home, and prevents any attempt to hold a large fair in its aid. We must depend upon the efforts of individuals and we look to our Corps to support this noble institution in its time of need. The $125.00 covers the expense of furniture, mattresses and pillows; all other articles are in addition to this sum.

"Fourteen Corps have already applied for rooms in the new addition, Union Corps No. 52 of Peabody leading off with the first payment of $125.00 in cash."

At the Department Convention in 1890, a vote was passed that three rooms be furnished by the Department, and named in honor of Sarah E. Fuller, E. Florence Barker and Lizabeth A. Turner, and a committee was appointed to have charge of the rooms, viz.: Mrs Emma B. Lowd, Mrs. M. Susie Goodale and Mrs. S. Agnes Parker.

Appended herewith is the letter of acknowledgment received from Treasurer George W. Creasey of the Soldiers' Home: —

BOSTON, March 20, 1890.

Mrs. EMMA B. LOWD,
Chairman Committee Mass. Dept. W.R.C.

DEAR MADAM: — Permit me by this to acknowledge the receipt of $300.00 from the Department of Massachusetts, Woman's Relief Corps, to be expended in the furnishing of the rooms in the addition now about completed to the Soldiers' Home at Chelsea.

Will you kindly convey to the Department President the thanks of the trustees for this additional expression of the earnest devotion of the ladies of your organization to the good work of our Soldiers' Home.

I am, very truly yours,

GEO. W. CREASEY,
Treasurer of the Board of Trustees.

When the Convention met a year later, Mrs. Mary E. Knowles, Department President, acknowledged in her annual address the courtesy extended by Col. Allen Corps 77 of Gloucester, in naming its room at the Soldiers' Home in her honor, and referring to the Home, said: —

"On the 7th of last June I was honored with an invitation from the Board of Trustees to be present and take part in the dedication of the new portion of the Home, and the interesting exercises and incidents of the occasion will be remembered with pleasure as long as life shall last.

"I have visited the Home whenever it was possible for me to do so. One very pleasant visit was made in company with our

National President and members of our council. That the comfort of its inmates is very near and dear to the members of this Department is shown in the tasteful, and in some cases luxurious, furnishing of the rooms that are cared for by a large number of the Corps; and the managers of the Home may feel assured that if a call is made upon us during the coming year we shall be ready to answer 'Here,' and we will do our part to the *best* of our ability."

Mrs. Harriette L. Reed, Department Treasurer, reported at this Convention the sum of one thousand dollars in the Department Soldiers' Home Fund, this being given by vote of the General Committee of Arrangements for the Eighth National Convention, from a surplus remaining after all expenses of entertainment had been paid.

In General Orders No. 5, issued June 8, 1891, by Mrs. Augusta A. Wales, Department President, reference is made to a proposed fair, viz.: —

"In response to a call from the Trustees, the Ladies' Aid Association of the Soldiers' Home in Massachusetts will hold a fair in Boston during the month of November for the benefit of the Home. Mrs. Julia K. Dyer, President of the Association, in a communication to the Department President announcing the above fact, says: 'Will you take your numerous family and come over and help us?' As this is in the direct line of the work of the Woman's Relief Corps, it is hoped that all who can will assist in this effort to increase the Hospital accommodations for the needy veterans."

At the semi-annual meeting of the Department Council, held June 22, 1891, it was voted to furnish a Department table in the fair, and Mrs. Emilie L. W. Waterman was appointed chairman of a committee to have charge of the same.

The following circular was mailed to all the Corps: —

HEADQUARTERS DEPT. OF MASS. WOMAN'S RELIEF CORPS,
AUXILIARY TO THE GRAND ARMY OF THE REPUBLIC,
657 WASHINGTON ST., ROOM 17,
BOSTON, Nov. 6, 1891.

CIRCULAR LETTER }
No. 1.   }

The fair in aid of soldiers will open in Music Hall, Feb. 8, 1892, and continue one week.

As the Annual Convention of the Woman's Relief Corps will be held on the 10th and 11th, an opportunity will be given for many to visit the Fair who might not otherwise find it convenient to do so. Meals will be served each day in Bumstead Hall. Dinners, twenty-five cents.

Any Corps which can furnish a table is cordially invited to do so, and will please notify Mrs. Micah Dyer, Hancock St., Dorchester, of such intention.

The Department of Massachusetts Woman's Relief Corps table will be under the charge of the following ladies : Mrs. Emilie L. W. Waterman, President; Mrs. Clara C. Lovering, Secretary; Mrs. Mary E. Knowles, Treasurer.

Executive Committee : Mrs. Augusta A. Wales. Mrs. D. S. Davis, Mrs. S. C. Walkley, Mrs. Mary M. Perry, Mrs. Clare H. Burleigh, Mrs. Mary G. Deane, Mrs. Annie K. Day.

All Corps which are not otherwise pledged are invited to send contributions of money or of articles useful or ornamental, to this table.

Communications or packages can be sent to Mrs. Waterman, 657 Washington St., Boston, Room 17. Make all money orders payable to Mrs. E. L. W. Waterman, Boston. Cash contributions should not be taken from the Relief Fund for this purpose.

Mark all articles *plainly* and *securely* with value and name of Corps donating the same, in order that credit may be given each Corps.

Articles remaining unsold at the close of the Fair will be returned to the Corps by which they were donated, except such as may be useful at the Soldiers' Home, to which they will be sent.

Articles may be sent as soon as convenient, and Corps should at once notify the Committee of their intention to assist in order that proper space may be secured.

Corps will receive credit for all tickets sold by them.

Season tickets, $1.00. Admission, 25 cents.

By command of

AUGUSTA A. WALES,
Department President.

EMILIE L. W. WATERMAN,
President Dept. W.R.C. Table.

Mrs. Waterman presented a summary of the work of the Department for this fair, at the Annual Convention in February, 1893, viz. : —

CONSOLIDATED REPORT OF THE COMMITTEE ON DEPARTMENT TABLE AT MILITARY FAIR.

No. of Corps donating to table .	88	
Estimated value of articles received	$696.99	
Cash received for articles donated .	. .	$450.28
Cash contributions received . .	. .	517.33
Cash received for tickets . .	. .	154.00
Total from all sources	.	$1,121.61
Expenditures . .	.	19.60
Turned over to Treasurer Fair Committee	.	$1,102.01

Respectfully submitted, in F., C. and L.,

EMILIE L. W. WATERMAN,
President Department Table.

Mrs. Mary G. Deane in her annual address as Department President in 1893, reported as follows, regarding the Soldiers' Home : —

"The demands of the hospital are constantly increasing, and to aid as far as possible in meeting these requirements is an important branch of our work.

"The last Annual Report issued by the Board of Trustees contains a list of rooms furnished, and of numerous contributions given by our Corps. The Trustees and Superintendent acknowledge in this, as in all their former reports, the active interest of our Corps. The Department rooms at the Home are carefully cared for by the committee having them in charge. Four rooms bear the names of honored members of this Department.

"In answer to numerous questions received during the early part of my administration I rendered a decision, that all articles contributed to the Department Table in the Fair held February last in Music Hall, should be reported as 'relief other than money.' This decision also refers to all articles contributed by our Corps from any source.

"According to a vote of the Tenth Department Convention, all cash contributions to the Home are credited to the Relief Fund.

"The value of donations to the Home by our Corps during the past year amounted to over $1,200, which includes the receipts from the Department Table at the Fair in Music Hall.

"On a recent visit to Powder Horn Hill, I thought what a monument of gratitude is there erected to the veterans who are sheltered within its walls! What a privilege as loyal women to show our respect for those who but a few years ago were honored as among the heroes of the Republic! Their record during those days can never be effaced, and their dependent condition should increase our regard for them.

"The death of the efficient Superintendent, General James A. Cunningham, and the subsequent retirement of his widow, the beloved Matron, were keenly felt by our members, who had often received their kindly greetings.

Capt. George W. Creasey, the successor of the late General Cunningham, is a true friend of this Department; and Mrs. Creasey, who, as Matron, carries sunshine to the inmates by her womanly tenderness and sympathy, is a member of our Order. We feel assured that all our endeavors will be appreciated in the future as they have been in the past."

At this Convention (1893), Mrs. E. Florence Barker said : —

"Mrs. President and Ladies of the Convention, I have been requested to bear to you the greetings of the Treasurer of the Board of Trustees of the Soldiers' Home in Massachusetts*, and

---
*Col. Thomas E. Barker.

his appreciation of the substantial aid rendered the Home by the Woman's Relief Corps. He wished me also to say that the fact that so many hundred women in our State were interested in that Home, convinced him that the Relief Corps of Massachusetts were on a more substantial basis than he had ever before realized." Mrs. Barker further stated that the Superintendent of the Home intended to establish a new industry — a large hennery.

On motion of Mrs. Barker it was voted, That each Corps be requested, through its President, to donate one pullet to the Home.

Mrs. Turner, as Committee on Soldiers' Home Hennery, reported a year later that $196.88 had been received from the Corps for the purchase of hens. There were contributed in addition thirty-eight hens and three cockerels.

Mrs. Barker (who introduced this subject at the last Department Convention) said: "We have set a ball rolling that has added $1,200.00 to the value of the Home, the Ladies' Aid Association having provided the hen-house after hearing of the vote of our Convention last year."

Mrs. Emily L. Clark, in presenting her annual address as Department President at the Fifteenth Annual Convention (1894), devoted a paragraph to the Soldiers' Home, viz.: —

"It has been my privilege to visit this grand Home for the Veterans several times during the year; and when on one occasion I had the pleasure of addressing these men in Sargent Hall, I felt as I saw them gathered together, and realized the services they had once rendered to the Union, that they *deserved* this pleasant Home, the grandest monument of gratitude to the living that could be erected.

"Of the rooms contained in the Home, sixty are furnished by Relief Corps of this Department; and it is a credit to the Corps that all calls from the Home presented to them have received a noble response.

"This noble institution, which shelters so many of the veterans who went out in the strength of their early manhood to battle for the Union and returned crippled or disabled from loss of health, is dear to the heart of every loyal Relief Corps woman; and whenever the Trustees of that Home call upon our organization in this Department for funds to aid in their noble work, let us respond cheerfully and promptly. One by one, in quick succession, the comrades are carried out from the Home to return no more; but others fall in and the vacancies are filled. Not one room is vacant, and this must always be so. Many who are admitted to the Home live but a short time and are thankful for all they receive during their last few days on earth.

"Our Corps have contributed the handsome sum of $243.36 for the Home, for the year ending Dec. 31, 1893.

"During the year just closing thirteen new rooms have been added for hospital purposes; and a call was made to assist in furnishing the same, to which the following Corps responded, subscribing one hundred dollars each: Corps 62, W. Acton; Corps 102, Weymouth; Corps 124, Plymouth, and Corps 37, Pittsfield, making a total of $643.36, exclusive of amount donated for the hennery."

As nearly as can be estimated the sum of $17,440.93 has been expended by this Department for the Soldiers' Home since it was established. This represents only the sums forwarded through Department Headquarters. Corps and individual members frequently send articles to the Home, and plan entertainments that are appreciated by the inmates; for the veterans in their homeless condition, many of whom are invalids, appeal to our sympathies, and we realize that they still have deserving claims.

Visitors to the Home in passing along its corridors, may see through the open doorways the little bannerets and monograms W.R.C.,— letters which are talismans of the blessings the Order has often bestowed.

I was once a sufferer on a battle-field and long afterwards, and every morn I could feel as if a silver cord was twined around a capstan in the regions of glory and reached to my heart, where it was anchored by the hand of woman.

I thank God, as a member of the Grand Army of the Republic, that He has brought to the front this auxiliary; that there was mind enough, charity enough, generosity enough to bring into existence the Woman's Relief Corps. — General JOHN A. LOGAN, Past Commander-in-Chief, G.A.R.

CHAPTER V.

FORMATION OF THE NATIONAL WOMAN'S RELIEF CORPS. THE TRIP TO DENVER AND ITS RESULTS—INTEREST OF THE DEPARTMENT OF MASSACHUSETTS IN THE NATIONAL ORGANIZATION.

ALLUSION was made in a previous chapter to the formation of a National Woman's Relief Corps. A communication recently received from Past Commander-in-Chief Paul Van Der Voort, through whose efforts the first National Convention was held, will be read with interest: —

OMAHA, NEB., July 6, 1894.

MISS MARY E. ELLIOT, Boston, Mass.,

Dear Friend: I have received your letter relating to the history of the Woman's Relief Corps in Massachusetts. During my term as Commander-in-Chief of the Grand Army of the Republic, I met Mrs. Kate B. Sherwood of Toledo, Ohio, Mrs. A. M. Sawyer of Portland, Maine, and others engaged in performing work relating to the Grand Army.

I found great results had been accomplished at Toledo and Portland, but they were merely local and pertained only to the Posts with which they were associated. When I visited Boston in the winter of '83, I made a careful investigation into the work of the Massachusetts Woman's Relief Corps. I visited their Department Convention, and was, I believe, the first Commander-in-Chief who did so. I examined carefully all books and papers relating to the Relief Corps.

I was strongly impressed with the capacity and ability of the members of that Department Convention. I made up my mind that if it was in my power, a National Relief Corps should be organized. I corresponded with a great many people on the subject. All had a differ-cut idea, and were thoroughly wedded to their own methods. The women of Massachusetts were fully organized.

Their plan could be taken right into the National work. It had been tried, and proven a success. I was satisfied that Mrs. Sherwood would be willing to adopt the Massachusetts plan in order to establish a National organization. I took a great deal of pains to see that there should be no failure.

Nearly all the Grand Army leaders were opposed to the organization, so when the call was issued for the National Encampment at Denver, all women interested in this work were invited. The result is well known.

Had it not been my privilege to visit your Convention, with the opposition that I met with the call might not have been issued. You have achieved a grand history. The wonderful work performed by the Woman's Relief Corps of Massachusetts will never be surpassed, and during all that time you have been harmonious and united.

I wish you the most abundant success in the future, congratulate you on your past history and thank you for the many courtesies you have shown to myself and wife.

Yours truly,
PAUL VAN DER VOORT.

While a resolution offered by Chaplain-in-Chief Lovering, endorsing a Woman's National Relief Corps, had been adopted by the National Encampment in session at Indianapolis, June, 1881, no further progress was made until Paul Van Der Voort, as Commander-in-Chief, determined upon a definite plan of action, after his visit to Massachusetts.

In a General Order dated February 16, 1883, he officially promulgated the following: —

The Commander-in-Chief is delighted to learn that the loyal women of the land are forming Auxiliary Societies everywhere. The grand work done by these organizations is worthy of the highest praise. The Woman's Relief Corps of Massachusetts is hereby particularly mentioned on account of the work they have done and their perfect organization. The President of the same, Mrs. E. Florence Barker of Malden, Mass., will be happy to furnish information.

By command of

F. E. BROWN,	PAUL VAN DER VOORT,
Adjutant-General.	*Commander-in-Chief.*

In General Orders issued May 1, 1883, announcing the arrangements for the Seventeenth National Encampment to be held in Denver, Colorado, July 24-28, Commander-in-Chief Van Der Voort inserted the following paragraph: —

"The representatives of the Woman's Relief Corps and Auxiliary Societies to the Grand Army of the Republic are cordially invited to meet at Denver and perfect a National organization. They should bring their rituals, rules, by-laws, and plans of organization, and if possible agree on a uniform mode or system of procedure throughout the country. I pledge the noble women who compose these societies that they will be warmly greeted and given all the encouragement possible. Miss Clara Barton has promised to be present."

At a meeting of the Board of Directors of the Department of Massachusetts, held in Boston June 27, 1883, Mrs. E. Florence Barker, Mrs. Sarah E. Fuller and Mrs. Lizabeth A. Turner were chosen delegates to represent this Department at the Convention in Denver. They were instructed to secure if possible the adoption of the Massachusetts work. It was voted, That the Department of New Hampshire be invited to unite with Massachusetts in sending delegates.

This movement had the hearty endorsement of George S. Evans, Department Commander, and Alfred C. Monroe, Assistant-Adjutant General, Grand Army of the Republic, of Massachusetts; and when arrangements for the trip to Denver were in progress, the comfort of the three representatives of the Auxiliary was not forgotten. On the evening of July 18, 1883, the official train started from the Fitchburg railroad station on its westward journey. A description of the trip and its results was given by Mrs. Fuller soon after her return, as follows: —

"After looking at each other in silence a few moments we began to realize that we were indeed *off for Denver* and must look about our quarters. Thanks to the kind thoughtfulness of Comrade A. C. Monroe, Assistant Adjutant-General of the Department of

Massachusetts, G.A.R., we had been assigned to the drawing-room apartment of our Pullman car for our trip to Chicago on the Grand Trunk road. We began to look about to learn who were our travelling companions, for as our journey would take about five days, this was quite an important item in our calendar. First we found we were in the car with the entire Maine, Vermont and Rhode Island delegations of the G.A.R. — Massachusetts and New Hampshire occupying the next forward car. With the Maine delegation we found Gen. I. S. Bangs, Junior Vice-Commander-in-Chief, wife and son, also Department Commander Shaw of Maine, wife and son. I mention these as they became an important part of our company.

"Early the next morning we found that to be perfectly happy veterans must smoke, and in order to *secure* their happiness and *ensure* our welcome among them, we invited them to smoke all they wished. This settled the matter, and sealed our friendship.

"Arriving at Chicago, Friday evening, July 20, we were met by Comrade George G. Bailey of Hyde Park, Mass., a member of the national staff. Past Department Commander John G. B. Adams of Lynn, Mass., also met us here, but left in advance of us.

"The delegations from Michigan and Ohio joined the train at Chicago, with about a dozen ladies who were also to attend the Convention.

"Sunday noon we arrived at Omaha, where the car with Commander-in-Chief Van Der Voort and party was attached to our train. Mrs. Kate B. Sherwood and daughter of Toledo, Ohio, joined our party here. She found a warm place in all our hearts, and will ever be remembered for her cordial and lady-like treatment of her stranger sisters.

"We arrived in Denver on the afternoon of Monday, July 23. As we neared the depot the air resounded with martial music, in honor of the arrival of the Commander-in-Chief and staff.

"While the honors of the city and State were being paid him, we took carriages to the Windsor House, which was National Headquarters. We had previously secured quarters at the American House, but were specially requested to give them up, and Department Commander A. B. Valentine of Vermont kindly tendered us the use of rooms already secured for the Vermont delegation of comrades.

"The comrades of each State seemed to vie with each other in kind attentions to us, in every possible way. Indeed, so unremitting had been their courtesies, that we felt it to be a most pleasant duty to tender them our thanks in a set of resolutions, which were offered by Junior Vice-Commander-in-Chief I. S. Bangs of Waterville, Maine, who called the entire New England delegation to meet in our car, and in his very happy manner presented them. They were received with three ringing cheers, and Department Commander Evans of Massachusetts in turn offered resolutions complimentary to the ladies of the party, which were unanimously adopted with a hearty round of cheers.

"The ladies of Denver had secured a parlor for a reception-room for the delegates to the Convention, and during all the week we met many prominent comrades and ladies from almost every State.

"Tuesday afternoon we were invited to view the grand parade, when it was estimated that there were twelve thousand veterans in line. The city was very profusely decorated with flags and bunting, some buildings having special designs which were very fine. Tuesday evening was spent in the parlors of the hotel, when we met those who were identified with the auxiliary movement.

"Wednesday morning (July 25) a preliminary meeting was held at Headquarters, and in the afternoon the ladies assembled at the hall of the Patriotic Sons of America, who had very generously tendered the use of their hall. The Convention was opened by Mrs. E. K. Stimson of Denver in an address of welcome. Mrs. E. Florence Barker of Malden, Mass., was invited to preside and Mrs. Kate B. Sherwood of Toledo, Ohio, was chosen Secretary. After a prayer had been offered all present were invited to express their views upon the advisability of forming a National Relief Corps, and also the character of the work to be adopted, eligibility to membership, etc. Several ladies spoke, and all with deep feeling and earnestness. During the addresses, the Commander-in-Chief, Chaplain-in-Chief and others of the National Staff of the Grand Army of the Republic were announced.

"Commander Van Der Voort gave a very eloquent address, strongly urging the immediate organization of a National Order. He was followed by all the other comrades in earnest sympathy with the movement."

An interesting letter was received from Miss Clara Barton (who was detained at home on account of illness) in which she expressed great interest in the movement.

At the second day's session, after a lengthy discussion, it was voted to form a National Woman's Relief Corps on the same basis as that of the Department of Massachusetts, provided the National Encampment of the Grand Army of the Republic should decide to recognize this action.

Meanwhile a resolution of endorsement was offered in the Encampment by Chaplain-in-Chief Foster, viz.: —

Resolved, That we cordially hail the organization of a National Woman's Relief Corps and extend our greeting to them.

We return our warmest thanks to the loyal women of the land for their earnest support and encouragement and bid them Godspeed in their patriotic work.

Several comrades who believed in a National organization opposed this resolution, as they favored restricting the membership to relatives of soldiers. The Massachusetts plan, which formed the basis of the proposed National organization, made *personal loyalty* the only requisite to membership. An earnest discussion in the Encampment was the result, during which Corporal Tanner said: —

"As I understand this question it is all in a nutshell. The Commander-in-Chief invited the ladies to come here and form an organization, giving them such sort of consideration and benefit as the Grand Army could. Now the ladies have had an earnest canvass. A part were in favor of one thing and a part in favor of another, and when that is the case, somebody is always defeated and some one wins. On this question a part were in favor of confining their membership exclusively to those who were the mothers or the wives or sisters of soldiers. Others, and they prevailed, were in favor of taking in every woman whose heart beat loyally for the soldier. When you ask me to decide on that question, I tell you, from my hospital days there comes up the memory of a woman's presence which was like a ministering angel to us. Yet you tell me that the loyal women of the North, who had so high a type of loyalty that they did this work with no ties of love to bind them to it, should be barred out. I will go as far as Grand Army rules will allow me to go in helping a movement that would include every one of the sex on earth. So, I say, comrades, that I believe we have nothing to lose, but everything to gain, by adopting the resolution of the Chaplain-in-Chief, and I hope we will do it, and I hope that that thing which is next to cowardice, — a motion to table, — will not be made on this subject."

Past Commander-in-Chief George S. Merrill of Massachusetts said: "We certainly, comrades of the Grand Army of the Republic, cannot afford to do anything that can by any possible means be construed as discourteous or hostile to any of the loyal women of America."

Comrade William Warner of Missouri (since Commander-in-Chief) participated in the debate by saying: —

"I come from a State that has no organization, and that has no interest in any differences between the various organizations.

I come from a State in which there does not breathe a loyal man who does not extend the right hand of welcome to every sister, mother or sweetheart within her borders, whose heart beats in sympathy with us. Is there a comrade in this Encampment, is there a man that was brave enough to bear arms in defense of the flag of his country, that will not say to every loyal woman, North or South, whether she was mother, sister or sweetheart, 'We bid you Godspeed'?"

The resolution was adopted, and at noon a messenger was sent to the Convention with an invitation for its members to attend the installation of officers of the G.A.R., which they accepted, adjourning their meeting for this purpose until 3 o'clock. Proceeding to the Tabor Opera House they were officially notified that the highest body of the Grand Army of the Republic had endorsed their work, and this news was received with great rejoicing. Some of the women present had been working, praying and hoping for many years that such a result as this might be realized.

In referring to the welcome given at the installation service Mrs. Fuller recorded at the time the following facts: —

"Mrs. Barker, Mrs. Turner and myself with Mrs. Bangs of Maine and a few others, were invited to seats on the stage which we accepted, and were introduced to all the newly-elected officers of the G.A.R. — Gen. Logan, Jack Crawford and others. In all the addresses the work of our Order was most heartily endorsed; and when our President, Mrs. Barker, was called to the front and presented by the Commander-in-Chief as the National President of the Relief Corps, Auxiliary to the G.A.R., we felt that our frail bark which was launched in stormy waters February, 1879, in our own city of Fitchburg, and since piloted so anxiously and ofttimes fearfully, was now safely out on the great ocean of Grand Army fellowship and support. Heaven grant it may ever be freighted with Fraternity, Charity and Loyalty for the veteran soldiers or sailors who stood like a wall of fire when our country's honor was assailed."

Robert B. Beath of Philadelphia was installed as Commander-in-Chief to succeed Paul Van Der Voort; and upon assuming the office and addressing the Encampment he said: "One subject I desire to touch upon. I have not been able to enter into the details of the proposed organization of a Ladies' Aid Society by the good ladies who have assembled in this city of Denver for this purpose; but whatever they have done and whatever they shall do that tends to perpetuate the great humane work of the war, that has now devolved on the Grand Army of the Republic and upon all their wives and sisters and friends, I can assure them of my most hearty support. (Applause.) If I did not say that I would be false to all my soldier career, I would be false to that hour when, lying in a hospital tent, my eyes opened and I saw daylight once more from the sleep in which I had been placed but a short time before, and awoke to find myself a cripple for life. I found by my bedside the first one in whose face I was able to look, one of the women nurses of the Army of the Potomac. (Applause.) She cared for me then in my helpless condition. Hers were the first words of cheer and encouragement that entered my ears, and I would be false to the recollections of that hour if I did not say God bless every woman who is engaged in this great and holy work."

Other speakers who gave a cordial welcome to the Auxiliary were Maj. William Warner, Senior Vice Commander-in-Chief; Walter H. Holmes, Junior Vice Commander-in-Chief; Rev. I. M. Foster, Chaplain-in-Chief; Gen. John A. Logan, Maj. George S. Merrill, Past Commanders-in-Chief, and Capt. John G. B. Adams, Past Department Commander of Massachusetts.

Upon reassembling in the afternoon the Convention voted to hold its sessions at the same time and in the same town or city as the National Encampment of the Grand Army of the Republic. It was voted to adopt a uniform badge and Mrs. Sarah E. Fuller, Mrs. E. Florence Barker, Mrs. Kate B. Sherwood, Mrs. Mattie B. Moulton and Mrs. E. K. Stimson were appointed a committee to prepare and issue the same.

The following is a list of the officers elected: —

President: Mrs. E. Florence Barker, Malden, Mass.
Senior Vice-President: Mrs. Kate B. Sherwood, Toledo, Ohio.
Junior Vice-President: Mrs. E. K. Stimson, Denver, Col.
Secretary: Mrs. Sarah E. Fuller, East Boston, Mass.
Treasurer: Mrs. Lizabeth A. Turner, Boston, Mass.
Inspector: Mrs. Emily Gardner, Denver, Col.
Chaplain: Mrs. Mattie B. Moulton, Laconia, N.H.
Conductor: Mrs. P. S. Runyon, Warsaw, Ind.
Guard: Mrs. J. W. Beatson, Rockford, Ill.
Corresponding Secretaries: Mrs. Mary J. Telford, Denver, Col., and Mrs. Ellen Fay, Topeka, Kan.

Mrs. Barker accepted an invitation to install the officers-elect, and after performing the ceremony she was duly installed as National President by Mrs. Fuller.

In grateful appreciation of the services rendered by the Commander-in-Chief, the following resolution was adopted: —

Resolved, That the loyal women of the Union tender their heartfelt thanks to Commander-in-Chief Paul Van Der Voort, in behalf of the widows and orphans of the Grand Army of the Republic, for his earnest, persistent, long and tender regard for their welfare, and for his efforts in bringing about a National Woman's Auxiliary to the Grand Army of the Republic, charged with devising practical aid in their behalf. His words of confidence and encouragement, his ringing appeals for united and harmonious action, and the enthusiastic spirit he has inspired into the hearts of all interested in woman's work, have been a source of inspiration to all who love to work for the dear old soldier and those to him most dear. In the name of loyal women everywhere, and their consecrated work, we say, God bless our noble commander about to retire from his high post of trust, and may the God of the widow and fatherless hold him and his in His everlasting care.

DENVER, July 25, 1883.   E. FLORENCE BARKER,
KATE B. SHERWOOD, } *Committee.*
LAURA McNEIR,

At the close of the Convention its members were guests at a reception tendered in the evening (July 26) to Commander-in-Chief Beath and Past Commander-in-Chief Van Der Voort.

An invitation was extended to our representatives to accompany the Commander-in-Chief's party on a trip through the Colorado cañons, which was accepted. This afforded an excellent opportunity for conference upon the work of the year, and the mutual interests of the two national bodies were considered by their leaders.

When returning to Massachusetts the National President, Secretary and Treasurer were tendered a reception by S. C. Lawrence Corps No. 5 of Medford, which was also an occasion of rejoicing over the victory at Denver. Many prominent guests were present, and several hundred comrades of the G.A.R. and members of the W.R.C. enjoyed the exercises and banquet.

Through the courtesy of George S. Evans, Department Commander, National Headquarters were established at the Headquarters of the Department of Massachusetts, G.A.R., in Pemberton Square, Boston.

At a meeting of the Union Board held October 10, 1883, Miss Elliot, Mrs. Goodale and Mrs. Turner were appointed a committee to prepare a suitable testimonial to be presented to George S. Evans, Department Commander, in recognition of his services for the Order.

Mrs. E. Florence Barker, Department President, in her annual address at the Department Convention held Jan. 29, 1884, reported the following in regard to the work at Denver: —

"The delegates departed amid the well-wishes and Godspeed of their sister members, but with many fears and doubts, feeling the burden of responsibility in their great undertaking. They realized that the Convention would be composed of representatives of the various orders in the land, interested in the charity work of the Grand Army of the Republic, and that among the number there would be many prominent members of recognized ability, devoted to their form of work, and prepared to press their own order to the front. Thus we started, without even the guiding star of the East — three lone disciples of our Order, representing a membership of nearly two thousand, whose only stronghold was the records of the Order we represented and faith in our work.

"With the fears and doubts of the true soldier entering the field of battle, we questioned, will it be defeat or victory?

"Wonder not that we felt we were travelling to the city of doubts. But before entering the city there arose the star of the East, not five-pointed, but with three shining letters — G.A.R.; and like him of old our hands were upheld and we were sustained in our darkest hour.

"Gathered in convention with ladies from nearly every State, representing twenty-six different orders, the work of uniting on any common ground seemed at one time very doubtful. The diversity of opinion as to the basis of the National Order resulted in much earnest discussion, and to Mrs. Kate B. Sherwood, one of the pioneers of a National Society, is due the honor of presenting *Massachusetts'* work as the basis of its formation. Too much praise cannot be accorded Mrs. Sherwood for her loyalty to the National Organization. Preferring, as she stated, open Parliamentary meetings, she waived a point to secure harmony, and desiring that the best ritualistic work should be adopted, if any, favored that in the hands of the Massachusetts ladies.

"We felt honored almost beyond our deserts when she proclaimed her preference for Massachusetts. Thus the assistance rendered by our sister from Ohio secured the Massachusetts work as the foundation of the National Relief Corps.

. . . .

"The confidence of the Grand Army of the Republic was our only stronghold, and when Comrades Tanner, Foster, Hazzard and Warner in warmest terms endorsed our work, and Massachusetts' electric orator, Past Commander-in-Chief Merrill, called upon his comrades to extend a welcome to the Order knocking at their door, which that day had joined hands to prevent the soldier ever wanting the necessaries of life, supplemented by the statement of Past Department Commander Adams, that without woman's aid the efforts to establish a Soldiers' Home in Massachusetts would have proved a failure, we passed the ordeal, and, with pride be it recorded, bridged the waters under whose smooth and shining surface the record of the brave soldiers' hardship of camp, march and battle lay side by side with woman's mental anguish, weary waiting, hope deferred, duty in hospital and the sacrifices that engraved the war of the Rebellion indelibly upon her heart.

"The resolution welcoming the aid of loyal women was adopted ; and thus in the Centennial State was founded an organization which we trust will prove the Right Hand of the Grand Army of the Republic. In delivering up the office to his successor, Commander-in-Chief Van Der Voort issued the following in his farewell order : —

"'I ask all the comrades as the last official request I shall ever make the Order, to give to the Woman's Relief Corps their warm, hearty and loving support.'

"With this benediction from him I trust that the assurance which I gave the National Encampment that their trust would not be misplaced, and that they should never have reason to be ashamed of the Organization, will be the study of every member of the Woman's Relief Corps. We have now to sustain our record — bright and clear must it be kept.

"Let us strive to retain the confidence of the veterans, and make the study of *how best to serve them* our work for the coming years. Soon the annual report of the Adjutant-General will record not how many gained during the past year, but instead, the number of comrades moved on to report to the Commander of All.

"I would suggest that every Corps have an Employment Committee whose duty it shall be to interest themselves in procuring work for those who are unwilling to accept other assistance than an opportunity to work for themselves.

"This record shows the year one of increasing labor. The fact that the active officers of the Department were also placed in responsible positions in the National Relief Corps gave to your President and her associates unlimited work during the remaining months of 1883."

Miss Elliot offered the following resolution at this Convention, which was adopted: —

Resolved, That the Department of Massachusetts, in Sixth Annual Convention assembled, realizing that the extension of our work to a National Relief Corps has given our Order a character and an influence which places it in the foremost rank of the organizations of the country, hereby places on record its high appreciation of the devotedness and ability of Mrs. E. Florence Barker, Mrs. Sarah E. Fuller and Mrs. Lizabeth A. Turner, delegates to Denver, Col., whose excellent judgment deserves our sincere thanks, and without whose services the grand results attained could not have been accomplished.

Department Commander Evans was invited to visit the Convention, when a framed testimonial, suitably engrossed on parchment, was presented him, the text of which reads as follows: —

To GEORGE S. EVANS,
  Department Commander, G.A.R.,
    State of Massachusetts.

Greeting: The Woman's State Relief Corps of Massachusetts, Auxiliary to the Grand Army of the Republic, remembers with pleasure and gratitude the eminent service you rendered its cause at the annual session of the National Encampment. G.A.R., held in Denver, Col., July 25, 26 and 27, 1883, and in recognition thereof this testimonial of regard is tendered you.

Your able endorsement of the Massachusetts work contributed largely to its final adoption, and we rejoice that the success of the Woman's Auxiliary Corps has sustained your judgment in claiming for the Order national recognition. May the Grand Army of the Republic, with its enduring ties of Fraternity, riveted on the battle-field, with its golden deeds of Charity, which time can never tarnish, and with its spotless record of Loyalty, which confers honor upon every comrade, never regret having extended to women the privilege of co-operating in its work of benevolence and mission of justice.

With assurances of appreciation and sentiments of respect, we remain,

Very truly yours,

MARY E. ELLIOT,
M. SUSIE GOODALE,
LIZABETH A. TURNER,
Committee.

Presented at the Fifth Annual Convention of the Woman's Relief Corps of Massachusetts, in Boston, Jan. 29, 1884.

E. FLORENCE BARKER, *President.*
SARAH E. FULLER, *Secretary.*

Commander Evans in responding expressed the pride he felt in the success of the Order, his faith in which was stronger than ever. He congratulated the Relief Corps upon the gain of last year, and as their charity had been exemplified in the past, he counselled " continued loyalty to country, to the Grand Army of the Republic and to their own Order."

In 1884, when the National Convention gathered in that magnificent city of the Northwest, Minneapolis, nine representatives from Massachusetts were present.

When New England welcomed the veterans at Portland in 1885, this Department united in paying them homage and every delegate to the Convention was present. Again we returned home with the National President, Mrs. Sarah E. Fuller, who was unanimously elected to that office.

The Convention roll was called in 1886 on the Pacific Shore, and many from the Bay State answered to California's greeting.

Twenty-nine voting representatives attended all the sessions, and Massachusetts was one of the three States having a full delegation.

The respect everywhere shown by the comrades to the members of our Order on that eventful journey, the pleasant companionships of the trip, and the greetings of co-workers in far-distant sections, the interweaving of our badge and monogram in the floral tributes so liberally displayed in that "land of fruit and flowers," the enthusiastic public receptions attended by thousands, at which our work was indorsed by officials of the Grand Army of the Republic, the sessions of the Convention, so ably conducted by *our own* National President, Mrs. Fuller, and so harmonious in results, are inspirations which will ever linger in memory.

When our Order the next year again met beyond the Mississippi (at St. Louis), this Department was numbered among its guests, and every delegate to the Convention attended its sessions.

The cordial welcome at Columbus in 1888, and the hospitalities extended by Milwaukee in 1889, are pleasantly remembered by our delegations.

An event that still has its influence was the great gathering of 1890, in the success of which 130 Corps of Massachusetts were interested, and a report of that memorable week in Boston is recorded in Chapter V.

Mrs. Harriette L. Reed, Delegate-at-Large to the Convention which met at Detroit in 1891, gave an interesting account of the part taken by our members, an extract from which is given as follows : —

"The custom of our Order requires that the Delegate-at-Large shall report to the Department Convention something of the doings of the last National Convention ; therefore, I turn back the leaves of memory's pages and review some of the scenes and incidents connected with the journey of the Massachusetts delegation en route to the National Convention of the Woman's Relief Corps, which was held in Detroit, 'The Gate City of Midland America,' last August.

"The arrangements for the trip were in the hands of the Department President, Mrs. Augusta A. Wales, and most satisfactorily to all were they carried out. In previous years, one car only has been needed for the accommodation of delegates and friends; but this year so large a number of the women of Massachusetts had turned their faces westward that two cars were filled with enthusiastic travellers. The day of departure from Boston, August 1, was most propitious, and a large crowd gathered at the station to wish us goodbye and Godspeed. The number leaving Boston was so large that the train was made up in three sections; and through the courtesy and kindness of the committee of the Grand Army of the Republic in charge and our friend, Mr. Watson of the Fitchburg road, our two cars were assigned to the official train of the Department Commander, which privilege was much appreciated. The route chosen was a long one, but the journey was rendered exceedingly pleasant by the frequent interchange of visits between the occupants of the various cars, many of whom were personal friends, and the kindly courtesies extended to us by all. The Department Commander, Arthur A. Smith and staff, the Past Department Commanders who were with us, — indeed, all the comrades of the Grand Army of the Republic who were our fellow-travellers, — were untiring in their efforts to make our journey easy and agreeable, and we were constantly indebted to them for their thoughtful care and consideration.

"One of the cars was the home of the Massachusetts members of General Alger's staff, and most graciously was their hospitality extended to us; a hospitality which was not confined to kindly words and happy greetings, but reached out to the dispensing of such creature comforts as ice cream and crackers, cold ginger ale and apollinaris, most grateful to dusty, weary travellers during this August excursion.

"Tuesday was the day of the grand parade, and it opened clear and bright, with a cool breeze from Lake St. Clair. The whole city was astir at an early hour in anticipation of the coming event — which was to be specially magnificent in commemoration of the silver anniversary of the Grand Army of the Republic. There were about forty thousand men in line, and it was six hours in passing a given point. Nearly every State bore some purely distinctive emblem, besides flags innumerable, both new and old. Ohio was gorgeous with strings of buckeyes; Kansas disported large ears of corn and sunflowers innumerable; Texas proudly carried an immense pair of steer's horns polished like a mirror; Montana was brilliant with white umbrellas, with a dash of blue in the centre; Vermont wore sprigs of cedar in their hats. The special insignia of Maine was the pine cone; Little Rhody revelled in the clam; New Hampshire displayed the granite block; Wisconsin bore aloft the badger; and the codfish, bean pot and shoe were conspicuous in the Massachusetts ranks. 'Our Massachusetts boys' were present in large numbers, and made a splendid showing, to the great delight of their lady admirers. Seats upon the grand stand had been provided for us for viewing the procession, but as our Headquarters at the Cadillac were available, we remained there. Our beautiful banner, which the Department President waved from the balcony of the hotel, received a salute of recognition from the comrades of the Old Bay State, again proving to us that they never forget us. Tuesday evening was reserved for the reception of the Massachusetts delegation, to which invitations had been sent to *all our friends everywhere.* Through the extreme courtesy and kindness of the proprietor of Hotel Cadillac, the doors of the large public parlor opening from our room were thrown back, thus affording a much larger space, and materially adding to our comfort. The receiving party were Department President Wales, Department Senior Vice-President Davis, Department Junior Vice-President Ralph, Past Department Presidents Lowd and Knowles, National Senior Vice-President Turner and our beloved Clara Barton, whom Massachusetts is so proud to claim and welcome always among her daughters. A large number of distinguished guests honored us by their presence : among them, Commander-in-Chief Veazy and Mrs. Veazy, all the past Commanders-in-Chief and wives who were in the city, Department Commanders of very many of the States, and comrades from Maine to California, National and Department officers, and members of our own Order from all parts of our country. One of the pleasantest features of the evening, and the one dearest to our hearts, was the visit of the entire delegation of Massachusetts comrades in a body, headed by Department Commander Arthur A. Smith."

Mrs. Mary G. Deane, Department President, in her annual address at the Department Convention in 1893, referred to the gathering in the city of Washington, as follows : —

"The announcement that the National Encampment of 1892 would be held in the city of Washington aroused enthusiasm among our members in every part of the State. Entertainments in behalf of a 'Washington Fund' were frequent, and the proceeds helped to increase the funds being raised by Posts for this purpose.

"Several hundred members of our Order accompanied the Grand Army of the Republic on this memorable excursion, and the demand for the popular ribbon badge of the Department of Massachusetts Woman's Relief Corps was greater than the supply.

"Many of the Posts on this occasion marched under banners presented by the women of our Corps, recalling the darker days of the Rebellion, when the colors they then carried through the streets of Washington were consecrated by woman's devotion to their cause. The usual invitation extended the Department W.R.C. to accompany the Department G.A.R. official train was cordially accepted.

"Two parlor cars were required for our delegation, which left Boston Sunday morning, September 18, via Old Colony, Shore Line and Baltimore & Ohio Railroad. We appreciate the courtesies extended by Mr. A. J. Simmons, New England Agent Baltimore & Ohio Railroad, in the arrangement for the transportation of our party.

"A largely attended meeting of the delegates was held at Department Headquarters at the Ebbitt House, on Monday morning, September 19; and when the Convention was called to order on Wednesday the Massachusetts representatives were prompt in their attendance.

"The assembling in National Convention of so many representatives from various parts of the country, shows the magnitude of this work.

"The fact reported that our Order is organized in every State and Territory of the Union save one (Alabama), impressed upon us the thought that the pioneer workers in this grand Order builded upon a firm foundation.

"I will not intrude upon the report of the Delegate-at-Large, which will contain the more important proceedings of the four days' Convention at the National Capital.

"Believing that members who are not delegates should have the privilege of wearing a State Woman's Relief Corps Badge, I *recommend*, That the next Department Council be authorized to adopt a distinctive Massachusetts badge when making arrangements for National Convention at Indianapolis."

A few items from the report of Mrs. Emilie L. W. Waterman, Delegate-at-Large, are given, viz.: —

"From the time it was decided that Washington, D.C., would be the meeting place of the Tenth National Convention of the Woman's Relief Corps, a large proportion of the members of the Order in this State began active preparations to avail themselves of the opportunity to visit the 'Capital of the Nation.'

"Consequently on Sept. 17 and 18, 1892, the various railroad companies sent out train after train heavily freighted with members of the Grand Army, Woman's Relief Corps and their friends. The one carrying nearly all the Department Officers left the Park Square Station, Boston, at 8.30 A.M. the 18th, and without accident arrived in Washington early Monday morning.

"Headquarters Massachusetts W.R.C. was established at the Ebbitt House, parlor 47. In response to request of the Department President, the delegates and alternates met promptly at 9.30, Monday morning. Badges were distributed and final arrangements for Convention made.

"The afternoon was spent in sight-seeing. In the evening, a reception given by the Citizens' Committee in the Rotunda of the Capital was attended by thousands. The following prominent workers in the Order from Massachusetts were among those who received: Past National Presidents E. Florence Barker and Sarah E. Fuller, Past National Senior Vice-President Lizabeth A. Turner and Harriette L. Reed of the National Pension Committee.

"A more perfect day than Tuesday, September 19, cannot well be imagined. Early in the morning strains of martial music were heard in all sections of the city; and every member of the Grand Army was astir, preparing for the parade, which was a magnificent spectacle and will never be forgotten by those privileged to witness it. Notwithstanding the fact that the veterans were tired with their long march, the receptions given by Mrs. General Logan at her home, the Potomac Relief Corps at the Congregational Church, corner of Tenth and G streets, and the Department of Potomac W.R.C., were largely attended. Through courtesy of the comrades, the spacious parlor at the Ebbitt House occupied by the G.A.R. as National Headquarters was from 5 o'clock to 9 P.M. the scene of a brilliant reception given by the Department of Massachusetts W.R.C. to their friends. Over three thousand were in attendance. The receiving party consisted of Department President Mary G. Deane, Senior Vice Department President Emily L. Clark, Junior Vice Department President Clare H. Burleigh, Department Secretary Mary E. Elliot, Past Department Presidents Emma B. Lowd and Augusta A. Wales, Past National Presidents E. Florence Barker and

Sarah E. Fuller, and Past National Senior Vice-President Lizabeth A. Turner. Department Inspector Helen A. Brigham, chairman of the Reception Committee, was assisted by Department officers and aides. Music was furnished through courtesy of Post 46, Fall River. One of the pleasant features of the evening was the presence of large delegations from Post 46 and Relief Corps 106 of Fall River, of which the Department President is a member. Massachusetts was honored in the unanimous election of Past Department President Mary E. Knowles as National Chaplain."

Extract from report of Mrs. Helen A. Brigham, Delegate-at-Large to the Convention at Indianapolis, 1893 : —

"One of the principal events of the year in connection with our work is the Annual Convention of the National Woman's Relief Corps.

"Since its organization in 1883, when at Denver, a cordial welcome was extended by the National Encampment of the Grand Army of the Republic, the Woman's Relief Corps gatherings have been a special feature of Encampment week.

"The pioneers from Massachusetts who founded the National organization travelled to Denver under the guidance of the officials of the Department of Massachusetts, G.A.R. The custom then inaugurated, of inviting the representatives of our Order to accompany the official Grand Army train, has been continued in this State, and extended almost universally to other States.

"Two cars were secured by the Department President, Mrs. Emily L. Clark, for the trip to Indianapolis, September last, and were nearly filled by our delegates and friends. The Headquarters train, which left the Fitchburg station at 9 o'clock on the morning of September 2, arrived at its destination about ten o'clock the following night. The Sabbath journey was a pleasant but uneventful one.

"When, however, we entered the Union station at Indianapolis, already crowded with visitors from every section of the country, we realized that the remaining days of the week would be crowded with events of National interest.

"Monday morning a meeting of the delegates was held at Headquarters — which had been established at the Denison — and several matters of interest were considered, among which was a unanimous vote to support Mrs. Sarah C. Mink of New York for the office of National President.

"In view of the fact that Capt. John G. B. Adams, one of the loyal friends of our Order, would probably be chosen Commander-in-Chief of the Grand Army of the Republic, Mrs. Turner was appointed a committee to procure a floral offering to be sent him, with the regards of the Massachusetts delegation.

"In the afternoon the corridors of the hotel were thronged with members of the Order, who had received special invitations from the local committee of arrangements to ride through the principal streets of the city. Through the thoughtfulness of this committee a printed card was given each guest, as she entered the carriage, on which was printed the itinerary of the trip, places of historic interest being specially noted.

"The avenues and residences, with their flags and other decorations, the arriving veterans, whom we met marching to their camps and headquarters, reminded us of the busy times three years ago, when we had the honor of greeting the veterans in Boston.

"We lingered to pay our tribute to the beautiful Soldiers' Monument, said to be the finest memorial of its kind in the world.

"We passed the home of that honored soldier and statesman, ex-President Harrison, and the mansion that was the home of Indiana's War Governor, Oliver P. Morton, whose memory is revered by every soldier in the State.

"Camp-fires were lighted Monday evening. The one attracting the largest number was held in the spacious Tomlinson Hall, where thousands assembled. It was a welcome by the

Citizens' Executive Committee; and the addresses by ex-President Harrison and other distinguished guests, with a programme of music, rendered the occasion one of enjoyment and inspiration.

"The 'grand parade' on Tuesday was witnessed from Headquarters at the Denison. During the day prominent officials of the Grand Army of the Republic called to register and to express again their interest in the Woman's Relief Corps of Massachusetts.

"Nearly a thousand people attended the reception, under the auspices of this Department, Tuesday evening, although there were numerous other receptions and entertainments at the same hour. The large parlors of the Denison were tendered for the occasion; and among those who were present, in response to invitations, were members of ex-President Harrison's Cabinet, and prominent citizens of Indianapolis; officers of the National Encampment, G.A.R.; the Department Commander and Staff of Massachusetts; Past Commanders-in-Chief, Department Commanders, and other comrades from almost every State in the Union; National and Department officers of the W.R.C.; showing the regard in which the Department of Massachusetts is held throughout the country. Later in the evening several of the delegates attended the reception given in Tomlinson Hall, by the Ladies' Executive Committee of Indianapolis, to all the patriotic organizations of women.

"Thousands of veterans who had honored Indianapolis by their presence gathered at the 'World's Fair' grounds in Chicago, Saturday, which had been assigned by the management of the fair as Grand Army Day.

"The glorious camp-fire, one of the most enthusiastic ever held, was a fitting close to an eventful week in the history of the Grand Army of the Republic and the Woman's Relief Corps. Many of our delegates lingered to enjoy the wonders of the Columbian Exposition, and all, we trust, returned to their homes with a truer love for the Union, and an added appreciation of its defenders."

A list of those who have served as voting representatives in the various National Conventions is herewith given :

DENVER, COLORADO, JULY 25 AND 26, 1883.
Delegates
E. Florence Barker of Malden, Sarah E. Fuller of East Boston, Lizabeth A. Turner of Boston.

MINNEAPOLIS, MINNESOTA, JULY 23-25, 1884.

E. Florence Barker, National President; Sarah E. Fuller, National Secretary; Lizabeth A. Turner, National Treasurer; M. Susie Goodale, Department President.
Delegates.
Kathrina L. Beedle of Cambridge, Mary E. Adams of Lynn, Annie J. Brown of Amesbury, Mary E. Elliot of Somerville; Mary E. Chipman of Waltham, Mrs. W. H. Chamberlain of Pittsfield.

PORTLAND, MAINE, JUNE 24-26, 1885.

M. Susie Goodale, Department President; S. Agnes Parker, Department Senior Vice-President; Sarah E. Fuller, National Senior Vice-President; Lizabeth A. Turner, National Treasurer; E. Florence Barker, Past National President.

Delegates.
Kathrina L. Beedle of Cambridge, Elizabeth C. Lovering of Worcester, Helen F. Johnson of Somerville, Susan S. Monroe of Fitchburg, Mary A. B. Fellows of Chelsea, Florence L. Wentworth of Danvers, Maria E. Ball of Ashland, Laura E. Baldwin of Melrose, Eliza F. Talbot of Holliston, Eleanor B. Wheeler of South Boston, Annie J. Brown of Amesbury, Mary E. Elliot of Somerville, Cinderella E. Clement of Merrimac, Mary E. Chipman of Waltham, Sarah B. Creasey of Newburyport, Mary E. Adams of Concord, Annie E. Tuttle of Lowell, Annie E. Bailey of Hyde Park, Augusta C. Randall of Arlington, Mary F. Merchant of Fitchburg, II. Abbie Sawyer of Lynn, Lucretia A. Rice of Worcester, Mary E. Swan of East Boston, Anna M. Boynton of Boston, Sarah G. M. Hill of Danvers, Helen M. Packard of Springfield, Jane L. Crann of Lowell, Hattie A. Ralph of Somerville.

SAN FRANCISCO, CAL., August 4-7, 1886.

Sarah E. Fuller, National President; Eleanor B. Wheeler, National Secretary; Lizabeth A. Turner, National Treasurer; S. Agnes Parker, Department President; Mary E. Elliot, Department Secretary; E. Florence Barker, Past National President.

Delegates.

Harriette L. Reed of Dorchester, Sarah B. Creasey of Newburyport, Gertrude Kenney of Danvers, Susan E. Richmond of Shelburne Falls, Mary P. Lloyd of Gloucester, Sarah F. Gallup of Leominster, Fannie T. Hazen (Corps 2) of Cambridge, Rosetta H. Hauscom of East Boston, Amanda Smith of Lynn, Louisa A. Morrison (Corps 28) of Boston, Clara A. Trask of Beverly, Emma F. Haskell (Corps 39) of Charlestown, Angela H. Scranton (Corps 27) of Cambridgeport, Ada G. Harrington of Waltham, Hittie M. Wilder of Hyde Park, Marion L. Burge of Westfield, Henrietta Palmer of South Boston, Amanda W. K. Bardwell of Greenfield, Ellen M. Gill of Medford, Adelia R. Burtt of Springfield, Abbie Norton of Salem, Pamelia W. Knight of East Cambridge, Mary J. Morse of Southbridge.

ST. LOUIS, MO., Sept. 28–Oct. 1, 1887.

S. Agnes Parker, Department President; Emma B. Lowd, Department Junior Vice-President; Mary E. Elliot, Department Secretary; Lizabeth A. Turner, National Treasurer; E. Florence Barker and Sarah E. Fuller, members National Council of Administration.

Delegates.

Louisa A. Morrison (at large) of Boston, Lucinda M. Farrar of Easthampton, Eliza F. Stiles of Lynn, Emma M. Barrett of Melrose, Annett Bell (Corps 67) of Boston, Clara A. Trask of Beverly, Amanda W. K. Bardwell of Greenfield, Pamelia W. Knight of East Cambridge, Eleanor B. Wheeler of South Boston, Harriette L. Reed of Dorchester, Mary McDonough of South Boston, Etta Morris of South Boston, Mary E. Kenney of Danvers, Mary E. Bedell of Charlestown, Mary E. Hunter of Cambridgeport, Eva T. Cook of Gloucester, Lizzie N. Wade of Plainville, Annie Howard of East Boston, Mary M. Graham of Lynn, Phœbe Rollins of South Boston, Mary P. Lloyd of Gloucester, Lucy A. Smiley (Corps 33) of Lowell, Emily L. Clark of Northampton.

COLUMBUS, OHIO, Sept. 12-14, 1888.

Emma B. Lowd. Department President; Mary M. Perry, Department Senior Vice-President; Mary E. Knowles, Department Junior Vice-President; Mary E. Elliot, Department Secretary; Lizabeth A. Turner, National Treasurer.

Delegates.

Rose A. Knapp (at large) of Somerville, Lulu A. Mann of Montague, Clare H. Burleigh of Athol, Jeanette P. Babbitt of Worcester, Harriette L. Reed of Dorchester. Nina B. Lovejoy of Ayer, Mary A. Bailey of Lynn, Mary T. Hawkes of Danvers, Eliza M. Bliss of New Bedford, Flora A. Smith of Colrain, Abbie L. Whitney of Stoneham, Albina C. Barker of Springfield, Sarah E. Johnson of Boston, Harriet Howe of Cambridge.

MILWAUKEE, WIS., Aug. 28-30, 1889.

Emma B. Lowd, Department President; Augusta A. Wales, Department Junior Vice-President; Mary E. Elliot, Department Secretary; Lizabeth A. Turner, National Treasurer.

Delegates.

Abbie L. Whitney (at large), Pamelia W. Knight of East Cambridge, Eleanor B. Wheeler of South Boston, Harriette L. Reed of Dorchester, Mary H. Vaughn of South Boston, Annie K. Day of Groveland, Emily L. Clark of Northampton, Margie E. B. Hutchins of Lawrence, E. Francena Gray of Brighton, Susan E. Parmenter of Athol, Sarah F. Gallup of Leominster, Sarah E. Woodard of Greenfield.

BOSTON, MASS., Aug. 13-14, 1890.

Mary E. Knowles. Department President; Mary M. Perry, Department Senior Vice-President; Elizabeth V. Lang, Department Junior Vice-President; Mary E. Elliot, Department Secretary; Lizabeth A. Turner, National Treasurer; E. Florence Barker and Sarah E. Fuller, members National Executive Board; M. Susie Goodale, Past Department President, S. Agnes Parker, Past Department President, and Emma B. Lowd, Past Department President.

Delegates.

Hattie A. Ralph (at large), Augusta A. Wales of Dorchester, Leocardia F. Flowers of Cambridge, Marion E. Bridgman of Northampton, Emilie L. W. Waterman of Boston, Mary G. Deane of Fall River, Hattie M. Tuttle of South Boston, Sarah C. Walkley of Westfield, Amelia J. Parker of Lynn, J. Victoria Simmons of Worcester, Louisa J. Savage of Haverhill, Lucia A. Knapp of Plymouth, Maria C. Walker of Greenfield, Carrie S. L. Bagley of Fitchburg, Clara A. Pillsbury of Danvers.

DETROIT, MICH., Aug. 5-8, 1891.

Augusta A. Wales, Department President; Delilah S. Davis, Department Senior Vice-President; Hattie A. Ralph, Department Junior Vice-President; Mary E. Elliot, Department Secretary; Emma B. Lowd, Past Department President; Mary E. Knowles, Past Department President; Lizabeth A. Turner, National Senior Vice-President.

Delegates.

Harriette L. Reed (at large), of Dorchester, Elizabeth V. Lang of Hyde Park, Mary M. Perry of Springfield, Abbie T. Usher of Newburyport, Josie A. Burdick of North Adams, Sarah A. Woodside of Woburn, M. Lizzie Bullock of Everett, Margie A. Sawyer of Westboro, Clara H. Smith of Lynn, Abbie D. Danforth of Plymouth, Elizabeth E. Hayward of Walpole, Ellen M. Gill of Medford, Mattie A. Fay of Spencer, Carrie S. L. Bagley of Fitchburg, Dorcas H. Lyman of Brighton, Mary H. Andrews of Essex.

WASHINGTON, D.C., Sept. 21-24, 1892.

Mary G. Deane, Department President; Emily L. Clark, Department Senior Vice-President; Clare H. Burleigh, Department Junior Vice-President; Mary E. Elliot, Department Secretary; S. Agnes Parker, Past Department President; Emma B. Lowd, Past Department President; Mary E. Knowles, Past Department President; Augusta A. Wales, Past Department President; E. Florence Barker and Sarah E. Fuller, members National Executive Board; Lizabeth A. Turner, Past National Senior Vice-President.

Delegates.

Emilie L. W. Waterman (at large) of Boston, Annie K. Day of South Groveland, Maria A. Brown of South Boston, Flora A. Smith of Colrain,

A. Lizzie Wood of Haverhill, Cynthia M. Caldwell of New Bedford, Harriette A. Burrows of Charlestown, Mary L. Nason of Roxbury, Etta A. Lockhart of East Cambridge, Sarah J. Hall of Georgetown, Lulu A. Mann of Montague, Cora P. L. Walker of Barre, Eva T. Cook of Gloucester, Lizzie N. Wade of Plainville, Emma F. Lanman of Plymouth, Helen A. Brigham of Hyde Park, Harriet A. Chamberlain of Somerville, M. Alice Carey of Malden.

INDIANAPOLIS, IND., Sept. 6–8, 1893.

Emily L. Clark, Department President; Eva T. Cook, Department Junior Vice-President; Mary E. Elliot, Department Secretary; Emma B. Lowd, Past Department President; Mary E. Knowles, Past Department President; Mary G. Deane, Past Department President; Lizabeth A. Turner, Past National Senior Vice-President; Eleanor B. Wheeler, Past National Secretary.

Delegates.

Helen A. Brigham (at large) of Hyde Park, Abbie T. Usher of Newburyport, Dorcas H. Lyman of Brighton, Harriette L. Reed of Dorchester, Mary M. Perry of Springfield, L. Stuart Wadsworth of South Boston, Abbie D. Danforth of Plymouth, Jessie R. Webber of Salem, S. Jennie Tirrell of Lynn, Ray E. Lane of Wakefield, Carrie A. Gibbs of Charlestown, Emma Collier of Brighton, Lila D. Lovering of Springfield, Mary H. Vaughn of South Boston, Sarah C. Bodman of Northampton, Fanny T. Hazen of Cambridge, Abbie L. Robson of Salem, Lulu A. Mann of Montague, Mary P. Lloyd of Gloucester.

PITTSBURGH, PENN., Sept. 12–14, 1894.

Clare H. Burleigh, Department President; Eva T. Cook, Department Senior Vice-President; Helen A. Brigham, Department Junior Vice-President; Mary E. Elliot, Department Secretary; Emma B. Lowd, Past Department President; Mary G. Deane, Past Department President; Emily L. Clark, Past Department President; E. Florence Barker, Sarah E. Fuller, members National Executive Board; Lizabeth A. Turner, Past National Senior Vice-President; Eleanor B. Wheeler, Past National Secretary.

Delegates.

Harriette A. Burrows (at large) of Charlestown, Mary J. Parkhurst of Gloucester, Annie M. Warne of Waltham, Rose A. Knapp of Somerville, Lizzie E. Jose of Brighton, Cappilla M. Ladd of Cambridge, Abbie T.

Usher of Newburyport, Sarah F. Kittredge of Peabody, Angela H. Scranton of Cambridgeport, Alice M. Goddard of Brockton, Emma M. Barrett of Melrose, Hattie A. Bray of Lynn, Abbie D. Danforth of Plymouth, Roxy A. Mellen of Orange, Rebecca A. Pickett of Beverly, Lila D. Lovering of Springfield, Ray E. Lane of Wakefield, Mary M. Graham of Westminster, Lucinda M. Farrar of Easthampton, Harriette L. Reed of Dorchester.

While journeying thousands of miles through States and Territories where the Woman's Relief Corps has become a successful reality, our delegates to National Convention have recalled its early aspirations and rejoiced at their grand fulfilment.

In all the work of the National organization the Pioneer Department has been loyally interested. The unknown graves in the South have not been forgotten on Memorial Day. Every appeal from National Presidents has met with a prompt response. Aid has been rendered sufferers by fire, flood and drouth in far distant sections. The National Woman's Relief Corps Home has received our cordial support. In helping to erect monuments and memorial halls, in teaching patriotism in the public schools and sustaining other special objects, the Department of Massachusetts has maintained its promise made in 1883.

Those who have watched the progress of our Order from the time when it had only a local influence to the present, when its beneficent work extends across the continent, feel a just pride in its success.

EMMA B. LOWD

Fifth Department President 1888, 1889

CHAPTER VI.

NATIONAL ENCAMPMENT WEEK IN BOSTON, AUGUST 11-16, 1890 — PART TAKEN BY THE WOMAN'S RELIEF CORPS OF MASSACHUSETTS.

WHILE the Seventh National Convention of the Woman's Relief Corps was in session at Milwaukee, Wis., in 1889, a message was received from the Twenty-third National Encampment, Grand Army of the Republic, then in session, stating that the Twenty-fourth National Encampment would be held in Boston.

Mrs. Emma B. Lowd, Department President of Massachusetts, and Mrs. Lizabeth A. Turner (of Boston), National Treasurer, immediately invited the Convention to hold its Eighth Annual Session in Boston, and the invitation was by vote accepted. Upon the return of our delegates to Massachusetts, a meeting of the Department Council was held to inaugurate plans for the success of the great gathering of 1890.

An Executive Committee of Arrangements was chosen, consisting of the members of the Department Council of 1889 and '90 and twenty-five additional members.

A General Committee of Arrangements was subsequently formed, which included all Corps Presidents of 1890.

A list of the various committees, as finally organized, is as follows: —

President, E. Florence Barker.
Treasurer, Lizabeth A. Turner.
Secretary, Sarah E. Fuller.

Vice-Presidents.

M. Susie Goodale, Medford.
S. Agnes Parker, Brockton.
Mary E. Knowles, Charlestown.
Mary M. Perry, Springfield.
Emily L. Clark, Northampton.
Eleanor B. Wheeler, S. Boston.
Mary A. Livermore, Melrose.
Matilda E. Lawton, S. Boston.
Ann E. Tucker, Boston.

Executive Committee.

Emma B. Lowd, Salem, *Chairman*.
Sarah E. Fuller, Medford, *Sec'y*.
Emma F. Lowd, *Ass't Sec'y*.
Lizabeth A. Turner, Boston, *Treas*.
E. Florence Barker, Malden.
Mary E. Knowles, Charlestown.
Augusta A. Wales, Dorchester.
Mary E. Elliot, Somerville.
Harriette L. Reed, Dorchester.
Leocardia F. Flowers, Cambridgep't.
Eliza F. Stiles, Lynn.
Mary M. Perry, Springfield.
Hattie A. Ralph, Somerville.
Elizabeth V. Lang, Hyde Park.
Eva T. Cook, Gloucester.
S. Agnes Parker, Brockton.
Emily L. Clark, Northampton.
M. Susie Goodale, Medford.
Marion E. Bridgman, Northampton.
Josephine A. Burdick, North Adams.
Carrie S. L. Bagley, Fitchburg.
Abby M. Weldon, Pittsfield.
Eleanor B. Wheeler, S. Boston.
Eliza F. Talbot, Holliston.
Hannah B. Belcher, Randolph.
Mary A. Livermore, Melrose.
C. Della Locke, Wakefield.
Clare H. Burleigh, Athol.
Sarah C. Walkeley, Westfield.
Lizzie N. Wade, Plainville.
Mary G. Deane, Fall River.
Annie K. Day, Groveland.
Sarah F. Gallup, Leominster.
Matilda E. Lawton, S. Boston.
Sarah B. Creasey, Newburyport.
Mary P. Lloyd, Gloucester.
Lucy M. James, New Bedford.
Clara C. Lovering, Medford.
Angela H. Scranton, Waverly.
Angie A. Robinson, Worcester.
Prudence H. Stokes, Wollaston Heights.

WOMAN'S RELIEF CORPS. 113

Executive Council.

Emma B. Lowd. Salem, *Chairman.*
Mary E. Knowles, Charlestown.
Hattie A. Ralph, Somerville.
E. Florence Barker, Malden.
Mary G. Deane, Fall River.
Lizabeth A. Turner, Boston.
Augusta A. Wales, Dorchester.
Elizabeth V. Lang, Hyde Park.
Mary E. Elliot, Somerville.
Hannah B. Belcher, Randolph.
Eliza F. Stiles, Lynn.
Angela H. Scranton, Waverly.
Sarah B. Creasey, Newburyport.
Clare H. Burleigh, Athol.
Harriette L. Reed, Dorchester.
Sarah E. Fuller, Medford.
S. Agnes Parker, Brockton.
M. Susie Goodale, Medford.
Mary M. Perry, Springfield.
Eleanor B. Wheeler, South Boston.

Conference with the Grand Army of the Republic.

Emma B. Lowd, Chairman of the Executive Committee.
Sarah E. Fuller, Secretary Executive Committee.
E. Florence Barker, President of the General Committee.

Reception.

Mary E. Knowles, Dept. Pres., *Chair.*
Sarah E. Fuller, Past Dept. Pres.
E. Florence Barker, Past Dept. Pres.
M. Susie Goodale, Past Dept. Pres.
Harriette L. Reed, Dorchester.
S. Agnes Parker, Past Dept. Pres.
Emma B. Lowd, Past Dept. Pres.
Mary M. Perry, Springfield.
Matilda E. Lawton, South Boston.
Elizabeth V. Lang, Hyde Park.
Lizabeth A. Turner, Boston.
Eva T. Cook, Gloucester.
Lizzie V. Innis, South Boston.
Eleanor B. Wheeler, South Boston.

Finance.

Hattie A. Ralph, Somerville, *Chair.*
Harriette L. Reed, Dorchester, *Sec'y.*
Marion E. Bridgman, Northampton.
E. Florence Barker, Malden.
Emma B. Lowd, Salem.
Sarah E. Fuller, Medford.
Lizabeth A. Turner, Boston.
Mary E. Knowles, Charlestown.
M. Susie Goodale, Medford.
Hannah B. Belcher, Randolph.
Mary A. Fellows, Chelsea.
Mary A. Bailey, Lynn.
Sarah F. Gallup, Leominster.
Martha M. Allen, Walpole.
Sarah P. Billings, Dorchester.
M. Alice Carey, Malden.
Sarah E. Woodard, Greenfield.
Mary P. Lloyd, Gloucester.
Sara K. A. Porter, Randolph.
May McKennie, Lynn.
Kate T. Dimon, Lowell.
Helen A. Brigham, Hyde Park.

8

Angie A. Robinson, Worcester. Lizzie N. Wade, Plainville.
Jane M. Chase, Westboro. S. Agnes Parker, Brockton.
Mary A. Yasinski, Salem. Ella J. Bailey, Milford.
Mrs. C. A. Stott, Lowell.

Transportation.

Mary G. Deane, Fall River, *Chair.* L. Annie Grant, Brockton.
Mary A. Ingram, Fall River. Lucy M. James, New Bedford.
Mary E. Goodwin, Foxboro.

Accommodations.

Lizabeth A. Turner, Boston, *Chair.* Hattie M. Tuttle, South Boston.
Eleanor B. Wheeler, S. Boston, *Sec'y.* Belle J. Noble, Charlestown.
Margaret T. Blanchard, Dorchester. Belle C. Stone, Dorchester.
Mary E. Swan, East Boston. Augusta A. Wales, Dorchester.
Augie K. Trask, Roxbury. Ellen A. Jarvis, Cambridgeport.
Maria A. Brown, South Boston. Mary E. King, Somerville.
Josephine R. Lescher, Somerville. Fannie T. Hazen, Cambridge.
Angie B. Chase, Chelsea. Cornelia F. Robinson, Boston.
Jennie T. Ray, Boston. Susan M. Dimond, Brookline.
Nettie D. Hill, Roxbury. Emilie L. W. Waterman, Boston.
Mary E. Bedell, Charlestown. Emma F. Haskell, Charlestown.
Lucinda Wakefield, Boston.

Information.

Elizabeth V. Lang, Hyde Park, *Chair.* Lizzie I. Fielding, Somerville.
Emilie L. W. Waterman, Boston, *Sec'y.* Kate M. Howard, Wakefield.
Helen A. Brigham, Hyde Park. Mattie A. Atwood, Dorchester.
Hattie M. Tuttle, South Boston. Emma Gillespie, Boston.
Addie A. Nottage, East Boston. Mary F. Young, Boston.
Annie Gurney, East Boston. Jennie Rogers, Boston.
Charlotte A. Hewins, Dorchester. Cornelia F. Robinson, Boston.
Abby E. Graves, Roxbury. Lena W. Niles, Boston.
Mary L. Merritt, Braintree. Helen M. Houghton, Randolph.
Belle J. Noble, Charlestown. Mary F. Croak, Randolph.
Sara K. A. Porter, Randolph. Harriet K. Wilson, E. Boston.
Ella M. Whittle, Malden. Mary A. Bird, Dorchester.
Martha C. Wakefield, Hingham. Abbie A. Haddock, Dorchester.
Prudence H. Stokes, Wollaston H'gts. Anna F. Adams, Boston.
Elizabeth E. Jones, Boston. Laura A. Merrow, Hyde Park.
Rose E. Eldridge, Hyde Park. Hattie B. Leonard, Hyde Park.

WOMAN'S RELIEF CORPS.

Susie E. Young, South Boston.
Sarah J. Williamson, Wollaston Heights.
Electa E. Field, Quincy.
Agnes S. Jones, Dorchester.
Mary Long, Randolph.
Alfrina J. Whittredge, Malden.
Nellie M. Barnard, Malden.
Nettie E. Cruff, Roxbury.
M. Jennie Simmons, Hingham.
Lizzie Allen, Charlestown.
Lizzie Daggett, Braintree.
Belle Alexander, Hyde Park.
Elizabeth Bickmore, Hyde Park.

Mary A. Laudt, Hyde Park.
Emma Leavitt, Quincy.
Lizzie M. Farrell, Quincy.
Susie Nelson, Norwood.
Mary T. Cobb, Dedham.
Mary I. Poland, Reading.
Mary G. McCollough, S. Boston.
Florence Kinsley, Dorchester.
Mary E. Kenney, Dorchester.
Emma F. Payne, Randolph.
Edith Taylor, Randolph.
Abbie M. Chamberlain, Braintree.
Susan M. Dimond, Brookline.
Sarah Addison, Somerville.

Entertainment.

Augusta A. Wales, Dorchester, *Chair.*
Lizzie V. Innis, South Boston.
Lizabeth A. Turner, Boston.
Leocardia F. Flowers, Cambridge.
Annie K. Day, Groveland.
Camilla E. Jenks, Worcester.
Lucia A. Knapp, Plymouth.
Nellie B. Mitchell, Roxbury.

Sarah A. Darling, Lexington.
Lizzie M. Richards, Charlestown.
Mary W. Whiton, Hingham.
Sarah W. Merchant, Lowell.
Elizabeth T. Beane, Lowell.
Mary A. Johnson, Malden.
Mary A. G. Robinson, Salem.
Clara H. Smith, Lynn.

Louisa M. Howe, Waltham.

Decorations.

Hannah B. Belcher, Randolph, *Chair.*
Lizabeth A. Turner, Boston.
Leocardia F. Flowers, Cambridge.
Carrie Dickman, Cambridge.
Etta A. Lockhart, East Cambridge.

Mary S. Hathaway, Randolph.
Prudence H. Stokes, Quincy.
Ellen M. Gill, Medford.
Carrie M. Hamblin, Hyde Park.
Lydia Palfrey, Dorchester.

Press.

Mary E. Elliot, Somerville, *Chair.*
E. Florence Barker, Malden.
Hattie A. Ralph, Somerville.
Lydia A. W. Fowler, Dedham.
Emma B. Lowd, Salem.
Mary E. Knowles, Charlestown.

Eva T. Cook, Gloucester.
Helen A. Brigham, Hyde Park.
Edith K. Perry, Malden.
Marion A. McBride, Boston.
Margaret J. Magennis, Dorchester.
Charlotte E. Berry, South Boston.

Charlotte Freeman, Cambridgeport.

Lunch.

Angela H. Scranton, Waverly, *Chair.* Sarah A. Woodside, Woburn.
Clara C. Lovering, Medford, *Sec'y.* Cora E. Snow, Dorchester.
Anna M. Conden, Watertown. Sarah F. Gallup, Leominster.
Mary A. Shattuck, Cambridgeport. C. Della Locke, Wakefield.
Mary A. Fellows, Chelsea. Mary H. Vaughn, South Boston.
Kate Tufts, Malden. Margie E. B. Hutchins, Lawrence.
Rose A. Knapp, Somerville. Leocardia F. Flowers, Cambridge.
Lizzie M. Dow, Watertown. C. O. Roberts, Malden.
Dorcas H. Lyman, Brighton. F. Lizzie Hubbard, Worcester.
Emilie L. W. Waterman, Boston. Mabel MacGill, Cambridgeport.

Halls.

Sarah B. Creasey, Newburyp't, *Chair.* Caroline M. McGlenen, Boston.
E. Florence Barker, Malden. Ida Meech, Boston.
Annie K. Day, Groveland. Augusta A. Wales, Dorchester.
Harriette L. Reed, Dorchester. Leocardia F. Flowers, Cambridge.

Banners.

Eliza F. Stiles, Lynn, *Chairman.* Eleanor B. Wheeler, S. Boston.
Clare H. Burleigh, Athol. Lizabeth A. Turner, Boston.
E. Florence Barker, Malden. Sarah A. Stiles, Dorchester.

Invitations.

E. Florence Barker, Malden. Emma B. Lowd, Salem.
Mary E. Knowles, Charlestown.

Auditing.

Clare H. Burleigh, Athol. Elizabeth V. Lang, Hyde Park.
Harriette L. Reed, Dorchester. Clara C. Lovering, Medford.
Leocardia F. Flowers, Cambridge.

Badges.

Emma B. Lowd, Salem, *Chairman.* Lizabeth A. Turner, Boston.
E. Florence Barker, Malden. Sarah E. Fuller, Medford.
Sarah B. Creasey, Newburyport.

Printing.

Harriette L. Reed, Dorchester, *Chair.* Lizabeth A. Turner, Boston.
Mary E. Elliot, Somerville, *Sec'y.* Augusta A. Wales, Dorchester.
Emma B. Lowd, Salem. Elizabeth V. Lang, Hyde Park.

MARY E. KNOWLES

Sixth Department President 1890
National Chaplain 1892-1893

Mary E. Knowles, Charlestown.   Hannah B. Belcher, Randolph.
Hattie A. Ralph, Somerville.   Eliza F. Stiles, Lynn.
E. Florence Barker, Malden.   Angela H. Scranton, Waverly.
Mary G. Deane, Fall River.   Sarah B. Creasey, Newburyport.
           Clare H. Burleigh, Athol.

Circulars were issued by the several committees which met frequently at Department Headquarters.

Mrs. Mary E. Knowles, who was chosen Department President at the Annual Convention in February, 1890, issued an appeal in General Orders, viz. : —

In consideration of the fact that this year promises to be the most important one in the history of this Department, I feel that this Order would be incomplete if I did not say to the Corps of Massachusetts, do all you can to make our coming National Convention a grand success. This dear old State of ours will be honored above all others during the month of August. From all parts of the country the veterans of the G.A.R. and our sisters of the W.R.C. will come to us. Prove to them that the "Mother Department" of our Order can be as royal in her hospitality as she is generous and tender in her care and protection of the country's defenders.

Local committees were appointed by the Corps throughout the State and the work outlined made daily progress. As early as March 7 the chairman of the Executive Committee was able to report the receipt of money and the promise of floral decorations for special headquarters.

Mrs. Turner, Chairman of the Committee on Accommodations, forwarded a circular March 26 to the Corps Presidents throughout the country, from which we copy the following : —

"The DEPARTMENT OF MASSACHUSETTS WOMAN'S RELIEF CORPS sends through you a most cordial greeting and invitation to each of their sister-members throughout the nation upon the coming TWENTY-FOURTH NATIONAL ENCAMPMENT, GRAND ARMY OF THE REPUBLIC, and the EIGHTH ANNUAL CONVENTION, WOMAN'S RELIEF CORPS, upon the 12th, 13th, 14th and 15th of August, 1890.

It is, at the present writing, impossible to announce the Programme of Ceremonies or any statement of the anticipated festivities happening through the several days and evenings of the Convention; but the preparations of the various committees and the assurances of both organizations throughout the country give promise of the largest and most memorable gathering of the old volunteers of the war for the Union and their friends in the history of the last quarter of a century.

It is estimated that there will be in the grand parade of August 12 upwards of 50,000 of our defenders in line.

Each of the yearly returning Encampments of the Veterans gathers about it new interests and emotions. The lengthening days of the living; the loving, tender memories of the dead; the added histories and recollections; the old friendships renewed and new ones created; the consideration of the best care of the sick and indigent, and the best direction of the holiest beneficence of our Nation, call most touchingly upon us as the Auxiliary of the Grand Army in their noble work of perpetuating the story and result of the Civil War.

The Department of Massachusetts, Woman's Relief Corps — the parent and pioneer — finds a peculiar pleasure in extending a most cordial entreaty to all of its sister Corps to unite in the coming Anniversary."

An appeal for funds was made to the Corps May 1, by Mrs. Ralph, Chairman of the Finance Committee, who stated in a circular that "The National Convention of the Woman's Relief Corps to be held in Boston the second week in August, will be a gathering of such interest and importance that every Corps in this Department will be benefitted thereby.

"Representatives are expected from thirty States where our Order has been established, and it is desired that our guests receive a greeting which will assure them that Massachusetts is imbued with a spirit of hospitality.

"Money and effort have been promptly given by Corps in States where the National Convention has met in former years. It is essential that Massachusetts, so often referred to as the 'pioneer,' should prove her interest in the work throughout the country, by extending a welcome to co-workers from abroad worthy the oldest Department. The plans which are being considered for the reception and entertainment of visitors include a lunch each day of the business sessions to the thousand delegates of the Grand Army Encampment and the delegates of our own organization.

"In order to properly proceed with the arrangements, the Executive Committee must know the amount that will be placed at their disposal as early as possible. Corps are therefore earnestly requested to inform the Chairman of the Finance Committee not later than May 15 the sum which they are willing to *pledge* for the expenses of National Convention."

Mrs. Mary E. Knowles, Department President, in her visits to Corps and at public gatherings of the Order, eloquently presented the subject and helped to awaken an interest in it. Nearly five thousand dollars were received from the Corps, and by July 12 the arrangements were so nearly completed that the Press Committee was authorized to publish the following programme in the leading papers throughout the country.

1883.   1890.
HEADQUARTERS EXECUTIVE COMMITTEE
EIGHTH NATIONAL CONVENTION, WOMAN'S RELIEF CORPS,
AUXILIARY TO THE GRAND ARMY OF THE REPUBLIC.
657 WASHINGTON ST., ROOM 17.

BOSTON, July 12, 1890.

The Woman's Relief Corps, as the recognized auxiliary to the Grand Army of the Republic, holds its annual sessions during Encampment week in the city and on the date selected by the Grand Army of the Republic.

The Eighth National Convention Woman's Relief Corps will assemble in Boston, August next, when delegates representing a membership of over ninety thousand will be in attendance from thirty States of the Union, and detached Corps from States where there are no Departments.

Arrangements for the week, as far as completed, are hereby announced.

Members of the Committee on Information (designated by badges) will be at depots and prominent hotels on Monday and Tuesday, August 11 and 12, to furnish strangers arriving in the city with information desired.

Through the courtesy of the National Encampment Grand Army of the Republic Committee, a grand stand will be erected in Copley Square for members of the Woman's Relief Corps, who will be admitted by tickets, to view the procession Tuesday A.M., and on that evening the Woman's Relief Corps will unite with the Grand Army of the Republic in a reception at Mechanics' Building, Huntington Ave.

The sessions of the Convention will open in Tremont Temple (Tremont Street), Wednesday, August 13, at ten o'clock A.M., when the delegates will be assigned to seats designated by the banners of their respective Departments. All other members of the Order desiring to visit the Convention and listen to its proceedings, will be admitted to the galleries.

A lunch will be served the delegates Wednesday and Thursday noon, in the Meionaon, Tremont Temple Building.

The badge of the Order will admit members to the Grand Army Camp-Fire, in Mechanics Hall, Wednesday evening.

The delegates will be the guests of the Grand Army of the Republic on Friday, August 15, in an excursion to Plymouth. Collingwood Corps, in this historic town, is preparing to extend a hearty greeting to all members of the Order.

On Friday evening, a Woman's Relief Corps Camp-fire, open to the public, will be held in Tremont Temple, presided over by Mrs. E. Florence Barker, the first National President.

Addresses will be made by His Excellency Governor Brackett, Speaker Barrett of the House of Representatives, Mrs. Annie Wittenmyer, National President, and Past National Presidents Woman's Relief Corps, Past Commanders-in-Chief Grand Army of the Republic, Corporal Tanner, and others.

Mrs. Mary E. Knowles, Department President of Massachusetts, will read a poem written for the occasion by Mrs. Kate B. Sherwood, Past National President.

An excellent programme of music will be presented.

An excursion to Nahant, complimentary to Woman's Relief Corps delegates and invited guests, is being arranged for Saturday, August 16.

A committee has been appointed to escort visiting delegates to places of interest in Boston and vicinity, and all members of the Order who may visit Boston during Encampment week are assured of a hearty welcome.

Headquarters have been assigned as follows : —
National Woman's Relief Corps Headquarters : Hotel Vendome.
Department of Massachusetts, Woman's Relief Corps and Executive Committee : Hotel Vendome.
New York : Hotel Brunswick.
Indiana : Hotel Vendome.
New Hampshire : Quincy House.
California and Kansas : Department Headquarters, Room 17, Boylston Building, 657 Washington street.
Michigan and Iowa : Woman's Educational Rooms, 98 Boylston street.
Pennsylvania and Nebraska : Woman's Educational Rooms, 98 Boylston street.
Wisconsin : Tremont Temple.
Illinois, Minnesota, Missouri, Maryland and New Jersey : Pilgrim Hall, Congregational Building, No. 6 Beacon street.
Maine, Ohio, Vermont, Rhode Island, Connecticut, Colorado, Washington, Oregon. North Dakota, South Dakota, Kentucky, Tennessee, Texas and New Mexico : Barnard Memorial Building, No. 10 Warrenton street.

MARY E. ELLIOT,
MARION A. McBRIDE,
Official : *For Press Committee.*
EMMA B. LOWD,
Chairman Executive Committee.

We quote from the report of Mrs. Barker in the *Republic Magazine* a few references to some of the events of that memorable week : —

"As the thousands upon thousands came thronging into Boston by every train, it seemed to the Committee on Accommodations that they might be called upon to fulfil the promise made by Mrs. Turner, ' to open the doors of New Hampshire, Rhode Island and Connecticut if necessary.' But so well systematized were the arrangements that all were comfortably provided for. The various committees had been engaged for months preparing for their guests, and on that Sabbath morning of August 10, everything was in readiness for the greeting.

"Sunday and Monday were busy days indeed for the Committees on Information, Reception and Accommodation.

"While the Grand Army received the Commander-in-Chief, General Alger, the Woman's Relief Corps welcomed Mrs. Alger to her apartments at the Vendome, which had been beautifully decorated by S. C. Lawrence Corps No. 5 of Medford.

"Our Honorary member, Paul Van Der Voort, who, as Commander-in-Chief, gave such official and valiant endorsement of the auxiliary societies, his estimable wife and the noble Clara Barton, were guests of the Relief Corps during Encampment Week. They were entertained at the Vendome, where were gathered many notable visitors, it being the headquarters of both organizations. The impressive parade of Tuesday was witnessed by National officers from the grand stand in Copley Square, where also the President of the United States, members of his Cabinet, General Sherman, Mrs. Logan, Clara Barton and other distinguished guests of the Grand Army of the Republic, received the battalions of marching veterans who saluted as they passed. And along the crowded streets many a wife, mother, daughter and sister watched for their own loved soldier in the line during the six hours' march.

"There was a brilliant reception in Mechanics' Building under the auspices of the two Orders, on the evening of the parade, when addresses were made by President Harrison, General Sherman, Governor Brackett, General Alger, the Commander-in-Chief, Mrs. Wittenmyer, National President, Mrs. Knowles, Department President of Massachusetts, and others.

"The sessions of the Convention were opened Wednesday morning in Tremont Temple, which had been elaborately decorated by the Grand Army Committee.

"The National Convention badge, distributed to the delegates, was a medallion of Mrs. Wittenmyer, attached to a yellow ribbon, — the National color. Each delegate also received a souvenir badge presented by the Executive Committee Woman's Relief Corps of Massachusetts. The design consisted of a pin with an oval plate, on which was embossed a hub, above being the words, 'Boston, 1890,' and below, the letters, 'F., C. & L.'

"From this gold pin hangs a medal on which is a cradle and the figures ''76.' Below this, suspended by chains from the pin, hangs a gold shield, on which is a representation of Faneuil Hall.

"The desk of the President was adorned with flowers presented by E. V. Sumner Corps No. 1 of Fitchburg, and other floral courtesies were subsequently received.

" Mrs. Wittenmyer fully rounded out her successful year's administration by an able address, summarizing the work of the past and the prospects of the future.

" The Convention was honored early in its sessions by distinguished guests, among whom were Gen. Jeremiah Rusk of the President's cabinet, Mrs. General Alger, Mrs. John A. Logan, Mrs. Mary A. Livermore and Miss Clara Barton.

" The visit of Secretary Rusk was specially interesting by reason of the presentation of a badge through him to his daughter, Mrs. Charity Rusk Craig, Past National President, who was unable to be present.

" As has been the custom since the National Order was formed, a committee from the National Encampment conveyed to the Convention the official greetings of the Grand Army of the Republic.

" Greetings were also received from representatives of the Union Ex-Prisoners of War Association, from Past Commander-in-Chief Van Der Voort and Department Commander Clarkson of New York, all of whom were cordially welcomed to the Convention.

" The sessions closed Thursday at midnight, after transacting important business connected with the Order.

"On Friday came the long anticipated excursion to Plymouth, and thousands were attracted to this historic spot, among them many of our members who were guests of the Executive Committee of the Grand Army of the Republic. The ancient streets and relics, the cordial hospitality of the people, the mammoth clambake and the fine decorations made the visit a memorable one in the history of the week.

"Collingwood Corps co-operated with the Post in making it a gala day. Its President, Mrs Lucia A. Knapp, made an address of welcome. Lunch was served by the Corps and three bushels of water-lilies distributed. Many souvenirs of this interesting place were borne away by the visitors, who will ever retain pleasant memories of the hours passed at Old Plymouth."

The novelty of a Woman's Camp-fire and the distinguished list of guests announced to participate, attracted thousands of people to Tremont Temple on Friday evening.

Three thousand people were admitted, filling every seat and the aisles, and as many more were turned away disappointed, unable to gain admittance.

Mrs. E. Florence Barker, Chairman of the General Committee of Arrangements, presided. After music by an orchestra, and singing of "The Star Spangled Banner" by Mrs. Nellie Brown Mitchell, a welcome was extended by Mrs. Barker, viz. : —

"Ladies of the Woman's Relief Corps, members of the Grand Army of the Republic and Friends : I bid you welcome to our camp-fire. Here in Massachusetts where twenty-three ladies joined together to form our Order, we tonight hold this, our grand festival. The child that we watched and prayed for, we have seen walk, but not without the aid of the brave men of the Grand Army of the Republic.

"We have invited the Governor, the Mayor, and the friends of the Woman's Relief Corps of Massachusetts to join with us in our camp-fire. But it is asked, 'How can you ladies build a camp-fire? You have no smoke.' Still we have plenty of dry wood and I propose to light it.

"Friends, we have with us this evening one of the greatest friends of the Union soldier, one who has furnished, perhaps, as much inspiration to our army as any person in this land. I have the pleasure of presenting to you Mrs. Julia Ward Howe."

Mrs. Howe said in responding: "I have been asked to recite something that I suppose is very familiar to you, 'The Battle Hymn of the Republic,' and when the President of this Association said that she would provide dry wood for the camp-fire, I thought that in presenting me she had brought forward a tolerably seasoned piece of timber. I could not do the noble hospital service that many did, but I went again and again to see the soldiers in their camp. The result of one of these visits, the first that I made, was the hymn that I will now recite to you. The first time I ever attempted to speak in public was when I visited a regiment in the neighborhood of Washington. Colonel Greene, I do n't know why, said to me, 'Mrs. Howe, you shall speak to my men.' I said, 'I never spoke; I cannot speak;' and I ran away three or four times. Finally he brought me back; and when I stood face to face to those gallant soldiers, I could only say how glad I was to see them, how proud and happy I was to be in their presence, and that is what I say to you tonight." She then read the

BATTLE HYMN OF THE REPUBLIC.

Mine eyes have seen the glory of the coming of the Lord :
He is trampling out the vintage where the grapes of wrath are stored ;
He hath loosed the fateful lightning of His terrible, swift sword,
    His truth is marching on.

I have seen Him in the watch-fires of a hundred circling camps;
They have builded Him an altar in the evening's dews and damps.
I can read His righteous sentence by the dim and flaring lamps,
    His day is marching on.

I have read a fiery gospel writ in burnished rows of steel:
"As you deal with My contemners, so with you My grace shall deal."
Let the Hero born of woman crush the serpent with his heel,
   Since God is marching on.

He has sounded forth the trumpet that shall never call retreat;
He is sifting out the hearts of men before His judgment seat.
Oh, be swift, my soul, to answer Him! be jubilant, my feet!
   Our God is marching on.

In the beauty of the lilies Christ was born across the sea,
With a glory in His bosom that transfigures you and me.
As He died to make men holy, let us die to make men free;
   While God is marching on.

Mrs. Barker introduced His Excellency, Governor Brackett. The Governor referred to his visits the past year to Grand Army gatherings, where on several occasions he had listened with pleasure to the eloquence of the Department President of Massachusetts. He said : —

"I am very much gratified to be present in behalf of the Commonwealth to give you a cordial welcome, to pay my respects to this organization, and to join with others in commendation of its noble work. It is an Auxiliary of the Grand Army of the Republic, and, like it, it is based upon the principles of Fraternity, Charity and Loyalty.

"I am informed that the delegates attending the National Convention represent a membership of nearly 100,000 women of this country; that there are some thirty State Departments and also Corps in States having no Departments. Such a band of American women joined together for patriotic and benevolent purposes, and actively fulfilling their mission, constitutes an institution for which the nation may well be grateful."

A vocal march was then rendered by the Swedish Quartette, after which Mrs. Barker introduced His Honor, Mayor Hart, saying: "The Mayor ordered the weather and has been working in his flower garden on the Common ever since the spring opened, preparing for this Encampment."

His Honor said : " We did commence in the garden early in the season. In my judgment we have shown you the handsomest Public Garden and the handsomest array of flowers that there is in the world.

" All this week I have been attending your camp-fires, and have been hearing how much Boston has done for you. My time has now come to tell you how much we respect the Grand Army, and I mean the Woman's Relief Corps just as well. By their combined efforts we have seen what the Grand Army and the Relief Corps are enabled to do. In thanking you for your invitation and reception I want to tell you as to the character of your presence in Boston. It was said that we should need an extra police force for the Public Garden to protect everything we had there. We had no occasion for the police which we had there before. I have received a letter from Mr. Doogue (Superintendent of the Public Garden) in which he said that there wasn't even a blade of grass missing. Your President has given me the credit of ordering the weather. I certainly prayed for it, for I heartily believe in prayer, and I believe the prayer is answered. I prayed for sunshine. The sunshine didn't immediately come; but the clouds lifted, and it has been pleasant up to this time. I hope and trust that it will be just as pleasant for you all, from the time you leave Boston until you get to your homes, and for all your natural lives."

" The Flag's Come Back to Tennessee," was sung by Mrs. Flora E. Barry.

Mrs. Wittenmyer, the retiring National President, was introduced, and in referring to the work of our Order, said : —

" Seven short years of existence has gathered together 100,000 of the very best women in the land. We are on dress parade tonight; but we work three hundred and sixty-five days in the year, Sundays excepted, and we have spent this year, in our charity work, $375,000. We are in the work to stay, for the veterans, and have at our finger-tips thousands of dollars to help those brave men who have fought for us."

Mrs. Mary E. Knowles, Department President, read the following poem written for the occasion by Mrs. Kate Brownlee Sherwood, Past National President: —

THE MASSACHUSETTS WOMAN.

A salute! And yet another!
A salute while the bugles play!
For the peerless Puritan mother,
For the mothers of Plymouth Bay!
For the Royal Relief Corps women,
The glory of Boston town!
For the Women of the grand old Commonwealth
Who share in her bold renown!
Through the ice and the snows
The Mayflower goes,
Through the racking, roaring sea,
And the breakers that dash on the lee;
And the old hull knocks
On the ragged rocks;
And the Puritan kneels to pray
To the Lord whom the winds obey.
Matrons and maidens are there
With their soothing hands on the head
Of the fainting and famished,
And the wrinkled brow of care;
Maiden and matrons are there
Where the savage has made his lair,
Heartsick, homesick and weary,
Bravest when all is most dreary;
Gaining courage and trust
From the frost and the snows and the rust,
And the fever and famine sore,
And the shadow of death at the door.
Matron and stately maiden,
Mothers and mates of men,

Of invincible Puritan men;
Sowing with hands full laden,
Seed that shall blossom again; —
Blossom in Revolution
And the birth of a Constitution
Brought forth in the freeman's fight,
In the daring defence of right;
In the splendor of right made might;
In the century flower of State;
In a Union grand and great,
The fruit of a mighty endeavor,
   One and forever.

Aye, it is brave to be going
Forth to the pipe and the drum,
Out where the bugles are blowing,
Hearing the drum say, " Come";
Loosed is the voice of the dumb,
And the halt and the lame
They leap in acclaim,
And the beardless boy says, " Come";
And the horses are neighing,
And the trumpets are braying,
And the heroes are shouting, " Come."
Aye, it is brave to be going
Where the bugles are blowing;
Where free men are met,
With faces firm set;
And they hold up strong hands,
And they vow to be true,
To dare and to do,
For their land of all lands;
And the shells are a-screaming,
And the rockets are gleaming;
And the roar of the cannon says, " Come,
   Come, patriot, come."

But the mother at home in her sorrow,
Or the wife with the babe on her knee,
No cymbals shall gladden her morrow,
No mourner so mournful as she;

And she swoons in her pain
When she hears the refrain
Of the jubilant marches afar;
Of the thunderous chorals of war.
O son, with the golden locks
All crimpled and crimsoned and wet,
With the dews of death in them set,
Where the surge of the battle shocks!
O brother, so stark and still,
Where the gunners charge over the hill,
And the mowers of death are thick,
And the heart of the hero is sick!
Do you hear her calling you, " Come."
Above the fife and the drum,
And the cannon that roars and rends
Both foes and friends?

But O for the Puritan mother,
Or the maiden of Plymouth Bay,
When husband, father and brother
And lover are marching away!
When the last bread is broken,
And the last vows are spoken;
And the kisses are sweet on the lips
As honey from the comb as it drips;
And the sword and the belt are in place,
And the horror of death creeps apace!
And she smiles a farewell,
And she whispers, " Be true
To the cause that is calling for you;
For death is the portal of life,
And dearer than mother or wife,
The truth that is calling for you,
From the scorn and confusion of hell;
And better the bonds of the grave
Than the gyves of the slave!"

Do you hear them? The Minute Men marching?
They have leapt the dread valley of bones;
Above them the brow overarching,
Beneath, the sacrificial stones

Where the martyrs are making their moans.
Do you hear them? The Minute Men marching?
They are shaking the kingdoms and thrones.
They are marching and marching and marching,
The bow of the Lord overarching,
And the son takes the place of the sire,
And their path is a pillar of fire,
As they're marching and marching and marching,
The promise of God overarching.
Do you hear them? The Minute Men marching?
In the Baltimore streets they are marching,
And the drops of their fiery baptismal
Have crimsoned the cup of their chrismal.
Do you hear them? The Minute Men marching?
The shadows of death overarching,
And beneath them confusion abyssmal?
Do you hear them? The Minute Men marching,
O imperious Puritan mother?
Lo, the ruddy red cross overarching,
She comes, keeping time with her brother!
When he faints she is there to relieve him;
When he falls she is there to receive him:
When the cannon roars out,
In the charge and the rout,
And the frenzy of wrath
Cuts its lurid long path,
'Til the rider and horse
Are down in its course;
No horror shall force her to leave him,
No disaster to question or grieve him,
And her voice is the tinkle of timbrels
When the battle is crashing its cymbals :
"By the Stars and the Stripes floating o'er you,
By the mothers and wives who adore you,
By the Commonwealth blazing with glory,
By a Union transfigured in story,
By the Puritan pride of endeavor,
Be freemen forever and ever."
And the hosts of the Lord overarching,
Massachusetts goes marching and marching.

O heroes of siege and of battle,
Recounting your conquests again,
When the drum-throbs of victory rattle
Make room for the angels of pain!

For the angel who sang in the dawn
Of the glory of God marching on!

For the white-ribboned angel of right
Lifting up pleading voice in the night!
For the angel who carries unfurled
The bannered red cross to the world!

For the angel who bears on her breast
The badge of sweet charity's quest: —
The cradle of liberty swung
From the cross that the crusader sung!

A salute and yet another!
A salute while the bugles play!
For the peerless Puritan mother,
For the mothers of Plymouth Bay!
For the regal Relief Corps women,
The glory of Boston town!
For the women of the brave old Commonwealth
Who share in her bold renown!

Mrs. Barker referred to the interest that the late General Logan had shown in our Order, and to the fact that "we owe very much to his companion who taught him this noble faith in woman." She then called upon Mrs. Logan who was given an enthusiastic greeting as she arose to acknowledge the compliment.

Miss Ella Chamberlain then whistled Fior Di Margherita in such a manner that the audience demanded an encore, and continued to applaud, causing Mrs. Barker to remark: —

"We always call upon the Commander-in-Chief to help us when we get into danger. I have the pleasure of presenting General Alger. He has just retired from the chair, and we have not yet learned to say Past Commander-in-Chief." Gen. Alger said : —

"As I have travelled over this great country during the past year, visiting many places, perhaps I have seen one hundred kindred organizations of yours. I have found in every place willing and glad testimony to the fact that you are doing the major part of the work of charity and relief for our disabled comrades, for their wives, for their widows, for their old fathers, their old mothers and their children. And it seems to me that it is superfluous talk to tell you that you are doing the noblest work on earth.

"You may be sure your work is appreciated. I am certain that you never find a man whose heart beats beneath the blue, who does not wish to show in his every act that he is grateful to you and appreciates your magnificent work."

Gen. William T. Sherman entered the hall during General Alger's address and the old hero was greeted with cheers. After the applause had subsided, General Alger addressed him, saying: "General Sherman, you came in at the last and best part of my speech; but I want to say to you, sir, that you are the dessert for any man's speech, and I gladly surrender my place to you."

Mrs. Barker then said: "It is impossible to outrank the comrade I now have the pleasure of introducing to you. All who outrank him have passed over. His equals in rank have passed over. He alone is left to speak for his representatives. I have the honor to introduce to you General Sherman." (Great applause. Mayor Hart called for three cheers for the General which were enthusiastically given.)

General Sherman said: "I hardly suppose that I can interest an audience of this kind; but so far as manifesting an interest in the objects of this association, the Woman's Relief Corps, I certainly will add my mite of praise and approval. I wish the Corps prosperity, I wish them success in their movement. I hope they may be spared the care of the wounded and of the sick, or of making provision for those who are at the front. They know their interests quite as well as we do. We must bear the brunt of the battle and they can alleviate its necessities and sorrows. I am sure, from what I have seen of the ladies connected with this association, that they will fulfil it all over this land of ours.

"We stand here on historic ground. We stand beneath a temple whose historic fame is world-wide. Here have occurred scenes which every patriot loves to dwell upon. And wherever we go, whether it be in the streets of Boston or in the suburbs of Boston, or in the villages which lie round about, we see repeated the names which were made dear to us as boys and girls in our schools. Who has not heard of Bunker Hill and Lexington and Concord? They are here now today. Their children are here, their grandchildren, their great-grandchildren, yea, it may be the fourth generation. And so of Dorchester Heights, and so of many other places you could name around Boston, every one of which recall memories of which even I only remember from books: for, gentlemen and ladies, I was not in the Revolutionary war. It sometimes makes me feel old when I see boys twenty-five and twenty-six years of age turning up their ears to hear more distinctly about the war of the Rebellion. They are just as innocent of it as we were of the Revolutionary war when we went to school.

"But these organizations — the Grand Army of the Republic, the various army societies, the Ladies' Relief Association — all aid in teaching the young what their fathers and grandfathers did before them: the lesson of patriotism, an object lesson stronger than any ever spread before you in types, whether of gold or silver or common black ink. Yes, my friends, you of the Grand Army of the Republic, your wives and children, whether they belong to the Relief Corps or not, spread before the youth of the rising generation a better knowledge of the principles which begot our Constitution, which were developed as we progressed, and which finally met a glorious result in giving us a united country, one and indivisible, now and forever, to the end of time."

Mrs. Nella Brown Pond then recited "The Bivouac on the Battlefield," after which Corporal Tanner was presented and spoke as follows: —

"Last night we thought that we had reached the altitude of Boston's possibilities, but we are tonight again surprised by the magnificence of this great gathering. This would not be the city of John A. Andrew in the past if it would not be ready at all times to welcome the men who made this gathering possible.

"Tonight we are the guests of the Woman's Relief Corps — I wish I could say more in praise of their work. Some of them may grow grayhaired with time, but they will always be young to us. Thank you, and God bless you for your great work."

Mrs. Barker: —

"The Commander-in-Chief has issued his first order to his comrades, and we are now ready to receive it for the Woman's Relief Corps."

General Veazy, Commander-in-Chief, said: "When your committee came into our Encampment yesterday and told us of your great numbers and of your great contribution to charity, amounting to many hundred thousand dollars, it occurred to me how much more potency and power there is in simple facts than in any words, and how much loftier is the eloquence of such facts than any that can fall from human lips.

"When I was elected to the great office to which your presiding officer has been pleased to allude, I was depressed and well-nigh overcome at the thought of the tremendous responsibility that was resting upon me. But then, when I thought again that the Woman's Relief Corps is the right hand of the Grand Army of the Republic, I felt that I should be equal to this great undertaking. But again tonight, when I just heard from my predecessor that this grand and great occasion of the Woman's Relief Corps is but the beginning of what I have got to encounter for twelve months to come, my heart again sank, until I thought: We have another auxiliary force, that is the left hand of the Grand

Army of the Republic, upon which to call to sustain me on such occasions as this and others, and that is the Sons of Veterans of war.

"In closing I wish to say that if there is any act, any influence of mine that can be of any aid or assistance to your organization, I hope you will freely call upon me, because while I shall freely give it I know that I shall receive an hundred fold more from you than it will be possible for me to do for you."

Miss Clara Barton was next introduced and bowed her acknowledgments.

The "Veteran's Last Song," written by Chaplain J. H. Lozier, was read by Corporal Tanner.

Other addresses were made by Past Commander-in-Chief Van Der Voort, Mrs. Mary S. McHenry, National President, Alfred C. Monroe, Assistant Adjutant-General, Department of Massachusetts, G.A.R., Mrs. Elizabeth D'Arcy Kinne, Past National President, Hon. Willard Howland, Judge Advocate of the Sons of Veterans and Hon. William H. Haile, Lieutenant-Governor of Massachusetts.

The camp-fire closed at a late hour, the immense audience listening with enthusiastic interest to all the exercises.

The closing festivity of the week was a harbor excursion to Nahant arranged by the Entertainment Committee of the Woman's Relief Corps, and a social day was enjoyed by many.

On the return trip to Boston, the party lingered a while at Lynn to accept hospitalities extended by General Lander Corps No. 29 of that city.

Mrs. Lizzie F. Mudgett, President, greeted the visitors with an address of welcome, lunch was served and a social hour passed by the company.

Through the interest taken by the Corps and the efficient work of all the committees, Mrs. Turner, Treasurer of the Executive Committee, was able to report that the contributions received amounted to over five thousand dollars, and that after all

AUGUSTA A. WALES

Seventh Department President 1891

expenses had been paid there was a balance on hand of one thousand dollars. This sum was transferred by vote of the Executive Committee to the Department Soldiers' Home Fund. In addition to the amount expended by the Executive Committee, the sum of $1,320.62 was appropriated by Corps for the local entertainment of guests.

The following correspondence is of interest: —

SALEM, Sept. 5, 1890.

GEORGE L. GOODALE,
   Chairman Executive Committee.

Dear Sir: At the recent meeting of the Executive Committee of the Woman's Relief Corps we were enabled to so far complete our reports as to assure us that, through the liberality of the Corps of this Department, the Executive Committee will be able to meet all expenses contracted by the Woman's Relief Corps for the Eighth Annual Convention.

I am, therefore, instructed to inform you that we shall not call upon the Executive Committee of the Grand Army of the Republic for any portion of the $3,000 appropriated by it for the use of the Woman's Relief Corps.

We desire to express our thanks for the courtesy tendered us, and while not needing to avail ourselves of it, we fully appreciate the fraternal spirit which prompted it. With congratulations to your committee upon the great success of the Encampment, I am,

                  Fraternally yours,
                          EMMA B. LOWD,
                Chairman Executive Committee, W.R.C.

HEADQUARTERS EXECUTIVE COMMITTEE,
NATIONAL ENCAMPMENT, GRAND ARMY OF THE REPUBLIC.
BOSTON, Sept. 13, 1890.

Mrs. EMMA B. LOWD,
   Chairman Executive Committee, Woman's Relief Corps.

Dear Madam: At a meeting of the Executive Committee, National Encampment, Grand Army of the Republic, 1890, held on the 10th inst., your communication of the 5th inst. was presented.

The Executive Committee desire to convey to the Woman's Relief Corps their acknowledgment and high appreciation of the work performed by its members, in so generously and abundantly providing lunch for the Delegates to the National Encampment, Grand Army of the Republic, and for their invaluable aid in the labor of preparation and successfully performing the pleasant duties of Encampment week.

That your grand work, so cheerfully undertaken and completed with such glorious results, has been done entirely through the aid and efforts of the ladies of your organization, and without any pecuniary assistance from our committee, makes a record for the Woman's Relief Corps, Department of Massachusetts, of which its members may well have a just feeling of pride.

We extend to your committee our congratulations upon the grand success attending the entertainment of the Eighth National Convention, Woman's Relief Corps.

No feature of the week of duty and of pleasure was more enjoyable than the camp-fire at Tremont Temple on the evening of Friday, August 15. We wish to express to your committee, and through it to the members of the organization you represent, our sincere, cordial thanks for the aid rendered us, and the hope that the fraternal bond uniting the Woman's Relief Corps and the Grand Army of the Republic may strengthen with each succeeding year of duty and of pleasure.

Sincerely and fraternally yours,

GEORGE L. GOODALE,
Chairman Executive Committee.

In presenting her annual address to the Department Convention of 1891, Mrs. Knowles, Department President, officially thanked the members for their hearty interest, viz. : —

" When the word was brought back to us from Milwaukee that the Eighth National Convention would be held in Boston, every member of our Order in this Department began to feel that she must do her part towards welcoming those who would come from all over our broad land, wearing the little bronze badge, the sight of which causes the hand to be given in the grasp of fraternity and the lips to speak words of welcome to the ' stranger within our gates.' The work of preparation for this memorable event in the history of our Department occupied many weeks of careful and untiring labor, and the grand results accomplished elicited words of praise and gratitude from the visiting members of the

Grand Army of the Republic and the Woman's Relief Corps. But while we feel a just pride in our committees, who were guided by the able women whose wise counsel and untiring zeal combined to render every arrangement for the comfort and enjoyment of our guests a *perfect* success, it is to you, my sisters, that our grateful thanks are tendered; without your aid and co-operation we could have done nothing; and the generous response given to our call by the Corps of this Department proved to us your loyalty and devotion, and the record you have made places this Department in the foremost rank of the Order."

Mrs. Hattie A. Ralph, Delegate-at-Large to the Eighth National Convention, gave a complete report, from which the following is taken: —

"The testimonials hanging upon the walls of many of our Corps rooms, the cordial letters received, and reports coming to us of Corps having been formed in other States through the good impressions formed of our Order here, are evidences that the results were worthy of the effort.

"As we watched the marching files passing along our streets on the morning of the parade (Tuesday, August 12), it seemed as though Heaven was weeping over the memories of those 'who returned not with the rest'; but later in the day it rejoiced with us over the victories of those who formed the grand parade, the inspirations of which still linger and cannot fail to impress our members with the value of our work as the auxiliary of the Grand Army of the Republic.

"The lunch provided by the Woman's Relief Corps for the Delegates of the Grand Army was a departure from previous encampments, but proved to be one that was highly appreciated by the comrades; and the efficient committee having this in charge also made successful arrangements for lunch for our own delegates.

"At the opening session, Wednesday morning, August 13, in Tremont Temple, delegates were present from twenty-nine States (including the full representation from Massachusetts) and eight detached Corps.

"Mrs. Sarah E. Fuller, Secretary of the National Pension and Relief Committee, rendered an interesting report referring to the petition 3,110 feet long, containing 160,000 signatures, which was presented to Congress in behalf of pensions for army nurses.

"The election of our beloved member, Mrs. Lizabeth A. Turner, to the office of National Senior Vice-President, whose nomination was greeted with the most hearty applause, must ever be a source of pleasure and pride to the Department of Massachusetts."

A few days after Encampment week, the badges of the Grand Army of the Republic and of the Woman's Relief Corps no longer greeted the passer-by or encircled the State House dome.

The arches, covered with flags and portraits and patriotic designs — all object lessons that had their influence — were removed from the streets, and closed were the halls where speech and story, where waving banners and music, had aroused enthusiasm. But the inspiration of that eventful week will ever linger in our memories, for there were gathered within our borders the heroes of a hundred battle-fields. The walls of our temples echoed not only to the sound of martial music and sweetest song, but to the eloquence of men who had led armies to victory, to the voices of women who had ministered to those armies in war and peace.

CHAPTER VII.

RELIEF AND PENSIONS FOR ARMY NURSES — DEPARTMENT
RELIEF WORK — MEMORIAL FUND — AID EXTENDED
NATIONAL W.R.C. HOME.

IN addition to the local relief which our Corps have extended to needy soldiers, sailors and marines, aid has been given army nurses, those " ministering angels of the battle-fields and hospitals " whose services were invaluable to the Union Army. Their cause was presented at the Second National Convention, held at Minneapolis, July, 1884, when it was voted to establish an army nurse fund at National Headquarters and in every Department.

An appeal was issued, and eleven corps from Massachusetts responded, viz.: Charles Beck Corps No. 2, Cambridge, S. C. Lawrence Corps No. 5, Medford, George H. Ward Corps No. 11, Worcester, E. K. Wilcox Corps No. 14, Springfield, Col. Prescott Corps No. 15, Ashland, U. S. Grant Corps No. 16, Melrose, Col. C. R. Mudge Corps No. 24, Merrimac, Gen. Lander Corps No. 29, Lynn, Phil H. Sheridan Corps No. 34, Salem, Timothy Ingraham Corps No. 35, Hyde Park, and Gen. James Appleton Corps No. 42, Ipswich.

Mrs. Kate B. Sherwood of Ohio, in her report at the Minneapolis Convention as National Senior Vice-President, recommended that " The Woman's Relief Corps memorialize Congress to grant pensions to the women who gave their best services for their country and for the care of the men who fought their country's battles."

This resulted in the appointment of a National Pension Committee, and at the Fourth National Convention at San Francisco in 1886, the Committee recommended that a petition be prepared, asking Congress to grant pensions to army nurses. This measure being adopted, sixty-seven Corps in Massachusetts circulated the petitions, and obtained over eight thousand signatures.

Blanks for compiling the records of army nurses were issued from National Headquarters, and the Department officers of this State rendered every aid possible to secure a complete and accurate list of nurses, and to promptly forward their certificates of service.

Mrs. E. Florence Barker served as Chairman of the National Pension Committee three years. Mrs. Sarah E. Fuller was Secretary of this Committee from October, 1889, to September, 1890, and working in Washington in the summer of 1890 for the success of the pension bill which was pending in Congress, when a sudden illness compelled her to resign, and, upon her recommendation, Mrs. Harriette L. Reed of Dorchester was appointed her successor. Thus, the Department of Massachusetts has from the first been identified with the movement which has resulted in securing pensions for army nurses who can prove that they served six months or more.

There are some nurses who have failed to prove their claims, owing to the fact that the officials under whom they served are not living, and the required evidence, therefore, cannot be secured. And there are many among those receiving pensions who are unable to live comfortably on the small sum of eight dollars per month, this, in some cases, being their only income.

A record of these is kept on file at Department Headquarters, and relief given from a permanent fund, which is supplied by donations from Corps and by a certain per cent appropriated from the *per capita* tax, by vote of the Convention.

A Department Relief Fund was established in 1888, and a Department Relief Committee appointed in 1890, by authority of National Convention. This Committee had charge of the disbursements from the Army Nurse Fund, until the latter was transferred to the Memorial Fund in 1893.

An idea of the work of the Department Relief Committee is given in the following extracts: —

From the report of the Chairman, Mrs. Emilie L. W. Waterman, 1892: —

"On Sept. 9, 1890, in accordance with the recommendation adopted by the Eighth National Convention, a Department Relief Committee was appointed, of which I was made chairman. The other members were Leocardia F. Flowers of Cambridgeport and Hattie M. Tuttle of South Boston. During the remainder of the year, thirty-one cases were attended to and seventy-one calls made.

"Mrs. Wales again appointed me chairman. Addie A. Nottage of East Boston and Lizzie B. Raymond of Charlestown have served with me and have been ever ready to do any duty assigned them. During the year ending Feb. 6, 1892, fifty-two applicants have been investigated and twenty-eight veterans or members of their families assisted, showing an expenditure from the Relief Fund of $107.35; from the Army Nurse Fund six have been assisted at an expenditure of $63.00: making a total of $170.35 expended in cash. This does not by any means show all that has been given in this work, but simply what has been taken from the Department funds. We have tried to take as good care of the Department pocket-book as we would of our own; and in many of these cases have succeeded in interesting G.A.R. Posts which have no auxiliary, charitable societies, and circles of the King's Daughters, which have given liberally; therefore the full amount of good done cannot be estimated. Seventy-six visits have been made, not including the numerous calls at offices of the organizations before mentioned, and at the pension offices and hospitals.

"I took up this work, little realizing the responsibility attending it, and time that must be devoted to it. As the old soldier advances in years the work must increase and demands for thorough investigation will be greater. I therefore recommend : —

"1. That, in the appointment of this committee, women who have had some experience in charity work be selected.

"2. That, in the work of investigation the proper officers of the Pension and State Aid Committees and the Associated Charities be consulted — for this reason : Many who apply are already receiving pensions, State aid and perhaps assistance from one or more charitable organizations, therefore do not really need our help.

"I could fill a large book with my experiences during the past three years. While there are many disagreeable duties to perform — as, I am sorry to say, we sometimes find those who are unprincipled frauds — yet there is a bright side, as could be proven if I had time to tell of all the 'God bless you's' received, and to read some of the letters from those who appreciate what is done for them. I will give you an extract from one. Having had an appeal from a lady for warm clothing for a deceased soldier's daughter (at present an inmate of the Consumptives' Home), the goods were purchased and forwarded. A week later the following was received : —

"'I ought to have acknowledged the receipt of the beautiful goods which came to me in response to my request before this. I have cut the dress and nearly finished the skirt, and my protégé is coming tomorrow to try it on. I wrote her that the beautiful new garments were a gift *from her father*. I looked at them almost with awe, as if a hand had been stretched across the space of thirty years to give these to this destitute child. I thank the Woman's Relief Corps very much. God bless you in your work.'

"In closing, I wish to thank the Department Presidents who have had confidence enough in me to place the charge of this important work in my hands; also, to those who have served with me, I say, 'Thank you' for the prompt attention to whatever they have been assigned. Special thanks are due to Col. C. Hapgood of the Pension Bureau; Mr. Reuben Peterson, State Aid Agent; Mr. Frothingham of the Provident Association; and the officers, one and all, of the Associated Charities, who have always treated me in the most courteous manner, giving me all assistance in their power; and last, but not least, to many officers of the police force who have aided in every way possible."

From report of Mrs. Waterman at the Convention in 1893: —

"The demands upon this Committee having greatly increased, it was deemed necessary this year to appoint four instead of two, as heretofore, to serve with me. Mrs. Elizabeth B. Raymond of Charlestown, Mrs. Addie A. Nottage of East Boston, Mrs. Nettie D. Hill and Mrs. Elizabeth Killian of Roxbury were appointed and have cheerfully and faithfully attended to all duties assigned them. Their experience in relief work has made them valuable co-workers; and the meetings held have been pleasant and harmonious.

"The surface work of the year may be summed up as follows: 110 applications for aid have been received; and after investigation 58 have been assisted from the Department Relief and 5 from the Army Nurse Fund. Eleven committee meetings have been held and 183 calls made, exclusive of those at pension offices, hospitals and Associated Charities. Nearly 200 letters have been written, numerous money orders, registered letters and checks sent, as this work is not by any means confined to the city of Boston. Itemized reports of all relief work have been forwarded each quarter (and to date) to the Department President. Two books of reference (to be kept at Headquarters) have been prepared; one in which the names of all soldiers or their relatives who apply for aid, and the results of investigation, are recorded, and the other for record of Army Nurses."

From the report of Mrs. Elizabeth B. Raymond (Chairman), at the Annual Convention in February, 1894: —

"I have the honor, as Chairman of the Department Relief Committee, to submit the following report for the year ending Feb. 7, 1894, inclusive: —

"The prediction of the able Chairman who preceded me has become a veritable fact, and, as stated one year ago, the work has nearly doubled.

"The present depressing state of affairs throughout the country is at least significant that all our energies will be required, in the ensuing year, and that the increase of our charities will go on proportionately.

"The following items, although they express nominally our work, are not truly indicative of the requirements of this Committee in its ministrations among the old soldiers and those dependent on them.

"All cases are thoroughly investigated, and many urgent cases of destitute soldiers require immediate relief before they can be properly brought before the Grand Army Post for investigation.

"One hundred and seventy-four calls for aid have been made upon the Committee, and 107 have received assistance from the Relief Fund.

"We have the names of thirteen army nurses on our list, five of whom have been assisted from the Army Nurse Fund.

"I have received 213 letters and written 232. Have placed four soldiers in the Chelsea Home. Have obtained admission for one soldier's widow to the National Home in Ohio.

"Have procured pension for one army nurse and State aid for three soldiers' widows.

"One soldier's wife, totally blind, has been placed in a pleasant home with board and is well taken care of. I refer to these few cases that you may know some of the special work of your Committee.

The amount expended from the Relief Fund	$269 26
Expended from the Army Nurse Fund	143 40
Relief other than money	82 65
Making a total of relief during the year of	$495 31

"Many soldiers have been placed in public and private homes and in many ways their sickness and suffering assuaged.

"I here desire to thank my able and patient co-workers, Mrs. Nettie D. Hill, Mrs. Rose A. Knapp, Mrs. Tryphena C. Berry and Mrs. Dorcas H. Lyman, for their ever-ready and heartfelt interest shown in this work.

"The army nurse has become a prominent factor in our charities. These noble women, who so faithfully nursed our sick and wounded soldiers, have been generously dealt with; and may they always receive from this Department, when occasion shall require, that grateful acknowledgment of their services which is so justly their due.

"I desire to thank the Department President, Treasurer and Secretary for their kindly advice and assistance.

"In closing I will call your attention to the fact that the old veteran and his dependents will require increasing solicitations as the years roll on. Volumes have been written in reference to his status since the war closed. But his courage and patriotism have never been questioned. Whatever standing our country has today among other nations, he made it. And our duty shall always be to him as long as he shall live or this organization exist."

During 1894, the sum of $380.00 was expended from the Department Relief Fund, by the Committee, Elizabeth B. Raymond, Annie J. E. Perkins, Margie E. B. Hutchins, Annie M. Warne and Angie B. Chase, who had charge of this work during the past year.

The work of the Memorial Fund Committee, which now has charge of the disbursements from the Army Nurse Fund, is fully explained in the following report presented by the Chairman, Mrs. Mary G. Deane: —

BOSTON, Feb. 7, 1894.

At the Fourteenth Annual Convention of this Department, in February last, the subject of a Memorial Home in Massachusetts for the widows and orphans of the deceased veterans was presented in the annual address of the Department President, who offered the following recommendations: —

"My experiences the past year have convinced me that a Home is needed in Massachusetts for the destitute widows and orphans of her veterans and for army nurses who are dependent. We take pride in the loyalty of our Corps to the Posts to which they are auxiliary; and no appeal in their behalf should ever be ignored. I have faith enough in the energy and devotion of our membership to believe that this additional work can be undertaken and successfully accomplished without lessening our efforts for the Grand Army of the Republic. There are soldiers' widows and orphans to whom such a Home as proposed would be a blessing; and this is a movement in keeping with the veteran's cause.

"In order to present the subject before the Convention for action, I *recommend*, That a plan be inaugurated for the establishing of a Home in Massachusetts for the destitute widows and orphans of her Union veterans, and for dependent army nurses on our roll; also, That the Home be dedicated as a memorial of the patriotism of the women of Massachusetts during the Civil War, and under the management of the Department of Massachusetts Woman's Relief Corps.

"As it may take several years to accumulate a fund sufficient for the purpose, I *recommend*, That some definite action be taken at this Convention toward starting a fund to be designated the 'Memorial Home Fund.'"

The Convention voted to adopt the recommendations, and also *voted*, That a committee be appointed to prepare and present a plan to

MARY G. DEANE

Eighth Department President 1892

the Convention for action, and that the Department President, Mrs. Deane, be Chairman of that Committee. Mrs. Emma B. Lowd and Miss Mary E. Elliot were added to the Committee, and the following report was subsequently presented: —

REPORT OF COMMITTEE ON MEMORIAL HOME PLAN.

Mrs. President: The Committee appointed to draft a plan that can be acted upon by this Convention present the following report: —

Recognizing the urgent demand in our State for a Home for the needy widows and orphans of Union soldiers and sailors, also for army nurses, and believing that such a memorial would be a practical aid in our relief work, a help to the Grand Army of the Republic, and would enlist the sympathy of the public, we *recommend*, That this Convention take the following action, viz.: —

That a bazaar or fair be held during the present year for this specific object, — a Memorial Home, — provided a sufficient number of Corps endorse the plan to warrant its undertaking.

We further *recommend*, That the Past Department Presidents and the incoming Department President be appointed a committee, empowered to prepare and issue to the Corps a circular explaining fully the project proposed and asking their co-operation.

If the responses received are encouraging, we *recommend*, That said Committee be authorized to proceed with arrangements for the bazaar and have charge of the same.

Respectfully submitted, in F., C. and L.,

MARY G. DEANE,
EMMA B. LOWD,
MARY E. ELLIOT,
Committee.

The above report having been adopted by the Convention, the Committee was called together by Mrs. Sarah E. Fuller, the Senior Past Department President, and organized with Mrs. Mary G. Deane as Chairman and Treasurer, and Mrs. Sarah E. Fuller, Secretary.

The first step taken by the Committee after organization was to correspond with the Department Commander of the Grand

Army of the Republic relative to a conference with the Department Council, G.A.R., as we did not desire to make any movement that would conflict in the least with that grand body of men to which we are auxiliary.

In answer to this request a communication was received that a meeting of said Council would be held May 17, 1893. This date was therefore selected for the second meeting of your Committee. After presenting the subject in question to the Department Council, G.A.R., the Committee convened at Headquarters; and after discussing the question it was decided to prepare a circular to be issued to the Corps, and present the same at an adjourned meeting of the Committee, to be held May 25, 1893, and the Chairman was empowered to prepare the same. On the date designated the meeting was held and the following circular presented for action, viz.: —

HEADQUARTERS DEPT. OF MASS. WOMAN'S RELIEF CORPS,
AUXILIARY TO THE GRAND ARMY OF THE REPUBLIC,
657 WASHINGTON ST., ROOM 17.

CIRCULAR LETTER
No. 1.
BOSTON, May 27, 1893.

In accordance with a vote of the Fourteenth Annual Convention, the matter relating to a Memorial Home for the widows and orphans of Union veterans and for destitute army nurses was referred to a Committee consisting of the Department President and Past Department Presidents. This Committee was authorized to issue a circular to the Corps asking their aid in holding a bazaar or fair in behalf of this project, and to proceed with arrangements for the same, provided the responses from the Corps warranted the undertaking.

The subject has been fully considered by the Committee; and while we realize the urgent need of such a Home in Massachusetts, it is not deemed advisable to hold a bazaar this year; but we are convinced that (as the recommendation presented in the Department President's address was adopted) a Memorial Fund should be established by this Department — a fund to be used for the maintenance of the women who never faltered in their devotion to the soldiers' welfare, and for the orphans of the defenders of our Union, that they may feel that their claims upon our gratitude are not unheeded.

The co-operation of every Corps in this Department is most earnestly desired, that a permanent fund may be established which may result in the erection of a Memorial Home whenever deemed expedient.

It is desirable that we know as far as possible what support the Corps are willing to give this movement. All communications in regard to this matter, either money or pledges voted, you will please forward to the Chairman of the Committee, Mrs. Mary G. Deane, Fall River, Mass., Box 672.

By order of the Fourteenth Annual Department Convention.

MARY G. DEANE, *Chairman.*
EMILY L. CLARK, *Dept. Pres.*
SARAH E. FULLER,
E. FLORENCE BARKER,
M. SUSIE GOODALE,
S. AGNES PARKER,
EMMA B. LOWD,
MARY E. KNOWLES,
AUGUSTA A. WALES,
Committee.

This was adopted, and, in accordance with a unanimous vote, a copy was sent to every Corps in the State. As a result of this letter, contributions and pledges were received, also letters assuring us that favorable action would be taken upon the matter by many Corps after the summer vacation. The correspondence relating to the project was large; and so numerous were the inquiries, both verbal and written, that the Chairman of the Committee, with the consent of the Department President, decided to issue a type-written letter to many of the Corps; this action was later endorsed by the Committee. The letter read as follows: —

FALL RIVER, Oct. 12, 1893.

Mrs. President: Will you kindly inform me what action Corps —— has taken in regard to Circular Letter No. 1, referring to the Memorial Home Fund? This is a movement that earnestly appeals for aid to all the Corps in this Department. The fact that there are soldiers' widows in Massachusetts destitute and homeless, also aged army nurses in our own vicinity struggling with disease and poverty, is sufficient proof that a permanent fund for their support should be established.

To whom shall they look for help if not to the Order whose special object is the care of those who suffered for the Union cause?

We trust that *every* Corps in this Department will take favorable action concerning the matter and promptly report said action or forward all contributions to the Chairman, Mary G. Deane, Box 672, Fall River, Mass.

It will be a grand record and one worthy the great Department of Massachusetts, if we can report at the next Annual Convention that every Corps responded to the appeal of the Committee in behalf of the Memorial Home Fund.

Yours sincerely, in F., C. and L.,

MARY G. DEANE,
Chairman Memorial Home Committee.

In answer to this the Corps responded promptly and liberally, and cash contributions from interested parties, with promises of building site, were received. Promises for the future are many, and we know of no reason why this fund should not be continued. The thanks of this Committee are hereby tendered to all who have manifested an interest in so noble an object.

Cash contributions from Corps and interested friends have been received to the amount of $1,167.53, which with pledges received amounts to $1,389.53.

We offer the following recommendations for your consideration, viz. : —

1. That this amount ($1,167.53) be placed in charge of the Department Treasurer, and that it be kept distinct as a Memorial Fund for the individual support of the mothers, widows and orphans of veterans; also army nurses who are homeless, and who, after proper investigation, may be deemed worthy of our care.

2. That contributions to this fund be continued, and that a committee be appointed by this Convention to have charge of soliciting donations and raising funds for the object specified, said committee to have charge of said fund; also, That the present Department Army Nurse Fund be merged into this fund.

We believe that this work should be continued until the women who suffered for our country " in her hour of peril," and the homeless orphans of veterans, receive the practical blessings that it is in our power to bestow. We commend this work in their behalf to all the Corps in the Department of Massachusetts.

Respectfully submitted, in F., C. and L,

      MARY G. DEANE, *Chairman.*
      SARAH E. FULLER,
      E. FLORENCE BARKER,
      M. SUSIE GOODALE,
      S. AGNES PARKER,
      EMMA B. LOWD,
      MARY E. KNOWLES,
      EMILY L. CLARK.
         Committee.

The sum of $317.00 has been expended the past year from this fund, leaving a balance of $1,224.70 on hand Jan. 1, 1895.

Quarterly meetings of the Committee are held at Department Headquarters and much interest is taken in this branch of our work.

When the National Woman's Relief Corps Home was founded, the Department of Massachusetts responded to its appeals with zealous interest, and has forwarded sums for its support amounting to nearly one thousand dollars.

Massachusetts has been represented on the Board of Directors the past five years by Mrs. Emma B. Lowd, Past Department President.

This Home is beautifully located at Madison, Ohio, and many aged widows and army nurses receive its sheltering care.

The managers of the Home are assured that the Order in Massachusetts will continue to assist in caring for the women who were so closely identified with the Civil War, and who are now worthy claimants upon our gratitude.

* * * *

"*We work for those whose valor
    From Treason saved our land.*

*For those, alas, whose numbers
    Grow less each passing year:
For those who fought to save us
    The homes we hold so dear.
We work for those brave martyrs,
    The army of the slain,
Whose nameless graves are scattered
    O'er many a Southern plain.*"

EMILY L. CLARK

Ninth Department President 1893

CHAPTER VIII.

SKETCHES OF THE CORPS IN MASSACHUSETTS — A
RECORD OF THEIR WORK.

WHEN outlining the plan of chapters for the Department History, it was decided by the Committee to devote one chapter to Corps sketches.

A circular was accordingly issued to every Corps in the State, soliciting " information relative to the work of the several Corps since their organization," and requesting that all information regarding this matter be directed to Mrs. Mary G. Deane, Secretary of the Committee.

To obtain all the facts necessary for a sketch of one hundred and sixty-five Corps required an extensive correspondence, and several hundred letters have been written by Mrs. Deane, explaining the design of this chapter.

We have endeavored to obtain complete information from every Corps, but in some cases the facts received are meagre and do not fully represent the work accomplished.

Several thousand pages of letters, manuscripts, etc., have been examined by the Secretary of the History Committee, who has gleaned from them the most important items, and arranged the desired material for publication as follows : —

E. V. SUMNER CORPS No. 1, FITCHBURG.

This Corps was formed Jan. 10, 1878, as an independent organization, and immediately began active work for E. V. Sumner Post No. 19. The Corps was recognized at Department Headquarters of the Grand Army of the Republic, and on the 19th of December, Assistant Adjutant-General Meech counseled with the Corps in regard to extending the work. Forty meetings were held during 1878, and out of a membership of ninety there was an average attendance of fifty members at each meeting.

A joint installation of Post and Corps officers was held Jan. 2, 1879. A few weeks later the Department of Massachusetts was organized in Fitchburg, and March 6 we voted to procure a charter from the Department. Corps 1 was formally instituted May 17, 1879, by Mrs. Sarah E. Fuller, Department President, Post 19 joining in a part of the proceedings.

In April, the Corps sent $10.00 to the Department treasury. Early in May it was voted to provide a collation on Memorial Day for comrades engaged in the services of the day; since that time this has been a regular custom. The Corps also twined wreaths for Memorial Day and has annually continued this custom.

In all the earlier years sewing for needy ones was a feature of every meeting. The Corps has faithfully done its duty as an auxiliary to Post 19, in both work and financial assistance.

Owing to the lack of statistics for the years 1879 to 1881 the amount expended in relief work cannot be exactly stated, but will exceed $2,000 for the past fifteen years. Two rooms at the Soldiers' Home have been furnished, besides a gift of $400, forwarded at the time the Home was started. The amount of work which the Corps has quietly done cannot be realized by one who has not carefully followed it.

Membership, one hundred and twenty-three.

PRESIDENTS.

Susie E. Goodrich	1879
Rosella J. Sibley	1880, 1881
Mary J. Peck	1882, 1883
Anna Davis	1884
Estella V. Glazier	1885, 1886
Emma L. Littlehale	1887
E. Annie Bruce	1888
Carrie S. L. Bagley	1889, 1890
Estella V. Glazier	1891, 1892, 1893
Martha M. Jaquith	1894

CHARLES BECK CORPS No. 2, CAMBRIDGE.

Previous to May 20, 1879, a band of earnest women had served Post 56, G.A.R., as a Relief Association for six years; feeling that they could do more effective work in a larger field, they deemed it advisable to come under the banner of the Woman's Relief Corps, and on this date Mrs. Sarah E. Fuller, Department President, instituted Charles Beck Corps No. 2, and installed its officers.

Ten days after, the Corps began its first Memorial Day work, preparing a collation for the Post, which it has continued to do each year. A donation of $5.00 was sent to the Department to aid in prosecuting its work.

In the fall of 1879, Corps 2 co-operated with Post 56 in arranging a fair and the members had charge of the tables, and in December, 1882, the Corps also assisted the Post in another successful fair. For several years the Corps held sewing circles to prepare for fairs and sales, and enjoyed a social gathering in the evening.

In May, 1882, the Corps presented Charles Beck Post No. 56 with a flag for its new hall, also a piano cover, and later a State flag.

In 1884 we asked the privilege of caring for a room at the Soldiers' Home, Chelsea. Room No. 25 was duly assigned and immediately furnished, and is cared for at the present date.

In July, 1884, the sum of $100.00 was voted to defray the expenses of Mrs. Kathrina L. Beedle to the National Convention at Minneapolis.

In 1887 the Corps sustained an irreparable loss in the death of Mrs. Kathrina L. Beedle, its first President, who passed from this to the higher life November 24. Words cannot express the esteem, respect and confidence which the sister members entertained for her. A conscientious, self-sacrificing spirit of Fraternity, Charity and Loyalty was exemplified in all her work. The burial service of the Order was, by her request, used at her funeral.

In October, 1891, on completion of the new addition to the Soldiers' Home, the Corps voted to take Room 85, as a memorial to Kathrina L. Beedle; and the room was formally dedicated by the Corps Oct. 31, 1891.

Amount expended in Relief since organization	$741 60
Turned over to Post	707 32
Relief other than money	300 00
Expended for articles presented to Post . .	80 50
Total .	. $1,829 42

For many years Corps 2 has decorated the Cambridge Soldiers' Monument on Memorial Day, arranged flowers for the soldiers' graves, and button-hole bouquets for the comrades, and has attended the services in a body.

Mrs. Fannie T. Hazen, who is an active member of this Corps, served as an army nurse in 1864-65, in the Columbian Hospital, Washington, D.C.

As a band of earnest, loyal women the Corps has served Charles Beck Post No. 56 as an auxiliary to the best of its ability.

Membership, ninety-four.

PRESIDENTS.

Sarah A. Torrey	1879, 1880, 1881
Elizabeth Miles	1882, 1883
Kathrina L. Beedle	1884, 1885
H. Annie Allen	1886, 1887
Leocardia F. Flowers	1888, 1889, 1890
Harriet L. Howe	1891
Anna E. Sanborn	1892, 1893
Cappilia M. Ladd	1894

JOHN A. HAWES CORPS No. 3, EAST BOSTON.

John A. Hawes Relief Corps No. 3 was instituted in East Boston, Oct. 12, 1883, by Mrs. E. Florence Barker, Department President, assisted by Mrs. L. A. Turner, Department Conductor, with forty-six charter members. The Corps was organized by the unanimous vote of John A. Hawes Post No. 159, G.A.R., and it has never failed to recognize its "auxiliary" in a most soldierly and courteous manner. On each Memorial Day and also on Memorial Sunday the Corps has been among the special guests of the Post and united with the comrades in all their services.

At the conclusion of the Post exercises in Woodlawn cemetery, Chelsea, special services are held in memory of the unknown dead, at the grave of Helen Gilson, an army nurse who gave her life while faithfully serving the Union Army, the Post acting as escort to the Corps, and otherwise assisting in making the service impressive and instructive to the great number of people who attend.

At the three fairs held by the Post since its organization, Corps 3 has taken entire charge of all tables, and as the result has turned over to the Post $4,100. By special request of the Post, Corps 3 had charge of the cake and ice cream tables at the Carnival in aid of the Soldiers' Home in 1885, and made returns to the Treasurer of $1,408.17, exclusive of $364.27, the amount of popular subscription given by the citizens of East Boston, but collected by the members of Corps 3. Also by invitation of Post 159 we contributed $28.00 for a Memorial window in the Meridian Street M.E. Church, upon which appears the beautiful badge of the Woman's Relief Corps beside that of the Grand Army of the Republic. The Corps has also presented to the Post a flag and guidons, and during the first year of its history inaugurated a series of social entertainments to which the families of the comrades and friends of the Corps were invited, literary and musical entertainment, with a collation, being furnished alternately by Post and Corps.

In 1884 Corps 3 assumed the care of Room 10 at the Soldiers' Home, and each year contributes all necessary bedding and articles of comfort for its occupants, besides giving two large reclining chairs to the hospital, and $58.71 in money.

In its work of relief the Corps has expended $943.00 and given valuable relief other than money; has aided in sending a soldier's daughter to a home in California; contributed to the National W.R.C. Home, and aided Southern Posts in observing Memorial Day. $25.00 were given to the Encampment Fund in 1890, and floral decorations were provided for Headquarters Department Mass. G.A.R. at the "Vendome" during that week. To the Camp of Sons of Veterans in East Boston the Corps contributed $25.00 for a silk flag.

This Corps has been honored by the Department and National Conventions in the election to the highest offices in the Order of one of its members, Mrs. Sarah E. Fuller. Mrs. Addie A. Nottage served as a member of the Department Relief Committee two years. The Corps has always received the support and endorsement of the public. Many of its receptions, notably that given in honor of present and past National officers in August, 1885, have been honored by the presence of leading citizens of East Boston. The clergymen of all the churches have attended its gatherings, and in every way possible co-operated in all its charitable work. Each succeeding year, officers and members have shown a deep spirit of loyalty to all the principles of the Order, and a willingness to bear their part in advancing all its interests.

Membership, one hundred and thirty-two.

PRESIDENTS.

Sarah E. Fuller,	from Oct. 1883 to Oct. 1885	
Addie J. Watson,	" Oct. 1885 to Jan. 1886	
Ada F. Sampson	. . .	1886
Thalia G. Higgins	. . .	1887
Addie A. Nottage	. . .	1888
Hattie B. Shurtleff	. . .	1889
Hattie I. Alexander	. . .	1890
Mary A. McConnell	. . .	1891
Sarah J. Woodside	. .	1892, 1893
Almira M. Maxwell	. . .	1894

EVERETT PEABODY CORPS No. 4, GEORGETOWN.

Twelve years ago, in 1883, through the instrumentality of Past Commander H. N. Harriman of Post 108, G.A.R., and his most estimable wife, thirty-one ladies of Georgetown decided to band themselves together to assist Everett Peabody Post No. 108, G.A.R., as its auxiliary, and on April 2, Corps 4 was instituted and its officers installed by Mrs. E. Florence Barker, Department President, assisted by Mrs. Sarah E. Fuller, Department Secretary.

The first assistance rendered to the Post was on Memorial Day, and every year since all possible aid has been rendered upon this occasion; dinners and suppers have been provided, wreaths and bouquets prepared, and the Soldiers' Monument decorated.

In May, 1883, the Corps presented the Post with a beautiful silk flag.

During the twelve years of its existence Corps 4 has given in charity (food, clothing and money) $922.87; turned over to Post 108, $150.00; also valuable and useful gifts. The Corps has contributed to the Soldiers' Home and also to the fund for the entertainment of the National Convention in Boston in 1890.

Since organization the Corps has had three treasurers (Mrs. Baylie serving seven years) and three secretaries (Mrs. Pickett, the present secretary, is now serving her eighth year).

Membership, sixty-four.

PRESIDENTS.

Susan S. Bickford		1883, 1884
Emma Howe		1885
Sarah A. Harriman		1886
Emily Wadleigh		1887
Sarah Nason		1888
Jane J. Merrill		1889
Sarah J. Hall		1890, 1891, 1892
Letitia A. Noyes		1893
Jane T. Merrill		1894

S. C. LAWRENCE CORPS No. 5, MEDFORD.

S. C. Lawrence Corps No. 5 was organized May, 1879, in the ancient town of Medford, a town so old as to date its history back to the year 1634, at which time we have record of the youth of ten years being drilled "in the exercise of arms, small guns, bows and arrows, in order to be ready at their country's call." In all the years following, down to the present day, the seed sown in the early days has been carefully nurtured, and gallant men and sacrificing women have held themselves in readiness to respond in their country's hour of need. It was not remarkable, then, that women born of such ancestry should early grasp the opportunity of enrolling themselves among the pioneers of the Relief Corps, such an opportunity being arranged by the Commander of Post 66, at that time George L. Goodale, one of the first comrades of the Grand Army of the Republic, who dared declare himself a champion of the little struggling organization known as the Woman's State Relief Corps. Medford Corps has ever been proud of this right to stand with the pioneers in this great work.

The Corps was instituted during the administration of Mrs. Sarah E. Fuller, Department President, by Mrs. Kathrina L. Beedle, Department Secretary, and so faithful and true were its first teachings, it has never swerved from a zealous observance of the principles of the Order, and today has a standing in the community and in the Department of which it has cause to be proud.

Its work in Medford has ever been commendable, expending for charity since its organization the sum of $3,038.41. The gifts to the Post have been valuable and numerous, and the response to every demand quick and generous. On Memorial Day the Corps has always assisted the Post in its tender observances, contributing floral tributes for the Soldiers' Lot, attending to the care of the vases, arranging buttonhole bouquets, and for many years preparing and serving a collation on the return of the comrades from their solemn duties at the cemetery. The Corps has also contributed money for the assistance of Phil Kearney Post of Richmond, Va., in its work on Memorial Day.

In addition to its local work the Corps took active part in the Soldiers' Bazar held in 1881, and in the Soldiers' Home Carnival, occurring in 1885, contributing praiseworthy sums on both occasions. It has had charge of a room at the Soldiers' Home from the moment permission was granted women to do so, and its interest in the welfare of this institution is constant and untiring, a most unique entertainment being given Oct. 27, 1893, of which the veterans cannot say enough. Directly and through the medium of the Bazar and Carnival, Corps 5 has contributed to the Home the sum of $926.33.

During the National Encampment of the G.A.R. held in Boston in 1890, the Corps stood side by side with its Post in entertaining Post 1 of Milwaukee. The Corps also contributed $78.00 to the Encampment fund called for by Department W.R.C.; also furnished floral decorations for General Alger's Headquarters and Department Headquarters on the opening day of the Encampment.

Among the many pleasant memories cherished by the Corps is the reception tendered by its members to Mrs. Barker, Mrs. Fuller and Mrs. Turner, delegates to Denver in 1883. The work of these ladies in securing the adoption of Massachusetts' work for the National organization was very gratifying, and well worthy the cordial welcome accorded them by the two hundred and fifty sister members called together to do them honor by Corps 5.

Several members of Corps 5 have been honored by election to National and Department offices, viz.: Mrs. E. Florence Barker, first National President; Mrs. M. Susie Goodale, Department President in 1884 and 1885; Mrs. Clara C. Lovering, a member of the Council in 1891 and 1892.

Membership, one hundred and forty-seven.

PRESIDENTS.

Cordelia Hutchins	. . .	1879
Ellen M. Gill . . .	. . .	1880
M. Susie Goodale . .	1881, 1882,	1883
Ellen M. Gill . . .	. . .	1884

Laura W. Beck	1885, 1886
Rebecca A. Peirce	1887
Clara C. Lovering	1888, 1889
R. Frankie Richards	1890, 1891
Adelaide S. Herriott	1892, 1893, 1894

P. T. WYMAN CORPS No. 6, HOLLISTON.

On Jan. 5, 1881, Mrs. Sarah E. Fuller, Department President, instituted Corps 17 of Holliston with twenty-two charter members, and was assisted by Mrs. Pamelia F. Sprague, Department Secretary.

The Corps, though small in numbers, has always been ready to assist Post 6, G.A.R., whenever called upon, and to relieve in every way the needs of the veterans and their dependent ones. It has expended in relief since institution $116.00 in cash, besides furnishing food and clothing to a large amount; has also turned over to Post 6, G.A.R., $320.00, and contributed to the Soldiers' Home.

On March 17, 1891, the number 6 having become vacant on the Department Roll, it was given to this Corps to correspond with that of the Post.

The Corps assists the Post in observing Memorial Day; dinner is provided for Post and Camp. This year its members made over a hundred bouquets besides filling four large vases at the Soldiers' Monument with choice flowers. Floral tributes were also placed in the cemetery in memory of the unknown dead.

A committee has been appointed to recommend some form of salute to the flag in our public schools, which we hope will soon be adopted in the schools of Holliston.

Membership, fifty-eight.

PRESIDENTS.

Elizabeth O. Farquhar	1881
Eliza F. Talbot	1882–1891
Lizzie F. Claflin	1892
Eliza F. Talbot	1893
Hattie I. Thomson	1894

FLETCHER WEBSTER CORPS No. 7, BROCKTON.

Was instituted Oct. 29, 1879, by Mrs. Kathrina L. Beedle, Department Secretary. Previous to this date its members had worked nine years as a sewing circle and rendered very efficient aid to Fletcher Webster Post No. 13, G.A.R., having raised and expended over two thousand dollars.

The first call upon the Corps was in aid of the Soldiers' Home, to which it nobly responded by supplying a table at the bazar held in 1885, from which it turned over to the Committee $626.00. A room at the Home has since been furnished and is in charge of the Corps. Since organization the Corps has assisted Post 13 in various ways to raise funds for a Memorial Hall, thereby turning into the treasury several thousand dollars. A piano and a silk flag have been presented to the Post by its auxiliary.

The Corps has always assisted the comrades in Memorial Day work, preparing wreaths and arranging baskets of flowers, serving the collation, and rendering financial aid whenever necessary. Socials and suppers are frequently held and every day the Corps is growing in popularity with the community. The Corps took active part in celebrating the twenty-fifth anniversary of Post 13, G.A.R., July 13, 1892, which was a very enjoyable occasion.

Expended in relief, turned over to Post 13, G.A.R., Soldiers' Home and other charities connected with the Order, $3,985.50; assisted nearly three hundred families, and contributed a large amount of clothing and food to the deserving poor.

Mrs. S. Agnes Parker, the first President, served the Department of Massachusetts W.R.C. as its President for two consecutive years, and at the National Convention held at Pittsburgh, Pa., September, 1894, was elected National Chaplain.

Membership, two hundred and three.

PRESIDENTS.

S. Agnes Parker	1879, 1880, 1881, 1882
Sarah W. Murdock	1883, 1884, 1885
L. Annie Grant	1886, 1887, 1888
M. Adah Pratt	1889
Margaret C. Hanson	1890, 1891
Margaret E. Andrews	1892, 1893
Mary A. Thorne	1894

E. W. PIERCE CORPS No. 8, MIDDLEBORO.

Was instituted Jan. 12, 1885, by Mrs. S. Agnes Parker, Department Junior Vice-President. Prior to this time the ladies had worked together as an Independent Order, but realizing that they could do more efficient work as an organization, decided to come under the banner of the Woman's Relief Corps. There were twenty-seven charter members. The growth of the Corps has been slow but sure.

The members have ever been ready to render all possible aid to the comrades, especially on Memorial Day, when dinners and suppers have been served to Post and Camp, also to families of both organizations.

The Corps has assisted at Fairs for raising funds for a Soldiers' Monument, and has turned over to Post 8, G.A.R., $300.00 toward a Memorial Hall.

The relief work is not as extensive as that of many larger Corps, yet the comrades of the Grand Army of the Republic never ask in vain; $263.76 have been expended in relief since organization. Many barrels of food and clothing for the sick have been sent to the Soldiers' Home, besides a cash donation of $33.00.

The calls from the Department for the several funds have been gladly answered, and the graves of the fallen heroes on southern battle-fields have not been forgotten on Memorial Day.

Membership, one hundred and eleven.

PRESIDENTS.

Susan M. Alden	1885, 1886, 1887
Lucy F. Perkins	1888
Dora F. Dempsey	1889, 1890, 1891
Susan M. Alden	1892
Lizzie E. Sampson	1893, 1894

MAJ. G. L. STEARNS CORPS No. 9, CHARLESTOWN.

Was instituted Oct. 16, 1879, with twenty-four charter members, by Mrs. Sarah E. Fuller, Department President, assisted by Mrs. Kathrina L. Beedle, Department Secretary. At first many discouragements were met with, but as time passed these were overcome and whatever Corps 9 undertook to do met with success. During the fifteen years of its existence the Corps has spent in relief $2,454.62 besides contributing clothing to the poor and needy. Presented to Post 149 an elegant silk flag, a State flag, an altar cloth and bible; furnished the comrades flowers and lunch on Memorial Days, and united with the Post in the exercises given at Mt. Auburn at the grave of Maj. Geo. L. Stearns; in the evening the Corps has always held Memorial services, having as their guests Post 149 and Camp 33, Sons of Veterans.

Corps 9 was one of the first Corps to assist in preparing the furnishings for the Soldiers' Home at Chelsea. Whenever hard work was to be done in the early days of our Order Corps 9 was ever ready with eager hearts and willing hands to carry forward the good work. A room at the Soldiers' Home is cared for and delicacies furnished for the inmates of the hospital. Thanksgiving dinners are always provided for the needy, and the Corps tries in every possible way to live up to the motto of the Order: "Fraternity, Charity and Loyalty."

This Corps started a "soup-kitchen" which was kept open daily from Dec. 26, 1893, to Feb. 28, 1894. Soup, hash and other food was solicited and prepared by the members, and the good work will always be remembered in Charlestown.

The Corps has always answered all calls from the Department, having contributed to the Monroe Monument Fund and other special funds, and to Phil Kearney Post in Virginia to decorate the graves of the fallen heroes.

Membership, seventy-three.

PRESIDENTS.

Esther Greenlaw	1879
Ellen Johnson	1880
Harriet A. Dana	1881
Susie Kimball	1882
Helen F. Johnson	1883, 1884, 1885
Ellen Johnson	1886
Mary E. Bedell	1887, 1888
Maggie M. Jones	1889
Martha M. Jenney	1890, 1891
Emeline Rugg	1892
Kate Dodsworth	1893
Emma F. Hutchins	1894

THEODORE WINTHROP CORPS No. 10, CHELSEA.

In the fall of 1879 an invitation was extended by Post 35 of Chelsea to the ladies interested in the work of the Grand Army of the Republic to attend a lecture by Mrs. Sarah E. Fuller on Relief Corps work, also to take steps to organize an auxiliary to the Grand Army of the Republic, which resulted in twenty-nine women signifying their desire to form such an organization. The officers were elected, an application made for a charter, and on Oct. 23, 1879, the Corps was instituted by Mrs. Fuller, assisted by Mrs. K. L. Beedle, Department Secretary.

The first work was to assist Post 35 in a fair, which was very successful, and Corps 10 has assisted in every fair to the present day. In some of the fairs nearly every table has been presided over by members of the Corps, turning in large amounts of money to their Relief Fund. Corps 10 has also assisted in furnishing G.A.R. Hall, and on Memorial Day prepared a collation, or furnished money for the same, for the Post and visiting comrades, and decorated graves of the unknown dead; also has for years sent money to Phil Kearney Post, Richmond, Va., to decorate graves there.

At the time of the National Encampment in Boston the Corps entertained visiting Posts and Corps, also supplying soap and towels where the comrades camped in the different halls.

It has assisted the Sons of Veterans in fairs and other enterprises and has always kept the Soldiers' Home in mind, and the various entertainments given by the Corps have been always accompanied by substantial aid for the veterans there, either in delicacies to tempt the appetite, or to add to the supplies of the hospital by leaving money or goods. We cannot enumerate *all* that has been done for the Soldiers' Home, and the room which is our special charge; the records of the Home should show what we have done.

There are instances where Corps have been unfortunate, and needing assistance, we have been able to respond to every call. We have contributed to the Department Relief Fund, the Patch Memorial Fund, the Army Nurse Fund, the Monroe Monument Fund, the Ladies' Aid Association, and the Memorial Home Fund for Widows and Orphans.

To be able to do this, the Corps has held several fairs, and many entertainments and dances. We have always tried to keep in view the object for which we are banded together, namely: to bear one another's burdens. We have watched with the sick and dying, buried the dead, and as far as lay in our power assisted the widow and the orphan.

It is not possible to estimate the amount of relief extended for the first two or three years, but we can say that we have expended in money for the Soldiers' Home $199.20. This does not include donations when giving entertainments, etc. For other objects we have expended $140.00; for soldiers and their families we have expended $708.00; making a total of $1,058.20. We have also done much in supplying food and clothing to the needy.

Membership, ninety-three.

PRESIDENTS.

Amanda M. Thayer	1879, 1880, 1881, 1882
Josie W. Connor	1883
Anna M. Boynton	1884
Mary A. B. Fellows	1885, 1886
Angie B. Chase	1887, 1888
Abbie O. Williams	1889
Josie W. Connor	1890
Angie B. Chase	1891
M. Emma Orcutt	1892, 1893
Eliza M. Baker	1894

GEORGE H. WARD CORPS No. 11, WORCESTER.

On May 4, 1883, Mrs. E. Florence Barker, Department President, assisted by Mrs. Sarah E. Fuller, Department Secretary, instituted Corps 11, with a charter membership of forty-five.

The Corps has gained steadily year after year. George H. Ward Post No. 10, G.A.R., has tendered the free use of the Grand Army Hall to Corps 11 since its organization, for which the Corps is deeply grateful.

Three years ago Corps 11 presented Post 10 with five hundred dollars, its *first* contribution, as the funds of the Post had been large heretofore, and the comrades are assured that whenever they wish assistance the Corps is ever ready to render aid, as its Relief Fund is ample at all times.

Much has been done by the Relief Committee for the worthy poor; since organization $2,096.21 have been expended in charity. The Committees, both Executive and Relief, have been very energetic, and to their efforts much of the success of Corps 11 is due.

Membership, two hundred and sixty-three.

PRESIDENTS.

Lucretia A. Rice	1884
Jeannette P. Babbitt	1885
Angle A. Robinson	1886
Mattie A. Denney	1887
J. Victoria Simmons	1888
Lizzie F. Hubbard	1889
Adelia J. Clough	1890
Anna H. Burbank	1891
Emma A. Savels	1892
Sybil H. Lincoln	1893
Gertie V. Bemis	1894

WARD CORPS No. 12, DANVERS.

On April 12, 1883, Mrs. E. Florence Barker, Department President, assisted by Mrs. Sarah E. Fuller, Department Secretary, instituted Corps 12, with fifty-five charter members. In the eleven years of its existence it has expended $638.12 in relief; turned over to Post 90, G.A.R., $300.00, besides furnishing food and clothing to the poor and needy. It also has charge of a room at the Soldiers' Home, Chelsea. On Memorial Day plants are furnished for the graves of the fallen comrades.

The gain in membership has been steadily going forward as the years fly by, and our work has been successful. Many entertainments have been held which netted large sums to the Corps treasury. April 12, 1893, its tenth anniversary was celebrated, at which were present many distinguished guests, both National and Department officers.

Membership, one hundred and twenty-eight.

PRESIDENTS.

Susan B. Sanger	1883
Sarah G. M. Hill	1884, 1885, 1886, 1887
Mary T. Hawkes	1888, 1889
Clara A. Pillsbury	1890, 1891, 1892, 1893
Mary T. Hawkes	1894

D. WILLARD ROBINSON CORPS No. 13, NORWELL.

Was instituted May 6, 1885, by Mrs. M. Susie Goodale, Department President, with twenty-one charter members. Public installation was held in the evening, at which D. Willard Robinson Post No. 112, G.A.R., and other friends, were invited guests. May 6, 1886, the Corps celebrated its first anniversary, a custom it has continued up to the present time, to which Post 112 and the Department President, W.R.C., are invited.

On Memorial Day the Corps accompanies the Post and assists in decorating the graves of the fallen heroes; it also furnishes the dinners on that day. Entertainments, picnics and socials have been held yearly, which have proved to be successful, both socially and financially.

Corps 13 has expended over $180.00 in relief. In May, 1890, it presented a beautiful State flag to Post 112 and has turned over to the Post $280.00. Misfortune having overtaken Post 112 and Corps 13 — losing their hall by fire — these two organizations were obliged for a while to live separately, but in 1891 the new hall was ready for dedication, and on November 13, with much rejoicing, Post and Corps took possession of their new home, the latter having proudly assisted in the furnishing of the same, providing the piano and many smaller articles.

On last Memorial Day the Corps dedicated an urn in the Washington Street Cemetery in memory of the unknown dead.

Membership, forty-two.

PRESIDENTS.

M. Jane Curtis	1885–1892
Lucy A. Thomas	1893, 1894

E. K. WILCOX CORPS No. 14, SPRINGFIELD.

In the early part of 1879, a public camp-fire was held in Springfield by E. K. Wilcox Post No. 16, G.A.R., at which the first action was taken toward the organization of a Relief Corps auxiliary to the Post, and on March 17, 1880, Mrs. Sarah E. Fuller, Department President, assisted by Mrs. Kathrina L. Beedle, Department Secretary, instituted E. K. Wilcox Corps No. 14 with twenty-five charter members. Mrs. Fuller's zeal and patriotism, combined with her devotion to the veterans, gave added inspiration to the work and the Corps started out with a firm determination to be to the Post all that the name auxiliary implies.

Sept. 29, 1885, the Corps prepared a box collation and served it to 1,800 veterans, who had gathered to dedicate a Soldiers' Monument in Hampden Park.

Jan. 1, 1886, the membership had increased to 148, and the Corps had about $750.00 in its treasury, besides having presented to the Post elegant Regulation and State banners, refitted its ante-rooms, furnished a new table for the Commander, also many other articles for use in Grand Army hall. This year (1886) the Corps began to make the floral tribute for Memorial Day and has continued this work each year.

A room at the Soldiers' Home is cared for by the Corps, and since its organization $2,112.76 have been expended in relief, besides making hundreds of visits upon the sick and needy.

The Corps has recently presented Post 16 fifty dollars for its library, and $345 00 as a fund toward a Memorial Hall, also $300.00 for the Relief Fund.

All of the charter members are living, and the membership to date is two hundred and thirty-six.

PRESIDENTS.

Mary B. Sawin	1880
Teresa Parkhurst	1880
Alice Wheelock	1881
Ellen C. Smith	1882, 1883
Mary M. Perry	1883, 1884, 1885
Mary E. Glover	1886, 1887
Adelia R. Burt	1888, 1889
Fannie B. Holbrook	1890
Albina C. Barker	1891, 1892
Lila D. Lovering	1893, 1894

COLONEL PRESCOTT CORPS No. 15, ASHLAND.

The comrades of Colonel Prescott Post No. 18, G.A.R., having circulated an application for a Relief Corps among the residents of Ashland, called a meeting on the evening of April 12, 1880, at which time Mrs. Sarah E. Fuller, Department President, assisted by the Department Secretary, Mrs. Kathrina L. Beedle, instituted Colonel Prescott Corps No. 15, with fifteen charter members, seven of whom are living.

The work of the Corps can never be recorded, for the labors of love can never be accounted for by the Relief Committee or Corps Treasurer. From time to time a testimonial to the unknown dead had been prepared, but on May 30, 1892, the Corps dedicated a handsome bronze urn which stands upon a granite base in which are cut the words "Unknown Dead." This is placed in the Soldiers' Lot in Welwood Cemetery, and annually filled with plants by the Corps. The Corps has disbursed for relief and turned over to Post since organization, $796.87.

Membership, fifty-nine.

PRESIDENTS.

Louisa A. Jones	1880
Maria E. Ball	1881, 1882, 1883, 1884
Addie A. Balcom	1885, 1886, 1887
Mary J. Holbrook	1888, 1889, 1890
Isabella H. Eames	1891, 1892
E. Minnie Greenwood	1893, 1894

U. S. GRANT CORPS No. 16, MELROSE.

Was instituted Jan. 6, 1881, by Mrs. Sarah E. Fuller, Department President.

Amount expended in relief, $607.71, which includes money turned over to Post, donated to Army Nurse Fund, given in aid of the Soldiers' Home and the Department Relief Fund. Estimated value of relief other than money, $70.00. Our work has been chiefly confined to the care of the children of deceased comrades.

Membership, eighty-two.

PRESIDENTS.

Mary E. Drayton	1881
Laura E. Baldwin	1882, 1883
Susan Brown	1884
Laura E. Baldwin	1885
Martha J. Ellis	1886
Susan Brown	1887, 1888
Amanda L. Johnson	1889, 1890
Emma M. Barrett	1891, 1892, 1893
Frances A. Roulstone	1894

GENERAL SEDGWICK CORPS No. 17, ORANGE.

Was organized June 12, 1888, with forty-two charter members, by Mrs. Mary M. Perry, Department Senior Vice-President, under the number 110, which was afterward changed to 17 to correspond with that of the Post to which it is auxiliary. In May, 1891, Corps 17 exemplified the work of the Order. Nov. 7, 1891, G.A.R. Hall was destroyed by fire and both Post and Corps were without a home; but the Odd Fellows kindly offering the use of their hall, it was accepted, and immediately active preparations were made to raise funds for a Memorial Hall, which were so successful that on March 8, 1893, the hall was publicly dedicated, and Post, Corps and Camp have once more a pleasant home valued at $8,000.

From October, 1893, to October, 1894, the Corps raised $530.00 by entertainments, suppers, etc., and during the year contributions were sent to the Soldiers' Home, the Department Relief Fund, Memorial Fund, and for Memorial Day in the South.

In November, 1893, Corps 17 united with Post 17 in a fair, and $500.00 of the money thus received were placed in the Building Fund the Corps refusing to accept any of the proceeds, although tendered one-half the amount by the Post.

On Memorial Day the Corps serves dinner to the Post, Camp and other friends, and prepares floral tributes for about one hundred graves, and for army nurses and the unknown dead.

Corps 17 has expended in relief since organization $269.00 and turned over to Post $1,611.43.

Membership, one hundred and sixty-four.

PRESIDENTS.

Mary A. Rand	. .	1888, 1889
Mary J. Shattuck	. .	1890, 1891
Enez E. Barrett	. .	. 1892
Lizzie Taylor	. .	. 1893
Enez E. Barrett	. .	. 1894

WILLIAM L. BAKER CORPS No. 18, NORTHAMPTON.

On May 13, 1885, Mrs. Mary M. Perry, Department Conductor, instituted Corps 18, with thirty-six charter members. During the nine years of its existence it has expended in relief and turned over to Post about $1,300, which does not include relief of members not relatives of soldiers.

Memorial Day has always been observed by Corps 18 in the preparation of floral tributes for the graves of comrades, in attending divine service and serving refreshments for Post, Sons of Veterans and drum corps at the close of the exercises. It has expended more than one hundred dollars upon the lot in the cemetery set apart as sacred to the "Unknown Dead."

Corps 18 has also furnished a room at the Soldiers' Home, Chelsea, at an expense of $135.00 and still continues its care for the same. It has presented to Post 86 a handsome altar cloth and united with the Camp of Sons of Veterans in presenting the Post with a beautiful silk flag.

The Corps had the pleasure of contributing $100.00 to the Encampment Fund for 1890. It has cared for and watched with the sick and fulfilled its obligation in full. Over all these years the sunshine of peace has hovered, and the mystic chain of Fraternity, Charity and Loyalty has been firmly cemented.

The first President, Mrs. Clark, has held the offices of Chaplain, Junior Vice-President, Senior Vice-President and President of the Department of Massachusetts. She is the present Department Counselor and is serving Corps 18 as Secretary.

Membership, one hundred and nineteen.

PRESIDENTS.

Emily L. Clark	1885, 1886, 1887
Marion E. Bridgman	1888, 1889, 1890
Mary H. Crittenden	1891, 1892, 1893
Harriet E. Kingsley	1894

E. P. WALLACE CORPS No. 19, AMESBURY.

Was instituted Jan. 27, 1882, by Mrs. Sarah E. Fuller, Department President, assisted by Mrs. Pamelia F. Sprague, Department Secretary, with twenty-four charter members. This Corps has done a large amount of local relief work, and has assisted some families that would not accept aid from the Post.

It has assisted the Post in building a hall at G.A.R. Park. The Essex County parade was held at this park and Corps 19 assisted in entertaining two thousand comrades. The Post has a Soldiers' Lot in

Mount Prospect cemetery and Corps 19 has expended quite a sum to improve it; has placed an urn in the centre which we take care of and fill with plants every year. On this lot we deposit our offering for the unknown dead. We always assist on Memorial Day at the different cemeteries and provide a collation when the comrades desire it.

In September, 1884, Corps 19 furnished a room at the Soldiers' Home and has cared for it ever since, besides contributing money at various times. We purchased a silk State flag and presented it to the Post on its twenty-first anniversary, and this year a gift of two silk markers.

Corps 19 has assisted the comrades of Amesbury at five fairs, at one of which $1,100.00 were realized, and one-half of this amount given by the Post to the Corps. Over one thousand dollars have been expended in relief and turned over to Post.

Membership, one hundred and thirty-eight.

PRESIDENTS.

Mary L. Tucker	1882, 1883
Mary F. Dennett	1884
Agnes E. Gale	1885
Lizzie A. Snell	1886, 1887
Georgia A. Collins	1888, 1889, 1890
Mary A. True	1891
Georgia A. Collins	1892
Alma A. Austin	1893, 1894

DAHLGREN CORPS, No. 20, SOUTH BOSTON.

This Corps, auxiliary to Dahlgren Post No. 2, G.A.R., was instituted April 10, 1882, by Mrs. E. Florence Barker, Department President, assisted by Mrs. Sarah E. Fuller, Department Secretary, with eighty-one charter members. During the past twelve years it has expended in relief $4,004.78 and extended relief other than money to the value of over $2,000. During this time, over eleven hundred persons have had their pathway brightened by the willing hearts and hands of the members of Corps 20. The Corps has always been ready to help in every good work that presented itself, and having a great many calls upon it for charity work has always responded nobly, being for a number of consecutive years the "Banner Corps" in the State for that work, and one year " National Banner Corps." It has also assisted Post 2 during four fairs, turning over to the Post since organization a total of $2,161.98.

Corps 20 has presented Post 2 with a State flag and a set of guidons, and presented to Dahlgren Camp Sons of Veterans a set of guidons.

The services on Memorial Day to the unknown dead have been observed by Corps 20 six times at the cemetery and twice in a church, with one or two exceptions the Post taking part with them.

Room No. 18 at the Soldiers' Home, Chelsea, is furnished and cared for by Corps 20. At the fair of the Ladies' Aid Association in 1892 for the benefit of the Soldiers' Home, the table in charge of the ladies from Corps 20 turned over to the Fair Committee $114.00. On the evening of Dec. 20, 1893, the Corps presented Dahlgren Post No. 2 with a handsome State flag, upon the staff of which was a gold plate, bearing the following inscription :

"PRESENTED BY W.R.C. No. 20,
DECEMBER 20, 1893."

On Feb. 6, 1894, Corps 20 gave a reception in honor of the National President, Sarah C. Mink, and the National Secretary, Sarah E. Phillips, to which invitations were extended to all Department officers, and all Corps Presidents and Secretaries in the State, also to the Department Officers of the G.A.R. and the comrades of Post 2. This event proved to be one of the "red-letter" days in the history of the Corps.

In May, 1894, the Corps turned over to Post 2 the sum of $588.00, as proceeds from Fair Committee, making total amount turned over to Post, since organization, $2,161.98. During the year of 1894, Corps 20 expended in relief $410.00, making total amount expended in relief since organization, $4,004.78.

On Memorial Day, 1894, an urn was erected to the memory of the unknown dead, in the Emerson St. Cemetery, South Boston.

This Corps was the first one in the Department to introduce a "Salute to the Flag" at each regular meeting, the same being given under the "Good of the Order."

All calls for help through National or Department Orders are answered by the Corps, and each year contributions are sent toward decorating the graves in the South.

Mrs. Eleanor B. Wheeler, Past National Secretary, is also a Past President of Corps 20.

Membership, one hundred and forty-one.

PRESIDENTS.

Matilda E. Lawton	1882, 1883, 1884
Eleanor B. Wheeler	1885, 1886
Mary H. Vaughn	1887
Maria A. Brown	1888
Hattie M. Tuttle	1889
Priscilla M. King	1890
Belle C. Stone	1891
Tryphena C. Berry	1892
Lue Stuart Wadsworth	1893, 1894

WILLARD C. KINSLEY CORPS No. 21, SOMERVILLE.

Was instituted May 11, 1882, with thirty-six charter members, by Mrs. E. Florence Barker, Department President, assisted by Mrs. Sarah E. Fuller, Department Secretary. In reality the Corps was an "offspring" of the old independent Corps which had been working in Somerville for over four years and was recognized as doing most excellent work, having expended about $500.00 in relief. Two of the charter members, Mrs. Hattie A. Ralph and Miss Mary E. Elliot, have held Department offices for several years. Mrs. Rose A. Knapp and Mrs. Harriet A. Chamberlain have been prominent in Department work.

In conjunction with Post 139, Corps 21 has worked in two large fairs, one of which netted nearly $2,000.00. Contributions have been made to the various relief funds of the Department, and although not furnishing a room at the Soldiers' Home, the many visits made by the members, and contributions left, show the interest and devotion to the veterans in the Home. The Corps has always co-operated with the comrades in Memorial Day work and has presented several gifts to Post 139, among them a handsome silk flag and guidons, a Bible and clock.

In May, 1892, the Corps exemplified the work of the Order with the Department President, Mrs. Mary G. Deane, and staff present; and the day was truly an interesting one for all present. In the evening the tenth anniversary of the Corps was observed, the Mayor and City Government, the Post and Department Officers W.R.C. being among the guests. Post 139, G.A.R., presented on this occasion a beautiful banner valued at $75.00, to its auxiliary Corps. Social gatherings of Post and Corps are frequently held. The regular meetings are largely attended and great interest is taken in all the work.

In December, 1894, a large and enthusiastic public meeting was held in the Unitarian Church on Highland Avenue and addressed by Mayor Hodgkins, several clergymen and others, in behalf of the flag salute in the public schools.

Miss Mary A. Gardner Holland, an army nurse, is a member of this Corps.

Nearly a thousand dollars have been expended for relief work and donations to Post.

Membership, one hundred and forty-two.

PRESIDENTS.

Mary E. Elliot	1882, 1883
Hattie A. Ralph	1884
Abbie J. Bean	1885
Ann C. Souther	1886
Rose A. Knapp	1887
Eveline P. Robinson	1888
Helen F. Johnson	1889, 1890
Harriet A. Chamberlain	1891, 1892
Helen M. McCully	1893
Fannie M. Jones	1894

LYON CORPS No. 22, WESTFIELD.

Was instituted Dec. 15, 1882, with a charter membership of forty, by Mrs. E. Florence Barker, Department President, assisted by Mrs. Sarah E. Fuller, Department Secretary. The first work of the Corps was to assist Lyon Post No. 41 in holding a six days' fair, which was a financial success; with their share of the proceeds they established a Relief Fund. From time to time entertainments of various kinds have been given for this purpose and the citizens at large have generously contributed whenever solicited.

In 1884 it was decided to take charge of a room at the Soldiers' Home, and Room 22 was comfortably furnished by personal contributions. Since organization several boxes have been sent to the Home, valued at nearly three hundred dollars. The Corps has presented Post 41 $55.00 in cash, besides assisting in furnishing its hall.

Through the efforts of the members an urn was placed in the Soldiers' Lot at the cemetery in Westfield, and each succeeding Memorial Day finds the two organizations, Post and Corps, working together to cover with garlands the graves of our fallen heroes.

With a present membership of seventy-two this Corps is doing all in its power to advance the interest of the Woman's Relief Corps and the principles to which it stands pledged.

PRESIDENTS.

Annie M. Watson	1882, 1883
Sarah C. Walkley	1884, 1885
Marion L. Burge .	1886, 1887
Kate P. Rich	1888, 1889
Lucy A. Tyler .	. 1890
May A. Graves .	. 1891
Jennie L. Kelsey .	1892, 1893
Carrie S. Smith .	. 1894

JOHN GOODWIN CORPS No. 23, MARBLEHEAD.

Early in March, 1885, steps were taken by John Goodwin Post No. 82, G A.R., toward the formation of an auxiliary, and after a number of preliminary meetings of Post and lady friends, on March 28, 1885, Mrs. Emma B. Lowd, Department I. and I. Officer, assisted by the officers of Corps 34 of Salem, instituted John Goodwin Corps No. 23 with a charter membership of forty-eight. The first work of the Corps was to assist Post 82 in holding a fair in January, 1886, which netted the sum of $489.59. The first anniversary was celebrated April 6, 1886.

Dec. 25, 1888, the Corps lost its home with all its furnishings by fire, saving only its Journal. Sympathetic letters were received from the Department President, Mrs. Emma B. Lowd, also from the Department Secretary, Miss Mary E. Elliot, stating that all supplies would be replaced by the Department free of cost; from Corps 30, Beverly, with a donation of $10.00; followed by donations from Corps 10, Chelsea, $15.00; Corps 34, Salem, $10.00; Corps 12, Danvers, $10.00; Corps 68, Dorchester, $10.00; Corps 50, Peabody, $25.00; total, $80.00. Though faint of heart and with serious thoughts of surrendering the charter, these tokens of sympathy, coming as they did with words of love and cheer, gave them fresh courage to start anew; and after due consideration Odd Fellows Hall was hired and the Corps started anew in its work of Charity.

March 15, 1889, Corps 29 of Lynn paid the Corps a fraternal visit and presented Corps 23 with a handsome Bible.

April 6, 1889, the Corps celebrated its fourth anniversary by inviting Post 82, G.A.R., to a social, at which time the Post was presented with an altar flag and staff, also a block and gavel and $9.58 in cash.

The Corps has spent in relief $289.65, besides donating clothing, flowers and fruit for the sick. It has always responded to all calls from Post 82 for assistance in sales, entertainments, arrangements for Memorial Day, or any service whenever required.

Membership, seventy-nine.

PRESIDENTS.

Mary C. Bowler	1885
Florence Gilley	1886
Mary J. Atkins	1887
Eliza W. Beedee	1888
Mary J. Atkins	1889, 1890, 1891, 1892
Abbie T. Trasher	1893, 1894

C. R. MUDGE CORPS No. 24, MERRIMAC.

Jan. 26, 1883, Mrs. Sarah E. Fuller, Department Secretary, instituted C. R. Mudge Corps No. 24 with fifty-two charter members. Notwithstanding the fact that the population of the town of Merrimac is less than three thousand, perhaps no Corps in the Commonwealth is so fortunate in its location as Corps 24.

At Department Convention in 1884 the Corps was ranked excellent, and it has continued to hold this rank up to the present time. It has expended in relief, $241.97; presented to individual Post members, $85.00, and turned over to Post $400.00. In October, 1884, the care of a room at the Soldiers' Home was assumed, and $143.87 has been expended for that purpose.

This Corps, in comparison with those situated in the midst of want and destitution, has not many cases under its supervision, but it does not allow any deserving case to pass by uncared for. It has always sustained the most friendly and cordial relation with the Corps that surround it,

with the Department to which it belongs, with the Post whose name it bears (and whose wives and daughters many of them are) and with the community in which it lives.
Membership, eighty-three.

PRESIDENTS.

Nellie H. Cushing	1883
Nellie Roberts	1884, 1885
Clara M. Howe	1886, 1887
Esther M. Guild	1888
Ida P. Hamilton	1889
Harriet O. Grant	1890
Lizzie Smart	1891
Elvira D. Churchill	1892
Cinderella E. Clement	1893, 1894

F. P. H. ROGERS CORPS No. 25, WALTHAM.

A number of meetings were held in Waltham at which were present by invitation F. P. H. Rogers Post No. 29, Mrs. E. Florence Barker, Department President W.R.C., and members of her staff, which finally resulted in the institution of Corps 25, Jan. 19, 1883, by Mrs. Barker and Mrs. Sarah E. Fuller, Department Secretary, with a charter membership of fifty-five. The good work of the Corps has steadily increased and prosperity has crowned its efforts, for the steady gain in membership and relief extended shows that harmony prevails both in its own ranks and those of the Post to which it is auxiliary. Since organization it has expended in charity and turned over to Post 29, G.A.R., $1,669.57. An Easter offering of $25.00 is sent to the Soldiers' Home each year, and the Corps has had charge of Room 13 since 1884.
Membership, one hundred and eighty-seven.

PRESIDENTS.

Nancy M. Daniels	1883, 1884
Mary E. Chipman	1885, 1886
Louisa M. Howe	1887, 1888
Minnie M. Sawin	1889, 1890, 1891
Annie M. Warne	1892, 1893
Lizzie M. Richards	1894

A. W. BARTLETT CORPS No. 26, NEWBURYPORT.

Auxiliary to A. W. Bartlett Post No. 49, G.A.R., was organized Feb. 14, 1883, with sixty-three charter members, by Mrs. E. Florence Barker, Department President, assisted by Mrs. Sarah E. Fuller, Department Secretary. The work of the Corps has been very successful. It has turned over to Post during the past ten years, $2,139.52; expended in relief, $210.15; donated to the Soldiers' Home, $159.59, and distributed in relief other than money, articles valued at $70.30. Public installations have been held with the Post, sisterly visits have been exchanged with neighboring Corps in Massachusetts, also with those of Seabrook and Exeter, New Hampshire. A reception was tendered Gen. A. W. Greeley on his return from the Arctic regions by Post 49 and Corps 26, Aug. 17, 1886.

Membership, one hundred and twenty-two.

PRESIDENTS.

Julia A. Talbot	1883, 1884
Abbie A. Wilson	1885–1887
Lydia M. Weston	1888
Abbie A. Wilson	1889, 1890
Abbie T. Usher	1891, 1892
Hannah C. Perkins	1893, 1894

WM. H. SMART CORPS No. 27, CAMBRIDGEPORT.

On Feb. 16, 1883, Mrs. Sarah E. Fuller, Department Secretary, instituted Corps 27 with twelve charter members. Previous to this time it had been an Independent Aid Society to Post 30, G.A.R., whose auxiliary it now became. With willing hearts and hands the members have worked for the Post whose name they bear; co-operating with the comrades in fairs and other occasions, assisting on Memorial Day and Children's Day (Fast Day), when the Post gives the children a grand time.

In relief work the Corps has labored in the interests of the Post, and transferred to it at various times, $1,157.37. The installations have occasionally been joint, and many invitations of a social character, as also presentations of flags and other kindly meant gifts, have passed between Post and Corps. During the Twenty-fourth National Encampment in Boston the Corps was associated with Post 30 in entertaining Post 30, Relief Corps 27, and Camp 14 Sons of Veterans, from Department of Pennsylvania, sufferers from the great Johnstown flood. An expression of their grateful thanks hangs in the Post hall, an object lesson of the Fraternity, Charity and Loyalty of Post 30. The Corps also donated $34.34 to the "Encampment Fund" for National Convention.

In the Soldiers' Home at Chelsea Corps 27 has always taken the greatest interest, furnishing Room No. 24, giving occasional entertainments, visiting the old veterans, carrying dainties to the sick, and even helping to establish the present hennery. The Corps also assisted the Post at the Carnival for the benefit of the Home, and contributed articles for the last fair valued at $36.50, besides expending in cash $319.31 for the Home since organization.

Of the great-hearted women who have had charge of the relief work too much cannot be spoken. No task has been too hard, no trouble too great, no weather too bad to keep them from carrying comfort and help to the dark homes of God's poor. In recognition of their work, Post 30 presented the Corps with $200.00 to aid in carrying it on. Contributions of garments, provisions and fuel amounting to $464.10 have been given to the needy; more than three thousand visits have been made, and in relieving the necessities of the veterans and their dependents, cash amounting to $1,975.80 has been expended. Neither have army nurses been forgotten: for the cash expenditure for them amounts to $227.42.

Mrs. Sarah M. Butterfield, an army nurse, is a member of this Corps.

In 1885, Corps 30 placed in the Soldiers' Lot in Cambridge cemetery a memorial vase to the memory of the unknown dead and keep it filled with blooming plants. They have expended in Memorial Day work $87.05, and sent cash contributions to the South to aid in this blessed work amounting to $25.25. At the last Corps meeting previous to Memorial Day, the entire Good of the Order is devoted to the memory of those whose narrow homes are scattered about our land, or above whose heads the great waters roll with a never-ceasing moan. The hands of little children build a pyramid of flowers to the unknown but never-to-be forgotten dead. The Post and Corps who attend in a body are always greatly interested in this part of the service, and many comrades' hearts are stirred to paint with glowing words those long-past scenes of "battle-cloud and fire." Once again we tenderly name those of our own band who have gone from among us; remembering with special reverence our first dear President, whose name heads the list of charter members. The remembrance of this service is a fragrance in our hearts through all the year. "They serve God well who serve His creatures."

Membership, one hundred and thirty-eight.

PRESIDENTS.

Maria A. Lull	1883, 1884
Angela H. Scranton	1885
Nannie Martin	1886
Mary E. Hunter	1887
Annie M. Walker	1888
Mary A. Shattuck	1889
Sarah E. Livingstone	1890
Addie P. Kinnear	1891
Etta B. Butler	1892
Ellen A. Jarvis	1893
Nettie S. Wheeler	1894

CHARLES RUSSELL LOWELL CORPS No. 28, BOSTON.

Was organized March 9, 1883, with twenty-five charter members, by Mrs. E. Florence Barker, Department President, assisted by Mrs. Sarah E. Fuller, Department Secretary. Nine of these members are still on the roll, including the first President, Mrs. Susie A. Perkins.

Corps 28 has expended for relief since its organization, $2,136.56, and $317.32 for relief other than money.

In June, 1887, the Corps presented Charles Russell Lowell Post No. 7, G.A.R., a naval and State flag, valued at one hundred dollars.

In March, 1891, a fair was held under the direction of the President, Mrs. Emilie L. W. Waterman, which netted $830.44; this was turned over to Post 7, and in July the same year a National flag valued at $75.00 was presented. The total amount turned over to Post 7 is $1,269.50.

This Corps, located in the city proper, has ever been the right hand of Department W.R.C. Headquarters, whenever called upon cheerfully and promptly extending aid to any veteran or his dependent ones who proved worthy on investigation. In April, 1884, the Corps voted to take charge of a room at Soldiers' Home, Chelsea. Post 7 endorsed this action, but through some misunderstanding the vote was rescinded and no further action was taken until June 12, 1886, when Room 36 was taken and has since that time been in charge of an efficient committee. During the past year a crayon portrait of Past President Emilie L. W. Waterman and a beautiful silk banner in honor of President Carrie Le

Favor have been placed in the room in appreciation of their devotion to the work for the soldier.

We have always been ready to respond to all calls in the name of Fraternity and good of the Order. One hundred dollars ($100.00) were subscribed in 1890 to National Encampment Fund. In addition to this, independent Headquarters were established in rooms E and I, Union Building, on Boylston street (where during the week over three hundred registered and were entertained), at a cost of $52.00. Flags and flowers for decorating tables, and waiters for one day of lunch furnished delegates, were volunteered from Corps 28. Many members of the Corps served on Information and Accommodation Committee for that time. Twice we have responded to calls from Department President and Inspector and exemplified the work of our Order to a large gathering. In 1891 more than 400 were present and in 1893 about 300. Honors have come to the Corps by election and appointment as follows: Emilie L. W. Waterman, Department Aide 1889, 1890 and 1891; Chairman Department Relief Committee, 1890, 1891 and 1892; Chairman Executive Board, 1892 and 1894; Department Inspector, 1893; Carrie Le Favor, Department Aide, 1892 and 1894. Corps 28 has had a delegate to National Convention every year since 1887.

Membership, one hundred and twenty-three.

PRESIDENTS.

Susie A. Perkins	1883, 1884
Olive Long	1885
Lillie Davis	1886
Louisa A. Morrison	1887
Ellen A. Gowell	1888, 1889
Emilie L. W. Waterman	1890, 1891
Ama J. Ellis	1892
Carrie Le Favor	1893, 1894

GENERAL LANDER CORPS No. 29, LYNN.

Has been organized nearly twelve years. Previous to this a patriotic organization known as the Ladies' Aid Society had been in existence, doing a most excellent work, and when, after due deliberation and consultation with prominent G.A.R. comrades, it was deemed advisable to come under the jurisdiction of the Department of Massachusetts W.R.C.

and become auxiliary to General Lander Post No. 5, G.A.R., an opportunity was given to the members of the Ladies' Aid Society at the last meeting before disbandment to sign an application for a charter in the Woman's Relief Corps into which the Ladies' Aid was merged, and on Feb. 20, 1883, General Lander Corps No. 29, with ninety-one charter members, was instituted by Department President Mrs. E. Florence Barker and her associate officers. In the evening a public installation of officers was held and their faithful services did much toward building a solid foundation for future work.

It is with a feeling akin to pride, though not of self-boasting, that Corps 29 has with but two exceptions maintained her position as the banner Corps of the Department of Massachusetts in regard to membership. The band of earnest women who at the beginning had taken the solemn obligation " to assist the Union veteran and his dependent ones," had not been lacking in zeal, and, with a sincere desire to assist in this noble work, all through the intervening years new members have been joining our ranks, the largest number being in 1890 when forty-nine were obligated.

In 1888 General Lander Post No. 5 G.A.R. tendered to Corps 29 the use of its beautiful hall free of expense in which to hold the regular meetings. On the evening of June 12, 1888, the first meeting in this hall was held, at which it was voted to send a set of resolutions expressing thanks to Post 5 in appreciation of the commodious quarters tendered.

The relief work has increased with the growth of the Corps and it has been benefited in ministering unto the needy, realizing " that it is more blessed to give than to receive." There has been expended for relief $3,994.79; relief other than money, $443.46; turned over to Post $494.75; making a total of $4,933.

In the Carnival which was held in Boston in 1885 in aid of the Soldiers' Home, the receipts accrued by Corps 29 were $644.53. The Corps has always maintained a room at the Home, and since the room has been taken for hospital purposes, and the demands for aid are less frequent, the monthly visiting committees usually carry delicacies for the sick. Corps 29 has also taken an active part in several G.A.R. Fairs, of which no definite report has been given, as the receipts were immediately taken in charge by the G.A.R. Committee. A union jack was presented the Post Aug. 16, 1884, Mrs. Hattie A. Bray making the presentation speech as Corps President.

Our thoughts often turn to the memories of the faces we miss, for during the ten years which have passed so swiftly by, twenty-one of our members have finished the lessons of life and answered to the last roll-call of the Great Teacher. Yet while we mourn their loss, the recollection of their deeds of loving kindness and their faithfulness to the work which is so dear unto our hearts, comes to us like a heavenly benediction.

It is with the tenderest feelings we speak of Memorial Day "when the nation pauses in its work and in its pleasure, and reverently gives place to veterans." The Corps has always considered it one of its highest privileges to assist in the sacred duties of Memorial Day, and whether we contribute our offerings to the brave boys who sleep in our own Northern cemeteries, or those unknown patriots who lie on Southern soil, yet we feel that

"Angels have heard their story
And God knows all their names."

We have traced with interest the experiences of the past, and we turn with eager faces to the future which seems to hold out to us so many bright hopes for usefulness. The principles of the Woman's Relief Corps, if sincerely adhered to, cannot fail to uplift and bless the life of any woman who espouses its cause, and make her of benefit to the community in which she lives. Our ranks are increasing as those of the veterans grow thinner, and our aim is to avail ourselves of every opportunity to be of service to the brave boys in blue who have made it possible for us to live a prosperous, peaceful nation under one flag.

Membership, three hundred and thirty-eight.

PRESIDENTS.

Mary A. Bailey	1883, 1884, 1885
Eliza F. Stiles	1886, 1887
Amelia J. Parker	1888
Clara H. Smith	1889
Lizzie F. Mudgett	1890
Emma P. Ward	1891
S. Jennie Tirrell	1892, 1893
Hattie A. Bray	1894

JOHN H. CHIPMAN CORPS No. 30, BEVERLY.

Was instituted with a charter membership of ninety, May 28, 1883, by Mrs. M. Susie Goodale, Department President, assisted by Mrs. Matilda E. Lawton, Department Treasurer. During the nearly twelve years that have passed the Corps has spent $2,524.22 for relief. In every way possible the Corps assists the Post, whether it is to raise money for its various needs or in strewing the graves of the fallen heroes with garlands on Memorial Day. All calls from the Department are quickly answered and no case of destitution left unattended.

Membership, one hundred and sixty.

PRESIDENTS.

Kate R. Hood	.	1884, 1885
Frances L. Murray	.	1886
Alice Creasey	.	1887
Rebecca G. Herrick	.	1888
Lizzie J. Dennett	.	1889
Lizzie Wallis	.	1890
Nancy M. Andrews	.	1891
Rebecca A. Pickett	.	1892
Caroline C. Merrill	.	1893, 1894

CHARLES H. STEVENS CORPS No. 31, LEOMINSTER.

Was instituted Dec. 29, 1885, by Mrs. M. Susie Goodale, Department President, assisted by officers of Corps 1 of Fitchburg. There were forty-one names on the charter roll and most of them were formerly members of an independent Corps which had disbanded. The new Corps received $195.00, which sum was in the treasury of the independent Corps at time of its dissolution. Charles H. Stevens Post of Leominster presented Corps 31 a check for $250.00 soon after it was instituted, which was placed in the Relief Fund. During the first year but little relief work was done, but this work has increased from year to year.

Since institution the Corps has received from fairs, entertainments, suppers, etc., $1,769.00, and has expended for local relief nearly $1,000.00, besides giving a large amount in clothing and food. Donations have been made to the Post, the various funds of the Department, the Soldiers' Home, etc., amounting to $1,273.43, and $125.00 were given to the National Convention Fund of 1890.

The calls made upon the sick have averaged over two hundred a year for the last six years. Our meetings are well attended, we have been prosperous in our work, and rank as one of the best organizations in Leominster. Corps 31 is striving to carry out the great principles of our Order.

Membership, one hundred and fifty-four.

PRESIDENTS.

Mary A. Flagg	. . .	1886, 1887
Sarah F. Gallup	. .	1888, 1889, 1890
Sarah E. Hicks	. . .	1891, 1892
Abbie M. Pratt	. . .	1893, 1894

C. D. SANFORD CORPS No. 32, NORTH ADAMS.

Auxiliary to C. D. Sanford Post No. 79, G.A.R., was instituted Sept. 18, 1883, by Mrs. Sarah E. Fuller, Department Secretary, with twenty-two charter members. This little band of devoted women bravely started on their loving work of caring for the veterans. The Corps has expended for relief $597.69; turned over to Post 79, G.A.R., $210.00, besides purchasing a piano valued at $500.00. It has also furnished a room at the North Adams Hospital at an expense of $175.00, where the veterans can be attended free of cost; also purchased furnishings for a room at the Soldiers' Home, Chelsea, at a cost of $72.00.

Every call for help from the worthy poor has been answered; the aim of the Corps has been to follow closely the motto of the Order, Fraternity, Charity and Loyalty. The work of the Order was exemplified during the administration of Mrs. Emma B. Lowd, Department President. Every Memorial Day the Corps erects a floral monument to the unknown dead. Letters of appreciation from the Commanders of Post 79 bear testimony of the gratitude of the comrades for the labors of love of the Corps members. The Corps raised by entertainments $900.00, to assist in sending Post 79 to Washington in 1892.

Membership eighty-five.

PRESIDENTS.

Minerva Illingworth	. .	1883, 1884, 1885
Harriet Eaton	. . . .	1886
Josephine A. Burdick	. .	1887–1892
Martha Cheesboro	. . . .	1893
Josephine A. Burdick	. . .	1894

JAMES A. GARFIELD CORPS No. 33, LOWELL.

Was instituted Nov. 21, 1883, by Mrs. E. Florence Barker, Department President, and Mrs. Sarah E. Fuller, Department Secretary, with thirty-six charter members. During Mrs. Tuttle's administration of nearly three years as President, sixty-two members were added.

In March, 1885, a room with three beds was furnished at the Soldiers' Home and boxes of supplies and other donations have since been sent to the Home, the value of which was over $300.00. In addition to this it has expended over $2,000.00 in relief.

Corps 33 has contributed to the Department Relief Fund and to other funds, and has pledged $50.00 to the proposed monument in honor of the unknown dead.

The Corps has at various times presented the Post over $200 00 and a very handsome silk flag. On Memorial Days the Corps decorates the Soldiers' Lot in the Lowell cemetery and the Soldiers' Monument and assists the Post in observing the day.

Membership, eighty-one.

PRESIDENTS.

Annie E. Tuttle	1883, 1884, 1885
Eliza J. Hall	1886
Dora Searle	1887
Sarah W. Merchant	1888, 1889
Viola A. Fifield	1890
Helen Hastings	1891
Hallie E. Perry	1892
Mary E. Offutt	1893, 1894

PHIL. H. SHERIDAN CORPS No. 34, SALEM.

To Phil. H. Sheridan Corps belongs the honor of being the first Corps instituted in Massachusetts (and probably in the Order) after the organization of the National Woman's Relief Corps. The Corps was instituted Sept. 7, 1883, with forty-one charter members, by Mrs. E. Florence Barker, National President, assisted by Mrs. Sarah E. Fuller, National Secretary.

At the time of institution it was numbered 31; but about a year later was numbered 34, corresponding with that of the Post to which it is auxiliary. On the institution of the Corps the use of the Post hall, rent free, was tendered by the Post; but after the first three months the Corps commenced paying, voluntarily, all expense incurred by use of the hall, and has continued doing so, believing that it was formed to aid the Post, not to expect aid from it, save by its loyal recognition of the services rendered by the Corps. On all occasions when it has been possible for Post and Corps to unite, they have been associated, and anniversaries, reunions, fairs and installations have been shared in common.

Memorial Day, that holy day set apart by the Grand Army of the Republic for the commemoration of all that was heroic in the lives of their silent comrades, has been devoted wholly to the service of the Post and anticipated by it in all arrangements made for that day. Thus, in every way, Post and Corps have devotedly worked together.

Year by year the Corps and Camp of the Sons of Veterans have drawn nearer together, as mothers love to lean upon their manly sons, and their endeavor is by united effort to more effectually serve the Post.

It is impossible to give in detail all that has been accomplished by the Corps. The statistics of the early work of relief and amounts expended in other ways are necessarily incomplete, owing to the methods then in use of reporting such expenditures.

Amount turned over to Post	. . .	$2,054 66
" expended in Relief .	. . .	1,712 97
" presented to Soldiers' Home .	.	500 00
" " " National W.R.C.Home,		37 50
Total .		$4,305 13

Amount expended in relief other than money not estimated.

The Corps has been selected to exemplify the work of the Order three times for the benefit of the Corps in its immediate vicinity. All of its Presidents have been honored by appointments on the staffs of National or Department Presidents, and one has risen to the rank of Department President of Massachusetts, and at the present time is serving a second term as a member of the Board of Directors of the National W.R.C. Home.

Eleven years have rolled on since the institution of the Corps, eleven busy years, making day by day the history of a Corps and the record of a band of loyal women, who have but simply endeavored to exemplify in word and deed the principles of the Order to which they belong. Whatever of success may have attained their efforts has been but in the line of duty towards the Union soldier and his dependent ones.

Membership, one hundred and fifty-two.

PRESIDENTS.

Emma B. Lowd	1883, 1884, 1885
Helen A. White	1886
Mary A. G. Robinson	1887, 1888
Abby L. Robson	1889
Mary A. Yasinski	1890, 1891
Jessie R. Webber	1892, 1893
Lizzie M. Peirce	1894

TIMOTHY INGRAHAM CORPS No. 35, HYDE PARK.

On the afternoon of Feb. 18, 1884, a number of ladies interested in the formation of a Relief Corps in Hyde Park met, and under the direction of Mrs. M. Susie Goodale, Department President, and Mrs. Sarah E. Fuller, Department Secretary, elected officers and received instructions. That evening, in the presence of the Post and friends, the officers were installed by Mrs. Goodale and the new Corps, with forty-six charter members, started out on its work for the veterans. Nearly eleven years have passed away and Timothy Ingraham Relief Corps bears an honorable name in the community. Its growth for the first five years was slow, the average number for many a quarter being sixty-five; but as the object of the organization became better known, ladies became interested and at the present time the membership is one hundred and twenty-five.

During the years since its organization Corps 35 has expended for relief. $1,154.68. A room at the Soldiers' Home has been fitted up and supported at an expense of $168.41. It contributed $150.00 toward the Encampment Fund of 1890. At the Soldiers' Home Carnival in 1885 this Corps assisted the Post with a table. In 1892 a creditable contribution was made to the Military Fair in aid of the Soldiers' Home. During the first year of its existence Corps 35 presented a silk flag to Timothy Ingraham Post No. 121; a few years later a silk altar cloth was donated to the Post, and within a few months a similar one has been donated to the Sons of Veterans. The money has been wholly raised by hard work,—fairs, suppers and entertainments have succeeded each other, most of them bringing into the treasury encouraging sums. In 1889 a fair was held which netted nearly $900.00.

It is about Memorial Day that we feel the work of the Corps centers. In assisting the Post to decorate the graves of their fallen comrades, and in caring for the comfort of those who perform this duty, comes an inspiration to remember, while life shall last, those whose bravery saved our beloved country, and when their hands fall helpless, to care for those near and dear to them. They saved this land that we might live in peace and comfort. Can we do less than remember to assist them in their hours of darkness?

Among the pleasant memories of the past come to us those of the receptions tendered members of our Corps. First, that of June, 1890, to Mrs. E. V. Lang, Department Junior Vice-President; September, 1891, a reception was tendered the Department officers, and in October, 1892, another to Mrs. Helen A. Brigham, Department Inspector, who is the present Department Junior Vice-President. In 1892, at the request of Mrs. Mary G. Deane, Department President, the School of Instruction for the Inspectors of the Department was held with the Corps.

Membership, one hundred and twenty-five.

PRESIDENTS.

Helen Bryant	1884
Annie M. Churchill	1885
Elizabeth V. Lang	1886
Lucy A. Reynolds	1887
Elizabeth C. Bickmore	1888
Belle B. Alexander	1889
Marietta Davis	1890
Helen A. Brigham	1891
Bertha L. Newell	1892
Abbie L. Day	1893
Jane Walker	1894

E. A. ANDREWS CORPS No. 36, SHREWSBURY.

Was instituted Feb. 21, 1884, with twenty-one charter members, by Mrs. Sarah E. Fuller, then National Secretary. During each year since its organization, entertainments have been held for the benefit of the Relief Fund; and sociables have been held with the Post which have been very pleasant.

The Corps has a Relief Fund, and has sent to the Soldiers' Home, $52.45; contributed to the Convention Fund, 1890, and to the W.R.C. Home; also to Post 135, G.A.R. It sustains a room at the Soldiers' Home in Chelsea. The calls for local relief are few, but whenever called upon Corps 36 gladly renders such aid as lies in its power. Memorial Day is also observed by the Corps.

Membership, twenty.

PRESIDENTS.

Isabella M. Loring	1884, 1885, 1886, 1887
Emily D. Mitchell	1888
Susan E. Winchester	1889, 1890, 1891
Nettie B. Foster	1892
M. Jennie Ball	1893
Ellen A. Rice	1894

W. W. ROCKWELL CORPS No. 37, PITTSFIELD.

Was instituted April 23, 1884, with forty-three charter members, by Mrs. Sarah E. Fuller, Department Secretary. Mrs. M. Susie Goodale, Department President, installed the officers.

The Corps has taken a deep interest in the Soldiers' Home and sent a box of articles valued at $80.00 to the Soldiers' Home Carnival in 1885, and in 1893 voted $100.00 for furnishing a room at the Home.

We have expended $414.25 in relief and have given clothing valued at $50.00. The sum of $400.00 has been turned over to the Post and we have expended $150.00 in refurnishing the parlor of Grand Army Hall.

Contributions have been sent at various times to the Department funds.

Memorial Day is appropriately observed by Corps 37.

Membership, eighty-two.

PRESIDENTS.

Agnes Bartlett	1884
Angeline A. Cooley	1885
Abbie M. Wheldon	1886
M. Jane Brewster	1887
Catherine Bagg	1888
Angeline A. Cooley	1889
Marietta I. Ayres	1890
Martha C. Read	1891, 1892, 1893, 1894

KILPATRICK CORPS No. 38, HOLYOKE.

Was instituted April 10, 1884, by Mrs. M. Susie Goodale, Department President, with a charter membership of forty-nine. The officers were publicly installed by Mrs. E. Florence Barker, then National President. The members of the Corps were full of enthusiasm and the prospects for the future were bright and promising. Entertainments, socials and Martha Washington tea-parties were held to raise funds to meet the many calls which were made for relief; the Corps has expended $1,012.90 in relief since organization, besides taking charge of a room at the Soldiers' Home.

Personal contributions have furnished a room at the City Hospital, where any member of the Post, Corps or Sons of Veterans can receive medical treatment. At the time of the National Convention in Boston, Corps 38 contributed $75.00 toward defraying the expenses incurred by the Department. Corps 38 turned over to Kilpatrick Post No. 71, $125.00.

Membership, one hundred and forty-four.

PRESIDENTS.

Ella M. Davis	1884
Ann J. Thorpe	1885, 1886
Olive L. Turner	1887
Harriet M. Smith	1888
Jennie P. Bishop	1889
Adaline P. Snell	1890, 1891, 1892
Ellen S. Cain	1893
Nettie M. Streeter	1894

ABRAHAM LINCOLN CORPS No. 39, CHARLESTOWN.

Was instituted April 22, 1884, by Mrs. M. Susie Goodale, Department President, assisted by Mrs. Sarah E. Fuller, Department Secretary, with a charter membership of twenty-five, and has gradually increased in membership. The Corps has endeavored to fulfill the object of its organization as an auxiliary to the Grand Army of the Republic by helping Post 11, G.A.R., at all times and in all ways that have seemed necessary. The Corps has assisted in two fairs and in the fall of 1892 held a fair the entire proceeds of which were given to the Post.

On April 23, 1888, the beautiful Hall in which Post and Corps hold their meetings was dedicated, when the Corps assisted the Post in entertaining over five hundred guests. One of the most enjoyable occasions in the history of the Corps was at the time of the National Encampment of 1890, when Post 11 entertained as guests Lincoln Post of San Francisco, Bosworth Post of Maine, and one member of George W. DeLong Post of Honolulu, Sandwich Islands.

During the past ten years the Corps has expended in Relief $839.14 and turned over to Post $1,057.29.

Many honors have fallen to individual members of the Corps, and the able manner in which each member has performed her duty reflects credit upon the Corps as well as upon themselves. Mrs. Mary E. Knowles entered the Department work in the second year of the Corps' existence as Assistant Inspector, passing on to the highest office in the gift of the State, that of Department President of Massachusetts. She was honored at the National Convention in Washington, 1892, by an unanimous election to the office of National Chaplain. Mrs. Elizabeth B. Raymond was for three years a member of the Department Relief Committee, and two years served as its Chairman. Mrs. Lizabeth A. Turner joined Corps 39 by transfer in 1891, at that time being National Senior Vice-President.

May the record of well doing in the future never be overshadowed by the past, but grow brighter and brighter to the end.

Membership, one hundred and twenty-three.

PRESIDENTS.

Emma F. Haskell . . .	1884
Mary E. Knowles . . .	1885
Ellen M. Dunton . . .	1886
Abbie H. Titus . . .	1887
Lizzie M. Richards . .	1888
Belle J. Noble . . .	1889
Ruth W. Bailey . . .	1890
Emily E. Marden . . .	1891
Harriette A. Burrows . .	1892
Ella H. Metcalf . . .	1893
Helen A. Atkins . .	1894

JAMES A. PERKINS CORPS No. 40, EVERETT.

Was instituted May 22, 1884, by Mrs. M. Susie Goodale, Department President.

It has expended in relief $286.34; turned over to Post $280.77; contributed to the Soldiers' Home $171.85 and to the Department Relief Fund, $42.00.

The members have made and presented to the Post the National Colors, a silk altar cloth, also a silk quilt from which $487.00 were realized.

Corps 40 has in addition presented the Post a storm flag, a State flag (which was carried for the first time at the Encampment in Washington) and a crayon portrait of James A. Perkins, which hangs upon the wall of Grand Army Hall.

The Corps has always provided a dinner for the Post on Memorial Day, and when decorating the soldiers' graves, also remembers the graves of two army nurses.

Membership, fifty-seven.

PRESIDENTS.

Addie W. Bullock	1884
Augusta K. Pettingill	1885, 1886, 1887, 1888
Mahala W. Batchelder	1889
Augusta C. Casler .	1890, 1891, 1892, 1893
M. Lizzie Bullock	1894

E. P. CARPENTER CORPS No. 41, FOXBORO.

At the request of E. P. Carpenter Post No. 91, G.A.R., a meeting was called April 14, 1884, for the purpose of forming a Corps, as an auxiliary to Post 91. The Department President, Mrs. M. Susie Goodale, instituted the Corps with seventeen charter members.

There has been expended in relief since organization, $356.57, $100.00 of which were appropriated towards furnishing a room at the Soldiers' Home at Chelsea. Turned over to Post, $218.11; Army Nurse Fund, $20.00; Invalid Veterans' Fund, $25.00. The Corps has assisted Post 91 in furnishing its hall, also in several large fairs and lawn parties; presented the Post a burial flag, and has always responded when called upon for aid.

Membership, seventy-three.

PRESIDENTS.

Susan E. Fuller	1884, 1885
Mary E. Goodwin	1886
Lydia R. Cobb	1887, 1888
Mary E. Goodwin	1889
Mary B. Folsom	1890, 1891
Susan S. Comey . .	1892, 1893, 1894

GEN. JAMES APPLETON CORPS No. 42, IPSWICH.

Auxiliary to Gen. James Appleton Post No. 128, G.A.R., was instituted May 19, 1884, by Mrs. M. Susie Goodale, Department President, assisted by Mrs. Sarah E. Fuller, Department Secretary, with a charter membership of forty-six. Like other Corps in small places, we have gained and lost membership, but a good work has been accomplished. Eleven of our members have passed on to the other shore. The calls for relief have not been as numerous as in some Corps, but there has been expended in relief about $810.00 since the Corps was organized. It has turned over to the Post in various ways $665.00. The funds to carry on the work of the Corps have been raised by fairs, entertainments and suppers, which have been liberally patronized by the townspeople.

Membership, ninety-nine.

PRESIDENTS.

Sarah E. Pickard	1884
Elizabeth R. Boynton	1885, 1886, 1887
Elizabeth H. Wait	1888, 1889
Anna F. Nichols	1890, 1891
E. Maria Stone	1892, 1893
Anna F. Nichols	1894

FRANCIS GOULD CORPS No. 43, ARLINGTON.

Was instituted June 30, 1884, by Mrs. M. Susie Goodale, Department President, with a charter membership of seventeen. The officers were publicly installed, Francis Gould Post No. 36, G.A.R., and Corps 5 of Medford being invited guests. At this time Post 36 presented the Corps $50.00 for its relief fund.

The Corps assisted Post 36 in a fair in 1885, and the aid rendered the Department of Massachusetts W.R.C. was turning over $100.00 worth of goods for the Soldiers' Home Carnival held in Boston in 1885. The same year the Corps presented the Post with an elegant silk banner. In 1886 a room was furnished in the Soldiers' Home at an expense of $125.00; and the same year the idea was conceived by the Corps of building a G.A.R. Hall; for four years the members worked energetically with that object in view and $1,000.00 was the result of their labors in this direction. A hall was leased at that time and furnished by the Corps and offered to the Post and Camp; to-day this home is used jointly by the three organizations. The local calls for relief have been few, but the Corps is ever ready to render assistance when required.

Membership, seventy.

PRESIDENTS.

Augusta C. Randall	1884, 1885, 1886, 1887
Georgianna Averill	1888
Violet C. Durgin	1889, 1890
Angelina B. Swadkins	1891, 1892
H. Ella Illsley	1893
Georgianna Averill	1894

DAVID CHURCH CORPS No. 44, MARSHFIELD HILLS.

Was instituted at the request of David Church Post No. 189, G.A.R., by the Department President, Mrs. Mary G. Deane, Jan. 4, 1893, with a charter membership of forty-one. The installation of its officers was publicly conducted in the evening and was attended by Post 189 and interested citizens.

For several years previous to this time these ladies had worked together as an independent society, but at this time it was thought they could do more effective work as an auxiliary to Post 189.

The charter of the Corps was presented by Mrs. Susan B. Guelpha, a charter member.

The first President is a daughter of David Church for whom the Post is named, having lost his life in his country's service. The first quarter the Corps raised by personal effort fifty dollars, which were presented to Post 189.

Membership, fifty-four.

PRESIDENT.

Alice M. Magoun	1893, 1894

W. A. STREETER CORPS No. 45, ATTLEBORO.

Was instituted Sept. 18, 1884, by Mrs. Sarah E. Fuller, Department Secretary, with twenty-two members.

The sum of $4,000.00 has been expended by the Corps for various objects, and the relief work has not been neglected. Several boxes have been sent to the Soldiers' Home.

Each year a dinner is served the soldiers on Memorial Day and flowers are furnished for decorating the cemeteries.

Corps 45 is in a prosperous condition.

Membership, forty-six.

PRESIDENTS.

Lucy B. Martin	1884, 1885
Lizzie Thompson	1886
Emma Adams	1887
Lucy B. Martin	1888, 1889
Maria A. MacDonald	1890, 1891, 1892
E. Jennie Sweet	1893, 1894

GEN. E. W. HINDS CORPS No. 46, SAUGUS.

Was instituted Jan. 16, 1885, by Mrs. Helen F. Johnson of the Department Executive Board, with a charter membership of fifteen.

Public installation was held in the evening, which was attended by Post 95 and invited guests, at which time Mrs. Lizabeth A. Turner installed the officers elect. The interest of the Post manifested at the time has continued, and is appreciated by the Corps during the nearly ten years of its existence.

The demands upon the Relief Fund have been few, but to such as have been presented the Corps has generously responded; over $204.50 have been expended in relief, and relief other than money extended to the amount of $35.00; $89.50 have been turned over to Post 95 and a piano has been placed in G.A.R. Hall. The Corps has experienced the usual trials, but the members do their best to exercise toward each other and the outside world that charity which is the grandest of its watchwords.

Membership, forty-eight.

PRESIDENTS.

Emma F. Mansfield	1885, 1886, 1887, 1888
Lizzie Graves	1889
Emma F. Mansfield	1890, 1891, 1892
Annie Gilman	1893, 1894

JUSTIN DIMICK CORPS No. 47, EAST BRIDGEWATER.

Was instituted Jan. 16, 1885, with a charter membership of twenty-nine, by Mrs. M. Susie Goodale, Department President, assisted by Mrs. S. Agnes Parker. Department Senior Vice-President.

During the nine and a half years since its organization Corps 47 has placed in the hands of Post 124 $148.25. This amount includes the cost of a silk flag which was presented to Post 124 by the President, Mrs. Hannah G. Churchill, in behalf of the Corps, Jan. 12, 1889.

Membership, forty-three.

PRESIDENTS.

Mary S. Hine	1885, 1886
Sarah J. Hayward	1887
Hannah G. Churchill	1888, 1889, 1890
Mary J. E. Poole	1891
Emily T. Smellie	1892, 1893, 1894

H. S. GREENLEAF CORPS No. 48, COLRAIN.

Was instituted April 28, 1886, with sixteen charter members, by Mrs. Mary M. Perry, Department Instituting and Installing Officer.

Although situated in the western part of the State, far away from Department Headquarters, the Corps has ever been awake to assist as far as possible in advancing the interests of the Order. Since organization the Post and Corps have worked together to raise funds to build a Memorial Hall; their efforts have been crowned with success, $2,366.62 having been raised by the Corps, and the building will soon be dedicated. The Corps has turned over to the Post $1,563.50; has expended in relief $100.00; contributed articles to the Soldiers' Home valued at $100.00.

Membership, thirty-six.

PRESIDENTS.

Flora A. Smith	1886, 1887
Julia M. Carpenter	1888
Flora A. Smith	1889, 1890
Mary A. Nelson	1891, 1892
Olive Howard	1893, 1894

GEORGE S. BOUTWELL CORPS No. 49, AYER.

Was instituted Jan. 26, 1885, with sixteen charter members, by Mrs. Helen F. Johnson, Department Guard, assisted by Mrs. Ellen Johnson of Somerville. A camp-fire was held in the evening with supper, speeches and war songs.

The Corps started a Relief Fund a few weeks later and raised money for this object in various ways. A fair was held the first year, from which about $300.00 were realized. A series of concerts were next arranged. Soldiers' families have been aided, donations sent to the Soldiers' Home and to the Department Funds, and contributions given the Post toward a lot in the cemetery, one hundred markers for soldiers' graves, and money to purchase flags which the comrades have carried in their processions. We also sent a contribution to the National (Boston) Convention Fund. We have expended about $150.00 for relief and given the Post $135.00, and have presented a flag to the Ayer High School.

The first hundred dollars toward erecting a Memorial Hall in Ayer was raised by the Corps.

Membership, thirty-seven.

PRESIDENTS.

Nina B. Lovejoy	1885
Mary L. Harlow	1886, 1887
Mary E. Pierce	1888, 1889
Lucy S. Richardson	1890, 1891
Nina B. Lovejoy	1892
Abbie A. Lewis	1893
Nina B. Lovejoy	1894

UNION CORPS No. 50, PEABODY.

Was organized May 27, 1885, as No. 52, by Mrs. M. Susie Goodale, Department President. In September, 1892, by consent of Mrs. Augusta A. Wales, Department President, it took the vacant number 50 to correspond with the number of the local Post.

The first work of the Corps was to assist Post 50 in a fair, in January, 1886, from which the Corps realized $359.33, which was immediately placed in the Relief Fund. In May, 1887, the Corps purchased a vase for the Soldiers' Lot in Cedar Grove Cemetery. In April a "Kirmess" was held, from which the Corps realized a handsome sum, and on its third anniversary presented Post 50 with a check for $775.00, also a silk flag valued at $55.00.

In February, 1889, the Corps presented Corps 23 of Marblehead a check for $25.00, as they had sustained a serious loss by fire. This year $100.00 was appropriated to furnish a room in the Soldiers' Home, Chelsea, and a clock was purchased for the hall in the Soldiers' Home.

In May, 1890, the Corps gave an entertainment, from the proceeds of which the Department was presented $25.00 toward defraying the expenses of Encampment week in Boston; and $50.00 to Union Post 50 to entertain friends from the South attending Encampment. In January, 1891, $25.00 were given to the National W.R.C. Home. The succeeding months found the Corps members busy at work and their endeavors were crowned with success.

The amount expended in relief can be summed as follows:—

For local relief	$581 36
Turned over to Post No. 50, G.A.R	1,194 50
Soldiers' Home, Chelsea	84 40
Room at Soldiers' Home, Chelsea	155 27
To Army Nurses, W.R.C. Home	115 00

The Corps provides refreshments for the Post on Memorial Days, and joins with it in keeping bright the memory of the brave soldier who so nobly served his country in its time of peril.

From a charter membership of twenty-three it has increased to its present number of seventy-one.

It has had but one President since its organization, Miss Sarah F. Kittredge filling that position so satisfactorily that the members are unwilling to make any change.

J. C. FREEMAN CORPS No. 51, PROVINCETOWN.

On March 31, 1883, J. C. Freeman Corps No. 51 was instituted by Mrs. S. Agnes Parker, Department Senior Vice-President, with a charter membership of twenty-three.

The Corps has conducted a good work, having assisted J. C. Freeman Post G.A.R., in furnishing its hall, and co-operated with the Post in all measures for the welfare of the veterans.

It has rendered practical assistance to soldiers and their families. specially remembering them during Thanksgiving week. In addition to local relief and Memorial Day work, Corps 51 has aided the following objects: Sailors' Reading Room, Provincetown, Department Invalid Veteran's Fund, Soldiers' Home, National Convention Fund, 1890, and in decoration of unknown graves in National Cemeteries.

Recognizing the services of Mrs. Mary A. Livermore during the Civil War, the Corps contributed $10.00 toward the fund of the W.C.T.U. of Massachusetts, for placing her bust in the Woman's Department at the World's Fair.

Over $600.00 have been expended in patriotic work, and Corps 51, though isolated on the borders of the Cape, is thoroughly imbued with the true spirit of the Order.

Membership, fifty-six.

PRESIDENTS.

Mary C. Nickerson	1885, 1886
Susie E. Young	1887, 1888
H. Louise Lyford	1889, 1890
Anne Snow	1891, 1892
Mira B. Conwell	1893, 1894

A. B. RANDALL CORPS No. 52, EASTONDALE.

Was instituted May 15, 1888, by Mrs. Harriette L. Reed of the Department Executive Board, with seventeen members. We are a small band of workers but have been very loyal to our Post, and unite each year with the comrades in holding a fair. Grand Army hall has been enlarged through the efforts of the Corps, and the hall is so commodious that the Post has no trouble in letting it at a financial benefit.

The larger part of the proceeds of our fairs and other entertainments are given to Post 52. The faithful hearts of our veterans are ever ready to help the widow and the fatherless of our soldiers.

We meet yearly on the evening of May 29, to prepare for Memorial Day and always attend the Sabbath memorial services with the Post and take an active part in the work of May 30. We are ever ready to lend a helping hand and to say "God bless you" to the organization we serve.

Membership, thirty.

PRESIDENTS.

Rosanna B. Morse	1888, 1889
Augusta M. Blood	1890, 1891
Mamie L. Willis	1892, 1893, 1894

WM. LOGAN RODMAN CORPS No. 53, NEW BEDFORD.

This Corps, auxiliary to Wm. Logan Rodman Post No. 1, G.A.R., was instituted and officers publicly installed by Mrs. M. Susie Goodale, Department President, Sept. 27, 1885, with twenty-five charter members. The present membership is one hundred and forty. Corps 53 has ever been active in the work of relief and from its institution until July 1, 1893, expended in relief the sum of $2,078.09, besides presenting to Post 1, cash, flags, silver, etc., to the value of $334.34, and paying rent of hall.

Corps 53 has also furnished and kept in good order a room at the Soldiers' Home since 1886, and contributed $100.00 toward defraying the expenses of National Convention in 1890.

In 1892 on Memorial Day, a very handsome granite sarcophagus was erected by Corps 53 and dedicated by Post 1, to the memory of the unknown dead "who sleep on Southern battlefields, or 'neath the ocean wave." It serves not only as a memorial to our fallen heroes, but also as a tribute to the devoted and patriotic women of Corps 53 whose patient and persevering work accumulated the sum that paid for this memorial stone. A most kindly feeling has ever been manifested for and returned by Camp 35, Sons of Veterans, connected with Post 1.

Mrs. Lucy M. James, who served the Corps four years as President, has served as Department Aide and as a delegate to National Convention.

Membership, one hundred and forty.

PRESIDENTS.

Mary H. Washburn	1885, 1886
Lucy M. James	1887, 1888, 1889
Eliza M. Bliss	1890
Lucy M. James	1891
Cynthia M. Caldwell	1892, 1893, 1894

E. BRIGHAM PIPER CORPS No. 54, WALPOLE.

Was instituted Sept. 28, 1885, by Mrs. M. Susie Goodale, Department President, with eighteen charter members. The Corps has expended about $375.00 for relief and contributed clothing and food, and sewed for families of soldiers when necessary. They have responded to all calls from Department Headquarters and performed their duties promptly and in a faithful manner.

Corps 51 has always been ready to assist Post 157 in all its work, and on Memorial Day the two bodies have worked together so earnestly and heartily that we have always had very interesting services, both at the hall and cemeteries, the children joining in the exercises. The Corps has always dedicated a floral piece of some form to the unknown dead. Many pleasant visits have been made on sister Corps and many Corps have been entertained, and we have reaped pleasure and profit by so doing. Each year brings more work and as the work increases so also the interest of the members increases, and they are ever ready to perform the work assigned them.

Membership, fifty.

PRESIDENTS.

Martha M. Allen	1885, 1886, 1887, 1888
Maria L. Brummitt	1889
Charlotte E. Fisher	1890
Maria L. Brummitt	1891, 1892
S. Jennie Nye	1893
Maria L. Brummitt	1894

NEEDHAM CORPS No. 55, LAWRENCE.

On Oct. 7, 1885, Mrs. Sarah E. Fuller, National President, instituted Needham Corps No. 55 with a charter membership of seventy-two.

Since organization there has been expended in relief over $838.67. Whenever called upon the Corps has always gladly responded.

In May, 1892, by request of the Department President, Mrs. Mary G. Deane, Corps 55 exemplified the work of the Ritual for the benefit of the neighboring Corps.

Membership, one hundred and forty-four.

PRESIDENTS.

Isabella G. Townsend	1885, 1886, 1887, 1888
Margie E. B. Hutchins	1889, 1890
Sarah J. Parsons	1891, 1892
Alice Curtis	1893, 1894

OZRO MILLER CORPS No. 56, SHELBURNE FALLS.

Was instituted Nov. 6, 1885, with a charter membership of twenty-one, by Mrs. M. Susie Goodale, Department President.

During the nine years of its existence considerable charity has been extended to the families of deserving veterans; watchers have been supplied in sickness; cash expended and money supplied when necessary. Over $100.00 has been presented to Ozro Miller Post, and money has been sent to Phil. Kearney Post, G.A.R., Richmond, Va., and articles to the Soldiers' Home.

In May, 1893, Corps 56 exemplified the work. Mrs. Emily L. Clark, Department President, Senior Aide Marion Bridgeman, and Emilie L. W. Waterman, Department Inspector, were present at this time.

All calls from the Department are promptly answered and the Corps, though small, is in a prosperous condition. While the expenditure of money has not been large, yet in many ways those left to us as precious charges by those who gave all that their country might live, have been cared for as precious legacies. Mrs. Gillett, the first President of Corps 56, attended the first State Convention in Fitchburg, 1879.

Membership, sixty.

PRESIDENTS.

Luanna R. Gillett	1885, 1886, 1887
Ellen A. Wilder	1888, 1889
Susan L. Russell	1890
Ellen A. Wilder	1891
Hattie G. Amstein	1892, 1893
Luella Meekins	1894

EDWIN E. DAY CORPS No. 57, GREENFIELD.

This Corps was instituted Nov. 13, 1885, with seventeen charter members, by Mrs. Mary M. Perry, Department Conductor.

Previous to the Encampment held in Boston, in 1890, the Corps presented to Edwin E. Day Post No. 174 a handsome silk flag, which the comrades proudly carried in the parade in Washington in 1892. On Memorial Day, 1893, the Corps presented Post 174 a large urn, which was placed in the public park.

Membership, sixty-six.

PRESIDENTS.

Eunice W. Moors	1885, 1886
Sarah E. Woodard	1887, 1888
Maria C. Walker	1889, 1890
Della B. Clark	1891, 1892
Calista A. Holden	1893, 1894

GEORGE C. STRONG CORPS No. 58, EASTHAMPTON.

An informal meeting was called on the evening of Oct. 27, 1885, by the members of the Post, to meet Mrs. Mary M. Perry of Springfield, and preliminary steps were taken toward forming a Relief Corps, which was instituted Dec. 7, 1885, with thirty-five charter members. One year from that time Corps 58 celebrated its first anniversary, at which time the Post in Easthampton was invited, and during the evening a life-sized portrait of Gen. George C. Strong was presented by the Corps.

Each anniversary the Corps presents something of value to the Post — rug, altar-cloth, officers' chairs, Bible, cash. In 1892 we placed a piano in the hall for the use of both organizations.

The amount of relief expended since organization is $412.04; turned over to Post $175.00, besides sending to the Soldiers' Home $32.00 and contributing to other objects.

Membership, sixty-seven.

PRESIDENTS.

Lucinda M. Farrar	1886
Nellie J. Ware	1887
Lora G. Taylor	1888, 1889
Lizzie Strong	1890
Helen Buzzie	1891
Sarah C. Caswell	1892, 1893
Maria E. Matthews	1894

ISAAC B. PATTEN CORPS No. 59, WATERTOWN.

This Corps owes its existence to the faithful missionary work of Mrs. Angela H. Scranton of Cambridge. It was instituted Nov. 30, 1885, with fifty-five charter members, by the Department President, Mrs. M. Susie Goodale, assisted by Miss Mary E. Elliot, Department Secretary.

Early in its life it assumed the care of room thirty-three at the Soldiers' Home, since known as the Watertown room, also of the Soldiers' Lot in the Common Street cemetery.

On the 31st of October, 1889, the Soldiers' Monument was dedicated with imposing ceremonies. Because of the zealous efforts of the Relief Corps, the President, Mrs. Lizzie M. Dow, was invited to unveil the statue, which she did, surrounded by her associate officers and most of those of the Department of Massachusetts. Probably Corps 59 was the first upon which this distinguished honor had been conferred.

Much charity work has been done in a quiet manner, and the worth of the Corps is recognized throughout the town. The beautiful silken flags borne by the Post and Sons of Veterans were gifts from the Corps, and bear silent testimony to the goodwill between these organizations. The following is an extract from a letter written since Memorial Day by the Commander of the Post: "The Corps is a blessing and a credit to the Post. May it live long and prosper, as the medium of comfort and blessing to the poor and distressed of the Grand Army."

Expended in relief $335 23
Turned over to Post 125 00
Furnished for National Convention, 1890 . 50 00

The Post has given the free use of the hall, and the Corps has furnished a set of handsomely carved oaken officer's chairs.

Membership, forty-five.

PRESIDENTS.

Mary A. Berry	1886, 1887
Abbie A. Smith	1888
Lizzie M. Dow	1889
Anna M. Condon	1890
Adell Elliot	1891
Abbie H. Stone	1892, 1893
Nellie F. Barney	1894

E. HUMPHREY CORPS No. 60, HINGHAM.

Was instituted Dec. 17, 1885, by S. Agnes Parker, Department Senior Vice-President, with a charter membership of twenty-six.

Although small in numbers it has worked with great zeal and energy to further the veteran's cause, and no call, however lowly, has been heard in vain.

A deep interest is taken in Memorial Day, and contributions have been sent to the various funds at Department Headquarters. The social gatherings of Post and Corps are very pleasant.

In May, 1893, Corps 60 exemplified the work of the Ritual, at which time the Department President, Mrs. Emily L. Clark and Staff were present and twenty-one Corps were represented.

Membership, seventy-eight.

PRESIDENTS.

Mary Whiton	1886, 1887
Martha C. Wakefield	1888, 1889, 1890
Martha C. Litchfield	1891
Hattie M. Low	1892, 1893
Georgie A. Stoddar	1894

JOHN ROGERS CORPS No. 61, MANSFIELD.

Was organized Jan. 6, 1886, by S. Agnes Parker, Department Senior Vice-President, with a charter membership of forty-four.

The Corps has helped various soldiers' families with clothing and groceries, of which no account has been kept. It has disbursed for relief in cash $152.40, and assisted John Rogers Post in two fairs.

It has always answered all calls from Headquarters, and aided whenever possible all who called for relief. Though small in numbers the Corps has been earnest in efforts to advance the cause and all the principles to which it stands pledged.

Membership, thirty-four.

PRESIDENTS.

Hattie E. Perry	1886, 1887, 1888
Carrie A. Tebbetts	1889, 1890
Laura A. Paine	1891, 1892
Ida J. Richards	1893
Alzadia M. Fisher	1894

ISAAC DAVIS RELIEF CORPS No. 62, WEST ACTON.

This Corps was instituted Jan. 20, 1886, with a charter membership of sixty-six, by Mrs. Emma B. Lowd, Department Junior Vice-President. Since organization, the Corps has held one fair and helped the Post in two others, thus aiding in adding to their treasury. In 1892 a lawn party was held, the proceeds of which helped defray the expenses of the Post to Washington, and the Corps has assisted the Post in every way possible.

In the spring of 1888 the Corps purchased a lot in the cemetery at West Acton, and on Memorial Day it was presented to the Post and dedicated with appropriate services to the unknown dead.

Donations have been sent to the Soldiers' Home in Chelsea, also to decorate the graves of the soldiers in the South; besides cash disbursements since organization of $103.00, we have also turned over to Post $200.00. While but little money has been expended in local relief, aid in other ways has been extended to soldiers and their families in sickness or trouble.

Membership, ninety-nine.

PRESIDENTS.

Frances A. Stevens	1886, 1887
Adeline Allen	1888
Sarah A. Hutchins	1889, 1890
Fannie Parker	1891, 1892
Almira M. Willard	1893, 1894

THOMAS G. STEVENSON CORPS No. 63, ROXBURY.

Was instituted Jan. 25, 1886, with a charter membership of nineteen, by Mrs. Sarah E. Fuller, National President, assisted by Mrs. L. A. Turner, National Treasurer.

Since organization the Corps has expended in relief $1,300.17; for the Soldiers' Home, $243.11; turned over to Post, $3,210.26; for soldiers' graves in the South, $25.00; National Encampment in Boston, 1890, $194.50.

In 1887 the Post held a fair and the ladies of the Corps had charge of three tables, turning over to the Post the sum of $2,062.33.

In 1889 Corps 63 purchased a lot in Forest Hill cemetery, placing therein a vase suitably inscribed, as a memorial to the army nurses, at a cost of $131.06; on each Memorial Day the Corps visit it in a body, conducting services and bringing their memorials of flowers. Joint services of Post and Corps are held each year at the Soldiers' Monument, the Corps furnishing a floral piece for the unknown dead.

Two rooms have been furnished and kept in order at the Soldiers' Home for a number of years, and annually Post and Corps have furnished a literary entertainment for the veterans, not forgetting to leave a substantial reminder of their visit, and donations to the Home from the Corps treasury amount to $243.11.

The Sons of Veterans have always found Corps 63 ready to assist them whenever needed. Whenever the Post has called on Corps 63 its members have responded and at the present time one hundred and forty-seven loyal women stand ready to do whatever is committed to their charge.

Membership, one hundred and forty-seven.

PRESIDENTS.

Alma A. Williams	. .	1886, 1887
Angie K. Trask	. .	1888, 1889
Abbie E. Graves	. . .	. 1890
Nettie D. Hill	. . .	. 1891
Mary L. Nason	. . .	. 1892
Mary L. Simpson	. . .	. 1893
Mary J. Parkman	. .	. 1894

MANTON E. TAFT CORPS No. 64, TURNER'S FALLS.

Was organized Feb. 15, 1886, with twenty-one charter members, by Mrs. Mary M. Perry, Department Instituting and Installing Officer.

In March, 1886, a dinner was served in G.A.R. Hall and $50.41 were cleared, of which $13.35 were sent to the Soldiers' Home. In October, 1892, a fair was held, at which time $150.10 were cleared and $50.00 of this amount turned over to the Post.

Since organization there has been expended for relief, $54.83; sent to Soldiers' Home, $30.35, turned over to Post, $250.00.

Membership, twenty-seven.

PRESIDENTS.

Phemie M. Goddard	. .	1886, 1887, 1888
E. Agnes Sherman	. . . .	1889
Harriet E. Mayo	. . . .	1890
Josie A. Adams	. .	1891, 1892, 1893, 1894

J. P. GOULD CORPS No. 65, STONEHAM.

Was instituted Feb. 17, 1886, with a charter membership of forty-eight, by Mrs. Lizabeth A. Turner, National Treasurer, assisted by Mrs. Hattie A. Ralph, Department Treasurer. The first year the Corps was instituted a room was furnished at the Soldiers' Home and has been cared for ever since that time.

Several fairs have been held by the Post at which the Corps has taken an active part, thereby considerably increasing the fund for the relief of members of the Post.

All calls for relief are gladly answered, according to the state of the finances, and we have expended between seven and eight hundred dollars.

Membership, eighty-one.

PRESIDENTS.

Margaret Brown	1886
Mattie C. Davis	1887
Jennie Brown	1888
Clara L. Buswell,	1889, 1890, 1891
Margaret Andrews	1892, 1893
S. Lizzie Campbell	1894

P. STEARNS DAVIS CORPS No. 66, EAST CAMBRIDGE.

Was instituted Feb. 22, 1886, by Mrs. Lizabeth A. Turner, Department Senior Vice-President, with a membership of seventy-three, at that time the largest charter membership of any Corps in the Department excepting one.

Immediately after institution a Relief Fund was established; money was also raised for the purchase of a piano.

During these years, $802.98 have been expended in relief, $709.55 turned over to Post and $90.95 to the Soldiers' Home. The Corps paid $100.00 for furnishing a room at the Soldiers' Home and dedicated it in honor of its first president, Mrs. Pamelia W. Knight.

During the week of National Encampment at Boston, Corps 66 assisted Post 57 in entertaining Post 7 of Philadelphia.

June 29, 1893, at the twenty-fifth anniversary of Post 57, Corps 66, through its President, Mrs. Mary E. Lincoln, presented a State flag in honor of its silver wedding.

Membership, two hundred and five.

PRESIDENTS.

Pamelia W. Knight	1886, 1887, 1888
Etta A. Lockhart	1889, 1890, 1891
Mary E. Lincoln	1892, 1893
Adelia A. Adams	1894

ROBERT A. BELL CORPS NO. 67, BOSTON.

Several ladies interested in Robert A. Bell Post united in forming a Relief Corps which was instituted Feb. 25, 1886, with sixteen charter members. Mrs. Lizabeth A. Turner, Department Senior Vice-President, conducted the ceremony, assisted by Miss Mary E. Elliot, Department Secretary.

The year following, the Corps presented Post 134, to which it is auxiliary, a State flag valued at $50.00, also a piano and other furnishings for Grand Army Hall. In 1888 the Corps assisted the Sons of Veterans connected with Robert A. Bell Post, in securing a flag. In 1890 Corps 67 presented Post Encampment $85.00, and placed chandeliers in Grand Army Hall. A picnic in the summer of 1890 netted $50.00 to the Corps treasury. The Corps has assisted the Soldiers' Home and responded to calls for other special objects. It has given public entertainments of interest and has co-operated with Post 134 in Memorial Day plans and other work.

With calls for help coming from every direction the Corps has found work to do, and the members have promptly responded to duty's call. It expended $268.75 in relief from 1886 to 1893; $258.39 for flag, furniture and other donations to Post, and $178.25 for assistance to the Sons of Veterans and families of comrades.

Membership, fifty-two.

PRESIDENTS.

Mary L. Hammond	1886, 1887
Sarah E. Johnson	1888, 1889
Mary L. Hammond	1890, 1891
Addie H. Jewell	1892
Susie A. Taylor	1893
Addie H. Jewell	1894

BENJ. STONE, JR., CORPS No. 68, DORCHESTER.

The Corps owes its existence directly to a reception given to the Grand Army of the Republic by the Seventh Annual Convention of the Department of Massachusetts, W.R.C., on the evening of Jan. 28, 1886. On that occasion the Commander of Benj. Stone, Jr., Post No. 68, became so enthusiastic that he declared as he left the hall: " Benj. Stone, Jr., Post 68 shall have a Relief Corps." Acting upon the impulse there received, Commander Stiles presented the matter to the Post at its next meeting, and a committee of comrades and ladies from the different sections of Dorchester was appointed to make the necessary arrangements for the formation of a Corps, which was instituted February 23, thereby securing to the Corps, No. 68, corresponding to the number of the Post, it being the first Corps thus fortunate at its institution. The Corps was instituted by Mrs. Emma B. Lowd, Department Junior Vice-President, assisted by Mrs. Lizabeth A. Turner, Department Senior Vice-President. The sixty-six ladies present enrolled their names as charter members. Two who had signed the charter application, but were not able to be present, were afterwards admitted by a special dispensation, thus completing the mystic number 68. Among the guests at the public installation in the evening were Department Commander Richard F. Tobin and Staff, Past Commander-in-Chief Paul Van Der Voort, Past Department Commanders George W. Creasey and George S. Evans, Department President S. Agnes Parker, Department Secretary Mary E. Elliot and Department Chaplain Mary E. Knowles.

The first public appearance of the Corps was on May 20, in response to an invitation from the Post to join in the dedication of Grand Army Hall. On this occasion a silk flag was presented to the Post, it having been secured by personal contributions from the members. Later on, in 1889, the Union Jack was presented by the Corps.

On Memorial Sunday of that year, as on all succeeding years, the Corps attended church by invitation of the Post, and on each Memorial Day has assisted in every way possible. Each year the Corps has furnished flowers for the five cemeteries which are under the charge of the Post; served the dinner to the comrades, held memorial services at the Soldiers' Monument and attended as special guests the orations given before the Post.

In 1889 the Post held a fair in Horticultural Hall, Boston, for the benefit of its Relief Fund, which proved very successful, and the Corps was presented with $987.70 for its Relief Fund, in recognition of its services, this amount being one-quarter of the net proceeds.

The year 1890 was one of unusual interest as well as responsibility, owing to the convening of the National Convention in Boston. Many of the members did good service on the various Department committees, while the Corps entertained as its special guest J. M. Wells Corps, Columbus, Ohio. A large hall was generously tendered by the Bethany Church Society, which was fitted up by the Corps as a dormitory and occupied by fifty ladies, meals being furnished at the Post Hall. Various entertainments were provided, including a trip down the harbor, a drive through the city and suburbs, reception at the High School Building, and seats from which to view the grand parade. Soon after, the Corps received from its guests an elegant silk banner, together with framed resolutions, in recognition of the fraternal courtesies extended. The sum of $459.00 was expended on account of the National Convention, $150.00 of the amount being contributed to the general fund of the Department.

This Corps has had the honor of entertaining many of the National Presidents, and one of the regular events of the year is the reception to the Department President and Staff, which always includes an invitation to Post 68. A "family party" on the 22d of February is one of the fixed festivals in which the Post and Corps and their families unite; this is an informal gathering, which the children especially enjoy. The Corps has pledged $500.00 towards defraying the expense of remodelling the Hall. Contributions to the various calls from the Department are always made cheerfully. The room at the Soldiers' Home which was furnished by the Corps, although now used for hospital purposes, will still be furnished with supplies as needed.

The Corps has been honored by the National and Department Presidents in the appointments of Aides, Department Inspectors and Assistant Inspectors, and in the election of Harriette L. Reed as Department Treasurer for three years, and Augusta A. Wales as Junior Vice and Department President. One item should be mentioned in this connection, viz.: the large number of young ladies and "loyal women" connected with the Corps. Special effort has always been made to secure such members, as it is upon these that the work of caring for the veteran must depend in the near future.

The Corps has expended for relief, $1,583.00, and turned over to Post, $2,306.30; and in all its work has had the support and respect of the public.

Membership, two hundred and fifty.

PRESIDENTS.

Augusta A. Wales	1886, 1887
Sarah A. Stiles	1888
Margaret T. Blanchard	1889, 1890
Abbie A. Haddock	1891
Annie E. Barnes	1892
Annie J. E. Perkins	1893
Susie R. Smith	1894

H. M. WARREN CORPS No. 69, WAKEFIELD.

Auxiliary to H. M. Warren Post No. 12, G.A.R., was instituted March 17, 1886, with seventy-six charter members, by Mrs. Lizabeth A. Turner, Department Senior Vice-President, assisted by Mrs. Mary E. Knowles, Department Chaplain.

This Corps has always endeavored to assist Post 12 in caring for the needy veterans and their families, and on each Memorial Day decorate the Soldiers' Lot and prepare a collation for the Post and its guests. It has co-operated with Post 12 in conducting two large fairs, at which time about $2,000.00 were realized, and the Corps has conducted one fair alone to swell the Post Building Fund, at which $450.00 were realized.

Since its institution the Corps has expended for relief, $346.73, and extended a large amount of relief other than money; for Memorial Day, $173.29; turned over to Post $573 61.

In January, 1892, we presented Post 12 with a handsome silk flag valued at $75.00.

Mrs. Margaret Hamilton, who served as an army nurse in the Union hospitals, is a member of this Corps.

Membership, ninety-eight.

PRESIDENTS.

Juliette H. Anderson	1886, 1887
C Della Locke	1888, 1889
Mary F. Aborn	1890
Abbie E. C. Eaton	1891
Ray E. Lane	1892, 1893
Susie A. Crosby	1894

CLARA BARTON CORPS No. 70, WARREN.

Was organized May 6, 1886, by Mrs. Mary M. Perry, Department Instituting and Installing Officer, with a charter membership of twenty-five.

This is a small, energetic Corps, and inspired by the name of the good samaritan they bear, endeavor never to be found wanting in any good work.

It has since its organization, turned over to Post, $138.75; expended in relief, $38.00; for Soldiers' Home, $73.00; also assisted the Post and the Sons of Veterans whenever called upon.

Membership, thirty.

PRESIDENTS.

Mary E. Jennings	1886, 1887
Lavinia B. Gage	1888, 1889, 1890
Hulda S. White	1891, 1892
Annie J. Bennett	1893, 1894

MALCOLM AMMIDOWN CORPS No. 71, SOUTHBRIDGE.

This Corps was instituted by Mrs. Mary M. Perry, Department Instituting and Installing Officer, May 27, 1886, with thirty charter members.

It has grown steadily, and has helped the needy and destitute, cheered the sorrowing, and tried to live up to its motto of Fraternity, Charity and Loyalty.

It has expended since organization, for relief, $453.35; turned over to Post, $423.75; value of relief other than money, $58 25.

Many socials are held by the Corps, at which the Post and Sons of Veterans with their families are guests.

Membership, seventy-six.

PRESIDENTS.

Mary J. Morse	1886, 1887
Ellen A. Corey	1888
Nellie F. Sanders	1889, 1890
Alvina Pratt	1891

MEMORIAL BUILDING

MILFORD, MASS.

Susie A. Morse	1892
Fannie Aldrich	1893
Hattie E. Morse	1894

MAJ. E. F. FLETCHER CORPS No. 72, MILFORD.

Auxiliary to Maj. E. F. Fletcher Post No. 22, was instituted May 27, 1886, by Mrs. L. A. Turner, Department Senior Vice-President, assisted by Mrs. Eliza F. Talbot of Holliston, with a charter membership of thirty-seven.

In November, 1886, the Corps assisted Post 22 in holding a fair, and one-half the proceeds ($378.05) was donated by the Post to the Corps, which placed the organization in a position to do effective relief work. Again in November, 1891, the two societies held a fair, realizing $1,033.52 which was shared equally. At all times the Corps has co-operated with the Post in entertainments, and always responded cheerfully to any calls for assistance that have been made.

At the election of officers Dec. 11, 1890, the faithful and efficient President, Mrs. Ella J. Bailey, who had so honorably filled that office for five years and had done such grand work for the advancement of the Order in Milford, resigned, much to our regret. Mrs. Ann M. Wilcox was elected President and has ably carried on the good work already established, and by her untiring fidelity to the principles of our Order has won the good will and respect of every member. Under her guidance the Corps has gained steadily in numbers and influence.

Since organization the Corps has expended over $400.00 in furnishings for the hall and banquet room.

The meetings of the Corps are held in the hall of Memorial Building, a fine granite structure which was built by the town of Milford to commemorate the services of her sons who were engaged in the Civil War. A flag presented by Corps 72 waves over the building; a piano has been purchased by the Corps and placed in the hall.

We have expended in local relief and turned over to Post $1,063.80, and take pride in adding to the furnishings of our beautiful hall, having recently procured an elegant silk cloth for the altar.

Annual receptions to the Post and Camp are held; also joint installations are the rule.

The Corps always attends Sunday memorial services, prepares the flowers for Memorial Day, and serves the banquet for the several bodies in the Memorial Hall.

We have contributed to the Soldiers' Home in Chelsea, Monroe Monument Fund, National Relief Corps Home at Madison, Ohio, Department Memorial Fund, and to various objects abroad that have been brought to our notice.

Membership, one hundred and forty.

PRESIDENTS.

Ella J. Bailey	. 1886, 1887, 1888, 1889, 1890
Ann M. Wilcox .	. 1891, 1892, 1893, 1894

JOE JOHNSON CORPS No. 73, NORTHBORO.

Instituted June 24, 1886, with thirty-five members, by Mrs. Hattie A. Ralph, Department Treasurer, assisted by Miss Mary E. Elliot, Department Secretary.

Since our organization, we have had little local relief work to do, assisting one family and one member in four other families to the amount of $5.00 each.

We have contributed articles of clothing to the Soldiers' Home at different times. We have also turned over to our Post small amounts of money. The result of co-operation with Posts in fairs and suppers has been successful, always adding to the Relief Fund of each organization.

As Memorial Day dawns near, we endeavor to interest the young by giving the decoration of the Soldiers' Monument to the first class in our high school each year, and by so doing they take a great interest in the work. The Corps always prepare the flowers for the decoration of the graves, and by invitation from the Post, decorate at the monument in memory of the thirteen soldiers who lie buried in unknown graves.

Membership, forty.

PRESIDENTS.

Charlotte A. Whitcomb	.	1886, 1887
Mary S. Wood . .	.	1888, 1889
Mary W. Corey . .		1890, 1891, 1892
Charlotte A. Whitcomb	.	1893, 1894

GEORGE H. MANTIEN CORPS No. 74, PLAINVILLE.

Was instituted by Mrs. Emma B. Lowd, Department Junior Vice-President, Oct. 19, 1886, with a charter membership of eighteen.

The Corps, though small in number, is fully alive to the needs of the veterans, and are always busy doing whatever their hands are able, to relieve the calls made upon them.

Contributions have been made to the various funds and to the Soldiers' Home; given to Post a silk flag and furnishings for Post hall, $250.00; and contributed to the funds for Southern battlefields and National Convention, 1890; given a flag for public school; cash expended in relief, $232.00; value of relief other than money, $175.75; total disbursements, $753.45.

Membership, thirty-nine.

PRESIDENTS.

Anna F. Mathewson	. . .	1886, 1887
Lizzie N. Wade	. . . .	1888, 1889
Carrie Coombs	.	1890, 1891, 1892, 1893, 1894

B. F. BUTLER CORPS No. 75, LOWELL.

In October, 1886, Comrade O. M. Cousins, at that time Chaplain of Post 42, G.A.R., and Mrs. Cousins brought together a few ladies, and the subject was discussed of forming an auxiliary to the Post. It was met with approval by the Post, and on Oct. 19, 1886, Mrs. S. Agnes Parker, Department President, instituted Corps 75 with seventeen charter members, assisted by Mrs. Annie E. Tuttle of Corps 33. At the time of institution Post 42 presented its auxiliary with ten dollars to assist in defraying the expenses of institution. The Corps has tried to fulfill its obligations, and during its existence has turned over to Post 42, $354.16. Its members have cared for the sick, also assisted in the care of an army nurse who was friendless and needed loving sympathy. Her last days were comforted, as our members cared for her until she was at last laid away forever.

Membership, fifty-seven.

PRESIDENTS.

Elizabeth T. Beane	1886, 1887
Kate T. Dimon	1888
Elizabeth T. Bean	1889, 1890
Ida I. Sleeper	1891
Mary C. Lynch	1892
Alfreda H. Perkins	1893
Truelove P. Kinney	1894

L. L. MERRICK CORPS No. 76, PALMER.

Was instituted by Mrs. Mary M. Perry, Department Instituting and Installing Officer, Nov. 19, 1886, with twenty charter members.

The Corps has always assisted the Post in whatever it has undertaken — on Memorial Day by providing a dinner, and flowers to decorate the graves of their fallen heroes. The Corps members accompany the Post to the different cemeteries of the town, and help distribute the flowers. The anniversaries of the Corps are annually celebrated, and as the Post hall is commodious these occasions have been thoroughly enjoyed by a great many people.

In 1890 the town erected a building as a memorial to the soldiers, to contain a library and hall for the G.A.R. It was dedicated in April, 1891, by Rev. E. A. Perry of Fort Wayne, N.Y. (a former member of Post 107), and Dr. C. H. Eaton, of N.Y.

In December, 1891, a camp-fire was held, when many Department officers of the G.A.R. and W.R.C. were present, also friends of the Order from adjoining towns.

A committee has been appointed to confer with the teachers of the public schools regarding the adoption of a flag salute.

The Corps has expended in relief, $287.97; for Soldiers' Home, $219.64; for National Encampment, Boston (1890), $35.00; turned over to Post, $291.00.

February 22 is annually observed by the Corps in a public manner. The community expect that the Corps will have something worth attending that day or evening, and no other order or church think of filling that date.

Membership, fifty-nine.

PRESIDENTS.

Delilah S. Davis	1886, 1887, 1888, 1889, 1890
Clara B. Ellis	1891, 1892
Abbie J. Lawton	1893, 1894

COL. ALLEN CORPS No. 77, GLOUCESTER.

Was instituted Dec. 29, 1886, with fifty-four charter members, of whom twenty-seven were formerly members of the first G.A.R. ladies organization in the country. The Corps was instituted and officers installed by Mrs. Mary E. Knowles, Department Chaplain. G.A.R. Hall, in which the meetings of the Corps were held, was destroyed by fire, Feb. 15, 1890, and the Corps lost its books of record, General Order File, Letter File, etc.; consequently a complete history of the Corps cannot be given. This necessitated a temporary home for the time being, but we soon returned to our old quarters.

Corps 77 has assisted the Post in conducting five fairs, and also assisted the Sons of Veterans, in two fairs; has turned over to the Post more than $4,000.00 in money, and presented a handsome piano to the Post for its hall; also twelve dozen silver spoons, on the Post's twenty-fifth anniversary. The Corps has charge of a room at the Soldiers' Home, named in honor of Mary E. Knowles who was Department President when the room was named in her honor.

Oct. 21, 1892, the Corps gave a reception to the Department officers in the evening, and the next day a drive was taken around Cape Ann and a visit made to the Bay View granite quarries.

Membership, one hundred and one.

PRESIDENTS.

Eva T. Cook	1886, 1887, 1888, 1889
Mary P. Lloyd	1890
Georgie A. Center	1891, 1892
Sarah E. Story	1893
Mary J. Parkhurst	1894

GEORGE K. BIRD CORPS No. 78, NORWOOD.

Was organized Jan. 22, 1887, by Mrs. Mary E. Knowles, Department Chaplain, with a charter membership of twenty-one. It was instituted as No. 80, but was subsequently changed to 78, by authority of the Department President, to correspond with the number of the Post to which it is auxiliary.

The Corps has given the Merchants' Carnival and other entertainments with good financial results and since its organization has expended in relief $143.82; turned over to Post, $130.00; for Encampment, Boston, 1890, $50.00. It has also presented the Post with a handsome flag, and a clock for its hall. Although small, the Corps entered into the work with a zealous determination to carry out the principles of the Order.

Many entertainments have been held, and every year new members are added to our roll.

Membership, forty-three.

PRESIDENTS.

Mary A. Pratt	1887
Ida M. Hayford	1888
Susie M. Nelson	1889
Ida M. Hayford	1890
Fannie Fuller	1891
Ida M. Hayford	1892
Mary A. Squires	1893
Georgie W. May	1894

FRANCIS WASHBURN CORPS No. 79, BRIGHTON.

Was instituted Jan. 11, 1887, with a charter membership of seventeen, by Miss Mary E. Elliot, Department Secretary, assisted by Mrs. Angela H. Scranton, Department Aid.

The object of its organization, to aid the Post in any way we can best serve its interests and to assist the veteran and his dependent ones, has been carried out from year to year to the best of our ability.

Relief extended to soldiers and their families	$586 24
Turned over to Post	454 05
Aid extended to Soldiers' Home	194 37
Total	$1,234 66

Aid has also been extended Southern Posts for Memorial Day, and the Camp of Sons of Veterans has been remembered.

In addition to the above, we have assisted the Post on all Memorial Days, taking part in the services by furnishing floral tributes for the unknown dead, army nurses and fallen comrades; also providing a collation for the Post.

We have striven to prove that we are truly an auxiliary, not only in name, but in deed. The Sons of Veterans attached to our Post we have aided whenever the opportunity presented, by selling tickets for their entertainments, by donations of money, by procuring their flags and by encouraging words and loyal support in carrying out the principles for which the association stands pledged.

For four years we have owned and cared for a room at the Soldiers' Home, doing our share in this way to make the declining years of the veteran more comfortable. We have given several entertainments at the Home for the enjoyment of the inmates. In addition to our local relief work we have paid the board of one of our sister members, who has been sick in another State; trying to make her pathway brighter by sending cheerful message and carrying into the work the teaching of the "Golden Rule." To Mrs. Angela H. Scranton credit is due for the missionary work which resulted in the Corps being organized.

Membership, ninety.

PRESIDENTS.

Lizzie W. Sanborn	1887
E. Francena Gray	1888
Emma Collier	1889, 1890, 1891
Mary L. Davis	1892
Dorcas H. Lyman	1893, 1894

ARTHUR G. BISCOE CORPS No. 80, WESTBOROUGH.

Was organized by Mrs. Hattie A. Ralph, Department Treasurer, Jan. 4, 1887, with forty-nine charter members; Miss Mary E. Elliot, Department Secretary, assisted in the services. The growth of the Corps has been steady and the work has prospered.

Installations have always been public, with Post 80 and Camp 76 as invited guests. Fraternal visits have been exchanged with Post and Camp, and in 1892 the Post instituted "Ladies' Night," which occurs the fifth Monday of the month; these meetings have been of mutual benefit and strengthened the bond existing between us.

The amount expended in relief has been upwards of $200.00 in cash and $188.00 other than money, including donations to Soldiers' Home, Chelsea, National W.R.C. Home, Army Nurse Fund, Memorial Fund, Richmond, Va. For the last three and a half years we have turned over to the Post $100.00 annually and assisted in a fair, the proceeds of which furnished the new Post hall; also contributed $63.00 to the National Encampment (1890). Under the direction of the Home and Employment Committee, a sewing circle was formed which has accomplished much good.

On Memorial Day it is our privilege to decorate the Soldiers' Monument and prepare the designs for the unknown dead and for army nurses; we form in hollow square around the monument during the services by the Post and march with the comrades to the hall for the concluding exercises.

> And on that hallowed Day of days,
> The one the patriot loves the best,
> We lay Spring's fairest, choicest sprays
> Upon the mounds 'neath which they rest.

At the dedication of our new hall, one of our number, Mrs. Essie M. Howells, gave the poem which she afterward published and with the proceeds presented the Post with a book-case, two silk flags for the altar; other small articles have been presented the Post by different members. We were honored guests at the silver anniversary of Post 80. In 1891, Corps 80 exemplified the work of the Order in the presence of Mrs. Wales, Department President, and delegates from eleven adjacent Corps.

We review the labors and results of the past with pleasure, and look forward to even greater usefulness in the future.

Membership, ninety-seven.

PRESIDENTS.

Mattie A. Fay	1887, 1888
Jane M. Chase	1889, 1890
Margie A. Sawyer	1891
Mary A. Giese	1892
Alice J. Forbush	1893
Mary J. Exley	1894

CHARLES DEVENS CORPS No. 81, OXFORD.

On Feb. 2, 1888, Mrs. Mary M. Perry, Department Instituting and Installing Officer, instituted Corps 81 with twenty-three charter members.

In the autumn of 1889 the Corps held a fair in Memorial Hall which was a great success financially, as well as socially, and netted §298.30. A year later we assisted the Post in a fair, which was also successful.

The history of Corps 81 has been very uneventful. Very pleasant relations have existed between our Corps and members of Camp 12, Sons of Veterans.

CLARE H. BURLEIGH

Tenth Department President 1934

It is needless to say that we have always assisted the Post whenever called upon, and in April, 1894, voted $50.00 to its treasury. Membership, nineteen.

PRESIDENTS.

Lottie M. Cushman	1888
Harriet M. Yeomans	1889
Ruth A. Bowdish	1890, 1891
Laura A. Humes	1892, 1893, 1894

HUBBARD V. SMITH CORPS No. 82, ATHOL.

Was instituted Feb. 22, 1887, with forty-one charter members, by Mrs. Mary M. Perry of Springfield, Department Instituting and Installing Officer, assisted by Mrs. Helen Packard of Springfield.

Corps 82 has been favored with officers of rare ability, including in its membership some of the most energetic, cultivated and influential women of Athol.

Its entertainments are of the first order, and are very popular among the citizens. During the eight years since the institution of this Corps it has presented a "Kirmess" and other elaborate entertainments, several fairs, and held concerts, etc., for the benefit of its funds. Its influence and example are valued by the patriotic townspeople.

The average attendance at regular meetings is sixty-four, and much interest is manifested in the work. It is the aim of the Corps to place a monument to the unknown dead in the local cemetery before next Memorial Day — this being a suggestion of the President, Mrs. Hamilton.

Amount turned over to Post 140, $998.84; relief extended in money, $386.00; other than money, $161.19.

Membership, one hundred and eighty-six.

PRESIDENTS.

Clare H. Burleigh	1887, 1888
Minnie K. Pitts	1889
Clare H. Burleigh	1890
Mercie S. Doane	1891, 1892
Julia Hamilton	1893, 1894

E. S. CLARK CORPS No. 83, GROTON.

This Corps has been organized but a few months, having been instituted May 21, 1894. Mrs. Flora A. Smith, Department Instituting and Installing Officer, conducted the institution ceremonies, and Mrs. Clare H. Burleigh, Department President, installed the officers.

The Corps was formed through the efforts of Mrs. Nina B. Lovejoy of Ayer, Department Aid.

It was given the number formerly belonging to Woburn Corps (83), as the number following the last Corps instituted (161) was assigned by special request of Woburn Post to its auxiliary.

There were eighteen charter members, and the present membership is twenty-five.

PRESIDENT.

Marcia W. Parkhurst . . 1894

BURBANK CORPS No. 84, WOBURN.

Burbank Corps, auxiliary to Burbank Post No. 33, was instituted March 17, 1887, by Mrs. Emma B. Lowd, Department Junior Vice-President. The charter membership, although not as large in number as that of many other Corps (being only thirty-three), was composed of women deeply interested in the noble work for which we are organized.

There were present at the installation in the evening comrades of Post 33 and a large number of invited guests, on which occasion Commander Colgate presented the newly-installed officers a set of badges as a gift from the comrades.

Only a short time elapsed before we were called upon to exemplify the work of our Order in assisting a soldier's family, none of whom were members of either Post or Corps. Since then we have had many calls, all of which have found ready and cheerful responses. The year following calls for relief increased and more work was done.

A handsome Bible was presented to the Post in February, 1888, and at the close of the year, learning that the Post was desirous of increasing its relief fund, arrangements were made to hold a Gypsy Encampment in February, 1889, for the benefit of the Post. This proved very successful and $200.00 turned over to the Post treasury.

On the evening of March 14, 1890, a beautiful silk parade flag was presented the Post, Mrs. Mary E. Knowles in her usual able manner making the presentation in behalf of Corps 84. The flag was one of the best made by Col. William Beals, and was obtained through the efforts of Mrs. Sarah A. Woodside, Past President, by contributions from members of the Corps and associate members of the Post.

On the evening of Memorial Day, a concert of war songs was given by one hundred school children.

The close of 1891 found Post 33 without a burial fund, having had many calls from this fund which exhausted it.

March 9, 1892, a fair was opened with Mrs. P. A. Whittier, President, as Chairman of the Committee, for the success of which the comrades worked with us. When the fair closed on the night of the 12th all felt repaid for their hard work, as $645.14 were realized. $300.00 of this amount were given to the Post, and $81.28 expended for hall furnishings. On May 13, a bunting flag was presented to the Post, and a week later an altar flag was purchased for use of Post and Corps.

Memorial Day has ever been a busy one with us; tributes to the unknown dead and those buried on Southern battlefields have been placed on the Common. Assistance is rendered the Post in preparing a banquet for about two hundred guests. Since we were organized suppers have been served at the close of all afternoon meetings, to which the comrades have been invited.

Corps 84 has a room at the Soldiers' Home, for which nearly $100.00 have been expended. Annual visits are made to the Home and donations left for the inmates. $25.00 were given to the Department towards defraying the expenses of the National Convention in Boston. Extensive repairs have been made on the hall and banquet room of Grand Army building, and a ready response has greeted all calls from the relief fund.

Cash expended for relief . . . $309 34
Relief other than money . . . 360 60
Amount turned over to Post . . . 762 56

Over one thousand calls have been made on the sick and those needing assistance.

Membership, one hundred.

PRESIDENTS.

Sarah A. Woodside	1887, 1888, 1889
Anna L. Randall	1890
Sarah A. Woodside	1891
Pauline A. Whitten	1892
Ruth Ward	1893, 1894

GALEN ORR CORPS No. 85, NEEDHAM.

Was instituted March 23, 1887, by Mrs. Mary E. Knowles, Department Chaplain, with a charter membership of twenty-three. The Corps has always realized that it was organized to assist the Post to which it is auxiliary, and has ever tried to do its duty. The amount of relief work is small, having expended only $46.50; turned over to Post in cash, $10.00; cash donation to Soldiers' Home, $8.00; to Phil. Kearney Post, $2.00. The Corps has held social meetings, and assisted the Post in one fair. No discordant notes have marred the rhythm of our work.

The Corps has been especially happy with its leading officers, who have held the highest stations since its organization. The President has been honored by the Department for two successive years by the appointment of Assistant Inspector, and each member feels it is an honor rightly bestowed. As a Corps we are, and wish to be, one of the willing auxiliaries of the Grand Army of the Republic.

Membership, forty-two.

PRESIDENTS.

Anna M. Adams	1887, 1888
Emily Henderson	1889
Addie S. Willgoose	1890, 1891, 1892, 1893
Jane B. Upham	1894

ALANSON HAMILTON CORPS No. 86, WEST BROOKFIELD.

Mrs. Mary M. Perry, Department Instituting and Installing Officer, instituted this Corps April 6, 1887, with seventeen charter members. That night the husband of one of our members was killed on the railroad. He was buried by the Post, and the Corps assumed all the care and assisted the family. During a long sickness of the afflicted member and her daughter, we were enabled in many ways to lighten their burdens. Thus we early learned and tried to show others our principles of Fraternity, Charity and Loyalty.

During the following winter we realized $50.00 from a supper and gave the money to the Post, and we have assisted the comrades in furnishing their hall. We have continued from year to year working in any way we could for the Post and helping whatever object seemed the most needy, to the amount of about $150.00.

We have taken special interest in caring for the sick; have contributed to the Soldiers' Home and other funds, and the calls for sympathy and assistance have been promptly responded to, and there have been many cases of sickness where a woman's hand and heart have lightened burdens almost too heavy to be borne.

Membership, twenty-nine.

PRESIDENTS.

Sophronia Griffin	1887, 1888, 1889
Carrie B. Gilbert	1890
Sophronia Griffin	1891, 1892
Jennie E. Allen	1893, 1894

CHARLES SUMNER CORPS No. 87, GROVELAND.

In the winter of 1887, Commander Isaac C. Day of Post 101 visited Boston and heard Miss Mary E. Elliot, Department Secretary of Massachusetts W.R.C., speak in Horticultural Hall in behalf of the Woman's Relief Corps; her words having made such an impression on his mind on his return home he immediately took the necessary steps toward the formation of a Corps in Groveland, auxiliary to Post 101, G.A.R.; and on March 31, 1887, Corps 87 was instituted by Mrs. Emma B. Lowd, Department Junior Vice-President, with thirty-three charter members. Miss Elliot assisted in the service.

The first two years the work of the Corps consisted in aiding Post 101 in furnishing its hall; officers' desks and chairs were purchased and a parlor was arranged and furnished throughout by the Corps.

The calls for local relief being small, the energies of the Corps were turned toward assisting Post 101 in enlarging its charity fund and keeping the Post hall in good repair. Cash donations amounting to $10.00 have been turned over to Post; many entertainments, sociables, dramas and fairs were held, which were successful socially and financially, and in this way the comrades were assisted in defraying their expenses to the National Encampment at Boston and Washington. A grand picnic was held in 1891, at which time many prominent members of the Grand Army of the Republic and Woman's Relief Corps were invited guests.

As Mrs. Annie K. Day had served as President for five years, the Corps decided to celebrate its birthday in April, 1892, and the Department President Mrs. Mary G. Deane, Department Secretary Miss Mary E. Elliot and Past Department President Mrs. Emma B. Lowd, were honored guests.

The work of the Corps from year to year is much the same. Contributions have been sent to the Soldiers' Home from time to time, amounting to $50.00, and calls from the Department answered whenever possible.

Membership, ninety-nine.

Mrs. Annie K. Day has served as President since organization. She has also served the Department as Instituting and Installing Officer and for two consecutive years as a member of the Department Executive Board. She has also been appointed Assistant National Inspector.

ROUSE R. CLARK CORPS No. 88, WHITINSVILLE.

Through the efforts of several ladies of Whitinsville (in the township of Northbridge), a Relief Corps, auxiliary to Rouse R. Clark Post, was organized May 3, 1893, by Mrs. Lizzie F. Mudgett, Department Instituting and Installing Officer, assisted by Mrs. Emily L. Clark, Department President. There were forty charter members.

A relief fund has been established and the Corps expects to do a good work in the future.

Membership, twenty-eight.

PRESIDENT.

Harriet N. Burr . . . 1893, 1894

FRANKLIN CORPS No. 89, FRANKLIN.

Was organized June 14, 1891, with twenty-three charter members, by Mrs. Annie K. Day, Department Instituting and Installing Officer.

The Corps has steadily increased in membership and interest. There is but little relief work required in Franklin, but the Corps stands ready to advance the principles of the Order, and is in a prosperous condition.

Membership, seventy-five.

PRESIDENTS.

Ellen A. Sanborn . . . 1891, 1892, 1893
Lena Holbrook 1894

D. G. FARRAGUT CORPS No. 90, GARDNER.

Was instituted May 17, 1887, by Mrs. Mary M. Perry, Department Instituting and Installing Officer, assisted by members of Corps 82, Athol, with twenty-five charter members.

The work has been very successful, and the Corps is noted for its excellent entertainments which have netted large sums to its treasury; $600.00 were added as the result of one — a fair and carnival. We presented the Post a silk flag in 1890.

The Post Building Fund Association received a gift of $500.00 from the Corps, and when the Memorial Building was completed in 1893, the Corps bought new desks, altars and pedestals for the Post, and also purchased a piano for the hall, and furnishings for the banquet-room.

The National Convention Fund of 1890 received $75.00 from the Corps. Several hundred dollars have been expended for local relief work, and contributions sent the Soldiers' Home, the Memorial Fund, the National W.R.C. Home, and in aid of Memorial Day in the South, amounting to nearly $1,500.00.

Membership, ninety-six.

PRESIDENTS.

Clara E. Howe	1887, 1888, 1889
Anna M. Whitney	1890
Ellen C. Wood	1891, 1892
Anna M. Whitney	1893
Francena M. Jillson	1894

WASHINGTON CORPS No. 91, SOUTH BOSTON.

Was instituted Oct. 9, 1893, by Mrs. Lizzie F. Mudgett, Department Instituting and Installing Officer, with twelve charter members.

A beautiful flag has been presented Washington Post, and in all its work this Corps has shown a sincere interest in the Post to which it is auxiliary.

Entertainments, socials, etc., are held for the benefit of its treasury; and the Corps has united with Washington Post in an appropriate observance of Memorial Day.

Membership. twenty.

PRESIDENT.

Frances M. O'Neil	1893, 1894

ARMSTRONG CORPS No. 92, MONTAGUE.

Was instituted June 22, 1887, by Mrs. Mary M. Perry, Department Instituting and Installing Officer. Since that time it has turned over to the Post $45.00, and has expended for Relief, $30.00. Aid has been given the Soldiers' Home at Chelsea and the National W.R.C. Home. Estimated value of relief other than money, $60.00.

Our members are widely scattered in a farming community, and have many claims upon their time, but the few who are enrolled in our Order feel a deep interest in its work.

Membership, eighteen.

PRESIDENTS.

Lulu A. Mann	1887, 1888
Laura A. Watson	1889
Almena S. Lougee	1890
Lulu A. Mann	1891, 1892, 1893
Josie A. Sewell	1894

PRESTON CORPS No. 93, BEVERLY FARMS.

Was instituted Oct. 14, 1887, by Mrs. Mary E. Knowles, Department Chaplain, with forty-six charter members.

The local calls for relief have been few, but the members of Corps 93 have ever been ready to render assistance; many calls have been made upon the sick, and $80.40 spent in relief. Donations to Soldiers' and National W.R.C. Homes amounting to $27.00 have been forwarded, also a donation of $10.00 toward furnishing flowers for southern cemeteries. The Corps has turned over to Post $110.00 in cash, besides presenting a silk flag and an altar at a cost of $85.00, and has presented the Sons of Veterans Camp with $10.00 toward purchasing a flag.

Since organization the Corps has always assisted Post G.A.R. in the observance of Memorial Day and twined wreaths and furnished flowers for the graves of the fallen heroes.

Membership, sixty.

PRESIDENTS.

Emma J. Abbott	1887, 1888, 1889
Alice L. Preston	1890, 1891
Mary E. Cullen	1892
Sarah E. Poole	1893
Alice P. Collamore	1894

GEN. SYLVANUS THAYER CORPS No. 94, SOUTH BRAINTREE.

Was instituted Nov. 14, 1887, with thirty-eight charter members, by Mrs. Emma B. Lowd, Department Junior Vice-President.

During the seven years of its existence it has turned over to Post money to the amount of $85.00 and has presented the Post with articles for hall valued at $87.25. Assisted in a large fair which netted $900.00.

The Corps expended in relief $137.00 and has ever responded to appeals from other Corps or from Department. In October, 1889, a barrel of bedding and clothing was sent to the Soldiers' Home in Chelsea. In 1890 Corps 94 sent $75.00 to Headquarters for the Encampment Fund. In January, 1890, sent $5.00 to the Army Nurse Fund and in November of the same year sent $5.00 to the Woman's Relief Corps Home in Ohio. In December, 1891, sent $5.00 toward the Fair for the benefit of the Soldiers' Home. In December, 1892, sent $5.00 for the Monroe Monument Fund.

Each year on the 14th of November, Corps 94 celebrates its anniversary, at which time Post 87 is always an honored guest.

On Memorial Days Corps 94 assists the Post in its services, and prepares a collation for all who take part in the services of the day.

Membership, ninety-six.

PRESIDENTS.

Mary L. Merritt	1887, 1888, 1889, 1890
Margaret V. Carmichael	1891, 1892
Mary L. Merritt	1893
Carrie M. Fisher	1894

R. A. PIERCE CORPS No. 95, NEW BEDFORD.

Was instituted Jan. 3, 1891, by Mrs. Mary E. Knowles, Department President, assisted by Mrs. Mary G. Deane of Corps 106, Fall River, and Mrs. Lucy M. James of Corps 53, New Bedford. There were thirty-seven charter members.

We have assisted our Post in every way possible, turning over to its treasury over $280.00, and presenting an altar and cover, a United States flag, a Post flag and guidons, and May 25, 1894, an elegant State flag, making contributions to the Post to the amount of $500.00. Over $350.00 have been expended in relief.

Corps 95 has contributed to the Soldiers' Home and to the Army Nurse Funds, also to Phil Kearney Post of Richmond, Va., to assist in decorating graves at the South.

We visit the sick and afflicted, assist needy soldiers and their families (always bearing in mind that we must not interfere with our sister Corps); we frequently have sociables for the benefit of the Post and Camp, and are busy most of the time working quietly, but doing with our might whatever our hands find to do.

When asking a Post Commander if he thought we had done anything worth referring to, he said: "You are always doing for us. Post 190 could not succeed without you."

Special interest is taken in Memorial Day, and Post and Corps unite in the plans for the day.

Membership, seventy-one.

PRESIDENTS.

Elizabeth P. Sawyer	1891, 1892, 1893
Abbie C. Gardiner	1894

MAJOR HOW CORPS No. 96, HAVERHILL.

Was instituted Jan. 23, 1889, with thirty-nine charter members, by Mrs. E. V. Lang, Department Instituting and Installing Officer, assisted by Mrs. Emma B. Lowd, Department President. A public installation was held on the evening of the same day, a large number of the comrades of Post 47 being present.

There has been much up-hill work since the organization of this Corps, but with true loyalty to the Post to which it stands auxiliary, it has worked onward and upward to its present standing, and has now a bright prospect of future success.

During its existence it has expended in relief, $292.44; estimated value of relief other than money, $286.89; turned over to Post 47 G.A.R., $1,187.09.

Membership, one hundred and fifty-six.

PRESIDENTS.

Louisa J. Savage	1889, 1890
Lucinda W. Martin	1891, 1892
A. Lizzie Wood	1893
Anna F. Shannon	1894

GEORGE G. MEADE CORPS No. 97, LEXINGTON.

Corps 97 of Lexington owes its origin to the energy and enthusiasm of Mrs. Augusta A. Randall, at that time a Department Aide and President of Corps 43, Arlington. It was instituted Jan. 10, 1888, by Miss Mary E. Elliot, Department Secretary, assisted by Mrs. Randall, with a charter membership of twenty-nine.

At the time of the National Encampment in Boston (1890) the Corps entertained a delegation from California, and many other visiting members. Through the combined efforts of Post and Corps both organizations are occupying homelike and comfortable quarters, consisting of hall, dining-room and ante-rooms.

During the nearly seven years of its existence Corps 97 has turned over to the Post more than $500.00; has donated over $50.00 to the National W.R.C. Home; has visited and donated to the Soldiers' Home in Chelsea and the Ladies' Aid Association, and has responded to almost all of the outside calls which are constantly being presented. There is not the opportunity in a country town for extended relief, but every case which has been presented has received immediate attention. The comrades gratefully acknowledge their indebtedness to Corps 97.

In February, 1892, at the suggestion of the Commander, color guards were formed in three schools in Lexington, having charge of their school flags and doing escort duty on Memorial Day and other important occasions. The swords and equipments for these guards were given by Corps 97. A patriotic spirit is thus inculcated in the children, and we feel that the work of the W.R.C. in Lexington is one of the influences for good.

Membership, fifty-three.

PRESIDENTS.

Sarah A. Darling . . . 1888, 1889, 1890
Maria L. Kirkland 1891, 1892
Julia C. Maynard 1893, 1894

FRANCIS A. CLARY CORPS No. 98, CONWAY.

Was instituted Jan. 18, 1888, with a charter membership of fourteen, by Mrs. Mary M. Perry, Department Instituting and Installing Officer.

In spite of small numbers it is in good working condition, doing all that lies in its power to promote the interests of the veterans.

Together with Post, and Camp of Sons of Veterans, many social gatherings are held, when each organization realizes a little for its treasury.

Memorial Day is always a busy day for Corps 98; wreaths, crosses and baskets of flowers are prepared each year for the graves of the comrades; the cross erected in one of the cemeteries in "Memory of the Unknown Dead," is covered with evergreens and flags. A dinner is provided for the Post, Sons of Veterans and their guests, as they halt in the center of the little town of Conway, in their march to the graves of their comrades in the different cemeteries.

In March, 1890, the Corps decided to take charge of a room at the Soldiers' Home, Chelsea, and contributed $120.00 for this purpose. The membership of both Post and Corps being small, the calls for immediate relief are few; $25.00 have been expended in relief, besides forwarding $10.00 for the Department Memorial Home Fund.

The Corps has sent contributions for the past two years to Phil Kearney Post, Va., to assist in decorating the graves of the unknown dead; it also sent a contribution toward the Encampment Fund of 1890.

Membership, twenty-seven.

PRESIDENTS.

Mattie J. Dill	. .	1888, 1889
Annie M. Pease	.	1890, 1891
Ellen Hamilton	.	1892, 1893
Elisabeth Johnson	. .	1894

A. ST. JOHN CHAMBRE CORPS No. 99, STOUGHTON.

On Jan. 20, 1888, a Relief Corps was instituted in Stoughton with fifteen charter members, by Mrs. L. A. Turner, Department Senior Vice-President.

But little progress was made during the first four years, as the membership did not exceed twenty. The Corps has increased since that time, and now has a membership of forty-six.

It has expended $105.00 for relief, and $350.00 (the proceeds from fairs, etc.,) have been turned over to Post 72 of Stoughton.

The members of the Post and Corps have always shown a united interest in the welfare of both societies. At all gatherings of the comrades where refreshments are in order, our members usually prepare the collation.

On each Memorial Day the Post extends an invitation to the Corps to assist in the services of the day. A collation is prepared by the Corps, and our members visit the cemetery in company with the Post and Camp, where services are held at the Post lot in memory of the loyal dead buried in distant and in unknown graves. It is expected that on next Memorial Day, through the exertions of Post, Corps and Camp, a monument will be placed on this lot and dedicated to the memory of "Stoughton's Patriot Dead in Unknown Graves."

PRESIDENTS.

Emma F. P. Monk	1888, 1889, 1890
Eliza M. Randall	1891, 1892, 1893
Carrie I. Pratt	1894

REVERE CORPS No. 100, CANTON.

Was instituted July 18, 1892, with a charter membership of twenty-five, by Mrs. Annie K. Day, Department Instituting and Installing Officer. Although its foundation is of so recent a date it had been carrying on a work corresponding to its own some nine years, as an independent organization known as the Ladies' Relief Society, established in 1883. This Society stood ready to render assistance to Revere Post No. 94 G.A.R., and did so whenever desired. It dispensed its charities to any in need throughout the town, working quietly, persistently, faithfully. Corps 100 has no history of the past as a Corps, but it has hopes in a future that may bear record of its faithful membership and good work.

Membership, forty-eight.

PRESIDENTS.

Harriett F. Holmes	1892, 1893
Emma F. Smith	1894

GILMAN C. PARKER CORPS No. 101, WINCHENDON.

This Corps was instituted with forty-nine charter members by Mrs. Emma B. Lowd, Department President, March 9, 1888. Great interest is taken in the work, and some of the members travel two miles to attend the meetings.

There is a relief fund of about $300.00, and the Corps has accomplished a good work in assisting the Post. Our members are very earnest in Memorial Day work and in all efforts for the cause. Corps 101 is in a very prosperous condition.

Membership, forty-nine.

PRESIDENTS.

Aurilla Cutter	1888
Ellen Stearns	1889, 1890
Finette Barnes	1891
Rebecca J. Holman	1892, 1893
Nancy H. Souther	1894

REYNOLDS CORPS No. 102, WEYMOUTH.

Organized Jan. 31, 1893, with seventy-four charter members, by Mrs. Mary G. Deane, Department President, assisted by Mrs. Emilie L. W. Waterman, Chairman Department Executive Board.

This Corps has furnished a room in Soldiers' Home, and in October forty-five of our members visited the Home and gave an entertainment to the soldiers, consisting of instrumental and vocal music, recitations, etc.

This Corps has in its several funds about $143.00; has contributed to Munroe Monument Fund, Soldiers' Home, and donated flags for Southern battlefields, also Memorial Home Fund.

Membership, one hundred and twenty-eight.

PRESIDENT.

Marion E. Hastings	1893, 1894

PAUL REVERE CORPS No. 103, QUINCY.

Was instituted May 7, 1888, by Mrs. S. Agnes Parker, Past Department President, with a charter membership of twenty-four.

In the fall of this year Post 88 invited the Corps to assist in carrying on a fair which resulted in a net gain of $465.64.

The Corps donated $60.00 toward the Encampment Fund of 1890, besides decorating and keeping fresh flowers in one room of the Congregational building in Boston, prepared meals and entertained Post 112 of Staten Island, N. Y., and supplied five of the Information Committee on duty in Boston.

In Mt. Wollaston Cemetery, Quincy, there is a lot dedicated to the soldiers and sailors who sleep in unknown graves. On this lot the Corps has placed an urn filled with growing plants, and on Memorial Day we hold a special service after assisting the comrades at their lot.

Corps 103 has assumed the care of a room at the Soldiers' Home, Chelsea, and has always responded to all calls from the Department or the Post to which we are auxiliary, and these efforts have met with appreciation.

Membership, eighty-five.

PRESIDENTS.

Prudence H. Stokes	1888, 1889
Isabel A. Souther	1890, 1891
Laura E. Holt	1892
Sarah J. Williamson	1893
Electa E. Field	1894

GEN. HORACE C. LEE CORPS No. 104, BLANDFORD.

Was instituted May 15, 1888, by Mrs. Mary M. Perry, Department Senior Vice-President, with thirteen charter members.

The Corps co-operates with the Post in preparing wreaths and flowers for Memorial Day and also furnishes a collation to the comrades.

Our membership is so scattered that the work is conducted under great difficulties. Over one hundred dollars have been expended from the Corps treasury for relief, and other assistance has been given soldiers and their families, the amount of which cannot be estimated.

Membership, twenty-four.

PRESIDENTS.

Celia R. Chapman	1888, 1889
Julia C. Loveland	1890
Ellen E. Hayden	1891
Celia E. Chapman	1892
Elvira V. Warfield	1893, 1894

J. ORSON FISKE CORPS No. 105, UPTON.

Was instituted July 19, 1888, with twenty-five charter members, by Mrs. Elizabeth V. Lang, Department Instituting and Installing Officer.

A Relief Fund was started immediately on formation and has increased with the growth of the Corps; every case which is presented is cared for by the Relief Committee.

The first assistance rendered to the Post was in holding a fair, the proceeds of which were equally divided between the three organizations, Post, Corps and Camp. On Jan. 2, 1889, the Corps held a joint installation with Post and Camp and these pleasant gatherings have been repeated yearly.

In October, 1890, the town of Upton erected a beautiful Soldiers' Monument. The Corps assisted at the dedication, and served the collation to several hundred guests from the neighboring Posts and Corps. In August, 1890, the Post and Corps entertained the 21st Regiment, furnishing dinner for four hundred people. In 1891 the Corps again assisted Post 105 in holding a fair for the purpose of raising funds to refurnish the Post hall; this was successful, netting $300.00. July 19, 1893, Corps 105 celebrated its fifth anniversary, at which Post 105 and Sons of Veterans were invited guests. The Corps contributed $30.00 toward the Encampment Fund for 1890.

On Memorial Day the Corps unites with Post 105 in holding services at the Soldiers' Monument, also in the cemetery at the grave of J. Orson Fiske, the comrade for whom the Post and Corps are named; a collation is served by the Corps at the close of the services to Posts, Corps, Camp and invited guests.

Entertainments, suppers and socials have been held to replenish the treasury, and a sewing circle, which was organized in the early days of the Corps, has proved to be very helpful, furnishing clothing for many a needy family. Donations of money and bedding have been forwarded to the Soldiers' Home, Chelsea. One case (a soldier's widow, totally blind) was visited by the Corps members, and many a weary hour lightened by tender acts of mercy; this lady was lately taken into the Corps and is at the present time a very interested member of the Order.

The Corps has assisted the Post to purchase a piano, and at different times turned over such funds as the state of its finances would permit.

Membership, fifty-six.

PRESIDENTS.

Abbie A. Morse	1888, 1889
Elsie S. Hood	1890
Abbie A. Morse	1891
Mary Walker	1892
Louise F. Despeaux	1893, 1894

RICHARD BORDEN RELIEF CORPS No. 106, FALL RIVER.

In the early spring of 1888, Richard Borden Post No. 46, G.A.R., of Fall River, John M. Deane, Commander, thinking that greater relief could be extended to the needy veterans if the patriotic and loyal women of the city were banded together, voted to have an auxiliary, and an urgent request was forwarded to the Department of Massachusetts, Woman's Relief Corps, that some one might be detailed to institute the Corps. Accordingly the charter was granted and Mrs. Emma B. Lowd, then Department President, personally answered the call, and on May 21, 1888, officially instituted Richard Borden Relief Corps No. 106, with a membership of sixty-three, and publicly installed its officers.

The first invitation from Post 46, G.A.R., to the Corps was to attend with them divine services Memorial Sunday, and this courtesy has been continued every year. The first call made upon the Corps for assistance was to furnish a collation May 30, 1888, for six hundred people; the Corps nobly responded and won the hearty approval of the Post.

Since the early days of its organization Corps 106 has been actively at work. In 1888, it sent its first contribution to the South to assist in decorating the graves of the fallen heroes, and this gift is annually repeated.

Each succeeding year brings its routine work for Memorial Day, and Corps 106 is ever ready to furnish flowers and collation, to attend the services, take charge of decorating the Soldiers' Lot in Oak Grove Cemetery, and yearly remember those fallen heroes, Grant, Sherman, Farragut and others; the unknown dead are not forgotten, for in 1889 the Corps erected an urn in this lot to their memory, and yearly fills the same with flowering plants.

In September, 1888, the Corps presented Post 46 with an elegant silk flag, also with curtains and articles of furniture for its Post hall. In December it was decided to extend our relief work and to take charge of a room at the Soldiers' Home in Chelsea, Mass.; one hundred and twenty-five dollars were forwarded and room No. 71 was assigned; the care of this has been continuous, many articles of comfort and convenience being added yearly. Thanksgiving offerings have been forwarded to the Home, and the Corps furnished its quota for the hennery when the call was issued by the Department.

In 1890 the Corps forwarded one hundred dollars to the National Encampment Fund, and its President, Mrs. Mary G. Deane, served the Department on important committees in the entertainment of its guests.

This year the Corps presented markers to Post 46, also one hundred dollars in cash toward a Memorial Hall.

The installations of Post, Corps and Camp have always been held jointly and publicly, thereby creating a greater interest in the minds of the public concerning our work. At the installation held Jan. 1, 1891, Post 46, through its Commander, Amos M. Jackson, presented Corps 106 with an elegant silk banner as a token of its appreciation of the work of the Corps.

In the fall of 1891 the Corps assisted the Post in holding a fair, which netted the Post over two thousand dollars. In 1892, another gift of twenty-five dollars was added to the Post Memorial Hall Fund, by the Corps. In 1893, the Post finding its hall inadequate to meet its demands, a change was made and Corps 106 gladly assisted in refurnishing the new hall, adding many pieces of furniture. On the 16th of January, 1893, the Post celebrated its silver anniversary and the Corps presented them with twenty-five silver dollars.

It has been the annual custom of Post 46, G.A.R., to hold a grand camp-fire, at which time the Department Officers G.A.R. and W.R.C. are honored guests; at these gatherings Corps 106 is always numbered among the guests.

The local relief work of the Corps is quite extensive; it is the annual custom to furnish a New Year's dinner at the Post hall for all the needy ones under their care, and many hearts are made happy on that day, as gifts of clothes, books and toys are also distributed.

While attending to the local calls, for relief the calls from the National and Department Presidents have not been unheeded, as the Corps has contributed to the National W.R.C. Home, National Relief Fund, Department Relief Fund, Army Nurse Fund, Soldiers' Home in Chelsea, Mass., Monroe Fund, also to the Johnstown, Nebraska and Sea Island sufferers, Department of Maryland, and was the first Corps to forward one hundred dollars to the Memorial Fund (a Department fund used to care for the widows and orphans, also army nurses).

The total amount of money spent in relief and turned over to Post since organization is one thousand six hundred dollars. The amount of relief extended other than money is so great that it cannot be estimated.

This Corps has been more honored than most Corps; its first President, Mrs. Mary G. Deane, served three years and three months, declining the fourth term. In 1890 she was appointed Department Aide by Mrs. Mary E. Knowles, Department President, serving the same year as National Aide for the National Convention in Boston; in 1891 she served as Department Inspector; in 1892 she was called upon to fill the highest office in the Department, that of President; in 1893, declining a re-election as President, she was appointed Department Counselor; this year she served as special National Aide under Mrs. Sarah C. Mink, National President.

Corps 106 stands ready to do whatever it may to assist the veteran and advance the cause of patriotism. If in an humble way its members can lighten the burden of one sorrowing heart, or brighten the life of a little child, they feel fully recompensed for all their labors.

Membership, one hundred and sixty-two.

PRESIDENTS.

Mary G. Deane	1888, 1889, 1890, 1891
Mary A. Ingram	1892
Sarah F. Dailey	1893, 1894

JAMES H. SARGENT CORPS No. 107, WEST MEDWAY.

Was instituted June 5, 1888, with nineteen charter members, by Mrs. Elizabeth V. Lang, Department Instituting and Installing Officer.

During the six years since its organization, the Corps has expended in relief, $70.00; relief other than money, $168.50. Fifteen soldiers have been assisted, and twenty-one members of soldiers' families.

The Corps has assisted the Post in furnishing its hall at an expense of $342.00, besides furnishing $60.00 for rooms for reception and sewing; also donated $35.00 to the Post for incidentals, besides $300.00 to furnish Post-room. It has also assisted Post 130, G.A.R., at two fairs which netted $500.00. The Corps has ever been active in good works, boxes have been filled and sent to Corps whose local relief work was larger than in West Medway, besides sending boxes to Soldiers' Home in Chelsea.

Membership, thirty-three.

PRESIDENTS.

Lizzie Pickering	1888
Nellie M. Pierson	1889, 1890, 1891, 1892
Sarah J. Bullard	1893
Carrie C. Hixon	1894

DEXTER CORPS No. 108, BROOKFIELD.

Auxiliary to Post 38, G.A.R., was organized June 2, 1888, with twenty-five charter members, by Mrs. Mary M Perry, Department Senior Vice-President. As a Corps we have confined our work first of all to Post 38, and the families of its members. We have contributed fifty dollars toward the Soldiers' Monument. There was an independent society before the Woman's Relief Corps was formed that worked with the Post in many ways. We have accomplished considerable relief work in these years as an auxiliary, and always readily respond to calls of relief, watching with the sick ones and rendering temporary aid.

Memorial Day always finds us doing our duty, and with willing hearts and ready hands working with the members of Post 38 in ways that are appreciated by them.

Membership, thirty-eight.

PRESIDENTS.

Lucy A. Sawtell	1888, 1889, 1890, 1891
Sarah A. Howe	1892
Carrie M. Ormsby	1893, 1894

CHARLES L. CHANDLER CORPS No. 109, BROOKLINE.

On June 8, 1888, Mrs. Mary E. Knowles, Department Junior Vice-President, instituted Corps 109 with twenty-seven charter members.

During the six years and a half of its existence, Corps 109 has expended for relief $177.80, and contributed to the following objects: National W.R.C. Home, Army Nurse Fund, Soldiers' Home, Chelsea, $166.27, and has expended in relief other than money, to the value of $387.60, besides furnishing Thanksgiving dinners to the needy soldiers' families each year.

The Corps took an active part in the bazaar held in Music Hall in February, 1892, in aid of the Soldiers' Home, having a table which realized some $200.00.

Each year Corps 109 attends Memorial services with Post 143, G.A.R., and assists in preparing the flowers for the graves of our heroes, besides furnishing a collation to Post and Camp.

It has presented a silk flag to Post 143, also presented one to the Sons of Veterans, and has recently given $250.00 to the Post.

Membership, seventy-two.

PRESIDENTS.

Susan M. Gross	. . .	1888, 1889
Amanda Richardson	. . .	1890
Lizzie M. Edwards	. . .	1891
Annie W. Farquhar	. . .	1892
Susan M. Gross	. . .	1893, 1894

CAPT. HORACE NILES CORPS No. 110, RANDOLPH.

Early in the year 1887, Capt. H. C. Alden, Commander of Post 110, G.A.R., having suggested that a Relief Corps should be organized auxiliary to the Post, active steps were taken toward the formation of the same; and on April 1, 1887, Mrs. S. Agnes Parker, Department President, instituted the Corps with eighty charter members. Post 110 with other friends were present at the installation of the newly-elected officers.

On Memorial Day, 1889, Corps 110 presented a beautiful silk flag to the Post, and a handsome bunting flag to Camp 4, Sons of Veterans.

Contributions given at various times to the Post amount to $269.42. The sum of $281.43 has been expended in relief and in furnishing a room at the Soldiers' Home. The sum of fifty dollars was forwarded to Department Headquarters for the 1890 Encampment Fund.

This Corps was originally organized as No. 89, but in 1890 the number 110 having become vacant, this number was given to Capt. Horace Niles Corps to correspond with the number of the Post to which it is auxiliary.

An entertainment is given quarterly to which members of the Post and Camp, with their families, are invited; these are very social occasions and help to increase the funds of the Corps.

While the work of some Corps is quite extended, the field for labor in Randolph is small, but all that has been given Corps 110 to do, has been faithfully attended to.

Membership, sixty-seven.

PRESIDENTS.

Hannah B. Belcher	. . .	1887, 1888
Mary S. Hathaway	. . . .	1889
Mary E. Page	. . . . .	1890
Lizzie S. Leach	. . . .	1891
Edith A. Taylor	. .	1892, 1893, 1894

JOSEPH E. SIMMONS CORPS No. 111, PEMBROKE.

At the commencement of the Civil War Pembroke "arose as one man," animated with love of home and country inherited from Revolutionary ancestors, to respond to the call of duty; and history tells us truly

> That the women and men were one that day
> In a purpose grand and great.

The women with sad but loyal hearts took up the work at home, in the path opened out before them, and nobly did they travel therein, heart to heart, auxiliary to father, husband, son and brother, who were in the field when the horror of war was upon our home and country. They met together forming themselves into the Ladies' Sanitary Aid Society, and did good, unwearying work all through the years of the war. When peace was declared, and the defenders of our country returned to their homes, they re-formed under the "Soldiers' Sewing Society," and out of this spirit of loyalty and gratitude which prompted that work, the Woman's Relief Corps has grown.

In March, 1891, ten years after the first resolution was adopted in regard to the recognition of the Woman's Relief Corps as auxiliary to the Grand Army of the Republic, Commander Charles A. Bryant called a preliminary meeting to form an auxiliary to Joseph E. Simmons Post No. 111. A charter was granted April 14, 1891, and Mrs. Annie K. Day, Department Instituting and Installing Officer, instituted said Corps on April 21, 1891, with thirty-two charter members. We are working to keep alive that spirit of patriotism and gratitude which prompted our organization. We have ever responded to all calls for relief as well as our means would allow. Oct. 29, 1894, Post 111 celebrated its twenty-fifth anniversary, at which the members of Corps 111 were guests.

Membership, fifty-nine.

PRESIDENTS.

Ellen Mann . .	1891, 1892
Jennie E. Sturtevant	1893, 1894

ERICSSON CORPS No. 112, EAST TEMPLETON.

Was instituted at Baldwinsville, Mass., Sept. 4, 1888, with thirty-six charter members, by Mrs. Leocardia F. Flowers of the Department Executive Board. This Corps is in some respects peculiarly situated, its members living in the four villages of Templeton, East Templeton, Baldwinsville and Otter River. Although the headquarters of the Corps is established at East Templeton, the meetings are alternately held in the four villages that all may have the opportunity of attending some of the meetings and assisting in the work.

This Corps has turned over to Post 109 G.A.R. about $100.00 each year since its organization, and in 1890 presented the Post with a beautiful silk flag; we have been ever ready to heed any call for assistance for needy soldiers or members of their families. Through the efforts of Mrs. Frances J. Smith, Past President of the Corps, flags have been presented the public schools of Baldwinsville.

Forwarded to National Encampment (1890) $40.00, also contributed to W.R.C. Home, Munroe Monument Fund, Army Nurse Fund, Soldiers' Home, Memorial Day, and for Southern graves.

Each year the Corps has assisted in the proper observance of Memorial Day and in many ways the institution of this Corps has proved not only an assistance to the Post, but an incentive to more expressions of loyalty and patriotism in the community.

Membership, seventy-six.

PRESIDENTS.

Frances J. Smith	1889, 1890, 1891
Ellen R. Hodge	1892
Sarah G. M. Hill	1893, 1894

JOSEPH P. RICE CORPS No. 113, WESTMINSTER.

The Corps was instituted by Mrs. Eva T. Cook, Department Instituting and Installing Officer, Jan. 27, 1890, with a membership of sixty-two.

During the three years and a half of its existence this Corps has expended $150.00 for the Post and $115.00 for charities. Entertainments and sales of various kinds have been held, and numerous social evenings spent with Post and Camp and Corps from other towns. Prosperity has attended these occasions as well as the every-day life of the Corps, and the outlook for the future career of Joseph P. Rice Corps No. 113 is very encouraging. Its members are very active in good works, and the Corps is honored in the community.

Membership, ninety-two.

PRESIDENTS.

Laura A. Raymond	1890, 1891
Julia L. Marshall	1892, 1893, 1894

O. H. P. SARGENT CORPS No. 114, ESSEX.

Was instituted by Mrs. Mary E. Knowles, Department Junior Vice President, Oct. 25, 1888, with seventeen charter members.

The first work undertaken by the Corps was the raising of funds for a memorial to the soldiers of Essex who sacrificed their lives in defence of the Union. Soon after the close of the war efforts to have a Soldiers' Monument erected by the town were unsuccessful. The Post, Corps and Sons of Veterans were considering the matter of uniting to build a memorial hall at the time of the death of Mr. T. O. H. P. Burnham of Boston, a former resident of Essex. Mr. Burnham bequeathed $40,000 to the town for the erection of a Public Library and Memorial Hall and also left a permanent fund for its support.

The Corps has contributed to the Soldiers' Home, the National W.R.C. Home, the Department Army Nurse Fund and the Monroe Monument Fund, and for local relief the sum of $243.46.

The value of gifts to the Post amounts to $132.13 and $336.37 have been expended in furnishings for Grand Army Hall. The Corps has but few calls from its relief fund, but has endeavored to stand side by side with sister Corps of the State in making our Order worthy of a hearty recognition from those we serve. The finances of the Corps are in excellent condition.

Membership forty-six.

PRESIDENTS.

Nancy C. Andrews	1888, 1889, 1890
Mary H. Andrews	1891, 1892, 1893
Sadie E. Haskell	. . 1894

J. W. LAWTON CORPS No. 115, WARE.

Was instituted Dec. 7, 1888, by Mrs. Mary M. Perry, Department Senior Vice-President, with a charter membership of forty-seven. The first year of our organization the Corps presented the Post with a handsome flag, and we were also able to send to the Johnstown sufferers the sum of eighty-four dollars. The second year we secured and furnished a room in the Soldiers' Home in Chelsea, No. 70, and have kept it supplied with necessaries and articles to make it more comfortable to those who occupy it. For several years a certain sum of money has been forwarded to Phil. Kearney Post, Virginia, for decorating the graves of unknown soldiers, and occasionally we have given different sums to the Post. The local relief work is small.

The services of Memorial Day are participated in by the three organizations — Post, Corps and Camp, — each willing to share in the work and thus rendering the duties of each as light as possible.

Membership, fifty-three.

PRESIDENTS.

Elvira J. W. Coney	1888, 1889
Emma Osgood	1890, 1891
Lucy E. Ainsworth	1892, 1893
Nellie M. Marsh	. 1894

E. M. STANTON CORPS No. 116, AMHERST.

On Jan. 25, 1889, Corps No. 116 was instituted by Mary M. Perry, Department Senior Vice-President, with a membership of twenty-eight.

On Memorial Sunday a large delegation attend divine service with the Post. They furnish wreaths and flowers to decorate the graves of the comrades and attend service at the cemetery besides furnishing a collation for the Post and their escorts.

We have not been backward in remembering our destitute and suffering sisters; have furnished warm clothing for the needy, nursed the sick, and in one instance raised a purse of twenty-five dollars for a loyal woman who was not entitled to help from our relief fund. We have always assisted E. M Stanton Post whenever necessary and assisted in furnishing the Post hall. Estimated amount of relief since organization, $38.80.

Membership, fifty-one.

PRESIDENTS.

S. Miranda Adams	1889, 1890
S. Jennie Thayer	1891, 1892
Ella M. D. Hall	. 1893
Kate W. Eddy	. 1894

PRENTISS M. WHITING CORPS No. 117, NORTH ATTLEBORO.

Was instituted Feb. 8, 1889, with one hundred and eight charter members, by Mrs. Mary E. Knowles, Department Junior Vice-President. It was an auspicious opening for the Corps. In April following Post 192 G.A.R. entertained the Bristol County G.A.R. Convention, Corps 117 furnishing and serving the dinner. On May 24, the citizens of the town, and Corps and Posts from neighboring towns, were invited to participate in an out-of-door festival, the principal feature of the evening being the presentation of an elegant stand of colors to Prentiss M. Whiting Post No. 192, G.A.R., valued at $100.00, by Miss Clara Merritt in behalf of Corps 117 and accepted by Commander Bugbee, Commander of the Post. An entertainment followed the presentation, which netted the Corps Treasury $63.00. On Memorial Day following, a dinner was served to the Post and other organizations at an expense of twenty dollars. In November a fair was undertaken at which was served a turkey dinner, netting the Corps $547.32. During all these months the Relief Committee was busy looking after all cases requiring assistance, and many hearts were cheered by sympathy extended as well as by more material aid.

Many fraternal visits were exchanged by Post, Corps, Sons of Veterans and neighboring Corps, and many members added to the Corps.

March 10, 1890, the Corps by vote assumed charge of a room at the Soldiers' Home at an expense of $145.95; many members of the Corps have contributed useful and ornamental articles. During the winter of 1890-1891 a lecture course of more than ordinary merit was provided by the Corps and $90.00 realized from it. At the time of the National Encampment in Boston $50.00 were forwarded toward defraying the expenses incurred by Department. Feb. 20, 1891, an entertainment was given by Corps 117 to which the Sons of Veterans were invited, and Mrs. Bugbee, the President, presented the Camp with a silk altar cloth and guidons. Salad suppers and entertainments have been given at various times, always with success, adding to the Relief Fund thereby. In 1889, the sum of fifty dollars was presented to the Post.

The Corps purchased a lot and built a hall where the three organizations could have a home, which was dedicated March 10, 1890.

In various ways there has been added to the Corps Treasury $1,151.85. There has been expended from the Relief Fund over $400.00 in money, besides furnishing many articles of clothing; and Christmas dinners have been given to those under the care of the Corps. Donations have been made to the National W.R.C. Home ($10.00) and $25.00 forwarded to the Plainville Corps for the benefit of a sick member.

Membership, one hundred and four.

PRESIDENTS.

Henrietta A. Swift	.	1888, 1889, 1890
Annie E. Bugbee	. .	1891, 1892
Martha A. Bennett	. .	1893, 1894

SAMUEL F. WOODS CORPS No. 118, BARRE.

Was instituted Feb. 14, 1889, by Mrs. Elizabeth V. Lang, Department Inspector, with twenty-three members.

Entertainments have been given for the benefit of the Corps treasury, and we have responded to calls for relief. For the past three years a sum of money has annually been donated to the Post, and Corps 118 has assisted the comrades in observing Memorial Day.

The sum of $10.00 was sent to the Executive Committee for the National Convention in Boston (1890). Contributions have been sent the Soldiers' Home, and a donation forwarded Department Headquarters for the Memorial Fund, and assistance given to other branches of the work.

Membership, twenty-four.

PRESIDENTS.

Ellen A. Hawes	. . .	. 1889
Emeline S. Egery	. . .	. 1890
Cora P. L. Walker	. .	1891, 1892
Ellen E. Hawes	. . .	. 1893
Maria N. Gilmore	. .	. 1894

ALLEN CORPS No. 119, MANCHESTER.

Auxiliary to Allen Post 67, G.A.R., was instituted March 14, 1889, by Mrs. Elizabeth V. Lang, Department Inspector, with twenty-two charter members.

This Corps has been steadily at work the years which have since passed, and in various ways, such as fairs, entertainments, concerts and sales, has raised funds amounting to $898.41 to carry on its work. It has expended for relief $126.11; presented to the Post, $225.00 for its

Relief Fund; and has visited the Soldiers' Home twice in a body, besides making two hundred and fifty visits to the sick and needy.
Membership, sixty-two.

PRESIDENTS.

Sarah E. Crombie	1889, 1890
Mary A. Smith	1891, 1892, 1893
Helen L. Willmonton	1894

WILLIAM H. BARTLETT CORPS No. 120, TAUNTON.

On Thursday afternoon, March 21, 1889, forty-eight ladies of Taunton met to organize a Relief Corps auxiliary to William H. Bartlett Post No. 3, G.A.R. Mrs. Mary E. Knowles, Department Senior Vice-President, instituted this Corps and installed its officers.

In October of this year, the Corps held a kettle-drum which was both socially and financially a decided success, netting the sum of $103.00. In November, William H. Bartlett Post No. 3, G.A.R., held a camp-fire, at which the members of Corps 120 were guests. The Post, Corps and Camp have worked jointly in a number of fairs, and in May, 1890, in appreciation of the services of the Corps, Post 3 presented it with $100.00. The Corps has presented to Post No. 3 a carpet for its Post hall valued at $100.00, also $25.00 at its silver anniversary, and a smaller donation since, besides tendering a reception and banquet to the Post in 1891.

It has expended in relief since organization $315.28, besides sending reading matter, clothing, a clock, two pullets and $5.00 in cash to the Soldiers' Home; $5.00 to the Army Nurse Fund; box valued at $25.00 to the military fair in aid of the Home; and $5.00 to National W.R.C. Home. Through the efforts of two of the members of the Corps, funds were raised, and a beautiful State flag purchased and presented to Post 3, G A.R., during the summer of 1892.

The Corps has always been faithful in assisting the Post in arranging flowers for Memorial Day, and always since its organization has served the comrades with a bountiful collation on that day without any expense to the Post.
Membership, seventy-three.

PRESIDENTS.

Harriett E. Howard	1889, 1890, 1891, 1892
Eliza W. Brown	1893, 1994

GEORGE W. PERRY CORPS No. 121, SCITUATE.

On April 5, 1889, through the earnest efforts of Mrs. Marion L. Bailey, Corps 121 was instituted by Mrs. Elizabeth V. Lang, Department Inspector, with nineteen charter members. The officers were publicly installed in the evening in the presence of the members of the Post and other interested friends.

A Relief Fund was started which has received additions from time to time, and although there are not many calls for relief in the quiet little town of Scituate, assistance is always cheerfully rendered whenever necessary.

The Corps takes great pride in appropriating funds to make Grand Army Hall attractive and comfortable. The Post is assisted by the Corps each Memorial Day in preparing garlands for the fallen comrades, and both organizations unite in a memorial service for those who sleep in unknown graves.

Membership, fifty.

PRESIDENTS.

Mandana C. Morris	1889, 1890
Mary F. Prouty	1891, 1892
Martha W. Pierce	1893
Annie M. Soule	1894

GEN. JAMES L. BATES CORPS No. 122, SWAMPSCOTT.

The Ladies' Aid Association connected with the Post in this town was organized as a Relief Corps June 6, 1889, with forty members, by Mrs. Eva T. Cook, Department I. and I. Officer.

This Corps responds to all calls for aid in the line of soldier work, and in addition to assistance rendered the Post, we have helped many worthy families of veterans. We have also remembered the Soldiers' Home by contributions. An unusual interest has marked our work the past year.

Membership, forty-eight.

PRESIDENTS.

Delia Ricker	1889, 1890
Lydia A. Andrews	1891, 1892
Lydia M. Adams	1893
Cornelia T. Damon	1894

C. M. PACKARD CORPS No. 123, AVON.

Was organized June 27, 1889, by Mrs. Eva T. Cook, Department I. and I. Officer, with thirty members. This Corps has assisted its Post in two fairs, clearing nine hundred dollars for the Post treasury. Memorial Day the Corps furnishes flowers for the comrades' graves and prepares a dinner for the Post and its escorts. In 1891 Corps 123 presented the Post with seventy-five dollars. The local relief work has been small, but all calls have been responded to cheerfully and willingly.

Membership, nineteen.

PRESIDENTS.

Emily W. Lothrop	.	1889, 1890
Lucia A. Stewart	.	. 1891
Esther Bryant	.	. 1892
Alice A. Hunt	.	1893, 1894

COLLINGWOOD CORPS No. 124, PLYMOUTH.

Corps 124 was instituted Dec. 3, 1889, by Mrs. Mary E. Knowles, Department Senior Vice-President, assisted by Mrs. S. Agnes Parker, Past Department President, with a charter membership of one hundred and thirty-three. The growth of the Corps during the first year was wonderful, and great interest manifested by all. At the end of the year the membership was nearly doubled.

The first fair was held in April, 1890, at which $713.94 were realized; and $500.00 of this sum presented to Post 76 for its expenses at the Encampment at Boston in August; two handsome guidons, costing forty dollars, were also presented at the same time.

Aug. 12, 1890 (Encampment week), was "Plymouth Day," at which time it was estimated that fifteen thousand comrades and members of the W.R.C. visited Plymouth. Corps 124 entertained its visitors at Odd Fellows Opera House and furnished lunch for all who were present. Amount expended by the Corps at that time was $842.53. Haversacks were made for the members of Post 76, G.A.R., and filled, thus making the day of the great parade much more enjoyable for those who were privileged to participate.

During this year a call was made by the Board of Directors of the National W.R.C. Home to which Corps 124 responded, sending articles valued at $32.63 and a cash donation of $3.55. Each anniversary has been observed by a social gathering.

The second fair to raise money was held in October, 1891, at which time the net receipts were $428.30. At the fair held in Boston February, 1892, Corps 124 furnished a table and realized therefrom $125.00 for the Soldiers' Home. During the summer of 1892 the Corps held a series of lawn parties and socials for the purpose of raising funds to assist needy Post members to attend the National Encampment at Washington, D.C., thereby turning over this year to Post 76, $271.30. The last fair held was in December, 1892, at which time $462.43 were realized and this sum was by vote placed in the Corps Relief Fund, making $728.85 the amount of said fund.

Among our most honored members is Miss Rebecca Wiswell, an army nurse, who, although eighty-seven years of age, is quite often able to be present at Corps meetings, and by her presence and interest cheers the hearts of the members and gives fresh impetus to the work in hand.

The Corps has always attended memorial services with the Post and furnished baskets of flowers for the graves of the fallen.

Amount expended in relief $918.62; turned over to Post $909.63.

Membership, two hundred and seventy-two.

PRESIDENTS.

Lucia A. Knapp	1889, 1890, 1891
Cornelia E. Brynes	1892, 1893
Anna E. Bowditch	1894

F. A. STEARNS CORPS No. 125, SPENCER.

Was instituted Jan. 30, 1890, with thirty-six charter members, by Mrs. Eva T. Cook, Department Instituting and Installing Officer.

Since organization Corps 125 has held various entertainments, socials, suppers and sales in order to supply its treasury and carry out the work which it had undertaken. Many fraternal visits have been exchanged between Post, Corps and Camp, also with sister Corps. In 1892 the Corps was called upon by the Department to exemplify the work, at which were present the Department President, Mrs. Mary G. Deane, Department Inspector, Mrs. Helen A. Brigham and delegations from numerous Corps.

The relief work of the Corps has been carefully attended to; more than one hundred visits made to the sick and needy, and about one hundred and fifty dollars expended, besides furnishing food and clothing when required. The Corps has ever been ready to assist the Post, and has at various times turned over cash amounting to $150.00. It also contributed to the Encampment Fund in 1890, and has expended in various ways $458.18 for relief. The Soldiers' Home at Chelsea has not been forgotten; visits have been made by the members upon the veterans and each time some contribution has been left to cheer the inmates.

Membership, seventy-six.

PRESIDENTS.

Mattie A. Fay	1890, 1891
Amelia R. Wheeler	1892
Caroline W. Hastings	1893
Cynthia L. Hancock	1894

WILLIAM B. EATON CORPS No. 126, REVERE.

On April 18, 1890, Mrs. Elizabeth V. Lang, Department Junior Vice-President, instituted William B. Eaton Corps No. 126, with a charter membership of forty-six. The relief work of the Corps has not been very extensive, but it has responded as far as possible to all calls.

We have assisted the Post whose name we bear in various ways, and on each Memorial Day contributed a small sum of money to help defray the expenses of decorating soldiers' graves, besides furnishing a floral offering in memory of the unknown dead; and serving a collation on the return of the veterans from the cemetery.

We have contributed fifty dollars towards furnishing the new Grand Army hall, and rendered aid in the three fairs held by Post 199.

Our anniversaries have been observed each year to which the Department officers, William B. Eaton Post No. 199, and other guests were invited.

Corps 126 has contributed to the Soldier's Home, and sent a barrel of clothing to a colored Corps in the South.

Membership, twenty-nine.

PRESIDENTS.

Caroline A. Fuller	1890, 1891
Clara J. Kimball	1892, 1893
Isannah Moore	1894

GEN. W. F. BARTLETT CORPS No. 127, ANDOVER.

On April 22, 1890, Mrs. Carrie S. L. Bagley, Department Instituting and Installing Officer, instituted Corps 127, with forty-seven charter members.

The Relief Corps work in Andover has prospered, and various entertainments have been given with grand financial results. Eighty Andover merchants were represented in the "Business Men's Carnival" held in 1891, and from the proceeds of this enterprise the Corps presented Post 99 of Andover a Christmas gift of one hundred dollars. In 1892, the Corps added one hundred and fifty dollars to the "Washington Fund" of the Post. The Corps has purchased a piano for Grand Army Hall, a clock and other useful articles, and has provided for the comfort of the families of Post and Corps in case of illness. Social gatherings are held between the two organizations, but the calls for local relief work are few. Corps 127 has contributed articles for the "Andover Room," at the Soldiers' Home, and has responded to special objects of relief outlined in General Orders issued from Department Headquarters.

Membership, seventy.

PRESIDENTS.

Jennie M. Bean	1890, 1891
Hannah S. Greene	1892, 1893
Phœbe L. Coleman	1894

VETERAN CORPS No. 128, READING.

Was instituted April 30, 1890, at Reading, with thirty-three charter members, by Mrs. Carrie S. L. Bagley, Department Instituting and Installing Officer.

Though small in numbers, the members of the Corps entered into the work for the veteran with hearty zeal; from the first the Post and Corps have worked unitedly in every undertaking.

The Corps has expended since organization $221.70 for the relief of soldiers and their families; presented to Post 194, G.A.R., $100.00, and a beautiful silk flag. The members have assisted in decorating the graves of soldiers in Southern cemeteries and also donated toward the support of the National W.R.C. Home. In every way they are striving to live up to the motto of our Order, Fraternity, Charity and Loyalty.

Membership, eighty-two.

PRESIDENTS.

Augusta K. Barrows	1890, 1891, 1892
Annie S. Nichols	1893, 1894

A. D. WELD CORPS No. 129, WINCHESTER.

Twenty-two ladies of Winchester, who were interested in A. D. Weld Post, united in forming an auxiliary Corps, which was instituted May 16, 1890.

Mrs. Augusta A. Wales, Department Junior Vice-President, conducted the service, and Mrs. Mary E. Knowles, Department President, installed the officers.

When organized we felt that our first duty was to encourage the Post and establish suitable Grand Army Headquarters in Winchester.

A hall was leased and furnished at an expense of nearly one thousand dollars.

There is but very little relief work for Corps 129, as fortunately there are no poor families in the town.

We have fulfilled our allegiance to the National and Department Woman's Relief Corps in all ways possible.

Several fairs have been held, in which the Post has assisted.

We have held several entertainments and arranged social gatherings which have been enjoyed by the Post members.

Over $1,500.00 have been raised by the Corps since it was organized.

We always serve a lunch to the Post on Memorial Day, which is appropriately observed by Corps 129 in the hall and at the cemetery.

Membership, thirty-three.

PRESIDENTS.

Pleasantine C. Wilson . 1890, 1891, 1892, 1893
Lydia L. Blood 1894

J. ARTHUR JOHNSON CORPS No. 130, STURBRIDGE.

On May 28, 1890, Mrs. Mary M. Perry, Department Senior Vice-President, organized Corps 130 and installed its officers.

Charter membership, twenty. With a feeble beginning, encountering obstacles that few Corps are called upon to meet, it has, notwithstanding the many discouragements, gained in membership and is noted for its patriotic work.

The Corps is in a prosperous condition, working with a zeal never excelled. It has cheerfully responded to every call for aid so far as its finances would allow. It has contributed to the Soldiers' Fair (1892),

Monroe Monument Fund, Soldiers' Home, Memorial Home, besides responding to local calls for relief.

In the work of Memorial Day Corps 130 has done much to lighten the labors of the Post, adding thereby greatly to the interest of that day. Divine service has always been largely attended on Memorial Sunday, and continuous effort made by its members to inculcate principles of patriotism and a sacred reverence for the day in the minds of the children of the town.

"Persevere" is the watchword of Corps 130 and the founders now have reason to be thankful that amid all the adverse conditions surrounding its advent they have persevered and secured to the Post to which they are auxiliary that support and encouragement of which it stood so much in need.

Membership, fifty-eight.

PRESIDENTS.

Sarah V. Anderson	1890, 1891, 1892, 1893
Mary L. Chamberlain	1894

THOMAS A. PARKER CORPS No. 131, EAST PEPPERELL.

Was instituted July 16, 1890, by Mrs. Carrie S. L. Bagley, Department Instituting and Installing Officer, with forty-one charter members.

The Corps has always been in a prosperous condition. In a town like ours the calls for help are few, yet from time to time money has been turned over to Thomas A. Parker Post No. 195, to be used for needy comrades.

In November, 1891, our Corps received an application for help from a soldier's widow over eighty years of age. She was sick, without fuel or sufficient food; she was immediately removed to a comfortable home, where she could be cared for and provided with medical aid. Steps were taken by the Corps to secure her a pension and with such energy that in six weeks the pension was granted with back pay. She is now well and happy and cannot say enough in praise of the Woman's Relief Corps.

Membership, thirty-seven.

PRESIDENTS.

Lucy P. Saunders	1890, 1891
Sarah M. Shattuck	1892, 1893
Sarah E. Ryder	1894

CHAS. CHIPMAN CORPS No. 132, SANDWICH.

Was instituted June 23, 1887, by Mrs. S. Agnes Parker, Department President, with twenty-three charter members, as Corps No. 91 — afterward changed to No. 132, to correspond with the number of the Post.

While the Corps has always been ready and willing to assist, the local calls for relief have been few, but we have helped six families of veterans; expended $150.00 in relief, besides furnishing clothing, food and delicacies to the sick, valued at $200.00. Every year a donation of money is forwarded to the Soldiers' Home in Chelsea, besides literature and delicacies for the hospital. The Corps has presented the Post with a handsome set of guidons.

There is not any cemetery in Sandwich, but on Memorial Day services are held by Post and Corps, and a place selected which is decorated in memory of the unknown dead; a collation is served by the Corps and the remainder of the day observed by all in honoring the fallen heroes.

Several large fairs have been held by the Post and Corps, with financial success.

Membership, fifty-five.

PRESIDENTS.

Emily M. Jones	1887, 1888
Marie A. Hunt	1889, 1890
Melissa M. Ellis	1891, 1892, 1893, 1894

HANCOCK CORPS No. 133, DALTON.

This Corps was instituted by Mrs. Mary M. Perry, Department Senior Vice-President, with a charter membership of thirty-seven, Oct. 21, 1890. The Corps, though small in number, has ever been active in good works. The local relief work has been carried on successfully, but much has not been done outside of that.

In 1892, Corps 133 exemplified the work of the Ritual at the request of the Department President, Mrs. Mary G. Deane, at which time representatives from many neighboring Corps were present.

On Memorial Day the Corps furnishes refreshments for Hancock Post and guests.

Membership, forty-three.

PRESIDENTS.

Ella S. Decker	1890, 1891
Ellen M. Phelps	1892
Mattie E. Lawrence	1893, 1894

HENRY CLAY WADE CORPS No. 134, COTTAGE CITY.

A little southeast of the coast of Massachusetts lie two famous islands, viz.: Martha's Vineyard and Nantucket. The first named is the one especially connected with this sketch, for upon this beautiful isle of the sea is situated the town of Cottage City, the headquarters of Henry Clay Wade Post and Relief Corps.

There are several towns on the island, among which are Vineyard Haven (where the terrible wreck of the *City of Columbus* occurred) and Edgartown,—the shire town of the island, and which furnished more than her quota to the late War of the Rebellion, and of which Cottage City was formerly a part. In these several towns were veterans, who in the summer of 1890 formed themselves into a G.A.R. Post which was named in honor of Henry Clay Wade, a native of the island and an acting master in the United States Navy during the late Civil War.

As Post 201 desired an auxiliary, an application for charter was forwarded to Department Headquarters, and on Dec. 4, 1890, Mrs. Prudence H. Stokes of the Department Executive Board instituted Henry Clay Wade Corps No. 134 with a charter membership of twenty-eight. The annual installations of the Corps officers are held jointly with the Post and are public. Since organization much good has been accomplished, and many *social gatherings have cheered the veterans' hearts.

About three hundred dollars have been turned over to Post and expended in relief. The Corps has also presented to Henry Clay Wade Post an elegant silk flag.

Membership, fifty-four.

PRESIDENTS.

Mary F. Tripp	1890, 1891
Abby B. Hillman	1892
Minnie E. Vincent	1893, 1894

CHARLES C. SMITH CORPS No. 135, SOUTH HADLEY.

On the afternoon of Jan. 5, 1891, this Corps, auxiliary to Charles C. Smith Post No. 183, G.A.R., was instituted by Mrs. Clare H. Burleigh, Department Inspector, the installation in the evening being conducted jointly with that of the Post. The members of this Corps are widely scattered, some living six or seven miles from our place of meeting, and a number coming three or four miles, which prevents a large average attendance at Corps meetings. Frequent visits and courtesies with Post No. 183 are exchanged, and its members assure us of their sympathy and approval.

Ways and means of raising money seem to be few, the work hard and returns small, which conditions we most cheerfully accept, if there is nothing better. These facts are shadows in the picture, bringing out in greater beauty our love for our Order, the many true friendships formed among its members, the sweet charity that grows up in our hearts, and our pride in and loyalty to the Grand Army of the Republic. We have done little relief work as yet, having had few calls, but should the demand come, as it will, we hope to be able to justify our title.

Membership, forty.

PRESIDENTS.

Fannie M. Barnes	1891
Maria S. Walkley	1892, 1893
Dorcas W. Clark	1894

DAVID A. RUSSELL CORPS No. 136, WHITMAN.

On Jan. 6, 1891, eighty-six women (including members of the G.A.R. sewing circle, wives and daughters of veterans and other loyal women) met in G.A.R. Hall to form a Relief Corps auxiliary to David A. Russell Post No. 78, G.A.R. The Corps was instituted by Mrs. Emma B. Lowd, Department Counselor, and Aides. On the evening of same date the officers-elect were publicly installed in the presence of a large company assembled to witness the joint installations of Post and Corps officers. The Corps felt largely indebted to Mrs. Agnes Parker and Mrs. Mary E. Knowles for their many words of advice and encouragement while they were undecided to enter a broader field of usefulness.

The calls for local relief work have been few, but it has always been the aim of Corps 136 to respond to all calls whether from Department or those nearer home. The Corps has presented Post 136 with a beautiful flag, also presented a flag to the public school of Whitman. We have repeatedly contributed to both the General and Relief Funds of the Post, assisted the comrades in carrying on two fairs, held entertainments, suppers and receptions, and tried in every possible way to be a helpmeet indeed to the Post whose name we bear. On Memorial Day the Post and Corps hold joint services, furnishing flowers for the graves of the fallen comrades, and attending services in a body.

Membership, one hundred and forty-two.

PRESIDENTS.

Laura A. Brown	1891, 1892
Lucy C. Howland	1893, 1894

HARTSUFF CORPS No. 137, ROCKLAND.

Hartsuff Corps No. 137, Rockland, auxiliary to Post 74, was instituted Jan. 14, 1891, with a charter membership of one hundred and twenty-six, by Mrs. Emma B. Lowd, Department Counselor.

But few calls for relief, considering the territory we represent, have been made. During our connection with Post 74 as its auxiliary, we have turned over to its quartermaster nearly one hundred dollars. It has been the custom for the Corps, in company with the Post and Camp, to attend divine service on the Sunday preceding Memorial Day; to provide wreaths and flowers to decorate the graves of the deceased soldiers, and floral designs for the mound dedicated to the unreturned, as well as for our own members who have been taken from us by death. In the years 1892 and 1893 the Corps provided dinner on Memorial Day for three hundred — Post, Camp and families, the clergy, town officers and soldiers' widows. In December, 1892, we contributed $5.00 to National W.R C. Home. In May, 1893, we sent $10.00 to Phil. Kearney Post, Va.

Picnics and fairs are held to encourage sociability, also to add to our treasury.

Membership, one hundred and thirty-three.

PRESIDENTS.

Martha A. Hopkins	1891
Emma E. Everson	1892, 1893
Susan E. Sheldon	1894

C. C. PHILLIPS CORPS No. 138, HOPKINTON.

It was early in the year 1891 when a movement toward the formation of a Relief Corps in Hopkinton was started. Preliminary meetings were held and arrangements made, and on the afternoon of March 12, 1891, under the direction of Mrs. Augusta A. Wales, Department President, Corps 138 was instituted by Mrs. Annie K. Day, Department Instituting and Installing Officer, with a charter membership of forty-six. On the evening of that day the officers-elect were installed in the presence of C. C. Phillips Post No. 14, G.A.R., and a large assembly of invited guests.

Since organization the Corps has assisted the Post on Memorial Days by providing baskets of flowers, furnishing dinners and attending services at the cemetery.

It has turned over to Post 14 sixty-two dollars and extended relief outside the regular work in town, which consists chiefly in visiting the sick. Interchange of visits with neighboring Corps have proved to be beneficial to all, and socials held with Post and Camp have been greatly enjoyed.

Membership, forty-nine.

PRESIDENTS.

Maria H. Parlin	1891, 1892
Mary L. Drawbridge	1893, 1894

D. G. ANDERSON CORPS No. 139, GREAT BARRINGTON.

Was organized March 18, 1891, with twenty-one charter members, by Mrs. Augusta A. Wales, Department President, assisted by Mrs. Annie K. Day, Department Instituting and Installing Officer.

We had worked hard for years on Memorial Day and at the installation of the officers of the Grand Army of the Republic, on which occasion a supper is always served. Those who are now members of the Relief Corps were in the habit of helping the Post at that time.

We do not have much call for relief. Have helped one poor family. About the 15th of last April we contributed $9.00 for articles for the Soldiers' Home in Chelsea.

Membership, twenty-four.

PRESIDENTS.

Hattie A. Sage	1892
Helen J. Huntley	1893, 1894

THERON E. HALL CORPS No. 140, HOLDEN.

Was organized April 13, 1891, by Mrs. Annie K. Day, Department Instituting and Installing Officer, with twenty-two members.

On our first anniversary we presented the Post with a silk flag, at the cost of $60.00, and also with $40.00 in January of the present year.

It has been our custom on each Memorial Day to provide the Post with a dinner and to assist the comrades in any way they may wish, both with flowers and decorations.

We are pleased to say we have a share in the hens at the Soldiers' Home in Chelsea.

We cannot speak of any large calls for charity at home, but it has been a little here and a little there nearly all the time. We have held two fairs and one miscellaneous entertainment, and the members have worked together very harmoniously and we feel we have done very well according to our numbers.

Membership, forty-two.

PRESIDENTS.

Martha E. Graham	1891, 1892
Mattie L. Holden	1893
Sophronia R. Hubbard	1894

F. D. HAMMOND CORPS No. 141, SOUTH CHATHAM.

Jan. 20, 1888, a charter was secured through Commander G. N. Munsell of F. D. Hammond Post No. 141, that resulted in the formation of a Woman's Relief Corps, starting with twenty-three charter members, representing the towns of Chatham, Harwich, Brewster, Orleans and Eastham. The Instituting and Installing Officer was Mrs. Mary E. Andrews of Brockton, a member of the Department Executive Board.

The Corps prospered during the year 1889. Meetings were well sustained and all members were ever ready and willing to do whatever work came to hand. The Corps has steadily gained a strong foothold in the community.

The Post and Corps work together very harmoniously, entertainments of various kinds being held by them jointly whenever deemed expedient.

Most of the members of both Post and Corps being in comfortable pecuniary circumstances, assistance from the Relief Fund is not often solicited, but the Order ever stands ready to give all necessary aid.

Meetings are held regularly with a fair attendance, the interest being well kept up.

Membership, fifty-three.

PRESIDENTS.

Hattie D. Condon	. . . .	1888
Abbie Small	. . . . . .	1889
Elizabeth K. Munsell	.	1890, 1891, 1892, 1893
Harriet Howes	. . .	. 1894

B. F. JONES CORPS No. 142, FALMOUTH.

This Corps was organized and officers publicly installed May 13, 1891, by Mrs. Annie K. Day, Department Instituting and Installing Officer, with a charter membership of twenty-eight. Since organization we have had little relief work to do; but have given "other than money" to the amount of $23.88. A Relief Fund has been established to be drawn upon if needed. In 1893 iron vases were purchased for the soldiers' graves by the Post, assisted by generous contributions from the citizens; in this work the Corps contributed its mite. The Corps has furnished Grand Army Hall with a new carpet and organ, and always contributed whenever called upon according to its means. It suffers under the disadvantages of many country Corps as the members are scattered, but the interest in the work constantly increases. We have contributed to the Soldiers' Home, Memorial Home, and for decorating Southern graves.

Membership, thirty-two.

PRESIDENTS.

Zibbie S. Thayer	. . .	1891, 1892, 1893
Mary J. Norton	. . . . .	1894

WILLIAM WADSWORTH CORPS No. 143, DUXBURY.

A Corps, auxiliary to William Wadsworth Post, was instituted at Duxbury with twenty-two members, Sept. 8, 1891, by Mrs. Emilie L. W. Waterman, a member of the Department Executive Board.

Realizing that we were organized as a helpmeet to the Post, we have endeavored to do our duty in this direction. The sum of $175.00 has been turned over to Post 165 and assistance given to comrades in preparing for Memorial Day.

Public meetings have been held, entertainments given, and efforts made to uphold the work and advance the interests of the Post and Corps.

Membership, thirty-two.

PRESIDENT.

Mercy A. Parker . . 1891, 1892, 1893, 1894

JOSEPH E. WILDER CORPS No. 144, HANOVER.

Joseph E. Wilder Corps No. 144 of Hanover was organized Oct. 20, 1891, by Mrs. Annie K. Day, Department Instituting and Installing Officer, with forty-seven charter members. This Corps has done all in its power to alleviate the sufferings of the veteran and his family, since its organization. It has held several entertainments for the purpose of swelling its funds that it might be able to respond, should its Post need help. When the Camp of Sons of Veterans was working for a flag the W.R.C. came to the rescue.

On Memorial Day a large number of the Corps work to prepare dinner for the veteran and flowers for the graves of departed heroes. In April, 1892, the three organizations held a fair which was a financial success, and the proceeds were shared by all.

Membership, fifty-three.

PRESIDENTS.

Lomyra H. Sturtevant . . 1891, 1892, 1893
M. Adele Waterman 1894

MARCUS KEEP CORPS No. 145, MONSON.

Mrs. Annie K. Day, Department Instituting and Installing Officer, assisted by Mrs. Delilah S. Davis, Department Senior Vice-President, instituted Corps 145, Monson, with a charter membership of sixty-five, Oct. 23, 1891.

Many socials and entertainments have been held to add funds to the treasury, and aid has been rendered soldiers' families in Monson, besides sending a small donation to the Soldiers' Home in Chelsea. Over seventy-five dollars have been expended in relief since organization.

Membership, eighty-one.

PRESIDENTS.

Susan E. Thrall . 1891, 1892, 1893, 1894

T. L. BONNEY CORPS No. 146, HANSON.

This Corps was instituted Dec. 29, 1891, with forty charter members, by Mrs. Annie K. Day, Department Instituting and Installing Officer.

The members are deeply interested in the work and the Corps has prospered, increasing in membership and meeting with financial success.

Assistance is rendered the Post in observing Memorial Day. At our first inspection we reported a Relief Fund of $50.00, and at the second inspection (September 1893), the sum of $100.00 was reported to the credit of this fund. From date of organization to September, 1894, $113.00 were expended for relief, and $45.00 presented T. L. Bonney Post.

Membership, seventy-two.

PRESIDENTS.

Isabella C. Scates	.	1891, 1892
Sarah D. Calder .	.	. 1893
Hannah B. Baker .	.	. 1894

THEODORE PARKMAN CORPS No. 147, CENTREVILLE.

Auxiliary to Theodore Parkman Post No. 204, G.A.R., was instituted Jan. 5, 1892, by Mrs. Annie K. Day, Department Instituting and Installing Officer, with a charter membership of nineteen. Since organization the Corps has assisted Post 204 in holding a fair which was a financial success, besides several smaller entertainments. We have turned over to the Post thirty-five dollars in money, besides a Bible and a costly silk flag.

While small in numbers, we are ever ready to do what we can to assist the veterans, and show our interest in the work by regular attendance at Corps meetings, many of us living from four to ten miles from Corps headquarters.

Membership, twenty-six.

PRESIDENTS.

Hannah C. Childs	1892, 1893
F. Albertine Childs	1894

ROBERT G. SHAW CORPS No. 148, NEW BEDFORD.

On Feb. 25, 1892, Robert G. Shaw Corps No. 148, auxiliary to Robert G. Shaw Post No. 146, G.A.R., was instituted by Mrs. Mary G. Deane, Department President, with a charter membership of thirty-one. Although this Corps has not the facilities for doing the good that many have, it is willing to assist as far as possible its Post and their needy comrades. The estimated value of relief other than money amounts to $48.50. In May, 1893, the Corps assisted Post 146 in giving an entertainment to raise money to purchase a flag and had the pleasure of seeing the Post carry its beautiful flag on Memorial Day. The Corps furnished refreshments Memorial Day, also a collation, and afterward a literary and musical entertainment.

Membership, forty.

PRESIDENTS.

Mary A. Jackson	1892
Harriette A. Chummack	1893
Johanna Maddox	1894

SCOTT BRADLEY CORPS No. 149, LEE.

Scott Bradley Corps No. 149, auxiliary to Scott Bradley Post, was instituted March 23, 1892, with a charter membership of twenty-four, by Mrs. Mary G. Deane, Department President, assisted by Mrs. Annie K. Day, Department Instituting and Installing Officer.

In the first year of its organization a box of comforts was sent to the Soldiers' Home in Chelsea.

The headquarters of the Corps at this time were not convenient, and the town of Lee becoming interested in the work which the Corps was endeavoring to accomplish, gave the Post and Corps the use of a large hall in Memorial Building, which was dedicated by both organizations with appropriate exercises.

The Corps, though small, was energetic and has continued to add to its membership, which is forty-seven.

PRESIDENTS.

Celina H. Spanes	. . .	1892, 1893
Sarah E. Horton	. .	1894

GEORGE C. MARSHALL CORPS No. 150, RUTLAND.

This Corps was instituted May 17, 1892, by Mrs. Annie K. Day, Department Instituting and Installing Officer, with a membership of nineteen. The following Memorial Day we assisted Post 136, by furnishing flowers to decorate the soldiers' graves, also wreaths and flowers for the Soldiers' Monument; also prepared a collation for the Post, band and school children on that day; this was continued each succeeding Memorial Day. Socials and a fair have been held to raise funds for the numerous calls which come to us. Jan. 3, 1893, we gave ten dollars to a soldiers' family during their illness. February, 1893, five dollars given to a family burned out. September, 1893, presented a soldier's family with a wool quilt; also met an afternoon and prepared clothing for destitute family of six children; expended two dollars for shoes. October, 1893, Corps and Post spent a pleasant social day with the Post Commander.

Membership, thirty-seven.

PRESIDENT.

Mary J. Dodge . . . 1892, 1893, 1894

WILLIAM T. SHERMAN CORPS No. 151, WAREHAM.

Wm. T. Sherman Corps No. 151, Wareham, auxiliary to Wm. T. Sherman Post No. 208, G.A.R., was instituted May 26, 1892, with thirty-two charter members, by Mrs. Annie K. Day, Department Instituting and Installing Officer, and its officers-elect publicly installed in the evening by

Mrs. Mary G. Deane, Department President. Since organization the Corps has steadily increased its membership. It has not been called upon by Post 208 for pecuniary assistance, but it has been helpful in fairs which have netted about five hundred dollars. The Corps has also presented an elegant silk flag to the Post. At the date of organization Grand Army headquarters were very small, but with prosperity for the Corps new headquarters have been provided, and Post, Corps and Camp have taken pleasure in fitting out their new home. The Corps has provided a new piano for the same. Calls from Department Headquarters whenever possible are answered. Installations have been joint with the Post and attended by the public.
Membership, fifty-seven.

PRESIDENT.

Emily V. Hurley . . 1892, 1893, 1894

GEORGE H. THOMAS CORPS No. 152, LEICESTER.

A meeting was called in Memorial Hall, Leicester, May 27, 1892, for the purpose of instituting a Corps auxiliary to Geo. H. Thomas Post No. 131. Mrs. Annie K. Day, Department Instituting and Installing Officer, conducted the services. Mrs. Mary G. Deane, Department President, installed its officers. Charter membership, twenty-eight.

This Corps, although in its infancy, has ever been ready to assist Post No. 131 whenever necessary, and during the past year has tendered to the Post a reception, successfully held a lawn party, Bellamy tea and Columbian entertainment, a yellow tea and candy sale and numerous other affairs to fill its treasury with necessary funds with which to successfully carry on the work of the Order. We have rendered aid to deceased soldiers' families, besides sending a small contribution to the Soldiers' Home. Situated in a prosperous country town the calls for local relief have been few.
Membership, forty-three.

PRESIDENT.

Moiselle Olmstead Biscoe . 1892, 1893, 1894

H. H. LEGGE CORPS No. 153, UXBRIDGE.

Was instituted Sept. 7, 1892, with twenty-seven charter members, by Mrs. Emilie L. W. Waterman, Chairman Department Executive Board.

Several entertainments have been given and a fair held with excellent financial results.

Our members are united and interested in the cause, and are loyal to the Post, co-operating with the comrades in Memorial Day plans, and in other patriotic work.

Membership, forty-seven.

PRESIDENTS.

Louise S. Southwick . .	1892, 1893
Florence L. Seagrave . . .	1894

EZRA BATCHELLER CORPS No. 154, NORTH BROOKFIELD.

Since the organization of Ezra Batcheller Post No. 51, G.A.R., two or three unsuccessful attempts were made to form a Relief Corps, and great credit is due to Mrs. Isabell C. Walker for her efforts, which met with success, for on Oct. 6, 1892, a Corps was instituted, as the result, by Mrs. Annie K. Day, Department Instituting and Installing Officer, with a charter membership of twenty-five. The interest manifested in the work has steadily increased.

The means of the Corps are somewhat limited, but its members have faithfully performed whatever has been required. They look forward to doing larger and more efficient work in the future.

Membership, forty-four.

PRESIDENTS.

E. Gertrude Spooner . .	1892, 1893
Isabell C. Walker . . .	1894

E. P. HOPKINS CORPS No. 155, WILLIAMSTOWN.

E. P. Hopkins Corps No. 155, auxiliary to E. P. Hopkins Post No. 209, G.A.R., was instituted with a charter membership of eighteen, by Mrs. Mary G. Deane, Department President, Oct. 21, 1892. The work in the

Corps is limited; we do not feel that we have accomplished all that we desire. On Dec. 15, 1892, we held a "C" supper and sale of fancy articles, from which we realized $133.00; of this amount $50.00 were given to Post 209. April 18, 19, 20, 1893, the Post and Corps held a fair which proved both a social and financial success; net proceeds, $131.13. May 1, 1893, Post and Corps visited a needy comrade, carrying with them a goodly stock of provisions, besides a purse of money which was equally contributed by both organizations.

The Corps attends services on Memorial Day in the forenoon at Williamstown, arranges flowers for the graves, and in the afternoon attends services at South Williamstown, the ladies from the latter place furnishing the dinner. August 16 the Corps tendered a reception to the North Adams Corps, and on October 21, the date of its anniversary, held a reception; at this time the President, Mrs. Nellie C. Crosier, presented the Corps with a life-size crayon of Mrs. Mary G. Deane, Past Department President, Mass. W.R.C., and "Mother" of Corps 155, which was a pleasing surprise to all. The calls from the Department have always been answered, and it is the earnest desire of Corps 155 that its members may be allowed to do all in their power to assist the veterans.

Membership, thirty-eight.

PRESIDENT.

Nellie C. Crosier . . . 1892, 1893, 1894

E. B. NYE CORPS No. 156, BOURNE.

This Corps on the Cape was instituted with forty-three members Oct. 27, 1892, by Mrs. Mary G. Deane, Department President.

A Relief Fund was promptly started, but the calls upon it are few, as this is a favored community.

A lunch is furnished the comrades at noon and again on the evening of Memorial Day, and we accompany the Post to the church where the exercises are held and also at the services on Memorial Sunday.

A fair was held in 1893, which resulted in adding to our treasury. A donation has been given to the Memorial Fund and other Department funds, and a pledge made to the proposed monument "in honor of the brave and true soldiers and sailors who never came back."

Of course we sometimes meet with discouragements, but we know that we are banded together to work for a most noble cause.
Membership, sixty-seven.

PRESIDENT.

Susan D. Phinney . . . 1892, 1893, 1894

BOSTON CORPS No. 157, BOSTON.

Organized Nov. 27, 1892, by Mrs. Mary G. Deane, Department President, with sixty-three charter members.

This Corps has expended in relief $17.53; assisted the comrades on Memorial Day and at the request of Boston Post No. 200, visited Mount Auburn, Mount Hope and Forest Hills Cemeteries to assist in decorating the graves of deceased comrades; also provided dinner for comrades and Sons of Veterans, furnishing a small bouquet for each.

Our calls for relief have been few, but we have expended in relief $17.50.

Membership, seventy-five.

PRESIDENTS.

Margie E. B. Hutchins	1892, 1893
Sarah A. Newell .	. 1894

MOUNTAIN MILLER CORPS No. 158, PLAINFIELD.

Was instituted Nov. 22, 1892, by Mrs. Emily L. Clark, Department Senior Vice-President, assisted by Mrs. Marion E. Bridgman of the Department Executive Board. Charter membership, twelve. Although not very old, this Corps shows by its interest that it is fully alive to the objects of our Order, having forwarded a box of supplies to the Soldiers' Home in Chelsea and established a Relief Fund.

Although organized but a short time we have gained in numbers, having at the present date a membership of twenty-three.

PRESIDENT.

Bessie S. Taylor . . 1892, 1893, 1894

SAMUEL SIBLEY CORPS No. 159, EAST DOUGLAS.

Organized Oct. 12, 1893, by Mrs. Lizzie F. Mudgett, Department Instituting and Installing Officer. Forty-five charter members. Our field of labor is comparatively small, but in every case brought to our knowledge we have rendered all assistance in our power. Expended in relief over $19.50. In all our undertakings to raise money have had the hearty co-operation of the townspeople as well as of Samuel Sibley Post No. 137.

Membership, fifty-seven.

PRESIDENT.

Loretta M. Sweet . 1893, 1894

GEORGE E. SAYLES CORPS No. 160, ADAMS.

Was instituted March 29, 1894, with fourteen members, by Mrs. Flora A. Smith, Department Instituting and Installing Officer. Mrs. Clare H. Burleigh, Department President, installed the officers.

The Corps has been organized such a brief time that there is little of public interest to record. But we have endeavored to be faithful to our obligation and to Post 126.

Membership, forty-one.

PRESIDENT.

Mattie E. Simmons 1894

WOBURN CORPS No. 161, WOBURN.

Woburn Corps No. 161, auxiliary to Post 161, was instituted March 17, 1887, with thirty-eight members, by Mrs. L. A. Turner, Department Senior Vice-President, assisted by officers of Corps 43, Arlington.

The number at date of institution was 83, but by request of the Post in 1892, the number was changed to 161, by authority of the Department President.

Success has crowned the labors of the Corps from its earliest days and its work is well known in the community. Many of its members are ladies of culture and prominence in society, and the influence of the Corps is felt in the city of Woburn.

One special feature is visiting the sick and over 1500 calls have been made, the committee taking with them delicacies, flowers, etc., to help and cheer the afflicted.

Through the efforts of Past President Miss Susan Tebbetts, a large sum of money was raised for a veteran's wife suffering with illness, and for eight weeks the Corps provided watchers and tenderly cared for her; when the final summons ended her sufferings, the Corps assumed charge of her burial.

Corps 161 has worked for the Post in its fairs and all proceeds are for the Post treasury.

A supper is given every fourth Tuesday evening in the month and the Post attends in a body. After each sociable flowers and delicacies are sent to the sick in the community.

Corps 161 has furnished the parlor of Grand Army Hall; a flag valued at $75.00 has been given the Post and was carried for the first time on Memorial Day, 1894.

Great interest is taken in Memorial Day and a collation is served in Grand Army Hall. Bouquets are always provided for the comrades and their guests, and this year the sum of fifty dollars was given the Post for use on Memorial Day.

The two Posts in Woburn alternate in decorating the Soldiers' monument, and every other year Corps 161 assists Post 161 in performing this sacred duty.

Our members are interested in the Soldiers' Home and arrange entertainments, etc., for the pleasure of the inmates.

In all cases of need, relief is promptly given; the Post is ably assisted at all its camp-fires, fairs and entertainments, and annually receives a gift of money from its auxiliary.

The ability and willingness to assist the Post on any and all occasions is recognized and fully appreciated.

During the existence of the Corps about $500.00 have been turned over to the Post from our treasury, and $80.00 given in relief and to the Soldiers' Home. This does not include all the relief work, as much has been given, the value of which could not be estimated.

During the year 1892, the number of candidates initiated was second to no other Corps in the State.

Membership, one hundred and twenty-eight.

PRESIDENTS.

Margaret B. Cutler	. .	1887, 1888
Octavia E. Dorr .	.	1889, 1890, 1891
Susan Tebbetts .	. .	1892, 1893
Eliza S. Tabor .	. . .	1894

GEN. JOHN G. BARNARD CORPS No. 162, SHEFFIELD.

This Corps was instituted May 16, 1894, with eighteen members, by Mrs. Flora A. Smith, Department Instituting and Installing Officer, assisted by Mrs. Clare H. Burleigh, Department President.

We united with the Post in observing Memorial Day, and although remote from other Corps and unable to gain inspiration by frequent visits to social gatherings, our members realize the importance of the work undertaken.

Membership, twenty-one.

PRESIDENT.

Julia A. Miller . . . 1894

MARTHA SEVER CORPS No. 163, KINGSTON.

Was instituted Aug. 20, 1894, by Mrs. Flora A. Smith, Department Instituting and Installing Officer, assisted by Mrs. Clare H. Burleigh, Department President, and also by a delegation from Collingwood Corps of Plymouth, who exemplified the Ritual. Our Post took for its name the name of a lovely young Kingston girl, who, thrilled with a desire to render acceptable service to her country in the hour of peril, went to the front as an army nurse and incurred a fatal fever, thus giving up her life for her country.

Dictionaries say, history is a narration of past events; and yet we are asked for our history when we have only just begun, are living in the present, and can only look forward to the future, not back to the past. Thus far we have given nothing outside of Post and Corps. We found it desirable to procure a musical instrument, and a piano was purchased at a cost of $150.00. In the meantime we have not neglected the interest of our Post, a special committee has repaired its flag, which with other help amounts to $25.00. We entertained the comrades in G.A.R. Hall in December, all declaring themselves as benefited by the social and fraternal gathering. A joint installation of officers was held on the evening of January 3, and being our first service of this kind was an important event in our history. Visitors from Collingwood Post and Corps were with us, Mrs. Lucia A. Knapp acting as Installing Officer in a very impressive manner.

We would not omit our first inspection held on the afternoon of Nov. 20. How we trembled! But the smiling face of our Inspector

Mrs. Cornelia Byrnes, Past President of Collingwood Corps, reassured us, and we shall remember with satisfaction our *first*. We can truly say as did our mother Corps No. 124, *that day*, "Long may Martha Sever Corps live and be an honor to this grand organization!"

This Corps was very successful as an independent organization, having worked in connection with Martha Sever Post several years. Its members have continued in the same earnest spirit since adopting the broader work of the Department.

Membership, fifty-nine.

PRESIDENT.

Emma P. Ford . 1894

HENRY H. JOHNSON CORPS No. 164, NORTHFIELD.

This Corps was instituted Dec. 20, 1894, by Mrs. Flora A. Smith, Department Instituting and Installing Officer, and the officers were installed by Mrs. Clare H. Burleigh, Department President.

The Corps was organized through the efforts of Commander Walter D. Crane of Post 171, Northfield, and has prospects of a successful future.

Membership, twenty-six.

PRESIDENT.

Ella L. Lazelle 1894

GEN. WILLIAM S. LINCOLN CORPS No. 165, ENFIELD.

Was instituted Dec. 22, 1894, by Mrs. Clare H. Burleigh, Department President.

Its members are interested in the work, and will well represent our Order in the extreme western part of the State.

Membership, twenty-five.

PRESIDENT.

Lizzie B. Moore . . 1894

WOMAN'S RELIEF CORPS.

As several of the preceding sketches refer to contributions given in 1890, for the entertainment of the National Convention in Boston, the following list is published that all the Corps represented in this Chapter may receive credit for their donations.

Corps		Amount	Corps		Amount
Corps	1	$53 10	Corps	36	$ 5 00
"	2	75 00	"	37	10 00
"	3	25 00	"	38	75 00
"	4	10 00	"	39	68 00
"	5	164 00	"	40	15 00
"	6	50 00	"	41	25 00
"	7	100 00	"	42	60 00
"	8	30 00	"	43	61 00
"	9	50 00	"	45	10 00
"	10	15 00	"	46	30 00
"	11	100 00	"	47	5 00
"	12	25 00	"	48	10 00
"	13	20 00	"	49	25 00
"	14	50 00	"	50	25 00
"	15	10 00	"	51	25 00
"	16	25 00	"	52	5 00
"	17	50 00	"	53	100 00
"	18	100 00	"	54	40 00
"	19	25 00	"	55	100 00
"	20	50 00	"	56	9 50
"	21	11 00	"	57	25 00
"	22	50 00	"	58	5 00
"	23	25 00	"	59	50 00
"	24	30 00	"	60	25 00
"	25	89 55	"	61	40 00
"	26	50 00	"	62	15 00
"	27	34 30	"	63	100 00
"	28	100 00	"	64	5 00
"	29	280 00	"	65	50 00
"	30	75 00	"	66	75 00
"	31	125 00	"	67	5 00
"	32	15 00	"	68	459 09
"	33	25 00	"	69	50 00
"	34	150 00	"	70	5 00
"	35	150 00	"	72	25 00

Corps 73 .	$ 5 00	Corps 104 .	$ 5 00
" 74 .	15 00	" 105 .	30 00
" 75 .	25 00	" 106 .	100 00
" 76 .	35 00	" 107 .	12 00
" 77 .	100 00	" 108 .	10 00
" 78 .	50 00	" 109 .	50 00
" 79 .	50 00	" 110 .	50 00
" 80 .	63 00	" 112 .	40 00
" 81 .	5 00	" 113 .	10 00
" 82 .	25 00	" 114 .	5 00
" 84 .	25 00	" 115 .	10 00
" 85 .	10 00	" 117 .	50 00
" 86 .	7 75	" 118 .	10 00
" 87 .	25 00	" 119 .	10 00
" 90 .	75 00	" 120 .	25 00
" 92 .	10 00	" 121 .	10 00
" 93 .	25 00	" 122 .	25 00
" 94 .	75 00	" 123 .	5 00
" 96 .	25 00	" 124 .	842 53
" 97 .	25 00	" 125 .	25 00
" 98 .	5 00	" 126 .	10 00
" 99 .	5 00	" 127 .	25 00
" 101 .	5 00	" 132 .	30 00
" 103 .	60 00	" 161 .	50 00

CHAPTER IX.

BIOGRAPHICAL SKETCHES.

ROM Feb. 12, 1879, to Jan. 1, 1895, there have been ten Presidents and four Secretaries of the Department of Massachusetts. A brief biographical sketch of each is given in this chapter, and also included in the list of biographies is a sketch of Mrs. Lizabeth A. Turner, one of the pioneers of the National organization, and of Capt. James F. Meech, the only Honorary Member of the Department of Massachusetts, W.R.C.

MRS. SARAH E. FULLER.

The first President of the Department of Massachusetts, Mrs. Sarah E. Fuller, has a record of thirty-four years' faithful service for the soldiers of the Civil War.

She was born August 1, 1838, in Portland, Me., and is of Revolutionary descent, both her father's and mother's ancestors having been soldiers in that struggle. Her father, Samuel Mills, was an intense abolitionist; his daughter, who is the only survivor of a family of ten children, was taught to take an interest in public affairs, and was given an opportunity in early life of hearing many of the leading orators and statesmen of the country. In 1851 her parents moved to East Boston, where, four years later, she married George W. Fuller of Canton, Me.

Among the thousands of homes in the North where the exciting debates in Congress were read with eager interest during the winter of 1859 and '60, was the quiet fireside of Mrs. Fuller. When, a few months later, the call for "seventy-five thousand men" aroused a spirit of patriotism that left its shadow on the threshold, her husband volunteered, but was rejected as physically unable to bear the hardships of war. He again volunteered in 1862 for naval service on the gunboat *Roanoke*, but his frail constitution was deemed a barrier, and he returned home disappointed, though not defeated.

He never abandoned the hope of serving his country, and Feb. 12, 1864, enrolled his name for the third time and was mustered into the service six days after enlistment as a member of Company C, Fourth Mass. Cavalry.

The regiment remained in camp at Readville until April 24, when it sailed from Boston for Newport News, Va., on the steamer *Western Metropolis*. It was ordered to Petersburg in the following June, where Mr. Fuller was stricken with malarial typhoid fever and removed to the hospital at Portsmouth, Va., surviving only until the 2d of July.

During this period Mrs. Fuller was rendering every possible aid to the Union cause, and represented Ward One of Boston on the Executive Committee of the Christian Commission. She assisted in preparing hospital stores and other comforts for the soldiers, and participated in many patriotic concerts given in various cities of Maine and Massachusetts, for the Hospital Fund. The day after the news of the battle of Antietam was received at the North, she arranged, with the help of a few others, a concert, from which $400.00 were realized and converted into articles which were forwarded to the front in less than two days after the concert was given.

In 1868, Mrs. Fuller visited the National Cemetery at Hampton, Va., where her husband is buried. Superintendent August Miller, in a letter to her a few years after, wrote: — "I have made it a rule to place a bouquet on grave 3544, George W. Fuller, 4th Mass. Cavalry, early in the morning on each Memorial Day. I noticed that other kind friends have also decorated the grave with choice flowers. Inclosed you will find a few rosebuds taken from the bush on the grave."

Remembering with gratitude that one of the noble band of army nurses ministered to her husband's comfort to the last, Mrs. Fuller consecrated her life to the soldiers' cause. She assisted in forming a Ladies' Aid Society, auxiliary to Joseph Hooker Post No. 23 of East Boston. This society began its work in April, 1871, and continued eight years. Mrs. Fuller served as Secretary, Vice-President and President, and was a delegate to the State Convention of Ladies' Auxiliary Societies held at Fitchburg, Feb. 12, 1879.

This convention resulted in the formation of the "Woman's State Relief Corps" of Massachusetts. Mrs. Fuller was chosen President, and re-elected to that office in 1880 and 1881. She realized that a great responsibility rested upon her, and looking into the years of the future with a faith that never wavered even amid discouragements, pledged her best efforts to this work in behalf of the Grand Army of the Republic.

It was no easy task, but one that required time and money, the best thought and judgment, a sincere purpose and a loyal womanhood of the highest type. That she won the support of many who were at first sceptical in regard to the success of the movement, and by her persistent energy established the Order on a firm basis, is now a matter of history.

Discouragements there were many, but voice and pen united to surmount them, for, eloquent in speech and convincing in argument, Mrs. Fuller wisely directed both for the best interests of the cause.

Upon retiring from the presidency at the Annual Convention in 1882, she was chosen Secretary of the Department. In her capacity as President and Secretary she travelled thousands of miles, instituted nineteen Corps in Massachusetts, five in Maine, and assisted Mrs. Barker and Mrs. Goodale at the institution of eighteen others. She conducted a large correspondence, writing hundreds of letters annually, and in this way aroused an interest in the Order outside of the limits of Massachusetts.

Mrs. Fuller was one of the three delegates who represented the Department of Massachusetts at the Convention in Denver, Col., which was called in 1883 by Commander-in-Chief Van Der Voort. She took an important part in its proceedings and improved every opportunity to advance the interests of a national organization and to secure the adoption of the Massachusetts work.

When the plans were recognized and the work completed by the election of officers, Mrs. Fuller assumed the duties of National Secretary, to which office she had been unanimously chosen. It was a busy year for her; over 1,500 letters and 500 postal cards were written and many hundred pages of written instruction copied by her, in addition to numerous other duties. From September 5 to February 23 she issued supplies for eighty-nine Corps.

At the Second National Convention held at Minneapolis, she was chosen National Senior Vice-President. During that year she instituted three Corps in Rhode Island, and visited Vermont on a tour of inspection, and then instituted a Department in that State.

At the Third National Convention, held in Portland, Me., in 1885, she was elected National President, and upon returning home tendered her resignation as Department Secretary. She was also obliged to resign her office as President of the local Corps in East Boston, which she had held nearly two years, as the National work required all her time.

That her efforts were appreciated by the comrades is shown by the following

RESOLUTIONS.

At a regular meeting of John A. Hawes Post No. 159, G.A.R., July 24, 1885, the following resolutions were unanimously adopted: —

WHEREAS, It has pleased the National Woman's Relief Corps in convention assembled at Portland, Me., June 25, 1885, to elect Mrs. Sarah E. Fuller to the highest honor in its gift — that of its National President; and

WHEREAS, She has shown by her loyalty and devotion to the principles of our Order, an affectionate remembrance of those, who, in a great crisis, saved the nation's life; therefore be it

Resolved, That while we recognize the high honor and trust reposed in her ability and integrity, we shall deeply feel the loss in our midst of one who was ever ready to offer the hand of aid to the distressed, the voice of sympathy and consolation to the sick and dying soldier and to the widows and orphans of those who fell in our "holy cause," whose utmost endeavors were exerted for the welfare and prosperity of the Grand Army of the Republic and Woman's Relief Corps by years of labor in the many fields to which she has been called.

Resolved, That in view of her retirement from the office of President of the Woman's Relief Corps 3, the members of John A. Hawes Post 159 desire to express to her their warm appreciation of the valuable services she has rendered them, both in her official and private relations, and whose deeds will long be remembered in the grateful hearts of her many associates.

Resolved, That the sincere and heartfelt good wishes of this Post will follow her day by day, as she labors for the good of the Order in the high position to which she has been called, that the present year may be one of great prosperity and growth.

Resolved, That a copy of these resolutions be spread on the records of the Post, that a copy thereof be transmitted to Mrs. Sarah E. Fuller, also to the *East Boston Advocate* for publication.

WM. G. SMITH,
CHAS. E. BUSHEE,
GEORGE S. PITTS,
Committee.

During her year as National President, Mrs. Fuller visited the Departments of New Hampshire, New York, Pennsylvania, Ohio and Illinois. She conducted a large correspondence and addressed many public gatherings. She issued eight General Orders, one of which was a memorial tribute to General Grant which was widely read, and being a document of historic interest is herewith published: —

HEADQUARTERS WOMAN'S RELIEF CORPS,
AUXILIARY TO THE GRAND ARMY OF THE REPUBLIC,
BOSTON, July 23, 1885.

GENERAL ORDERS, }
No. 2.

On this bright summer morning the bells are tolling the requiem of our country's noble dead.

Ex-President Ulysses S. Grant has closed his eyes and lain him down to rest. The long, weary months of pain and suffering are over, and our brave, lion-hearted Commander and Comrade is no more.

A nation is in tears, and the people sit in sadness. He whose courage and devotion to his country in her great hour of need led the people to look to him to lead us to victory, has heard the last "roll call," and in answering has laid down the weapons of warfare, wrapt his mantle about him, and is now numbered with that "Grand Army whose term of service is completed." No more will the bugle-call arouse his slumbers. His is a sleep that knows no earthly waking.

As an auxiliary to the Grand Army of the Republic, who today mourn the loss of their comrade, it is fitting that we, the members of the "Woman's Relief Corps," should unite with them in our expressions of sorrow and mourning.

Therefore, in recognition of the faithful services of this patriot, soldier and friend, and as a tribute of our respect and love for the "Hero of Appomattox," and our grateful remembrance of his heroic deeds, the charters of all Corps throughout our Order will be draped in the emblems of mourning for sixty days, and at the first regular meeting after the receipt of this order all Corps shall set apart one hour for special services commemorative of his life and glorious deeds as a soldier.

In this hour of great affliction and sorrow I would tender to the widow and family of this deceased comrade the loving sympathy and respect of the members of this Order. Twenty-five thousand women, who are banded together to work for the interest of the veteran soldier and sailor of the late Rebellion, will bear them on their hearts, praying the consolations of Heaven may be theirs.

Department and Corps Presidents are charged with a prompt distribution of this order.

By command of

SARAH E. FULLER,
National President.

ELEANOR B. WHEELER,
National Secretary.

When closing her year as National President at the Fourth Annual Convention held in San Francisco, in 1886, Mrs. Fuller was elected a member of the National Council of Administration, and at St. Louis, a year later, was made a life member.

In 1889 Mrs. Fuller was elected Secretary of the Committee of Arrangements for the Eighth National Convention to be held in Boston the following year. She was Secretary of the National Pension Committee for Army Nurses and was called to Washington to aid in securing favorable action by Congress in June, 1890, when, prostrated by the heat, she became suddenly deaf and was obliged to defer all active work for two years.

Mrs. Fuller was elected Department Treasurer at the Annual Convention of this Department held in 1892 and has continued to perform the duties of that office, taking an active interest in all that concerns the welfare of the Department. She resides at the home of her son in Medford.

She has been an active member of the Ladies' Aid Association of the Soldiers' Home and served in official positions from the date of its organization in 1882 to the present time. A room at the Home is furnished by the Department W.R.C. and named in her honor, and her portrait has been placed on its walls, a gift from Corps 3 of East Boston. William Logan Rodman Post No. 1 of New Bedford has placed her picture (handsomely framed) in its Post room, and the occasion was made an event of great interest in that city. Mrs. Fuller has delivered Memorial Day addresses in Maine and Massachusetts, and has addressed hundreds of camp-fires and other patriotic gatherings. She has friends in every State in the Union and they appreciate her grand service and her loyal womanhood.

Mrs. E. Florence Barker.

Mrs. E. Florence Barker, the first National President, was born March 29, 1840, in Lynnfield, Mass., where she passed her girlhood days and graduated from the public schools. She finished her education at the academy at Thetford, Vt.

Mrs. Barker is a daughter of William A. and Mary J. (Skinner) Whittredge. On the 18th of June, 1863, she married Col. Thomas Erskine Barker of Gilmanton, N.H., while he was at home on a furlough, recovering from wounds received in the battle of Chancellorsville. In July of the same year Colonel Barker was able to again take command of his regiment, the Twelfth New Hampshire. His bride joined him in August at Point Lookout, Md., and remained at the front until the following April. Naturally patriotic, this experience increased her regard for the Union soldiers whom she often met in the camp and hospital. Her tent was tastefully decorated and was a cheerful place of rendezvous for the officers.

When the Grand Army of the Republic was formed, Mrs. Barker, remembering that its members represented the veterans of the Civil War, became deeply interested in its success. She united with the Relief Corps in Malden in May, 1879, and served four years as its President, and at the convention of the Department of Massachusetts in 1880 was elected Department Senior Vice-President, and re-elected in 1881. Mrs. Barker was chosen Department President the following year and filled the office so acceptably that she was re-elected in 1883. Eighteen Corps were instituted during her administration, the number of Corps being doubled during her two years' leadership.

While presiding over the Convention that year she had the pleasure of welcoming Paul Van Der Voort, Commander-in-Chief of the Grand Army of the Republic, and other prominent comrades. The eloquent manner in which she presented the work of our Order helped to win the support of the Commander-in-Chief. When, a few months later, in response to his call for a convention of all the auxiliary societies, the

Union Board elected delegates to Denver, Col., Mrs. Barker was chosen chairman of the delegation. She presided with grace and tact over the deliberations of that convention, and accepted a unanimous election as its President when the National Organization was completed. How fortunate that the honor was bestowed upon one so worthy to guide the Order through its first year's trials!

Three hundred thousand comrades of the Grand Army of the Republic were looking upon the auxiliary with critical eyes, — many with words of encouragement, but some with doubts as to the advisability of the new movement.

To prove that a National Order was needed, that the plan adopted at Denver was the best, and that women were capable of managing a large organization with ritualistic forms and parliamentary rules, required judgment, tact, and a love for the work. These principles were combined in Mrs. Barker, who sought advice from officials of the Grand Army of the Republic and recognized the importance of harmonious co-operation with them.

Her first General Order, issued soon after her return home, shows that she realized the importance of the obligation she had assumed, and was competent to manage with success the great work she had undertaken.

An extract from General Order No. 1 is herewith given:

NATIONAL HEADQUARTERS WOMAN'S RELIEF CORPS,
AUXILIARY TO THE GRAND ARMY OF THE REPUBLIC,
12 PEMBERTON SQUARE. BOSTON, Sept. 1, 1883.

GENERAL ORDERS.
No. 1.

Upon assuming the duties of National President, I desire to express my grateful thanks to the members of our Order for the honor conferred by their action in placing me in this responsible position. Trusting I may prove worthy the same and praying the folds of the cloak of charity may fall over the many mistakes of my administration, and the earnest heart atone for the errors of the head, I commit myself to the Auxiliary of the Grand Army of the Republic.

Realizing somewhat the great responsibility, I assume the work of the ensuing year with many misgivings, yet the past record of the competent corps of officers associated with me assures me that, with the best efforts of every member of our Order, much good work may be accomplished during the first year of our National Organization. I trust we shall prove worthy the indorsement of the Seventeenth National

Encampment, having secured its approval, standing second to that most glorious charitable organization in this land, a society embracing every color, every nation and every religion: the Grand Army of the Republic. While working in unison with the G.A.R. we can accomplish great results and build well the structure which we hope will stand years after the watchful comrades have left, as they must, their unfinished work to our willing hands.

When presenting her annual address at the Minneapolis Convention July, 1884, she was able to say, "Our success far exceeds the high anticipation of our most sanguine friends."

Mrs. Kate B. Sherwood, in her report as National Senior Vice-President, complimented the "broad-minded policy" of the administration.

Mrs. Barker wrote over a thousand letters during her year as National President, visited the Departments of Maine, New Hampshire and Connecticut and performed numerous other duties. She declined a re-election, but as a life member of the National Executive Board she has a vote in shaping the affairs of the Order. Mrs. Barker is an eloquent speaker and has addressed many patriotic gatherings. She represented the Order at the International Council of Women held at Washington, D.C., in 1889.

She is deeply interested in the Soldiers' Home in Massachusetts and is one of the founders of the Ladies' Aid Association connected with the Board of Trustees of which Colonel Barker is Treasurer, and she has ever since been an officer and leader in the Association. One of the rooms at the Home was taken by the Department of Massachusetts and named in her honor, and her portrait has been placed therein. The room is designated by a banner on which is this inscription: —

"Dedicated in honor of Mrs. E. Florence Barker, First National President of the Woman's Relief Corps."

A patriotic spirit pervades the pleasant home of Colonel and Mrs. Barker in Malden. In a room devoted to relics may be seen a jewelled sword presented the Colonel by the officers of his regiment, his commission as military governor of Danville, Va., a lock from Libbey Prison in which he was confined several months, and hanging on the walls of this room is the engrossed testimonial presented Mrs. Barker by the Department of Massachusetts when she retired from the office of Department President in January, 1884. which reads as follows: —

To Mrs. E. Florence Barker, Past Department President, Woman's Relief Corps of Massachusetts:

Greeting: In appreciation of the fact that interwoven in almost the entire history of the Woman's Relief Corps are your counsels and your efforts, from the time when, as a small organization in Massachusetts, it struggled for recognition, to the date of the successful formation of the National Relief Corps at Denver, Col., your associates in the Department of Massachusetts have voted you this testimonial as a tribute of respect.

The excellent judgment ever manifested during the two years in which you served this Department as President — the fidelity with which you rendered service as First National President of the Order, your influence everywhere recognized, have conferred honor upon our work, and aided in giving it a permanent endorsement by the Grand Army of the Republic throughout the land.

As a loyal woman whose sympathies from the earliest days of the Civil War have been enlisted in the veterans' cause, as a faithful visitor to the Soldiers' Home in Massachusetts, whose inmates regard you as their friend, as the wife of an honored soldier, as our associate in the work of fraternity, charity and loyalty, we give you the assurance of our highest esteem.

(Signed)

MARY E. ELLIOT,
M. SUSIE GOODALE,
S. AGNES PARKER,
L. A. TURNER,
Committee.

Mrs. Barker has valuable scrap-books relating to the G.A.R. and W.R.C. and numerous autograph letters from distinguished friends in various parts of the country. Two daughters and a son have received a mother's devoted care, notwithstanding her public work.

Mrs. Barker has not confined her interests entirely to Grand Army or Soldiers' Home work. She is one of the Directors of the Union Prisoners of War National Memorial Association; is treasurer of the Woman's Club House Association of Boston, and is one of the Trustees of the Malden Hospital and a Director in the Hospital Aid Association. She exerts an influence in public work and social life, and thoroughly enjoys her associations in both.

Mrs. M. Susie Goodale.

Mrs. Goodale was a schoolgirl when the Civil War began, but the lessons of loyalty taught her by a patriotic father were deeply impressed upon her mind, and she inherited a love for the flag from revolutionary ancestors. She was determined to help the Union cause, and among other successful efforts, solicited money from citizens and furnished a Thanksgiving dinner to the soldiers' families in her neighborhood. Her father, being an invalid, could not enlist, but he aided the cause financially, and organized a society for the care of soldiers' families. He died shortly after victory and peace were declared, and Mrs. Goodale honors his memory by a continued interest in the cause he loved.

She is a charter member of S. C. Lawrence Corps No. 5 of Medford, which was instituted May 27, 1879, and served that year as Senior Vice-President.

She was installed as President in January, 1880, and re-elected three years in succession.

At the Department Convention in 1881 she proved very efficient in committee work and at a meeting of the Board of Directors held in April was chosen a member of the Committee on Soldiers' Home Bazaar, and also as one of a committee to purchase a flag for the Home. When the Board of Directors met again in October, Mrs. Goodale was elected Department Conductor to fill a vacancy in that office.

She was Secretary of the Union table in the Soldiers' Home Bazaar held in December at Mechanics Building, Boston. At the Annual Convention in 1882, she was re-elected Department Conductor, and was appointed a member of the Committee on Ritual and Rules and Regulations. Mrs. Goodale was elected Department Senior Vice-President at the Annual Convention in 1883 and a year later was chosen Department President.

During the first year of her administration sixteen Corps were added to the roster, being instituted by her, and there was a gain in membership of 733, making a total of 49 Corps and 2,608 members. Dec. 31, 1884. The sum of $3,039.78 was expended in relief and $257.55 turned over to Posts during the year. Her annual address contained many valuable suggestions. When the Convention met in 1885, Mrs. Goodale was urged to retain the office another year, and was unanimously re-elected. That the Convention acted wisely is shown by the results of her work.

Although prevented by serious illness from attending the Convention in 1886, she sent a report of great interest, and extracts from the same are given as follows: —

"The nervous strain upon my system by the duties devolving upon me as President, the travelling from place to place throughout the Department as Instituting and Installing Officer, has been too great and at almost the last hour I have been obliged to place my precious charge in other hands. This has been very hard for me to do, as I was looking forward with fond anticipations to the hours of the Convention when I should meet so many of those dear sisters whom I have learned to honor and love.

"The first large undertaking of the year was the work for the Soldiers' Home Carnival, and the earnest, unselfish manner with which the members responded to my appeal in General Orders No. 1, was gratifying and never will be forgotten by me, and I hereby tender to all the Corps my sincere thanks for the labor then performed.

"Since last Convention we have made a net gain of 16 Corps and 1,204 members. Our entire membership up to the last of my administration, Jan. 27, 1886, is a little over 3,800.

"I cannot give you full particulars of my labors during the year but will briefly say, that I have represented the Department on 73 different occasions, written 698 letters, and a large number of postal cards, travelled over 1,900 miles (not including the weekly trips to Headquarters on Wednesday).

"The work of the Department has assumed such proportions that I am led to recommend that this Convention adopt measures for the appointment of a corps of aides, corresponding to the aides appointed by the Department Commander of the Grand Army of the Republic. It would be the duty of these aides to become thoroughly acquainted with all the workings of the Order, holding themselves in readiness to act in any capacity.

"My sisters, I am compelled to be 'absent in the flesh, yet I am with you in spirit,' and most earnestly wish that the Convention of 1886 may prove a happy, successful and instructive one."

Mrs. Goodale was chairman of the Department table in the Soldiers' Home Carnival, the proceeds of which netted $4,000 to the Carnival treasury.

She is a member of the Ladies' Aid Association of the Soldiers' Home and rendered efficient service in the kettledrum held under its auspices at the Institute Building in Boston, and has been a grand worker for the Home.

She is a member of the Committee on Department Rooms at the Soldiers' Home and of other committees and retains an earnest interest in all branches of the work.

She is the wife of George L. Goodale, Past Department Commander, G.A.R , who served in the 43d Mass. Regiment, and who was Inspector-General on the Staff of Commander-in-Chief Weissert. They have three children, a son and two daughters.

Mrs. Goodale participated in the National Conventions at Minneapolis and Portland, serving on special committees, and in 1884 was appointed by Mrs. Sherwood, National President, to represent Massachusetts as National Corresponding Secretary.

She is an interesting speaker, and a woman of excellent judgment, whose counsel always has weight, and she has the love and respect of numerous friends. Mrs. Goodale is a member of the Woman's Club in Medford, and interested in the social and educational affairs of her city.

Mrs. S. Agnes Parker.

Mrs. Parker is a native of New London, N.H , where she was born in 1841, but has lived in Brockton, Mass., ever since she was three years old (the place at that time was called North Bridgewater).

Her husband, John Parker, has been Quartermaster of Fletcher Webster Post No. 13 of Brockton the past fifteen years. He served in Co. F, 58th Mass. Regiment, was wounded at Cold Harbor and honorably discharged for disability soon after the surrender of General Lee.

Early in 1873 a Grand Army sewing society was formed in Brockton to assist Post 13, and Mrs. Parker was chosen secretary. When the society was merged into Relief Corps No. 7, in October, 1879. she was elected President, and re-elected for three successive years.

A special feature of the Annual Convention in 1880 was a report from each Corps President relative to the work accomplished during the year. The Convention records referred to this as follows : —

"The various Corps Presidents gave good accounts of their Corps, that of Mrs. S. Agnes Parker of Fletcher Webster Corps of Brockton being specially interesting."

Mrs. Parker served on important Committees that year, and at the Convention in 1881 was elected Department Treasurer. She was Department Inspector in 1882, and also served as a member of the Committee on Ritual and Rules and Regulations, and was appointed Chairman of the Committee the following year. She was chosen Department Junior Vice-President in 1883, promoted to Senior Vice-President in 1884 and re-elected in 1885. Mrs. Parker presided over the Annual Convention of 1886, as the Department President, Mrs. Goodale, was detained at home by illness. She was elected Department President at this Convention.

When referring in her annual address, the following year, to the work undertaken, she said: —

"One year ago I had the honor to be elected Department President by the members of the Seventh Annual Convention of Massachusetts. I shall ever be indebted to you for the honor you conferred upon me, as well as for the pleasure it has afforded me to work for our noble cause as the recognized head of this Department. I took the obligation of my office with fear and trembling, knowing there was hard work before me, and if I wished to make the same record as my predecessors, I should have to put my whole soul into the work. I have always loved and honored the soldier; and it was no task to work for the brave men who wore the blue; but to always do that which was right and best for our beloved organization required much thought and deep study. I promised to strictly and impartially fulfil my duties to the best of my ability, and I stand here today feeling I have tried to keep my obligation. If you are satisfied with my work, I shall be happy; if I have not met your expectations, I beg of you to cover my faults with the mantle of charity.

"I have been absent from Headquarters but twice, and then on account of sickness. I have issued seven General Orders. In my first and second General Orders I appointed a Staff of Aides to assist the Department officers in their work, and be of service to those Corps in remote parts of the State, whenever they needed assistance or instruction. To reach Corps in every section of the State requires a great deal of travelling and considerable expense. This plan has proved successful, Department as well as Corps having been benefitted by the assistance of these aides, who have my warmest thanks for their efficiency.

"My duties as Department President have occupied the greater part of my time. No one can fill the chair or attempt to discharge the duties of Department President without giving her time and attention to the work before her. I have travelled in official capacity in the State of Massachusetts four thousand and seventy-one miles, have made forty-one visits with Corps, visiting thirty-three different Corps, having made four tours to visit the extreme northern, western, eastern and southern Corps. I hope these visits may be productive of much good. In my travels I have been cordially received, and have spent one of the happiest years of my life attending to the work of the Department President. I attended the National Convention at San Francisco, travelling a distance of over eight thousand miles.

"I have attended many anniversaries and inspections (by invitation). Have instituted one Corps and installed the officers in six Corps, and have paid other official visits too numerous to mention.

"We have expended in relief the past year $3,903.47. This sum does not include the entire amount, as much has been given in the way of clothing and other articles not mentioned. The Soldiers' Home has received $657.28."

A reception was tendered Mrs. Parker in Boston upon her return from California by the delegates who represented Massachusetts at the Fourth National Convention. Fletcher Webster Post and Corps of Brockton also gave her a reception in that city.

Mrs. Parker conducted such a successful administration that she was unanimously re-elected Department President at the Convention in 1887. When presenting her annual address a year later she referred to the work of the year as follows: —

"The growth of the Order in Massachusetts has been marked and quite satisfactory. Jan. 1, 1887, we had 77 Corps with a membership of 5,257; today we number 100 Corps with a membership of over 6,700. We have not lost or suspended a Corps during the year. Amount expended in relief the past year $5,624.40, and turned over to Posts $3,258.34. This amount does not cover the value of all clothing and food given, as in many cases the value is not estimated. The Inspector was unable to secure the full amount given to the Soldiers' Home the past year, but the sum reported is $679.18.

"My duties as Department President have occupied nearly all my time. I have issued seven General Orders and two Circular Letters; have visited headquarters ninety times; have travelled in official capacity in this State 5,844 miles, visiting thirty-eight different Corps. I have also attended many anniversaries, inspections, installations and fairs. Several Corps have given me receptions which were very enjoyable occasions.

"I have had the pleasure of installing the officers of seven Corps, instituted two Corps, and assisted at the institution of other Corps. I had the honor of attending the National Convention held at St. Louis, travelling a distance of 3,070 miles. Number of official visits made during the year, 207.

"The time has come when loyal women feel a pride and pleasure in doing something for the soldiers who fought for the Union.

"Mrs. Angela H. Scranton and Mrs. Augusta A. Randall deserve special mention for their missionary work, which has gained several Corps.

"We have ten applications for charter in circulation, and we hope to institute the Corps at an early date. The outlook for the coming year is an encouraging one for the Woman's Relief Corps."

Mrs. Parker gained the love of all her associates and won the regard of the Grand Army of the Republic during the two years of her administration. Upon retiring from the chair she was installed as Department Counselor. She was missed at the Annual Convention in 1889, illness preventing her attendance. Messages of sympathy and tokens of regard were sent her and she was reappointed Department Counselor by Mrs. Emma B. Lowd, Department President. In presenting her report as Counselor at the Convention of 1890, she said:—

"For nine successive years I have been honored by an office in this Department, and now, retiring, I wish to extend to the ladies of the Department of Massachusetts Woman's Relief Corps my sincere thanks for the many honors they have conferred upon me. I shall never cease to take an interest in this Department. I shall not forget the loving words spoken to me, or the deeds of its members."

Mrs. Parker was appointed at this Convention a member of the Committee on Department Rooms at the Soldiers' Home, and has been reappointed at every subsequent Convention. She is also a member of other committees. She was unanimously elected National Chaplain at the National Convention in Pittsburg, Pa., September, 1894. She has two children, a son and daughter.

Mrs. Parker is active in local affairs and when the Hospital Aid Society was formed in Brockton she was elected one of its Directors and the next year was chosen President. She was one of the founders of the Woman's Educational and Industrial Union of Brockton, which is supported by all the churches of the city, and has served continuously in official positions, being very active in raising funds for its benefit. She is also President of the Ladies' Aid Society connected with the Universalist Church of Brockton and is honored at home as well as abroad.

Mrs. Emma B. Lowd.

Mrs. Lowd, whose maiden name was Emma B. Sibley, was born Jan. 1, 1845, in South Danvers (now Peabody), Mass. Her maternal grandfather was a Revolutionary soldier who saw service at Long Island, Trenton and Valley Forge. Both branches of her paternal ancestry, Abbott of Andover and Sibley of Salem, were in the Revolution.

When she was about seven years of age her parents moved to Salem and she received her education in the schools of that city, graduating from the High School in 1859. She was preparing to enter the Salem Normal School in 1861, but owing to the death of her father and the serious illness of her mother, this plan was changed. In December, 1862, she married Albert J. Lowd of Salem, who served during the war in the 5th Mass. Regt. and who has been an officer of Post 34 of Salem for several years. They have three children — two sons and a daughter.

In 1877, Mrs. Lowd was elected a Director of the Salem Samaritan Society, continuing in that office until 1881, when she was chosen secretary, and for the past five years has also filled the position of treasurer. This organization is a large and beneficent one, expending over a thousand dollars annually for the worthy poor who are sick and aged. Mrs. Lowd has been active in church and Sabbath School work in Salem, and has also taken an active interest in educational matters. She was elected a member of the Salem School Board in 1879 and served one year.

When Phil. H. Sheridan Corps No. 34 was organized in Salem, Sept. 7, 1883, Mrs. Lowd was elected President. She was re-elected in 1884 and 1885 and declined to serve in 1886 on account of her work as Department Inspector, but has served on important committees and continued to work for the interests of the Corps. Mrs. Lowd was elected Department Junior Vice-President at the Convention in 1886 and re-elected in 1887. She was elected President of the Department in 1888, and again at the Convention in 1889.

In presenting her first annual address at the Convention of 1889 she gave the following statistics: —

"At the commencement of this year we numbered 100 Corps; today we number 117, with a membership of 7,941. The summary of all quarterly reports from Jan. 1, 1888, to Jan. 1, 1889, gives the amount expended in relief, $5,697.22; turned over to Posts, $5,146.58; value of relief other than money, $1,971.54; amount expended for Soldiers' Home, $564.50; total, $13,379.84.

"The duties of the year have included the attendance at anniversaries, fairs, camp-fires, etc., and in all I have made 76 official visits, visited 43 Corps, instituted two Corps and installed the officers of eleven Corps, visited Headquarters 185 times, written over 1,000 letters, issued eight General Orders and one Circular Letter."

When reporting to the Annual Convention of 1890, she said: —

"One year ago we were proud to claim 117 Corps, with a membership of 7,941. That the interest in the objects for which our Order is formed is not diminished in the hearts of the comrades in this Department is shown from the fact that we have made a gain of nine Corps.

"Today we have 125 Corps and 9,010 members. The amount expended in relief by the Department was $148.00, by the Corps, $7,275.62; turned over to Post, $6,776.63; value of relief other than money, $2,464.10; total, $16,664.35. From this sum $1,065.19 were expended for the Soldiers' Home: of this amount $632.86 have been contributed by Corps for the furnishing of rooms in the addition to the Home.

"My time has been almost wholly devoted during the year to the service of this Department. Besides attending the National Convention at Milwaukee, I have made 58 official visits, installed the officers of 11 Corps, visited Headquarters 213 times, written more than 1,200 letters, issued nine General Orders and a letter of instruction to Corps Presidents, besides assisting the Department Secretary in the preparation of the synopsis of the first seven years' records of our Department. This cannot convey to you all that has been done — it is only an outline."

Mrs. Lowd was appointed Department Counselor in 1890 by her successor, Mrs. Mary E. Knowles, and at the same Convention was elected Chairman of the Department Soldiers' Home Committee (which position she holds at the present time).

She was selected as Chairman of the Executive Committee of Arrangements for the National Convention in Boston, 1890, and rendered a detailed report of her stewardship at the next Department Convention.

At the National Convention held at Indianapolis, September, 1893, she completed a three years' term as a member of the National Woman's Relief Corps Home Board, to which position she was re-elected for a term of five years.

Mrs. Lowd has attended all the National Conventions for the past nine years and has been recognized by appointment on important committees. She is a member of the Ladies' Aid Association of the Soldiers' Home in Massachusetts. She has delivered Memorial Day orations and has often addressed public gatherings.

Mrs. Mary E. Knowles.

Mrs. Knowles was born in Boston, Feb. 14, 1847, and is a daughter of Jacob Clones of Revolutionary ancestry. She was educated at the Hancock school in Boston, and after graduating, studied elocution and is a successful teacher in the profession. She has gained popularity as a public reader, having natural talent as an elocutionist.

Her husband, Z. R. Knowles, was in the signal service of the army and is a Past Commander of Abraham Lincoln Post No. 11 of Charlestown. He was one of the comrades of the G.A.R. who early advocated forming auxiliary Corps.

Mrs. Knowles is a charter member of Abraham Lincoln Corps No. 39, auxiliary to Post 11. She was installed as its first Senior Vice-President, April 22, 1884, and in January, 1885, accepted the position of President, and has served continuously in office and on committees. Her first participation in a Department Convention was in 1886, when she was invited to present a banner which had been procured by contributions of members. Her remarks on this occasion made such a favorable impression that she was elected Department Chaplain and re-elected in 1887.

In her second Annual Report as Department Chaplain she recommended that a special service be prepared for use on Memorial Day in honor of the unknown dead and of army nurses.

Mrs. Knowles was elected Department Junior Vice-President in 1888, and in this capacity attended the National Convention at Columbus, Ohio.

Referring to her associations in the work, she said in her Annual Report at the Convention of 1889 : "The pleasant acquaintances formed during my Department work of the last three years, have brought the members of our Order very near to my heart."

Mrs. Knowles was this year elected Department Senior Vice-President, and in 1890, received the highest office in the Department. This being the year of preparations for the National Convention, many extra duties were placed in her charge.

She was a member of the Executive Committee of Arrangements; Chairman of the Reception Committee, and a member of the Committees on Finance, Press and Invitations.

Extracts from her Annual Address at the Convention in 1891, are given as follows : —

"The growth of our Order in Massachusetts during the past year has been most encouraging. At the end of the official year of 1890, our roster bore 125 Corps, with a membership of 9,010 in good standing. Today, we have 137 Corps with a membership of 10.600, a gain of 1,590. Thirteen applications for charters have been granted.

"As our Order has grown, so the receipts and expenditures have kept pace with the increased membership. During the year ending Dec. 31, 1890, $8,577.69 were expended in caring for those for whose benefit our Order was organized ; $2,457.78 represents the value of relief other than money, and $6,098.87 were turned over to the Posts of this Department — a grand total of $17,134.34. Surely, we may *well* feel proud of our record, and we ought not to fear for the future of those whose claims upon our care are constantly increasing; and every member of our Order should esteem it a privilege that she, by right of her membership, can do her part in this grand work of relief.

"It is my earnest desire to acknowledge at this time to the members of the first Corps I instituted, No. 77 of Gloucester, my heartfelt appreciation of the honor bestowed upon me, when they placed upon the walls of their room in the Home the beautiful banner bearing my name. Of all the testimonials of affection that have come to me during my year's work this is the most precious, and the respect and love that is represented by this act of 'my first Corps' fills me with emotions no words of mine can express.

"On the 7th of last June I was honored with an invitation from the Board of Trustees of the Home to be present and take part in the dedication of the new portion of the Home, and the interesting exercises and incidents of the occasion will be remembered with pleasure as long as life shall last.

"I have visited the Home whenever it was possible for me to do so. One very pleasant visit was made in company with our National President and members of our council. That the comfort of the inmates of the Home is very near and dear to the members of this Department is shown in the tasteful, and in some cases luxurious, furnishing of the rooms that are cared for by a large number of the Corps; and the managers of the Home may feel assured that if a call is made upon us during the coming year we shall be ready to answer ' Here,' and we will do our part to the *best* of our ability.

"The official correspondence of the year has been great, requiring much time and thought. I have tried to answer all communications as promptly as possible, and give advice and instruction whenever needed; and the letters of thanks for information rendered, of personal regard and kind encouragement, have cheered me many times, and will bring pleasant memories in the years to come. I have not kept an exact account of the letters written, but they number nearly one thousand. I have issued eight General Orders and one Circular Letter.

"Many invitations to camp-fires, fairs and anniversaries of Posts and Corps have been accepted and thoroughly enjoyed. I have always been received with much courtesy and cordiality, and I regret that it has not been in my power to accept all the invitations tendered me.

"I have assisted at the opening of four fairs, attended four receptions, eleven anniversaries, instituted two Corps, installed the officers of twenty-four Corps, visited thirty Corps, and delivered the Memorial Day address at Leominster. Have been present at Headquarters Tuesdays, Thursdays and Saturdays, with but few exceptions."

She served as Department Counselor in 1891, and continued her active interest, visiting Corps gatherings, and participating in camp-fires, sociables, etc., and has been an eloquent and faithful missionary for the Order.

She was Assistant Secretary at the National Convention at Detroit in 1891, and at the Convention in Washington in 1892 was unanimously elected National Chaplain, and served in that capacity at the National Convention at Indianapolis in 1893.

Mrs. Knowles has taken an important part in all the Department Conventions since her connection with the Woman's Relief Corps and has served constantly in local or Department Committee work.

She has filled reading engagements in many halls and churches in Massachusetts and in other New England States and has delivered Memorial Day addresses in New Hampshire and Massachusetts. Many Posts and Corps have been aided financially by the services she has rendered them as an elocutionist.

Her services as an Installing Officer are in great demand, and she is sure of appreciative audiences whenever taking part in any service.

Mrs. Knowles is a member of the Ladies' Aid Association of the Soldiers' Home, the New England Helping Hand Society and the Independent Order of Odd Ladies, and is interested in church and Sunday-school work, having for many years been a member of Rev. S. H. Winkley's church in Boston, and a teacher in the Sabbath school connected with it.

Mrs. Augusta A. Wales.

Mrs. Wales was born in Maine, but has resided in Massachusetts since 1866. She is the wife of Capt. B. Read Wales, formerly of the 42d and 45th Mass. Regiments, one of the Harvard students who responded to his country's call. Capt. Wales has been identified with the Grand Army of the Republic since its earliest days and has served as Department Inspector, Assistant National Inspector, and in other positions. He has always been an earnest supporter of the Woman's Relief Corps.

After her marriage in 1874 she became greatly interested in the work for the veterans and entered vigorously into the effort to raise money for the purchase of the property on Powder Horn Hill for a Soldiers' Home. She served on the first Board of Visitors from the Ladies' Aid Association of the Soldiers' Home in Massachusetts.

In June, 1885, she became a member of the Woman's Relief Corps by uniting with Hiram G. Berry Corps No. 6 of Malden, and at the Department Convention in February, 1886, was elected Delegate-at-Large to the National Convention, to be held that year in San Francisco, but was unable to attend.

By transfer from Corps No. 6, Mrs. Wales became a charter member of Benj. Stone, Jr., Corps No. 68 of Dorchester, organized in February of the same year, serving two years as its President, and was an Aide and Assistant Inspector on the Staff of the Department President, Mrs. S. Agnes Parker.

In 1888 Mrs. Wales was appointed Department Inspector by the Department President, Mrs. Emma B. Lowd. During that year the system of District Exemplifications was organized, which has been carried on each year since. In 1889 she was elected Department Junior Vice-President and at the close of the year declined further honors in order to take a much-needed rest. This, however, was not to be the case, as the year 1890 proved to be the most exacting of all, on account of the meeting of the National Convention in Boston. She was a member of the Executive Committee, also of several sub-committees, and was Chairman of the Committee on Entertainments which arranged the " Woman's Camp-fire " at Tremont Temple and the excursion for the delegates to Nahant. The following year she was elected Department President and devoted herself entirely to the work, visiting more than sixty Corps throughout the Department besides attending to the regular routine duties at Department Headquarters.

A few extracts from the annual report of Mrs. Wales, when summing up the work of the year, are herewith given : —

" We speak of closing the work of the year. It can never be closed. The cords which bind the old and new are so closely interwoven that, while untried hands may take the helm, the ship veers not a point, but keeps steadily on, bearing its precious freight of love and good works.

" Thus it was one year ago, when the new succeeded the old, and the Department of Massachusetts was placed in the charge of those who today offer for your consideration the record of the year.

" The membership on Jan. 1, 1891, was reported to be 10,305 ; on Jan. 1, 1892, 11,675 ; a net gain of 1,370.

" At the opening of my official year there were 136 Corps in the Department ; 11 have been added during the year, and we stand in an unbroken line 147 strong, and for the most part prosperous.

"The financial condition of the Department is 'sound.' The receipts and expenditures have been large, and the items 'Turned over to Posts, $8,310.88,' and 'Expended from Relief Fund, $6,975.66,' exemplify the objects of the Order. These amounts, with the cash value of food and clothing donated, $2,271.63, give a total which is very creditable.

"This does not fully report the charitable work of the Corps, as much of the assistance rendered to unfortunate members, and various donations for National W.R.C. Home, army nurses, Memorial Day, etc., which could not legitimately be made from the Relief Fund, are not included in this amount.

"A more correct estimate of the work accomplished is gained from the quarterly reports, which show a balance on hand Jan. 1, 1891, of $23,838.33; total receipts, $44,130.95; expended, $38,709.57; balance on hand, Jan. 1, 1892, of $29,259.92 in the treasuries of the Corps, which will keep the wolf from many a veteran's door for some time if properly expended.

"The days assigned for work at Headquarters have been busy ones and they have afforded an opportunity of meeting many of the members of the Grand Army of the Republic, and of our own Order, from other Departments as well as from Massachusetts

"The correspondence has been immense, which with the preparation of Orders and all matter of similar nature, have required a vast amount of time and labor; the work has of necessity been done in the quietness of home, and the numerous (143) visits to Headquarters have been devoted to the business incidental to the day.

"It has been a very great delight to me to be able to accept so many of the invitations. received; they have included anniversaries, camp-fires, fairs, receptions and social gatherings of various kinds, at which I have been called upon to represent the Department, and while the memories of the four magnificent camp-fires held in the western part of the State remain, I shall have no fear that our Order will decline for lack of appreciation by the comrades of the Grand Army of the Republic.

"I have attended fifty-six Corps anniversaries, receptions, fairs, etc., eleven exemplifications, nine Post camp-fires and anniversaries, eight regimental reunions and social assemblies, which have kindly recognized our Order by extending an invitation to the President. Illness, or the inability to become ubiquitous, has obliged me to decline over thirty invitations which otherwise I would gladly have accepted. The generous hospitality of those who have so pleasantly entertained me, I shall never forget. These social demands have been met without neglect of the legitimate work, and have served to bring me in contact with a very large part of the membership of the Department, which is very helpful to any woman who stands at the head of such an organization as ours; they have also proven the appreciation of the Grand Army of the Republic for its auxiliary and the fidelity of our Order to the principles of fraternity."

Mrs. Wales was specially interested in the relief work of the Order, in the Soldiers' Home and the National W.R.C. Home.

When at the Ninth National Convention in Detroit, an appeal was made to the Departments for funds to purchase additional land for the National W.R.C. Home, Mrs. Wales, who represented Massachusetts as its President, pledged the sum of $50.00 for the object. This action was subsequently endorsed by the Department Council.

About $230.00 were contributed to this Home in Ohio, during Mrs. Wales' year. A systematic plan of reporting amounts expended for specific objects was devised by her.

Mrs. Wales was appointed Assistant National Inspector by Mrs. Sarah C. Mink, National President, and was also one of a special committee on "Revision of Inspection" of the Order last year.

In addition to the work of the Woman's Relief Corps, Mrs. Wales is also an active member of the Ladies' Aid Association of the Soldiers' Home in Massachusetts, the Woman's Charity Club of Boston, the Dorchester Woman's Club, the Dorchester Associated Charities, and the Home and Foreign Missionary Societies of the Second Parish Church in Dorchester, of which she is a member.

Mrs. Mary G. Deane.

Mrs. Mary Gray Deane was born in Norwich, Conn., Nov. 16, 1846, and is a daughter of the late Abner T. Pearce, a railroad contractor who introduced the first railway into South America.

During the Civil War she was a school-girl in Providence, R. I., and her leisure hours were given to scraping lint and other work for the Union soldiers. Her parents moved to Freetown, Mass., in 1865, and a year later she married Major John M. Deane, a teacher by profession, but now a merchant in Fall River. They have four sons and one daughter.

Through the efforts of Major Deane, who was Commander of Post 46, G.A.R., of Fall River, an auxiliary Corps was organized in 1888, with his wife as a charter member. She was chosen President and re-elected three years in succession.

During the nearly four years of her service as President, Mrs. Deane met with success in her efforts to make Corps 106 one of the best in the State. Upon retiring from the Presidency she accepted the office of Treasurer. Mrs. Deane was a member of the Executive Committee of arrangements for the National Convention held in Boston in 1890, and was also appointed on sub-committees. She was a delegate to this Convention and has attended every subsequent National Convention and been recognized by appointment on committees.

In 1891 she was Department Inspector and at the Annual Convention the following year was elected Department President, having accepted the nomination at the urgent request of leading members.

She immediately sought to familiarize herself with all the details of the office, and possessing unusual executive ability, conducted a very able administration, being earnest, thorough and systematic in all her work.

She gave special attention to the work of organizing Corps, and issued a carefully prepared Circular to Post Commanders, which resulted in fourteen Corps being instituted.

Extracts from her Annual Address presented at the close of her administration are given as follows: —

"Having been unexpectedly called upon one year ago to assume the obligation and discharge the duties of President of this Department, I accepted the trust with a love for the Order and a desire to assist in its advancement.

"The experiences of the year have endeared me more closely to this work — to the Grand Army of the Republic and all that it represents.

"My entire time has been given to the service, and I have endeavored to perform the varied and responsible duties in a just and conscientious manner.

"I desire to express my appreciation of the services of Mrs. Emilie L. W. Waterman, Chairman of the Department Executive Board, in the successful missionary work accomplished, whereby Corps 44, at Marshfield Hills, was added to our Order. I also desire to acknowledge the faithful missionary work of Mrs. Josephine A. Burdick, Department Aide, through whose efforts we have been enabled to add to our number Corps 155, Williamstown.

"The Quarterly Reports received Jan. 1, 1893, gave a membership of 12,634, a gain of 959 during the calendar year. Adding the charter lists of Corps 44 and 102, instituted since January 1, will increase the membership to 12,751.

"The finances of the Corps are in excellent condition. $8,308.39 were contributed for relief, $9,816.49 turned over to Posts, and there remained in the Corps treasuries Jan. 1, 1893, the sum of $16,176.40 to the credit of the Relief Fund, and $14,873.98 in the General Fund.

Department Relief Fund, Balance, Jan. 1, 1892,		$1,333 20
Received during the year	. . . .	603 27
Total		$1,936 47
Expended	.	488 35
Balance, Jan. 1, 1893	.	$1,448 12

"The Department Treasurer's report gives an encouraging statement concerning the general financial condition of the Department, there remaining in the Treasury Jan. 1, 1893, the sum of $1,835.17.

"In my first General Order, issued February 12, the assignment of my office hours at Headquarters was announced; but two afternoons each week have not been sufficient to complete the duties given to my charge. Members and committees seeking advice and information, reports to be examined, correspondence requiring immediate attention, copy to be furnished the printer, and other duties, have required my presence many days at Headquarters. Whether in Boston or at my home in Fall River, every day has been fully occupied with the work of the Department, and with few exceptions my evenings have been devoted to its executive or public duties.

"I have issued nine General Orders, thirty-eight Special Orders, three Circular Letters, and other official documents, and have written several thousand letters, endeavoring to answer all correspondence with promptness, allowing no letter to remain unanswered.

"I have accepted all invitations to represent our Order at gatherings held by Posts or Corps whenever possible. When compelled to decline such invitations the Department has been represented by other officers.

"I have made four trips to western Massachusetts and visited every county in the State with the exception of two (Barnstable and Dukes counties).

"By special request, I have personally instituted four Corps, viz.: at Bourne, Williamstown, Marshfield Hills and Weymouth; have assisted at the institution of Corps at New Bedford, Lee, Wareham, Leicester and Boston; and it has been my pleasant duty to install the officers of nine Corps.

"The receptions tendered Department Officers by Corps 106 of Fall River, Corps 26 of Newburyport, Corps 35 of Hyde Park and Corps 68 of Dorchester, are remembered as among the pleasant occasions of the year.

"By invitation of the President of the New England Chautauqua Assembly, I presented a brief history of our Order at the 'Grand Army Day' exercises held at South Framingham July 25, under the auspices of the Assembly.

"The Silver Anniversaries of Fletcher Webster Post No 13 of Brockton and Richard Borden Post No. 46 of Fall River, which I had the pleasure of attending, will ever remain as delightful memories.

"A register, containing the names of comrades and others who have called at Headquarters 'to pay their respects,' is a memento of the year, that reminds us of pleasant incidents.

"In closing my year as President of this Department and transferring its duties to another, I do not surrender my love for the work that is so near my heart.

"In the future success of the Grand Army of the Republic and Woman's Relief Corps I shall ever have the deepest interest. I have witnessed the loyalty of their membership and the faithfulness of their service; and whenever I shall review in memory the work of the year, it will recall pleasant associations and friendships formed that will be treasured through life."

That portion of her report recommending that a Memorial Home Fund be established, is printed in full in Chapter VII.

Mrs. Deane is deeply interested in this object and, as Chairman of the Committee, has raised over $1,200 for the Memorial Fund.

The portrait of Mrs. Deane hangs upon the walls of Department Headquarters, placed there by the contributions of Corps Presidents of 1892. A large and handsomely bound album was presented her which contained the letters expressing the regard of the donors.

E. P. Hopkins Corps No. 155 of Williamstown has placed her picture in Grand Army Hall.

Mrs. Deane was appointed Department Counselor in 1893 by her successor in office, Mrs. Emily L. Clark, and has continued her active work in the Department and her interest in all the Corps. She is again serving Corps 106 of Fall River as Treasurer, and as Chairman of its Executive Committee, has added several hundred dollars to the Corps funds by her able management of entertainments.

Her husband has been an earnest friend to the Woman's Relief Corps and is an honored guest at many of its public gatherings. He was Major of the Twenty-ninth Massachusetts Regiment and has received a Congressional Medal of Honor for special bravery in the service. He was appointed Assistant National Inspector of the G.A.R. by Commander-in-Chief Lawler.

Mrs. Deane is a member of the Ladies' Aid Association of the Soldiers' Home in Massachusetts. She has been identified with church and charitable work in Fall River since 1868. As a member of the First Congregational Church she has served on active committees.

During the temperance revival in Fall River a few years ago, she was a member of the Executive Board of the Woman's Christian Temperance Union, and served as treasurer of the "Coffee House" which was established and conducted on a large scale by the Women's Christian Temperance Union.

She has taken an interest in the Woman's Auxiliary to the Young Men's Christian Association, and is one of the Board of Managers of the Children's Home of Fall River, a position she has held twenty years. A large brick building has recently been dedicated, where many destitute orphans can receive all the comforts of home.

Mrs. Deane is a regular visitor to the Home and takes a special interest in the welfare of the children. She is a member of Minnehaha Lodge Daughters of Rebecca of Fall River, and being a descendant from Revolutionary ancestry, has united with Quequechan Chapter, Daughters of the American Revolution.

Mrs. Emily L. Clark.

Mrs. Emily L. Clark was born in Becket, Mass., April 24, 1832, where her girlhood days were passed. When eighteen years of age she married Capt. Edwin C. Clark of Northampton and has endeared herself to the people of that city by her kindly deeds and active co-operation in benevolent objects.

When the civil conflict began Mrs. Clark had three children, the youngest only eleven months old. While unable to leave her home to engage in work for the soldiers she resolved to do her share, and opened her house as a rendezvous for all who desired to aid the Union cause. Days and nights were constantly devoted to work for the volunteers, and her house was a busy place, being continually thronged with people who were zealous in this patriotic work. Many boxes of supplies were thus sent from her home to the brave boys at the front.

In April, 1861, her husband assisted in recruiting Co. A, Twenty-Seventh Mass. Regiment and was commissioned second lieutenant. He served at Roanoke Island, Newbern and in other campaigns under General Burnside.

Lieutenant Clark resigned his commission and returned home in 1862, when he re-enlisted in the Fifty-Second Mass. Regiment and received a commission as first lieutenant and later was commissioned quartermaster. This regiment formed a part of the Banks Expedition and he performed active duty at Baton Rouge, Barry's Landing and Port Hudson until the regiment was mustered out of service in the fall of 1863. He is actively identified with the interests of Northampton and is one of its leading citizens.

Mrs. Clark has four children, two sons and two daughters.

When peace was declared, Mrs. Clark felt that her labors for the "boys in blue" were ended, but she soon realized that though the war had ceased, the suffering it had caused remained. Her patriotic work was continued and when W. L. Baker Post of Northampton was organized in August, 1882, Mrs. Clark entered heartily into plans for its success. She was a charter member and first President of Corps No. 18 (auxiliary to Post 86), which was formed May 13, 1885, and was re-elected President in 1886 and again in 1887. The year following she served as delegate from the Department of Massachusetts to the National Convention at St. Louis.

In 1888 she was chosen by the Department Council to fill a vacancy caused by the resignation of the Department Chaplain, and was re-elected to that office in 1889 and 1890.

Owing to severe illness Mrs. Clark retired from active work the following year, but in 1892, accepted the office of Department Senior Vice-President, and upon the expiration of her term was elected Department President. Mrs. M. Susie Goodale, Past Department President, made the nominating speech as follows: —

"I have the honor to place in nomination the name of one who has many qualifications for the position.

"First of all, she has a heart filled with love for humanity, and very few are the days when some poor, wounded soul does not seek and find comfort beneath her sheltering roof; in all this she is seconded by her soldier husband. Again, she is a pioneer in the Order, and has served you faithfully as Department Chaplain and Senior Vice-President.

"I believe her to be in every way qualified for the position."

Upon assuming the work of her office, Mrs. Clark gave special attention to the interests of the Corps throughout the State, especially those that needed encouragement.

Though living one hundred miles from Department Headquarters, she was on duty there several days each week. In her annual report she said: —

"During the year I have travelled more than twenty thousand miles and visited seventy-two Corps, besides attending many receptions, campfires, fairs, etc. I have endeavored to encourage all to persevere in the noble work in which we are engaged.

"The year has been too short to accomplish all I desired; but I trust that my successor will take up the work where I lay it down and do more than I have been able to accomplish.

"Three new Corps have been added to our roster, and today we have one hundred and fifty-nine Corps.

"I have issued nine General Orders, two Circular Letters, have granted many dispensations, and have written more than twelve hundred letters and postals, answering innumerable questions; and endeavored to instruct and encourage all who sought advice. The many personal letters I have received, expressing appreciation for help given, will be to me a storehouse of pleasure in the coming years when I shall have leisure to again read their words of commendation.

"The two days assigned as office days at Headquarters were not sufficient, and scarcely any week has passed that I have not been present at the rooms three and often five days; and when at home my entire time has been given to the work before me.

"I have accepted all invitations to social gatherings whenever it has been possible to do so, and especially when given by Posts and Corps jointly. I cannot refrain from mentioning two of these: one, the silver anniversary of Post 68 of Dorchester, as pleasant a gathering as I ever attended and one which will long be remembered. Senior Vice-Commander Wilfred A. Wetherbee represented the Department G.A.R. and spoke in enthusiastic terms of the Woman's Relief Corps. The other notable occasion was the reunion of the Twelfth Mass. Regiment, at the Thorndike, Boston, January 20, the current year. Many others I might mention, and all have been pleasant and productive of good.

"I have had many invitations to install the officers-elect during the month of January, but I could not accept all, as dates conflicted. It was my privilege, however, to install the officers of seven Corps, which I greatly enjoyed."

Mrs. Clark visited the Soldiers' Home several times during her official year and in General Orders issued an appeal to Corps to furnish some of the new rooms in the annex. She reported in her annual address that over $640.00 had been expended for the Home, by our Relief Corps, for the year ending Dec. 31, 1893.

Upon learning that the National President desired to establish a Relief Fund at National Headquarters, for cases of distress that required immediate attention, Mrs. Clark authorized that a check for $50.00 be forwarded, which was the first response to the request of Mrs. Mink.

Mrs. Clark also felt an interest in having the Department creditably represented in the National W.R.C. exhibit at the World's Fair, and $50.00 were sent by her order for this purpose.

In reporting the results of the year's work, she referred to the thousands of callers she had met at Headquarters, and to the mutual benefits arising from the greetings and encouragement thereby received.

Upon retiring from the chair, Mrs. Clark was appointed Department Counselor by her successor in office, and assisted Corps 18 of Northampton by accepting an appointment as Corps Secretary.

Mrs. Clark served as National Chaplain *pro tem.* at the National Convention in Boston in 1890, and at Indianapolis in 1893, and she rendered service on committees at Pittsburgh in 1894.

She will always have the regard of her associates who appreciate her friendship and her devotion to the work.

Mrs. Clare H. Burleigh.

Mrs. Clare H. Burleigh, Past Department President, is the daughter of the late Dr. George Hoyt, and sister of Col. George H. Hoyt, a Union cavalry officer known as "the lawyer who defended John Brown," and the widow of Judge Henry M. Burleigh, who served his country from April, 1861, until the close of the war.

Mrs. Burleigh's maternal ancestors came to Plymouth in the ship *Fortune* in 1621. Two great-grandfathers were Revolutionary soldiers, her parents were active anti-slavery workers, and she is devoted to the veteran's cause and interested in all progressive movements.

After a membership of many years in a local Aid Society in Athol Mrs. Burleigh joined Hubbard V. Smith Relief Corps No. 82, as a charter member, Feb. 22, 1887, and has managed entertainments for the benefit of its treasury and been active in shaping its affairs.

She was the first President and continued to hold the office three years. She served the Department as Inspector, Junior Vice-President and Senior Vice-President, and at the Annual Convention in February, 1894, was elected Department President.

At the camp-fire in the People's Church, Boston, held at the close of this Convention (February 8), Mrs. Burleigh made her first address as Department President, an extract from which is given as follows : —

Mrs. President, Comrades, Sons of Veterans, Members of the Woman's Relief Corps and Friends: I am sure it is not often that a newly-fledged President of the Woman's Relief Corps makes her *début* in such an assembly as this and among such distinguished guests. Yet I should be no apt pupil of the Woman's Relief Corps were I not happy to respond for the Department which I now have the honor to represent, and to extend to all a cordial greeting, with the hope that the evening's entertainment may be enjoyable. We believe that we shall hear from the eloquent speakers upon the platform some words of commendation for the work of our Order; and while we consider its wonderful growth, its munificent charities, its large reserve funds, its lessons in patriotism to the children of the nation, and its moral influence upon woman, let us remember the grand women who were pioneers in the work — who planned and built the foundation upon which we stand today.

* * * * * * * * *

In closing she said : —

" National President, it is now *my* privilege to renew our pledges of allegiance for the coming year.

" Commander-in-Chief, I am happy to repeat the congratulations of my predecessors in office, upon your elevation to the highest position in the gift of the Grand Army.

" Department Commander, your auxiliary is ready for duty. Command our services in all that relates to the interests of the veteran and his dependents.

" And may I be permitted to say to His Excellency the Governor, that if the 13,000 women of this Department shall be faithful to their obligations, they will confer blessings not only upon the Grand Army of the Republic, not only upon the communities in which they live, but upon the Commonwealth of Massachusetts "

Mrs. Burleigh assumed the duties of her office with the hearty co-operation of her husband, who was a member of the Department Council of the Grand Army of the Republic. But his sudden death a few weeks after cast a shadow over her administration.

She furnished Room No. 29 at the Soldiers' Home and named it in honor of her late husband, and continuing the work of her office gave much of her time to its public duties.

The amount expended for Relief during her year (including other than money) was $11,306 94
Turned over to Posts 8,585 07

A summary of her official work contained the following statistics : —

"I have issued nine General Orders and three Circulars; have made one hundred and forty-one visits to Corps, including twenty exemplifications, seven fairs, the delivery of five public addresses for the benefit of Corps funds, numerous anniversaries, camp-fires, etc.; have installed the officers of twenty-one Corps, assisting in the institution of six new Corps.

"It was also my privilege to address a Legislative Committee February 6, in the interests of the Bill 'making it unlawful for any person to print, stamp or impress any words, figures or designs upon the flag of the United States, with a penalty annexed.'"

Mrs. Burleigh wrote over twelve hundred letters and postals and travelled extensively in the discharge of her duties.

She served as a representative to the National Convention at Columbus, Ohio, in 1888, at Washington, D.C., in 1892, and as Department President had charge of the delegation to the National Convention at Pittsburgh, Pa., in 1894.

During the arrangements for the National Convention in Boston in 1890, Mrs. Burleigh was a member of the Executive Committee and also served on sub-committees.

She was appointed, in 1894, a member of the National Committee on Patriotic Teaching, by Mrs. Emma R. Wallace, National President.

Mrs. Burleigh has published a small volume of poems, is an extempore speaker, and has devoted much time to literature, painting and portraiture.

The banners designating the different Departments at the National Convention in Tremont Temple, Boston, in July, 1890, were painted by her. A crayon of the late Assistant Adjutant-General Monroe, which she gave to the military fair in 1891, was purchased by contributions of members in aid of the fair, and presented to Grand Army Headquarters.

Mrs. Burleigh is a member of the Ladies' Aid Association of the Soldiers' Home, the Daughters of the Revolution and other societies.

Mrs. Kathrina L. Beedle.

A history of our work in Massachusetts would be incomplete without some reference to the practical help rendered by Mrs. Kathrina L. Beedle, in the formation of the Department in 1879.

She was born in Boston Jan. 14, 1844, and educated at a private school.

Mrs. Beedle participated in the first Convention of the Woman's Relief Corps as a delegate from Cambridge and was elected Department Secretary.

At the adjourned meeting in Cambridge a few months later she took an active part in the work of revising the Rules and Regulations, and prepared the Installation Service of the Order, which (with the exception of a few changes) is the one now in use.

Miss Georgie Miles and Miss Augusta Sears of Corps 2, Cambridge, set the type for the first Ritual printed and Mrs. Beedle read the proof and in many other ways worked untiringly for the new organization.

At a meeting of the Board of Directors held May 12, 1880, she was chosen one of the Committee on Conference with the G.A.R. and she gave much attention to committee work in the early years of the Order.

Mrs. Beedle was re-elected Department Secretary in 1880, and chosen Department Inspector in 1881, and again in 1884, and was elected Department Treasurer at the Convention in 1885.

She served as a delegate to the National Convention at Minneapolis in 1884, and at Portland in 1885.

Mrs. Beedle served as Secretary of the Department table in the Soldiers' Home Carnival which was held in Mechanics Building, Boston, in March, 1885.

At the Convention of 1886, she was elected Chairman of the Department Executive Board, but later in the year felt obliged to resign on account of ill health.

The records of the Convention of 1887 refer to Mrs. Beedle as follows: —

"Remarks were made by Mrs. Turner complimentary to the services of Mrs. Kathrina L. Beedle (the first Department Secretary) during the early days of the Woman's Relief Corps, who is now prevented by illness from actively participating in its work. In closing, Mrs. Turner moved that some recognition of these services be tendered her. Amended by Mrs. Clara C. Lovering, of the Department Council, that the testimonial be accompanied with a letter of sympathy and appreciation. Carried."

KATHRINA L BEEDLE

First Department Secretary 1879—1881

DECEASED NOV. 24, 1887

Mrs. Turner was appointed a committee to procure the gift and selected a gold ring, which was suitably inscribed and greatly treasured by Mrs. Beedle, and the letter and gifts were a source of comfort to her during her last illness.

Her death occurred Nov. 24, 1887, and her funeral was largely attended by Department officers and other friends. Corps charters throughout the State were draped in mourning for thirty days.

Tributes were paid to her memory at the next Annual Convention by Mrs. Parker, Department President, Mrs. Turner and Mrs. H. Annie Allen, President of Corps 2 of Cambridge.

In the report of the Department Secretary at this Convention, the following reference was made to the death of Mrs. Beedle: —

"As we turn the pages on which is recorded the early history of this Department and remember the invaluable services of our first Department Secretary, whose useful life entered so zealously into this work, we feel that her memory should ever be held sacred. One page of our report (if the proceedings of this Convention are printed) should be set apart as a tribute to the worth and a memorial of the work of Mrs. Kathrina L. Beedle."

The following is a copy of the memorial which was prepared by Mrs. S. Agnes Parker, Department President.

MEMORIAL.

MRS. KATHRINA L. BEEDLE.

Earnest and faithful in life, true to the principles of our Order, she gave to the Woman's Relief Corps a noble example of woman's ability, loyalty and self-sacrifice.

As the daughter and wife of a soldier, next to home and husband and children, she always placed first in her life the sacred duty she owed to the Grand Army of the Republic and to the widows and orphans left by those who "sleep on Southern battlefields or 'neath the ocean wave."

She adds one more illustrious name to the roll of the truly great women of our State.

Let her name be honored and kept sacred throughout the Department.

The Department of New Hampshire also placed on record a memorial of Mrs. Beedle.

Her husband (Past Commander M. C. Beedle of Charles Beck Post No. 56 of Cambridge), was one of the earliest friends of our Order among the comrades of the Grand Army of the Republic. Mrs. Beedle was President of Corps No. 2, Cambridge, in 1884 and 1885 and was greatly beloved by the members. A room at the Soldiers' Home in Chelsea is furnished by the Corps and named in her honor as a tribute to her memory.

Mrs. Pamelia F. Sprague.

Mrs. Sprague, a member of the first board of Department officers, was born in Boston, Feb. 20, 1837, but her parents removed to East Boston in 1848, where she has continued to reside. Mrs. Sprague was educated in the public schools of Boston. Her husband, John W. Sprague, a prominent member of John A. Hawes Post 159 of East Boston, and its Commander for 1895, enlisted in the 12th Mass. Reg't July 1, 1861, leaving two small children, the youngest only two months old, to the care of their mother. Mrs. Sprague when referring to those days, said: —

"My experience during the three years that followed was one of anxiety, as was the lot of all who sent their loved ones to the front.

"After my husband's return my time was fully occupied with domestic duties until a short time before the formation of a Relief Corps. I was induced to join a Soldiers' Aid Society, and my name was enrolled as a member of the W.R.C. at the time of its birth."

Mrs. Sprague participated in the first Convention (1879) as a delegate from the East Boston Society, and was elected to the office of Department Guard. The following year she was a member of the Committee on Burial Service and at the Convention in 1881 was chosen Department Secretary. In addition to her duties as secretary which were faithfully performed, she served as a member of the Committee on Soldiers' Home Bazaar.

Mrs. Sprague has been of great service in helping Grand Army fairs in East Boston and has been a liberal contributor in aid of the financial work of the Corps.

She was elected Department Junior Vice-President at the Convention in 1882, and in 1886 was elected a member of the Department Executive Board, but resigned before the expiration of her term, owing to ill health. Mrs. Sprague has not been able for several years to take

PAMELIA F. SPRAGUE

Second Department Secretary 1881

an active interest in the Order. She is devoted, however, to the cause and never loses any opportunity to help it in a quiet way, and is proud of the fact that she is one of the pioneers of the Department of Massachusetts.

Miss Mary E. Elliot.

(By a vote of the History Committee this sketch was ordered to be inserted in this chapter, and it was by special request prepared by Past Department President Mrs. M. Susie Goodale.)

Mary E. Elliot was born in Somerville Feb. 2, 1851. She is a lineal descendant of two Revolutionary soldiers, Joseph Elliot and John Hicks, both of whom died in the service, and is a sister of Charles D. Elliot, who served in the Civil War from 1862 to 1864, at Port Hudson and elsewhere, on the staff of engineers of the Nineteenth Army Corps, under General Banks.

Her public work for the soldier began in the organization of Willard C. Kinsley Relief Corps in March, 1879. This Corps was an independent organization, working under a ritual prepared by Miss Elliot, who was its first President; but in 1882, at her urgent solicitation, it was reorganized as a branch of the State Department.

She was again elected President, and continuing in the position two years, rounded out a term of five years as leader of the Relief Corps in Somerville.

She served as delegate to the National Convention in Minneapolis in 1884, and has participated in every subsequent National Convention, serving several times as a member of the Press Committee, and twice as Assistant National Secretary.

In the summer of 1885, upon the resignation of Mrs. Sarah E. Fuller, a step made obligatory by her election as National President, Miss Elliot was appointed Department Secretary by Mrs. M. Susie Goodale, Department President at that time, and so thoroughly devoted has she been to the work, and so excellent her services, that they have been retained during a term of ten years. Her reports prepared for Conventions inspire every heart to renewed zeal, filled as they are with words of eloquence, and as a recording secretary, she has no superior, her records of Convention work proving more satisfactory than the work of a stenographer.

During her term of service as Department Secretary she has delivered five Memorial Day addresses, and her experience as a press correspondent has often enabled her to call the attention of the public, through the press, to the work of our organization.

She was chairman of a committee through the efforts of which the flag salute was introduced into the schools of Somerville. She has been an earnest worker in the Ladies' Aid Association of the Soldiers' Home, and is a member of several local societies. Quiet and unassuming, her strength of character is known only to the privileged few who are intimately associated with her in the work of our Order.

Mrs. Lizabeth A. Turner.

Mrs. Lizabeth A. Turner was born in East Windsor (now Windsor Hills), Conn. One of her grandfathers was in the battle of Bunker Hill and the other at Valley Forge and she is one of the Daughters of the American Revolution. Her parents were Charles and Betsey Thompson of Windsor, Conn. In 1857 she married F. F. L. Turner of Georgia who died three years later. Mrs. Turner inherited the patriotism of her Revolutionary ancestors and from April, 1861, has given her time and best efforts to aid the soldiers' cause. She packed and forwarded the first box of supplies sent from Boston to the soldiers at the front. In 1863 she was a constant visitor to the hospital which was located in Pemberton square, Boston, where the wounded sent from the battlefields of the South received the kindest care.

She became a member of the Woman's Relief Corps March 17, 1880, and was initiated by Mrs. E. Florence Barker, who was then President of Gen. H. G. Berry Corps of Malden. Mrs. Turner served the Corps as Treasurer two years and President two years. When it was proposed to establish a Soldiers' Home in Massachusetts, she promptly offered her assistance.

One of the principal attractions in the Soldiers' Home Bazaar held in Mechanics Building in 1881 was the military album containing autographs of President Lincoln and the original war cabinet, beside those of prominent generals and leaders in the Revolutionary and Civil Wars, which were collected and arranged by her. It was valued at a thousand dollars and is treasured in the library of the Loyal Legion.

LIZABETH A. TURNER

Department Senior Vice-President 1886, 1887
First National Treasurer 1883 — 1889
Thirteenth National President 1895, 1896

Mrs. Turner is a regular contributor to the Soldiers' Home and is a welcome visitor to its hospital. She is one of the founders of the Ladies' Aid Association, auxiliary to the Board of Trustees of the Home, and has served on most of its important committees as treasurer, also as a member of the Board of Directors and as vice-president. A room bearing her name is furnished at the Home by the Department of Massachusetts and contains her portrait.

Mrs. Turner is deeply interested in all the Posts of the Grand Army of the Republic and has an extensive acquaintance with the comrades in all parts of the country. Admiral Foote Post of New Haven, Conn., and Gen. H. G. Berry Post of Malden, have been presented by her with relic-gavels made of wood from Andersonville Prison and the tree under which Lee surrendered. The gift to Post 40 of Malden was accompanied with the request that when the Post shall cease to exist, the gavel be presented to the Trustees of the Malden City Library.

On the walls of Mrs. Turner's rooms at No. 29 Temple Place, Boston, may be seen two framed testimonials from the above-named Posts which express their appreciation of her gifts. As an additional token of respect the comrades of Admiral Foote Post presented her a costly gold badge, which she treasures among her many souvenirs.

At the Department Convention in 1888, she was elected Conductor and in June of the same year was chosen a delegate to Denver, Col., where it was proposed to form a National Woman's Relief Corps.

She was elected Department Junior Vice-President at the Annual Convention in 1884 and in 1885 and Department Senior Vice-President in 1886 and 1887.

At the Annual Convention in 1888 she declined to accept the position of Department President which was tendered her, and the following resolution, offered by Mrs. Augusta A. Wales, was adopted: —

WHEREAS, Mrs. L. A. Turner, Senior Vice-President Department of Massachusetts Woman's Relief Corps, has declined to allow the use of her name as a candidate for promotion; therefore,

"*Resolved*, That this Convention, recognizing her untiring devotion and manifest ability in the past, do hereby tender to her our sincere and heartfelt thanks for her faithful services and earnest interest in the welfare of the Order, and our best wishes for her future prosperity and success, feeling assured that her love for the Order will be in no wise diminished, although not officially connected with the Department."

Mrs. Turner was elected Chairman of the Department Executive Board and prevailed upon to accept the office, and was re-elected in 1889 and 1890. She rendered efficient service this year as treasurer of the Executive Committee of Arrangements for the Eighth National Convention in Boston. In 1892, she was appointed Department Counselor by Mrs. Mary G. Deane, Department President. At this Convention she proposed the erection of a monument in memory of the unknown dead, presenting the subject as follows: —

"Ladies, I have something to bring before you that is a little out of the common course of convention work. All through the South, in almost every little town and hamlet in the States which were enrolled as Confederate, there are hundreds of little monuments erected to the dead. Some bear only the inscription 'Our Dead,' some the 'Unknown Dead,' all erected to the men who never came back. Several say, 'Our Dead, who never came back.' Shall the people of the South do more for their dead who never came back than Massachusetts? I have seen how money has been poured in for those who did come back; and now I want this Department of Massachusetts to erect a monument in some public place which shall bear the inscription, — 'Erected by the Woman's Relief Corps, in memory of the men who never came back.'

"I would ask that a committee of one be appointed by this Convention to receive the amount each Corps is willing to pledge to such a monument, the committee to report at the next Convention. I think we can raise the amount necessary very easily. I am sure that the women who sent forth loved ones who did come back will give of the fullness of their hearts. The women whose loved ones sleep in unknown graves will surely give to the men who made it possible for us to live under one flag."

Mrs. Turner, who was appointed Committee on Monument, has secured pledges for the same amounting to several hundred dollars. She hopes to have the proposed monument erected on Boston Common or in the Public Garden.

Mrs. Turner has been as active in National as in Department work. She rendered great service in forming a National Order at Denver, and during the first seven years served as National Treasurer, the duties of which were very arduous during the early years of the Order. She was elected Chairman of the National Executive Board in 1889, and at the National Convention in Boston, in 1890, was elected National Senior-Vice President and the following year at Detroit declined to be a candidate for the highest office. She has attended every National Convention and taken a prominent part in their proceedings. She has visited the Colored Corps in the South as Inspector for several successive years and is recognized as the "patriotic missionary of the W.R.C." Mrs. Turner is an entertaining speaker, is personally popular with all her associates and is an indefatigable worker in all lines. She has finally consented to be a candidate for the office of National President, and will undoubtedly receive a unanimous election at the Thirteenth National Convention to be held at Louisville, Ky., September next. Mrs. Turner is a practical business woman and wherever known is regarded as one of the ablest of the *loyal women*.

JAMES F. MEECH.*

Capt. James F. Meech was born in Preston, Conn., Aug. 10, 1846, and graduated from the public schools of that town.

When about sixteen years of age he enlisted in the Twenty-sixth Conn. Infantry and was assigned to the Ninth Army Corps under General Banks, serving at New Orleans and in the siege of Port Hudson.

Taking up his residence in Worcester at the close of the war, he joined George H. Ward Post No. 10 of that city and served two years as Commander.

At the Department Encampment of the Grand Army of the Republic in 1876, Captain Meech was elected a member of the Department Council of Administration.

Gen. Horace Binney Sargent, who was elected Department Commander of this Encampment, appointed Comrade Meech his Assistant Adjutant-General.

He was a popular official and very efficient in the discharge of his duties, and was reappointed three successive years, but resigned in 1882 to accept a responsible position in the Thomson-Houston Electric Light Co., as manager of their plant at New Britain, Conn.

When the Company's works were established at Lynn, Captain Meech removed to that city and became identified with its interests. He travelled in Europe three years as foreign agent of the Company, and was manager of its exhibit at the Paris Exposition.

He was active in establishing the Board of Trade of Lynn, and was elected its secretary.

In the chapters of this history relating to the early work of this Department, reference is made to the part taken by Captain Meech, at whose suggestion the State organization was formed. His advice and

---

* Died May 2, 1895. For Memorial Order see Appendix A.

practical help were invaluable in those days, and in recognition of his faith and friendship, the following action was taken at the Sixth Annual Convention in 1885 : —

Voted, on motion of Mrs. Barker, that Past Assistant Adjutant-General Meech be elected an honorary member of the Department of Massachusetts W.R.C.

He was subsequently escorted to the altar and duly obligated, when a gold badge suitably inscribed was presented him.

At the Annual Convention in 1887, a beautiful floral emblem was placed upon the platform by order of Comrade Meech, who was temporarily residing in Belgium, and this tribute was each year continued during his absence.

A few days after the close of the Convention, the following letter was received : —

HOTEL ROYAL, NAPLES, Feb. 5, 1887.

MARY E. ELLIOT,
    Secretary Woman's Relief Corps, Department of Massachusetts.

My Dear Miss Elliot: I desire to acknowledge very gratefully the receipt of General Orders No. 7, together with a card to the reception to be given to Commander-in-Chief Lucius Fairchild, January 27. If I could have been there, I should have had the added pleasure of attendance upon the Annual Encampment of the Grand Army of the Republic and that of paying to the Woman's Relief Corps of the Department of Massachusetts my personal respects and devotion. I am sure you will pardon me for giving the Grand Army of the Republic the seeming preference, but it is because of the fact that it is my first love.

At the date of your reception I was in Sicily, and although far distant from yourself and associates and my comrades of the Grand Army of the Republic, your annual meeting was kept in mind by Mrs. Meech, who is with me, and myself.

Your Convention and attendant festivities must have been an unqualified success, full accounts of which I shall undoubtedly receive in the Boston papers, some of which are sent to me every day. I am sure that the condition of the Woman's Relief Corps, Department of Massachusetts, is such as to meet the most sanguine anticipations of its friends, and of course it has no enemies. I trust the time is not far distant when I shall be able to express to you all personally my renewed interest in your organization. Please convey to your associates my most cordial respects, and believe me to be

                Fraternally yours,
                          JAMES F. MEECH.

A hearty welcome was accorded our honorary member at the Department Convention in 1889, and he was greeted with enthusiasm when participating in the evening reception.

In 1890, a magnificent basket of flowers was sent to the Convention platform with the accompanying note: —

"Will the Woman's Relief Corps, Department of Massachusetts, accept the accompanying flowers as a slight token of remembrance and esteem from its honorary member, JAMES F. MEECH."

The gift was accepted with a rising vote of thanks.

When the floral offering was received at the Convention in 1892, Mrs. Turner said: —

"I should like to tell the members that through a three years' residence in Europe, he wore under the lapel of his coat the badge of the Woman's Relief Corps by the side of his Grand Army badge."

When visiting the Annual Convention in 1893, Captain Meech said: —

"Mrs. President, I appreciate the cordiality of our reception. I come to greet you and to pay my respects. My mind goes back to the early days of the inception of the Woman's Relief Corps. I have never regretted, and never shall, the work that was done to put this organization in a condition to meet the plaudits of the Grand Army of the Republic of this Department and of the Union. I desire, as one of the trustees of the Soldiers' Home, to thank you for the work you have done for that institution. I ask you to renew your efforts in its behalf. We have more than a hundred men unable to care for themselves. It has become what we anticipated it would become, simply a great hospital. We may have to ask more of your Corps to allow your rooms to be used as hospital rooms. I come again to thank you for the compliments you have bestowed upon me in former times. I bid you Godspeed, and am at your command to do whatever you may put upon me to do."

When addressing the Department W.R.C. camp-fire in the Peoples' Church, Boston, Feb. 8, 1894, he said: —

"It was my good fortune to assist in taking the first steps in the organization of this Woman's Relief Corps, which has now reached a membership of nearly 140,000 loyal, great-hearted, patriotic women. It has been possible for this organization to be a power for good wherever it has existed. It has been my privilege to speak in this same strain before, at the Departments of the Grand Army of the Republic and the Woman's Relief Corps in Maine, to encourage them to consolidate and make themselves more powerful. There are many thoughts that come to me. The power for good that the Woman's Relief Corps exerts — has always exerted in the communities where it has been organized — is beyond calculation. The love of the flag which it inculcates will make it celebrated if it has no other reason for being celebrated.

"The Woman's Relief Corps has come to that point where it is recognized as a great and growing power in this nation — as the supplement, perhaps, of the Grand Army of the Republic — a power that will be known long after the Grand Army of the Republic has passed away. I look to the Woman's Relief Corps and Sons of Veterans to maintain that loyalty to the flag that the Grand Army of the Republic fought to maintain.

"Mrs. President, I am glad to be here. Mrs. President-to-be, or who is now president in fact, I pledge my services to you, and you have but to command my services."

Captain Meech was a member of the Executive Committee for the National Encampment in Boston (1890), and also served on sub-committees. In December, 1890, he was chosen a member of the Souvenir Committee with Charles Carleton Coffin and B. N. Adams.

A copy of the souvenir, which is an elegant volume containing a report of Boston Encampment week (1890), was presented to our Headquarters' library.

Captain Meech was always a welcome guest at our Conventions, social gatherings and camp-fires.

As Adjutant-General on the Staff of Commander-in-Chief Adams, he gave his official influence and the same personal interest in the Woman's Relief Corps as in former years, and always appreciated the fact that he was the only honorary member of the Department of Massachusetts.

JAMES F. MEECH.

Honorary Member Dept. Mass. W.R.C.
Assistant Adjutant-General Dept. Mass. G.A.R. 1276 — 1992
Adjutant-General G.A.R. 1893, 1894

CHAPTER X.

RELATIONS OF THE DEPARTMENT OF MASSACHUSETTS WOMAN'S RELIEF CORPS TO THE GRAND ARMY OF THE REPUBLIC.

WHILE the Woman's Relief Corps received the endorsement of Department Commander Adams, Assistant Adjutant-General Meech and other prominent comrades of the Grand Army of the Republic, and local Posts extended courtesies to its Department officers, the exact relations of the two societies were not definitely settled during the first year of Relief Corps work.

At the Annual Encampment of the Grand Army of the Republic, held in Lynn Jan. 28, 1880, Department Commander John G. B. Adams in his Annual Address referred to the new organization as follows: —

> I feel that I should be remiss in duty did I not call the attention of comrades to the assistance we are receiving from the ladies' societies connected with the Posts. While many Posts have had auxiliary Corps connected with them for years, it was thought by some that a better work could be accomplished if these could be brought together as a State organization. And last year the Ladies' State Relief Corps was organized. I think the result has been all that could be desired. Several new Corps have been organized and as far as I can learn are rendering valuable assistance to Posts; and I urge comrades to give our lady friends the encouragement in their patriotic work they so richly deserve.

A resolution was framed by Col. Thomas E. Barker, and presented by George L. Goodale for action by this Encampment, viz. : —

Resolved, That we recognize in the Ladies' State Relief Corps, Department of Massachusetts, an auxiliary to our charitable association, whose power and influence for us comrades are inestimable. Heartily endorsing and approving of the organization, we learn with profound gratitude of their success during the past year, and we bid them Godspeed in the noble work they have taken up.

An earnest debate followed, and the resolution was cordially endorsed by Comrades George L. Goodale of Medford, Thomas E. Barker of Malden, Azel Ames, Jr., of Wakefield, W. W. Blackmer and A. B. Underwood of Boston, and several others.

There was, however, enough opposition to indefinitely postpone the subject.

At a meeting of the Board of Directors of the Woman's State Relief Corps, held May 12, 1880, a committee, consisting of Mrs. Sarah E. Fuller, Mrs. E. Florence Barker, Mrs. Kathrina L. Beedle, Mrs. Francelia P. Boynton and Mrs. Amanda M. Thayer, was appointed to confer with the Department Commander and Council of the G.A.R., "in order to determine the relative position of the Woman's State Relief Corps to the Grand Army of the Republic."

Arrangements were made for this conference which was held June 3, 1880, and in accordance with the advice of Department Commander John A. Hawes (the successor of Captain Adams), the term, "Auxiliary to the G.A.R." was added to the title of the W.S.R.C.

Department Commander Hawes pledged the women his support, and promised that a delegate from the Department Encampment G.A.R. would offer a resolution in the next National Encampment endorsing their work.

When presenting his Annual Address to the Department Encampment of 1881, Commander Hawes referred to the Woman's Relief Corps as follows : —

The relationship of the Woman's State Relief Corps to our organization was the subject of much debate at our last Encampment. Having since that time become more familiar with its objects and of the desire of its members generally to be "helpmeets," and upon consultation with its principal officers, having been convinced that there was no desire on the part of a large portion of its officers to have attached to the association any name which would interfere with the constitution or by-laws of our organization, and believing that its object is from a conscientious desire to aid us in our work of charity, and not from selfish motives; knowing that in its ranks are ladies who sorely suffered by the sacrifices which they made for loved ones while in the camp or on the battlefield, while years have not effaced from their memories the effect the war had on them as individuals, and that the old-time sympathy is still extended to our unfortunate comrades, I give the association my sincere and cordial support; but it is as a separate and distinct organization.

The Committee on Address of Department Commander consisted of Azel Ames, Jr., John D. Billings, G. M. Fiske, L. F. Currier, John T. Wilson and George H. Patch. They reported upon this subject as follows : —

Upon that portion of the Commander's address relating to the status of the Woman's Relief Corps, your Committee submits the following resolve, as the embodiment of its recommendation : —
Resolved, That the Department of Massachusetts, G.A.R., recognizes in the Woman's Relief Corps an invaluable ally in its mission of Charity and Loyalty and hails it as a noble band of Christian workers, who while not of the Grand Army of the Republic are auxiliary to it.

This report was adopted, and the resolution marks an important event in the history of both organizations.

Rev. J. F. Lovering, Chaplain-in-Chief G.A.R., who had been corresponding with Mrs. Sarah E. Fuller, Department President, in regard to a National Order, offered to present the matter to the next National Encampment, and requested a statement from Mrs. Fuller regarding the work in Massachusetts, which he read at the Encampment at Indianapolis in June, 1881, and then offered the following resolutions which were adopted : —

Resolved, That we approve the project of organizing a Woman's National Relief Corps.

Resolved, That such Woman's Relief Corps may use under such title the words "auxiliary to the Grand Army of the Republic" by special endorsement of the National Encampment, G.A.R.

This gave new impetus to the work in Massachusetts, and although no further action was taken at that time toward forming a National organization, it called attention to the fact that the women who had organized this work were in earnest, and that the movement was not a spasmodic one.

The word "state" was dropped from the title after the adoption of the above resolution.

When the next Department Convention met in Boston (Jan. 31, 1882), the newly elected Department Commander, George H. Patch, sent greetings and wished the Woman's Relief Corps "long life and prosperity." He proved the sincerity of this message by his helpfulness throughout the year and in his address as Department Commander, at the Sixteenth Annual Encampment held in Faneuil Hall, Boston, Jan. 29, 1883, said : —

The Woman's Relief Corps in this State now numbers nine hundred and forty-one members, a gain of two hundred and twenty-seven the past year, with a net gain of five regularly organized Corps. This certainly is an evidence of their vitality. They expended in the year 1882 the sum of $5,043.70, against $1,117.97 in 1881, and have a balance on hand in the treasury of $1,155.56. This surely indicates charity, and also united work which is necessary to secure substantial results. If the above are recognized as facts, then indeed does the Woman's Relief Corps deserve our hearty commendation. I am satisfied that the Corps, like the Grand Army, is gaining wisdom by experience, and is fast outgrowing what may have seemed to some to be vital defects in its organization; and while I may differ with them upon questions of policy, I certainly feel it to be my duty to commend their organizations to all Posts who can unite and work in harmony with them as an organization. In answer to my request for a few facts to present to this Encampment concerning their work during the past year, the Secretary of the Relief Corps says, after giving me the figures above used, " And we look forward to the coming year with hopefulness and deep earnestness that the results of our work as a band of women may prove financially and socially a benefit to that noble organization, the Grand Army of the Republic, for whose advancement and interest we most fervently pray."

To such statements we can all say Amen. And while we may not be able to reconcile individual opinions contrary to our convictions, we can stand upon that broad plane of fairness and justice, and as comrades and gentlemen pay to these honest, earnest women that tribute of respect and esteem due to all wives, sisters and mothers who, by their silent influence, exert such a power in our homes, our State and our nation.

A delegation from the Sixteenth Annual Encampment visited officially the Department Convention which was holding its session in Boston at the same time; Commander-in-Chief Van Der Voort and Staff being escorted to the Convention by Assistant Quartermaster-General Goodale, Col. Thomas E. Barker, E. B. Stillings and other comrades.

The custom then inaugurated has been continued, and each year since we have had the pleasure of welcoming to our Convention an official delegation from the Department Encampment, Grand Army of the Republic. A cordial greeting is extended by the Encampment to the official committee of the Woman's Relief Corps, visiting that body as representatives of the Annual Convention.

Department Commander George S. Evans gave the following testimony in his address at the Seventeenth Annual Encampment, Jan. 30, 1884 : —

The State Department, Woman's Relief Corps, has, as in the past years of its existence, been doing a noble work of charity, and has, in many instances which came under my own observation, been of great benefit and a material helper to some of our Posts. Having always had infinite faith in woman's work as auxiliary to the Grand Army of the

Republic, I am stronger in the faith today than ever, and I heartily commend the Massachusetts Department, as it now stands, as an organization whose only aim is to aid and co-operate with us in the noble work we are day by day accomplishing, and to in no way assume any of the prerogatives of our organization; but to help and care for the destitute comrade if need be, and to comfort and provide for the widows and orphans of our late comrades.

Department Commander John D. Billings expressed the following opinions in his address to the Eighteenth Annual Encampment, January, 1885 : —

I heartily indorse the work of this organization. I never shared the solicitude of those comrades who feared that it would usurp the name, the badge, the work and glory of the Grand Army, or even that it would "bury" us all before we needed it. While I have not been an enthusiast in its behalf in former years, I have not been an opponent, and my only question has been as to the need of a State or National organization, inasmuch as loyal women have always been ready to second us. But I am now satisfied on that point. My mother and sisters were as good soldiers in their sphere as I was in mine, and I must be a man much lower than the angels if I attempt to restrict them in times of peace on a simple question of methods. Several Posts have expressed great dependence on their Auxiliary Corps. In one case only, a lack of harmony has been reported, and in this the estimable Department President, who has shown a constant zeal to have the most harmonious relations on the part of her Corps, immediately resorted to measures to secure the desired end. I confidently predict the time is not far distant when they will be the right arm of our support in the community, and I give them Godspeed.

Department Commander John W. Hersey was glad to bid "Godspeed" to the Woman's Relief Corps in his address at the Nineteenth Annual Encampment held in Boston, Jan. 27, 1886 : —

I have no words at my command, my comrades, to express to you my appreciation of and thanks for the grand work which this organization is accomplishing in our Department. Filled with the same loyal devotion and self-sacrificing zeal that possessed them, their mothers and sisters, during the dark days of the Rebellion, they have gone out all over this Department as ministering angels, carrying sunshine and gladness into many a desolate home, and making glad many a sad and lonely heart.

During the year it has been not only my duty, but also my happy privilege, to assist them in word and deed as far as I possibly could, and my only regret is that I have not been able to do more to aid them. And I most heartily commend them and their noble work to the favorable consideration of the comrades of the Department, and for myself, I can only say that from my heart of hearts I bid them Godspeed in the noble work in which they are engaged.

It was during the year 1886 that the memorable excursion to California was arranged, and a special car was assigned the W.R.C. by the Grand Army officials, who planned for the comfort of our representatives. Many courtesies were extended our delegates by the Grand Army comrades of Massachusetts, who journeyed to the National Encampment at San Francisco.

It was now apparent that the Woman's Relief Corps was firmly established as a co-worker with the Grand Army of the Republic, and the value of such an auxiliary was being recognized throughout the State and Nation. Posts were urged to organize Corps, and Department Commander Richard F. Tobin, at Twentieth Annual Encampment in Boston, 1887, presented this matter in his address as follows : —

It has been my pleasure during the past year to meet the officers of the Woman's Relief Corps, both State and National. This patriotic auxiliary to the Grand Army of the Republic is entitled to our esteem, respect, confidence and protection; and wherever practicable, I would respectfully recommend that Corps, auxiliary to the Grand Army of the Republic, be instituted, as great good must result from such united action and mutual confidence in each other must naturally establish a patriotic zeal, and each will stimulate the other in its fraternal charity for the needy wards of our grand organization. Our gratitude should go forth to encourage the noble women in their efforts to smooth the paths of those who have few other earthly helpers. I commend to the protection of this Department of the Grand Army of the Republic this noble band of loyal women, who, as mothers, sisters, daughters and wives of our comrades, are so faithfully and earnestly fulfilling their mission of fraternal charity.

Department Commander Charles D. Nash, at the Twenty-first Annual Encampment in Boston, January, 1888, referred to the value of Corps in helping Posts in their relief work, viz. : —

To the officers and members of the Woman's Relief Corps I desire to extend my personal thanks for the many courtesies received at their hands during my term of office. I desire also to commend the loyal women of this Order for the good work they have undertaken. When I contemplate that in a few years the Posts of the Grand Army will, in consequence of their depleted ranks, be obliged to surrender their charters; when the fostering care of the Relief Committees of today shall cease, then it is that I can see that this institution, in addition to the great work that it is doing today, will be of incalculable benefit. They will be the great reserve upon which the thin picket-line of the Grand Army of a few years hence will be obliged to fall back to, and right nobly, I believe, they will care for the old veterans of the future, with a devotion and tenderness equalled only by the loyal women of a quarter of a century ago. Then in your name, comrades, I bid them all hail and God-speed.

Department Commander Myron P. Walker, at the Twenty-second Annual Encampment, 1889, inserted the following paragraph in his address : —

In all public and private utterances I have given cordial support to the Woman's Relief Corps; but I have never yet been able to find language adequately to express my admiration for the interest its members take, in all that concerns our organization. The President of the Department, Mrs. Emma B. Lowd, and her associate officers, have been true to their mission, and wherever duty has called me, I have found the officers and members of the several Corps, willing and anxious to share the burdens of the Post with which they are connected. Officially I bid them farewell and commend them one and all to our Department.

Greetings were sent the Department Encampment by our Convention Feb. 12, 1889, viz. : —

The Department of Massachusetts Woman's Relief Corps, in Convention assembled, send greetings to the Twenty-second Department Encampment, Grand Army of the Republic, with the renewed assurance of the hearty co-operation of eight thousand loyal women, in the noble work of caring for your unfortunate comrades, their widows and orphans.

L. A. TURNER,
ELEANOR B. WHEELER,
Committee.

This Encampment sent the following message in response : —

The representatives of twenty thousand comrades of the Grand Army of the Republic, Department of Massachusetts, in Convention assembled, acknowledge the kind greetings of the Department of Massachusetts Woman's Relief Corps, and hereby express to them our hearty appreciation of their valuable services as an auxiliary to our Order, their loyalty to all the interests of the Grand Army, and wish for their continued success and prosperity. Unanimously adopted.

A. C. MONROE,
Assistant Adjutant-General.

Department Commander, George L. Goodale, who had been our staunch and able friend from the first, gave the Woman's Relief Corps the same hearty endorsement when closing his administration, as his address at the Twenty-third Annual Encampment, February, 1890, shows : —

As in all the years of the past, since the organization of the Woman's Relief Corps, so in the year now closing, this noble band of loyal patriotic women have zealously, cheerfully, devotedly performed their mission as an auxiliary to our Order. May not we, the boys of the Old Bay State, have a just and proper feeling of pride in the remarkable growth and prosperity of the Woman's Relief Corps? It was here in this Department, that the organization had its birth : here it was first fostered and acknowledged as an auxiliary to the Grand Army of the

Republic. And when, in the progress of events, a National Woman's Relief Corps was formed, the ritual of our Corps was adopted, and Massachusetts ladies were elected as the pioneer leaders in a work which is now country wide. While other Departments have been formed, the loyal women of our State have so sustained our Corps, that it remains among the leading Departments of our Order.

Having ever been a friend of the organization, I have made, during my official year, careful observations, wherever duty has called me throughout the Department, and endeavored to ascertain if the work performed by the women of the Corps justified the high opinion their zealous friends entertained for them and their labors. I have found that where a Post has a Corps as its auxiliary, it is the universal testimony that it contributed greatly to the advancement of our Order and is constantly proving, by acts of loving kindness in aiding the poor, the sick and needy comrades, and the widows and orphans of those who are with us no more, that of all the blessings which have come to us as a Department, the greatest and best came in the formation of our auxiliary — the Woman's Relief Corps. Words are entirely inadequate to express the appreciation with which the services of the ladies of the Corps are held in the hearts of the comrades. With sincere gratitude for what they have done for us in the past, let us bid them a loyal hearty " Godspeed ' for the future.

The year 1890 was an eventful one for our Order in Massachusetts and Department Commander George H. Innis, at the Twenty-fourth Annual Encampment, 1891, expressed official thanks for aid rendered during the year, viz. : —

I have had occasion during my term of office to observe the workings of the Woman's Relief Corps. Wherever I have been I have met the women of this truly patriotic organization.

The President, Mrs. Mary E. Knowles, and her associate officers have been energetic and loyal to the Grand Army of the Republic and its sacred trust; and I feel I voice the sentiment of every comrade when I say to the Woman's Relief Corps, God bless you in your noble work. The valuable assistance rendered by this noble band of women during the National Encampment added greatly to its success. Being associated as I was at Headquarters of the National Committee, I had an opportunity to see the amount of work done by these ladies, and in your names, comrades, I sincerely thank them; and in the future I shall deem it my duty to be as loyal to them as they have been to the Grand Army of the Republic.

Department Commander Arthur A. Smith at Twenty-fifth Annual Encampment, 1892, referred to the W.R.C. as follows: —

In this noble organization of truly loyal women we see the same spirit manifested that prompted the loyal women of the North to noble sacrifices during the dark and uncertain period of our Nation's existence. To those loyal and patriotic women the credit must be given of doing their duty at home, not only in supplying the hospital, the camp and field with the products of their handiwork, but caring for the home and loved ones left in their charge; while many a brave woman followed the army, administering with loving, gentle hands to the distressed soldiers and sailors of the Union. Numberless almost are the brave boys who owe their lives to the timely presence and constant care of these devoted Army Nurses.

Is it strange, then, that the Grand Army of the Republic should love and respect its auxiliary, the Woman's Relief Corps? composed of women prompted by the same spirit which educated those brave and loyal women during the war of the rebellion, and whose objects are, "To assist the Grand Army of the Republic and to perpetuate the memory of their heroic dead." Let the increase in the number of Corps organized during the past year in the State answer the question so far as the Department of Massachusetts, Grand Army of the Republic, is concerned. I am free to say that if this Department of the Grand Army of the Republic during the past year should be characterized with a degree of success, much of it is due to the hearty co-operation of the Department President and her associate officers, together with every Corps in this Department.

May the Great Commander of us all bless them in their noble work!

At the Department Convention in 1893, Mrs. Mary G. Deane, Department President, referred in her Annual Address to the presentation of a flag, as follows: —

Since 1881 we have been working as the only recognized auxiliary of the Grand Army in this Department; and during all these years harmony and friendship have existed between the State organizations.

One incident of this was illustrated at the gathering in Grand Army Headquarters, Aug. 19, 1892, when the Committee chosen at the last Convention to purchase a flag for the Department Grand Army of the Republic, presented the gift. The occasion was one ever to be remembered, and was referred to in General Orders by the Department Commander as follows: —

It will be remembered that at the Thirteenth Annual Convention of the Department of Massachusetts, Woman's Relief Corps, it was voted that the Department present " a banner or flag to the Department of Massachusetts, Grand Army of the Republic," and that a committee be appointed to carry the vote into effect. As a result of that action, the following members of the Woman's Relief Corps, Department of Massachusetts, advanced upon, and I am pleased to confess, captured, our Department Headquarters on Friday afternoon, August 19, during a session of our Council of Administration: Mary G. Deane, President; Lizabeth A. Turner, Counselor; Mary E. Elliot, Secretary; Sarah E. Fuller, Treasurer; Augusta A. Wales, Past President; Emma B. Lowd, Past President, and Elizabeth V. Lang, Past Junior Vice-President. In behalf of our honored auxiliary, Mrs. Turner presented to the Department, through the Department Commander, a beautiful State flag, with the Massachusetts coat of arms emblazoned on both sides. In size the flag measures five feet two inches on the staff, and five feet eleven inches fly. On motion of Comrade Charles M. Whelden, of the Council of Administration, it was voted unanimously that a resolution of thanks be presented at the hands of the Assistant Adjutant-General to the ladies for their valued present.

Following the flag presentation, Mrs. Deane presented the Department with elegantly-bound copies of the Journals of Proceedings of the National Convention, Woman's Relief Corps, at Detroit, and the Department Convention at Boston in 1892. It was also voted that a vote of thanks be tendered the ladies for these valued gifts.

In the Annual Address of Department Commander James K. Churchill at Twenty-sixth Encampment, 1893, he said: —

It is with great pleasure that I take this opportunity to add my testimony of appreciation of the services of this organization to the Department of Massachusetts, Grand Army of the Republic. To them, my comrades, we owe a debt of gratitude which we can never repay. Their loyalty has been demonstrated substantially in numberless cases throughout the Department during the past year; and it is due to them that many Posts, whose names are today on the roster of this Department, would simply be a matter of record in its history, were it not for the loyal and generous support given to them by their auxiliary, the Woman's Relief Corps.

It has been my privilege and pleasure, in my official capacity, to meet on several occasions during my visits to the Posts of our Department the Department officers of the Woman's Relief Corps; and it has been a pleasure to witness the zeal and interest they have on all occasions manifested for the Department of Massachusetts, Grand Army of the Republic. One of the most noteworthy instances of this devotion to this Department was made in August last, when this noble band of women, forestalling the action of the last Encampment, presented to this Department the beautiful State flag which you see before you.

To the honored President Mrs. Mary G. Deane and her associates, I return my sincere thanks for the many courtesies extended to myself and associates during the past year. Long may you live in the grateful remembrance of the comrades of the Department of Massachusetts, Grand Army of the Republic; and may He who controls the destinies of us all spare you for many years to come, to aid us in performing the grand work of our beloved Order.

When our Department was organized in 1879, its officers were tendered Grand Army Headquarters for a weekly meeting. This courtesy extended by Department Commander Adams was continued by his successors until it was deemed advisable in 1887, owing to the increase of our Order, to establish headquarters of our own in Pemberton Square, adjoining the G.A.R.

When, in February, 1889, Headquarters of the Grand Army of the Republic were moved from Pemberton Square to Boylston Building, our Department established headquarters in the same building by invitation of Department Commander Walker.

Early in 1893 the rooms tendered by a vote of the legislature in the new portion of the State House were occupied as Grand Army Headquarters, and our congratulations were tendered the comrades upon this recognition, which they justly deserve from the Old Bay State.

Mrs. Emily L. Clark, Department President, in referring to this, said in her Annual Address at the Department Convention in 1894: —

You will rejoice, I am sure, to learn that rooms have been assigned at the State House as the permanent Headquarters of the Department of Massachusetts, Grand Army of the Republic.

The Commonwealth never did a more graceful act than in providing these rooms for "our boys," thus securing them Headquarters without expense.

She then called upon the Convention to *salute the Commonwealth*. The entire delegation then arose and gracefully saluted the Commonwealth of Massachusetts.

Department Commander Eli W. Hall, at the Twenty-seventh Annual Encampment, 1894, expressed his regard for the Woman's Relief Corps as follows: —

This noble organization has added another year of most efficient work to its history — a history which was already filled to repletion with records of loyal and charitable work.

As our gallant comrades were sustained in the fiery contests of their youth by the prayers, sympathy and assistance of multitudes of noble, loyal women — their mothers and sisters, their sweethearts and wives — so their advancing years are made to rejoice in comfort and happiness by the generous assistance and good cheer of the Woman's Relief Corps.

I have seen ample evidence of their good work, as my official duties have led me all over the State during my visits to the various Posts of this Department. I can testify to the fact that many Posts which are small in number and weak in financial resources have been strengthened and sustained by the timely assistance of this noble band of women.

We can fully realize that the spirit which actuated a Florence Nightingale or a Clara Barton is still active in the hearts of the women of our Commonwealth; and we may rest assured that as long as this sentiment prevails the brave soldiers of the Union will not lack for comfort and encouragement in their works of Charity and Loyalty.

I take this opportunity to express my appreciation and thanks to the President and Department officers of the Woman's Relief Corps for the many courteous attentions received by myself and other officers of this Department during the year.

I feel that I give voice to the universal sentiment of the Department when I extend to the Woman's Relief Corps the highest appreciation and best wishes of the comrades of the Grand Army of the Republic.

In a letter received from Past Department Commander Evans, dated Boston, Mass., Nov. 2, 1894, he gives a brief resumé of the work of the Woman's Relief Corps, viz. : —

It was my privilege to be present at the second Convention of your organization which took place at East Boston, in May, 1879, where I was very deeply impressed with the earnestness of the ladies who were at the gathering, and who afterwards proved to be the pioneers in the work for the veteran and those dependent upon him. For four years as the Massachusetts Woman's Relief Corps you did such grand work and the organization was of so much benefit to the Grand Army of the Republic, that I felt if anything could be done to promote the establishing of a national organization, so that the work could be spread all over the country, and that every State in the Union where the G.A.R. existed, could be benefitted thereby, I would render all the assistance possible to that end.

Being Department Commander of Massachusetts G.A.R. in 1883, when our warm friend, Paul Van Der Voort, was Commander-in-Chief, I fully co-operated with him in bringing the ladies together at Denver, Col., for the purpose of considering the feasibility of forming a national organization. I need not enter into details of the result, for the banding together of over one hundred thousand women in such a grand cause fully justifies the action taken at Denver that year, when the National Encampment indorsed the organization and made it auxiliary to the Grand Army of the Republic.

What was gratifying to the Massachusetts G.A.R. delegation at that Encampment was the fact that the work as exemplified by the Massachusetts women was adopted by the national organization of the Woman's Relief Corps, and that three of its leading women were selected to fill the highest offices, and to carry on the work which was to grow into such large dimensions.

How well the duties of that first year were performed is a matter of history and needs no commendation at my hands. Mrs. E. Florence Barker as National President, Mrs. Sarah E. Fuller as National Secretary, and Mrs. Lizabeth A. Turner as National Treasurer, with the hearty co-operation of the other noble women who were elected officers at that time, laid the foundation for one of the grandest organizations of women that exists in the land today.

I have been privileged many times to tender the greetings of the G.A.R. at both National and Department Conventions, and my feelings in relation to the W.R.C. have been so freely expressed that I do not think that it is necessary for me to say how highly I appreciate what has been done by your organization.

I desire to express my appreciation of all that has been done by the Department, and by the different Corps of the W.R C. of Massachusetts, in connection with our Soldiers' Home. Being a member of the Board of Trustees, and for many years its Secretary, I am fully conversant with the many kind and generous acts performed by members of your Order for the benefit of the inmates of the Home. The number of rooms furnished, and the money raised for the purpose of taking care of those who cannot be admitted for want of room, is but a small part of what has been done by your organization in the interest of the Home. The donations and entertainments given have been appreciated by the Board of Trustees, the officers and men of the Home.

In conclusion, let me say that I have never regretted the stand I took when there was opposition to such an organization as yours. The magnificent showing at your last Convention in the matter of relief fully justifies it, and I sincerely hope that in the years to come the record of the Woman's Relief Corps may be as glorious and as grand as it has been in the years that have passed.

Yours fraternally,

GEO. S. EVANS.

In accordance with the Rules and Regulations of the Woman's Relief Corps, each President is required " to forward to the Post Commander a quarterly report of the relief extended by the Corps, and confer with him concerning all matters in common between Post and Corps; appoint a Conference Committee of five to meet and counsel with a like Committee from the Post, in order to strengthen the relations and perfect the work for which these organizations stand mutually pledged."

Each Department President reports annually to the Department Commander the condition of the Order and expenditures for relief, and said reports are printed in the Journal of the Encampment.

Many camp-fires and social gatherings are held throughout the State where the interests of this great patriotic work are considered by Posts and Corps.

Joint installations of officers are held annually in many places, and when journeying to the National Encampment Posts frequently carry with them banners presented by their Corps.

In the great work of teaching patriotism to the young, and introducing the flag salute into the public schools, our Order has been specially active. This new line of educational work is being systematically planned by the National Committee, and in Massachusetts as well as in other States public flag meetings are teaching lessons of patriotism to the rising generation.

Since the Department of Massachusetts was formed in 1879 its Corps have expended over $130,000.00 in relief, assisted in establishing and maintaining the Soldiers' Home in Massachusetts, and have appropriated thousands of dollars for Memorial Day.

Corps have also co-operated with Posts in the erection of monuments and memorial halls and in many other efforts for the Grand Army of the Republic.

Our members believe that the services of the Union veterans should be recognized and their record honored in every community, and that

"'Tis ours while life remains
To garner up their glorious deeds
And make them live again."

For the suffering caused by the Civil War did not cease on the battlefield, and the cause which the *defenders of the Union* represent, is hallowed by sacred memories.

In Memoriam

IN MEMORIAM.

IN MEMORY OF GEORGE H. PATCH, RICHARD F. TOBIN, ALFRED C. MONROE AND JAMES F. MEECH, LOYAL SUPPORTERS OF OUR ORDER, WHO HAVE JOINED THE SILENT GRAND ARMY.

DURING the year 1887 the Woman's Relief Corps met with a great loss in the death (July 26) of Past Department Commander George H. Patch. A special train conveyed the delegations of the G.A.R. and W.R.C. to South Framingham, where the funeral services were held. In a circular to the Corps Mrs. S. Agnes Parker, Department President, referred to his "eloquent voice and pen," which have so often been at our command, and to the faithful service he gave to our work.

In 1890 we were called to mourn the death of another true friend, Richard F. Tobin. Mrs. Mary E. Knowles, Department President, issued the following Circular Letter as a tribute to his memory: —

BOSTON, Nov. 24, 1890.

To the Members of the Order in this Department.

Richard F. Tobin, Senior Vice Commander-in-Chief, and Past Department Commander of Massachusetts, Grand Army of the Republic, has, after many weeks of suffering, laid down his life-work and has gone to join that "Grand Army whose term of service is completed."

In his death our Order has lost a true and loyal-hearted friend — one who was ever ready with voice and hand to encourage and assist us in our work. His grand endorsement and words of appreciation of our services during the week of the National Encampment and Convention will never be forgotten by those who heard his eloquent words.

Our hearts are heavy with the burden of sorrow, and we feel that it would be fitting, as auxiliary to the Grand Army of the Republic, to unite with the comrades in this Department in an expression of sorrow and bereavement.

Therefore, we earnestly request that the charters of the Corps in this Department be draped in mourning for thirty days, as a tribute of love and respect to the memory of this gallant sailor hero.

May we remember those dear ones whose hearts are aching, and whose loss is so heavy to bear; let us take them in our prayers to our Heavenly Father, whose ear is ever quick to hear the cry of His children and who has promised that the widow and fatherless shall never be forsaken.

Department officers and several Corps attended his funeral which was held in Boston.

In 1891, that eloquent and loyal friend of our Department, Alfred C. Monroe, was also summoned to join the *Silent Grand Army*.

A Memorial General Order was issued June 19, by Mrs. Augusta A. Wales, Department President, in which she expressed the sentiment of every member, viz. : —

It is with a feeling of personal bereavement that the Woman's Relief Corps joins with the Grand Army of the Department of Massachusetts in paying homage to the memory of Assistant Adjutant-General A. C. Monroe, who died at Revere, Thursday, June 18, at 5 P.M.

To us and our work he was as loyal as to his own, not only in public speech, but in deeds as well, and none can bear stronger testimony to the value of his words of counsel and cheer than those to whom have been entrusted the cares and responsibilities of our Department during the years past.

Let us tenderly remember him as a brave soldier, true-hearted man and beloved friend.

Department officers and many other members attended the funeral services at East Weymouth, leaving Boston on a special train provided by the Department officials of the G.A.R.

The delegates to the Department Convention in 1892, having learned that Fletcher Webster Post of Brockton (of which the late Assistant Adjutant-General was a Past Commander) intended, in conjunction with the Department of Massachusetts, G.A.R., to erect a monument to the memory of its late comrade, voted that fifty dollars be appropriated for this object. A Monroe Monument Fund was started and voluntary subscriptions from Corps increased this amount to $251.00 before the monument was completed.

An invitation to attend the dedication of the Monroe Monument was extended Department officers and all Corps in the State by the Committee of the G.A.R. having the arrangements in charge. Among the thousands present at the services in East Weymouth, Sunday afternoon, Oct. 30, 1892, were many members of our Order.

The late Assistant Adjutant-General endorsed the Woman's Relief Corps before the formation of a Department — and never wavered in his loyal support of its work.

One of the last addresses which he gave in public was at the camp-fire in Tremont Temple, under the auspices of the Department of Massachusetts, W.R.C., Feb. 12, 1891.

Mrs. Mary E. Knowles, who presided as the retiring Department President, introduced the Assistant Adjutant-General as follows: —

When Memorial Day comes, all over this broad land the comrades of the Grand Army of the Republic, with the Woman's Relief Corps and the Sons of Veterans, unite in paying tribute to those who have answered to the roll-call of the Great Commander; and at this time I wish to present to you one whose courage and bravery no one doubts, whose faithful services to his country and his State entitle him to all the honors, respect and esteem that can be offered him. I have the pleasure of presenting to you the Assistant Adjutant-General of the Department of Massachusetts, Alfred C. Monroe, who will speak to you on "The Silent Grand Army."

Comrade Monroe's response was characteristic: —

Mrs. Chairman, Comrades and Friends: Before taking up the theme which you have given me, I wish to say a few words to congratulate you and your Department upon the grand work you have accomplished the past year. Mrs. Turner has said that the Woman's Relief Corps antedates the organization of the Grand Army of the Republic. Yes! You and I, comrades, as our minds go back to other days and other scenes, realize that woman was at the front, suffering all the hardships and privations of the common soldier, that she might carry to him some of the comforts of home. You know, comrades, how tender, delicate and kind were her ministrations. You and I know that there were heroines as well as heroes in that war; and beside the names of Grant, Sherman, Sheridan, Farragut and Logan, we will place in memory's type the names of Mother Bickerdyke, Harriet P. Dame, Helen Gilson and that Florence Nightingale of America — Clara Barton.

But I am asked to speak for the "Silent Grand Army"; and what a theme, my comrades! As we think of that "Silent Grand Army" how many faces come up before us, and we can almost imagine that we feel the magic touch of elbows again. We see that genial comrade. George H. Patch; the gallant sailor, Dick Tobin; the eminent jurist, gallant soldier, statesman and orator, Comrade Devens. They are bivouacked on the other side, but they are with us here. They live in our memories, and "To live in hearts we leave behind is not to die." Legions are resting upon the battlefields of the South: that fair land is dotted over with their graves. They are resting in the glades of the forest, along the streams by which they fought, on mountain peaks, in mossy glens. The mocking-birds sing over them, but they hear not the music. The summer sun beats down upon them, but they heed it not. The cold winds of winter sigh and moan through the pine trees, but they strike no responsive chord in their bosoms. Sleep on! your memory is enshrined in the hearts of your comrades living. We will not forget you or those you have left to our care and protection.

A few months ago our hearts were again made sad by the death (April 30) of Capt. James F. Meech, who was instrumental in forming the Department of Massachusetts W.R.C. in 1879, and who was proud of the distinction of being its only honorary member.

Department Headquarters were closed on the day of his funeral, which was attended by many representatives of the Order. The following Memorial Circular was issued by the Department President: —

HEADQUARTERS DEPT. OF MASS. WOMAN'S RELIEF CORPS,
AUXILIARY TO THE GRAND ARMY OF THE REPUBLIC,
657 WASHINGTON ST., ROOM 17,

CIRCULAR LETTER }
No. 1.   }

BOSTON, May 2, 1895.

"God calls our loved ones, but we lose not wholly
What He hath given;
They live on earth, in thought and deed, as truly
As in His heaven."

With saddened heart your Department President is called upon to announce to the Corps of this Department that our revered honorary member Capt. James F. Meech has responded to the last call. "Well done! good and faithful servant." Sad hearted that no more in this life can we see his noble, kindly face or receive his words of counsel and advice; grateful that such a man has lived and his influence for good been ours for so many years.

Our Department has lost its only honorary member and our Order a grand and loyal supporter. To his unqualified support, his unswerving loyalty to our cause, added to his faith in woman, is the success of our Department in Massachusetts largely indebted for all that it has attained or accomplished.

With our hearts overflowing with sympathy for the bereaved family and with grief for our own great loss, for our comrades of the Grand Army, who have another proof that their circle here is growing smaller, yet with faith we can still look up, and say, "Thy will, O God, be done."

While the Corps of this Department are preparing their offerings for Memorial Day, it is hoped that every Corps will arrange one as a tribute of love and respect for our honorary member.

Corps charters will be draped sixty days in his memory, which we can best honor by striving to make our Order all that he would have it be.

            EVA T. COOK,
             Department President.

MARY E. ELLIOT,
 Department Secretary.

A circular was issued by the National President, May 30, to every Corps in the country as "a Memorial leaf placed this holy day in memory of OUR FRIEND."

Several Corps sent beautiful floral designs on Memorial Day to his last resting place in Lynn, and nearly every Corps in the State placed floral offerings in local cemeteries with appropriate inscriptions to his memory.

EVA T. COOK

Eleventh Department President 1995

APPENDIX A.

ADMINISTRATION OF 1895.—MRS. EVA T. COOK, DEPARTMENT PRESIDENT.

SEVERAL months having passed since the close of the Sixteenth Annual Convention, it was decided by the Committee on History to include in the Appendix a sketch of the Department work of 1895.

At the Convention referred to, which was held in Springfield, February 13 and 14, Mrs. Eva T. Cook was unanimously elected Department President.

When accepting the office she said: —

"I pledge my best efforts in every way. Tenderly as I have guarded my own name and honor during my life, so I will guard the honor of the Department of Massachusetts."

Mrs. Cook was born in Manchester, Mass., June 26, 1849. She married Col. Benjamin F. Cook of the Twelfth Massachusetts Regiment (popularly known as the "Webster Regiment"), Feb. 24, 1869, and then moved to Gloucester, of which city her husband is the present mayor.

She was a charter member of Clara Barton Lodge, formed as an auxiliary to Col. Allen Post G.A.R., of Gloucester, May 13, 1870, and was elected its first Treasurer, and then served as President six consecutive terms.

Thus for over twenty-five years Mrs. Cook has been identified with the work for the Grand Army of the Republic.

When Col. Allen Relief Corps was instituted Dec. 18, 1886, she united with it and was elected President, holding the office three years.

She served as Department Instituting and Installing Officer in 1889, as Chief Aide on the Staff of Mrs. Knowles in 1890, and as Department Corresponding Secretary in 1891. At the Convention in 1892 she was elected a member of the Department Executive Board, and the following year was chosen Department Junior Vice-President. She was promoted to the office of Senior Vice-President in 1894, and at the Convention held in Springfield, February last, assumed the office of Department President, entering upon its duties with an earnest purpose and a determination to conduct her work in a just and loyal manner.

Mrs. Cook has issued seven General Orders. The Annual Memorial Day Order is worthy of note and is given on page 358.

She has delivered a Memorial Day address each year since 1889, and May 30, last, gave an address at Sturbridge in the afternoon, and at West Medway in the evening.

She is an earnest speaker who always commands attention, and has represented the Department of Massachusetts at many public gatherings.

Mrs. Cook has contributed articles for several Grand Army papers.

She assisted in preparing the history of the Webster Regiment, and in recognition of this valuable service was elected an honorary member of the "Webster Regimental Association," and participates in its annual reunions.

During the first three weeks in June, Mrs. Cook attended the annual exemplifications and addressed representatives from nearly every Corps, upon the ritualistic and general work of the Order. She was accompanied by a special staff appointed by her to exemplify the work, viz.: Hattie A. Bray (Department Inspector), Lynn, President; Fannie M. Jones, Somerville, Secretary; Rebecca A. Pickett, Beverly, Treasurer; Dorcas H. Lyman, Brighton, Conductor; Ray E. Lane, Wakefield, Guard.

Great interest was manifested in all the work, and as in former years, the gatherings with the Post at the close of the afternoon meetings were occasions of inspiration and social enjoyment.

In a General Order issued July 13, Mrs. Cook requested Corps Presidents to fill out an enclosed blank containing a list of questions regarding the efforts of Corps to introduce a flag salute in the schools, and forward the same to Mrs. Mary E. Knowles, Committee on Patriotic Teaching, not later than August 20, that a report of this work in Massachusetts might be presented to the National Convention in the consolidated report of its Committee.

In referring to this subject Mrs. Cook expressed the following sentiment in her General Order: —

At no time since the war has the fact been more apparent that lessons of loyalty and love of country should be inculcated in the minds of the children; and the members of this Department must realize that a grand opportunity is theirs to carry out one of the principles of our Order.

Mrs. Cook had charge of the delegation to the Thirteenth National Convention which met in Louisville, Ky., in September. She was Chairman of the Committee on Reception tendered by the Department of Massachusetts to the "Grand Army of the Republic, Sons of Veterans and other friends," at the Galt House, on the evening of September 11, and the Committee was assisted in receiving by Joseph W. Thayer, Department Commander, John M. Deane, Department Junior Vice-Commander, Hubert O. Moore, Assistant Adjutant-General, J. G. B. Adams and George S. Merrill, Past Commanders-in-Chief, G.A.R., and Col. B. F. Cook.

This reception was attended by several hundred invited guests.

Department Headquarters at the Galt House were in charge of Mrs. Mary L. Gilman, the efficient Chief of Staff, and friends of our work from every section of the country called to greet the Department of Massachusetts.

At the opening session of the Convention Mrs. Cook was appointed Chairman of the Committee on Appeals, and presented an able report.

She esteemed it a great privilege to have the honor of nominating Mrs. Lizabeth A. Turner of Boston as a candidate for the office of National President and her remarks on this occasion have been highly complimented. The *National Tribune* referred to this effort as "the gem of nominating speeches."

Upon returning from Louisville Mrs. Cook again entered zealously into the work for the Department, cheerfully responding to every call of duty, whether at Headquarters or in advancing the work in other directions.

Four Corps have been instituted under the present administration, viz. : —

CAPT. E. T. DRESSER CORPS No. 166, HOUSATONIC.

Instituted March 28, by Mrs. Annie M. Warne, Department Instituting and Installing Officer. Mrs. Eva T. Cook, Department President, installed the officers.

Membership, twenty-four.

President   Lucy G. McDonald.

MYRON E. STOWELL CORPS No. 167, SO. DEERFIELD.

Instituted April 24, by Mrs. Annie M. Warne, Department Instituting and Installing Officer.

Membership, thirty-one.

President .   Laura T. Delano.

JOHN C. FREMONT CORPS No. 168, WEST BRIDGEWATER.
Instituted May 7, by Mrs. Annie M. Warne, Department Instituting and Installing Officer.
Membership, seventeen.
President . . Carrie A. Charlton

BRIDGEWATER CORPS No. 169, BRIDGEWATER.
Instituted June 4, by Mrs. Annie M. Warne, Department Instituting and Installing Officer.
Membership, fifteen.
President . . Florence E. Phinney.

The membership of the one hundred and sixty-eight Corps in Massachusetts October 1, was 13,442. Value of relief expended from January 1 to October 1, $9,374.14. Amount turned over to Posts, $5,323.74.

By vote of the last Department Convention the sum of $534.08 was forwarded the National W.R.C. Home from the Department treasury, and also $50.00 for the relief of the Nebraska sufferers.

A meeting of the Department Relief Committee is held at Headquarters each month, and a good work is being accomplished by the Committee, which consists of Margie E. B. Hutchins, Boston; Hattie M. Tuttle, South Boston; Emilie C. Baker, Dorchester; M. Lizzie Bullock, Everett; Mabel MacGill, Cambridgeport.

In a General Order issued November 11, Mrs. Cook made an official appeal for additional contributions to the Department Relief Fund and also for the Soldiers' Home. She asked the Corps to make "this coming Christmastide one long to be remembered by sending boxes of clothing and delicacies such as are common to this festive season." In closing she said: —

> The season for entertainments, for festivities, is approaching. Open your doors and invite in your friends, the public, that they may see the good work we are doing and give us their encouragement and support.

Accompanying the General Order was a circular in behalf of the Memorial Fund, prepared by Mrs. Mary G. Deane, Chairman of the Committee, and our Corps, always loyal to the cause, have responded to these appeals.

The administration of 1895 has been a successful one. Mrs. Cook has been guided by a sincere desire to faithfully serve the Department over which she has had " the honor to rule."

Thoroughly patriotic, she is devoted to the Grand Army of the Republic, and considers it an honor to work for the soldiers and sailors of the Union.

HEADQUARTERS DEPT. OF MASS. WOMAN'S RELIEF CORPS,
AUXILIARY TO THE GRAND ARMY OF THE REPUBLIC,
NO. 657 WASHINGTON ST., ROOM 17.

GENERAL ORDERS,
No. 3.

BOSTON, April 27, 1895.

" Aye, bring the fadeless evergreens, the laurel and the bay,
A grateful land remembers all her promises today;
And hearts that gave their treasures up when manhood was the price,
Now bring the sweetest offerings and bless the sacrifice."

A year with all its varied experiences has come and gone since last we met to do honor to our Nation's dead. Let us then turn aside from the busy whirl of life and join with our comrades of the Grand Army in making the coming Memorial Day one worthy of its sacred memories. Let us twine the evergreen and the myrtle and join our hearts and voices in one grand anthem of praise and patriotism.

May we ever remember that we owe our Nation's life and prosperity under God to that host of brave soldiers and sailors, one grand division of which sleeps beneath the sod made sacred by their blood, while the other mingles with us, enjoying the fruits of their victories; and while we cherish the memories of the dead, we must still remember and honor the living.

The grave of every Union veteran in our land is a shrine of patriotism, and so long as the love of liberty shall continue to live in the human heart, their memories will grow brighter and brighter.

The flag floating above us suggests in its every fold the noble manhood and bravery of those we honor; its every star a gem saved by their blood to adorn these shrines.

As we scatter the chaplets and garlands, fragrant with the sweetness of Spring, on the spot of green which covers the mounds of our Nation's benefactors, may we open our hearts to the teachings of the hour and the sacredness of the ceremony, light anew the fires of patriotism and renew our pledges of life and sacred honor to transmit unsullied to our children this noble heritage of ours.

And while we meet around these altars of our love, may we give a thought of affection to those far-off graves marked with that one word "Unknown." Unknown perhaps the name, yet he was a soldier of the Union; unknown perhaps his rank, his birthplace, or religion, but known he was a brother, who gave his life for freedom. In this fair land are other graves still for us to approach with reverence: our sister women, whose love of country was shown in action, and whose sympathy for suffering was stronger than life; and while we may not lay our offering of love upon their graves, we can give a tender thought to their memories and strive to make our womanhood as true as theirs.

Bring into the day's service the young children and teach them by our example as well as what is said to them, that we hold the day sacred. Let them assist in preparing the flowers and the wreaths, and make them understand that it is a *holy day* as well as a *holiday* to be kept sacredly.

Let every member of our Order feel it her especial duty to join in the service of the day, and as in former years our Corps have furnished lunches for the comrades, on this day it is hoped that the custom will still continue.

Corps Chaplains are requested to attend to the filling of blanks furnished them as soon as possible after the exercises of the day are over, and forward to the Department Chaplain.

"Yes, honor and glory for them are eternal,
The nation they ransomed their memories will keep;
Fame's flowers immortal will bloom ever vernal
O'er the graves where our heroes in glory now sleep."

National Memorial Day General Order is hereby promulgated.

By order of

EVA T. COOK,
Department President.

MARY E. ELLIOT,
Department Secretary.

APPENDIX B.

MISCELLANEOUS INFORMATION.

THE badge of the Grand Army of the Republic and the "little bronze button" worn by its members, are emblematical of battles fought and victories won in defence of the Union.

They are distinctive emblems of honor which only a comrade can wear, and in the years of the future will be regarded as precious heirlooms.

The only recognized auxiliary to the Grand Army of the Republic, when adopting a badge, selected the red, white and blue as representing the principles of its work, and with the permission of the G.A.R. adopted the monogram F., C. and L. as an assurance that its work would be conducted in a spirit of Fraternity, Charity and Loyalty.

W.R.C. BADGES.

The first badges adopted for Corps Officers consisted of a tri-colored ribbon with an emblem suitable to the office. Members' badges were made with tri-colored ribbon of the same length and width as the officers' ribbons.

At a meeting of the Board of Directors, in 1881, it was voted, That Past Department Officers and Past Corps Presidents be entitled to wear a badge the same as that of the office represented, with the addition of the letter P above the emblem and a loop of the material above the pin.

The present membership badge of the Order was designed by a committee of which Mrs. Sarah E. Fuller was Chairman, and is described in Rules and Regulations as follows: —

"The membership badge of the Woman's Relief Corps shall be, in form and material, that adopted at National Convention held in Minneapolis, July 23, 1884, and no other shall be worn as the badge of the Woman's Relief Corps, except that prescribed for Officers and Past Officers, and must be obtained from National Headquarters through the proper channels.

"This badge is a maltese cross of copper bronze, with the Grand Army medallion suspended from a bar pin, bearing the initials " F.,C.,L.," (Fraternity, Charity, Loyalty) by a red, white and blue ribbon, one and one-half inches long in the clear, and one and one-fourth inches in width.

"The official badge is the same, except that the bar pin designates the office, and the ribbon is of solid color, blue designating the Corps, red the Department, and yellow the National."

Mrs. Lizabeth A. Turner stated at the National Convention in Columbus, Ohio, in 1888, that a request had been received for a set of Relief Corps badges, to be placed in the badge collection at the National Museum in Washington. She was authorized as National Treasurer to arrange and forward them.

A State souvenir badge was adopted at the Department Convention of Massachusetts in 1893, the design of which is a *fac simile* of Faneuil Hall attached to a white ribbon. While adapted for any gathering of the Order, it is intended principally as a souvenir for National Conventions.

HISTORIC GAVEL.

A pleasant incident of the Fifth Annual Convention held in Boston, Jan. 29, 1884, was the presentation of a gold-mounted gavel to the Convention by Mrs. Elizabeth C. Lovering, on behalf of her husband, Rev. Joseph F. Lovering, Past Chaplain-in-Chief, G.A.R.

It was made from wood obtained specially for this purpose — from the stockade at Andersonville Prison. It bore a Latin inscription, which translated, reads as follows: —

"*Let us, both small and great, urge on this work, this undertaking, if we would be dear to our country and to ourselves.*" — *Horace.*

An appropriate presentation speech was made by Mrs. Lovering, who said: —

"Whenever this gavel is struck, some echo from the past must come from its silent lips."

The response of Mrs. E. Florence Barker, as President of the Convention, was an eloquent allusion to the memories which the gift recalled.

A committee was appointed to transmit a suitable testimonial to Mr. Lovering.

RECEPTION TO COMMANDER-IN-CHIEF ROBERT B. BEATH.

At the Soldiers' Home, Chelsea, Feb. 22, 1884, by the officers of the National Woman's Relief Corps, representing Massachusetts.

No more appropriate observance of Washington's birthday could have been arranged than the reception tendered Commander-in-Chief Beath of the Grand Army of the Republic, Friday afternoon, at the Soldiers' Home, where he was the guest of Mrs. E. Florence Barker, President, Mrs. Sarah E. Fuller, Secretary, and Mrs. L. A. Turner, Treasurer of the National Woman's Relief Corps.

The Department W.R.C. was officially represented by Mrs. M. Susie Goodale, President, and Mrs. M. E. Lawton, Treasurer, and the G.A.R. by Junior Vice-Commander Tobin. There were also present several of the Past Department Commanders, Past Asst. Adj.-Gen. James F. Meech and his predecessor in that office, Henry B. Pierce, Secretary of State, and Asst. Adj.-Gen. Pease of the Department of Missouri. Dahlgren Post of South Boston, accompanied by the "fife and drum corps," arrived about three o'clock, by which time the parlor and hall of the Home were filled with ladies and gentlemen, all of whom were interested in work for the soldiers.

Several enlivening selections were given by the band, after which Mrs. Barker invited Capt. J. G. B. Adams, President of the Board of Trustees, to preside.

The inmates of the Home were provided with seats in front of the platform, and evidently were impressed with the thought that a "good time" was in store for them.

The scene was an inspiring one. Above the platform the "Flag of our Union" was tastefully arranged, and on one side of the platform-screen was a shield inclosed with the letters: "Ladies' Aid Association of the Soldiers' Home, Mass."; on the other, the familiar badge of the Grand Army, with the letters "G.A.R." The faces of the inmates, many of them with gray heads and forms bent with age, surrounded with men and women who had gathered from many sections of the State to pay honors to the Commander of the *Grandest Army* in the world, and to testify anew to their interest in a cause equalled only by that which Washington represented, tended to show the appropriateness of such a celebration.

Captain Adams made a few introductory remarks, paying a tribute to Philadelphia, the home of General Beath, and to the "two hundred and fifty thousand loyal boys who wear the blue, all united under the same banner of the Grand Army."

Commander-in-Chief Beath was then introduced and received an enthusiastic greeting. While he came from a State that has no soldiers' home, he was pleased to say that thousands of dollars had been expended in patriotic charity, and over six thousand children had been cared for in the orphan schools of Pennsylvania. "His State," he said, "was pressing forward a movement to found a home in Philadelphia where the deserving veterans shall die with sympathizing friends and the flag of our Union above them. The ladies now representing the Woman's Relief Corps were our friends from 1861 to 1865, and are now co-operating in the humanitarian, fraternal and charitable work of the Grand Army of the Republic, and his indorsement of the Order was most gratifying to the representatives of various Corps who were present." General Beath said that he had visited every soldiers' home in the United States, and he considered this more like a *home* than any of the others. He honored the men and women who sustained it, and he should bear to his comrades upon his return his warmest eulogiums of this Home.

Secretary of State Pierce added a few words of congratulation that Massachusetts had such a Soldiers' Home, and complimented the ladies who are as enthusiastic today as during the war. Massachusetts as a State is identified with the Home, and a resolve appropriating a sum towards its support would undoubtedly be adopted at the State House. He closed with: "God save the Commonwealth!"

Senior Vice-Commander Whiting of Dahlgren Post of South Boston was called upon, and responded by presenting a check for one hundred dollars to the Home in behalf of Dahlgren Post. Captain Creasey, Treasurer of the Board of Trustees, accepted the gift with thanks, saying an equivalent was received for every dollar expended for the Home. Past Department Commander Evans handed to the Treasurer the sum of twenty-five dollars donated by a gentleman present — Hon. Samuel P. Tenney, ex-Mayor of Chelsea.

The presiding officer, whose witty remarks in introducing the various speakers caused considerable merriment, suggested that the audience join in singing "Gather Them In." Speeches were also made by Hon. S. P. Tenney of the Board of Trustees; Mrs. E. Florence

Barker, President of the National Corps, who referred to the services of Capt. J. F. Meech in the early days of the Woman's Relief Corps; Mrs. M. Susie Goodale, President of the State Department; General Cunningham, Superintendent of the House; and Junior Vice-Commander Tobin of the Massachusetts G.A.R.

The audience united in singing "Marching Through Georgia," and "America" was sung as the "Benediction."

The exercises closed at five o'clock, when many of the company remained to inspect the various apartments of the Home.

It is a compliment to the officials of the Woman's Relief Corps that their management of the Order has been such as to receive the commendation of the highest officials of the Grand Army of the Republic, whose indorsement has been given after a thorough investigation of the plans and results of its work.

The Commander-in-Chief held a conference with the National Officers in the evening, upon matters relating to both organizations.— From report in *Grand Army Advocate*, Boston, March, 1884.

DEPARTMENT BANNER.

A beautiful Department Banner, procured through the efforts of Mrs. A. J. Parker of Corps 31, Leominster, was presented at the Annual Convention in 1885.

Mrs. Mary E. Knowles made the presentation speech, and it was her first attendance at a Department Relief Corps Convention.

Mrs. Parker, who was an indefatigable worker for the veterans' cause, died in 1891.

The elegant banner which hangs in a case on the walls of the large room at Headquarters was presented by the Executive Committee of the National (1890) Convention, in appreciation of the free use of headquarters for committee meetings.

THE PIONEER DEPARTMENT.

From the address of Mrs. Kate B. Sherwood, National President, at the Third Annual Convention at Portland, Me., June, 1885.

A State organization having been formed in Massachusetts, the character of the Association and the eligibility to membership was fully discussed. The decision was a secret association and the eligibility of all loyal women, and from this noble germ has grown and developed that benign and beautiful tree, shedding the dews of healing and distilling the fragrance of hope in every valley and on every mountain-top of this great land of ours. It was voted to adopt the name of Woman's Relief Corps, subordinate organizations to be designated by the name of the Post, as now. Committees on Rules and Regulations and Ritual were appointed, which six weeks later reported to a special convention. After important revisions, their work was accepted, and the work of organizing Massachusetts and of enlisting Soldiers' Aid Societies, wherever they were found to exist, began in earnest. Maine may be termed the pioneer Corps in woman's work, but to Massachusetts must be given the proud title of the army of possession, marching bravely forward and planting their banners on the outmost lines.

In Massachusetts we find these patriotic women laying their foundations broad and well. A faithful following of the Grand Army is the policy. Charters, badges, seals, blanks, returns, reports, inspections, everything is planned for the great National Association, which is in itself both a prophecy and a dream. Not until thirteen Corps were formed was there a ritual printed. Important revisions were made at each Convention, and not for two years was a printed copy to be had. In 1880 New Hampshire, having promptly taken up the work, united with Massachusetts in the formation of the Union Board. In 1882, Connecticut joined the advancing column, and in 1883, Massachusetts had the proud and well-earned satisfaction of having her work adopted in National Convention. Maine declined all overtures to unite, holding herself aloof on the eligibility question.

ARRANGEMENTS FOR THE CALIFORNIA EXCURSION.

From General Order issued by Mrs. S. Agnes Parker, Department President, June 28, 1886.

The Council of Administration met June 10, in Boston, and filled vacancies in the list of delegates to the National Convention at San Francisco.

It is earnestly desired that the Department of Massachusetts will send a full representation. It is expected every one entitled to act as a representative will promptly attend each session.

Headquarters will be established at the Occidental Hotel, where all members and friends of our Order are most cordially invited.

The New England delegation will leave Boston July 22. The route to and from California selected by this Department is the same as that selected by the G.A.R. of Massachusetts, viz.: *Outward* — Hoosac Tunnel, West Shore, Great Western, Chicago and Grand Trunk to Chicago; from Chicago, via Chicago, Milwaukee and St. Paul, Union and Central Pacific. *Return* — Southern Pacific Co. to New Orleans; from New Orleans via Queen Crescent route to Cincinnati, through the Kenesaw Valley, and the cities of Chattanooga, Mobile and Montgomery, and thence to Boston, via Fitchburg Railroad and its connections.

Tickets can be procured from J. R. Watson, No. 250 Washington Street, from July 3 to July 22, on presentation of a certificate from these Headquarters. Price, $87.50, round trip.

COURTESIES EXTENDED NATIONAL PRESIDENTS.

From report of Mrs. Rose A. Knapp, Delegate-at-Large to the Sixth National Convention at Columbus, O., 1888, to the Tenth Department Convention of Massachusetts, 1889.

Referring to her New England visit, Mrs. Emma R. Hampton, National President, said: —

"In Massachusetts the Convention was *large*, *enthusiastic*, and the work ably handled. The courtesies and friendliness extended by the officers to the National President (a comparative stranger) have grown by frequent interchange into warm and enduring friendship."

Mrs. Cora Day Young, National Senior Vice-President, also referred to the hospitalities extended her while in Massachusetts.

From General Order, Mrs. Mary E. Knowles, Department President, March 4, 1890.

During the Convention Mrs. Annie Wittenmyer, National President, honored us with her presence.

The eloquent words that came from her lips, the earnestness with which she urged us to remember the principles of our Order, Fraternity, Charity and Loyalty, made an impression on our minds and hearts which time will not efface.

At the Annual Convention in 1894,

Mrs. Sarah C. Mink, National President, after expressing thanks for the courtesies extended her, said : —

"I feel perfectly at home in Massachusetts. I recognize that my election to this office is due to the support given me at Indianapolis by the delegates from your Department. The first quarterly report received, and the first response to my call for the Relief Fund, came from your Headquarters. I have long sought to attend a Massachusetts Convention, and I am gratified with this visit, which will be a help to me during the rest of the year."

From address of Mrs. Sarah C. Mink, National President, at the Twelfth National Convention, Pittsburg, Pa., September, 1894.

The National Secretary accompanied me to the Department Convention of Massachusetts, where we were most cordially welcomed and hospitably entertained.

The reception tendered the Commander-in-Chief (their own much-loved "Jack Adams") and National President was the largest and most enthusiastic it has ever been my privilege to attend.

The Governor and his official Staff honored the occasion with their presence, and together with the Commander-in-Chief and Staff, Department Commander and Staff, Commander-in-Chief Sons of Veterans and Staff, all in uniform, united with the brilliant lights which shone on fair women and brave men, the music, flowers and eloquent words of commendation of the work of the Woman's Relief Corps, rendered it a never-to-be-forgotten occasion.

SONS OF VETERANS.

The most friendly relations have existed between the Woman's Relief Corps and the Sons of Veterans. The "Sons" have been invited to the annual receptions and other public gatherings of the Department and its leading officers have participated in the programme. Local Corps and Camps often co-operate together in work for the veterans.

WORLD'S FAIR.

At a meeting of the Department Council held Feb. 10, 1893, a telegram was received from Mrs. Margaret R. Wickins, National President, requesting that some action be taken by the Department of Massachusetts, in aid of the Woman's Relief Corps exhibit in the Woman's Building at the World's Fair.

Voted, on motion of Mrs. Deane, Department Counselor, That a reply be sent the National President, pledging the support of this Council.

The sum of $50.00 was subsequently forwarded by Mrs. Emily L. Clark, Department President, who also secured, through the kindness of Mr. Charles O. Eaton, a silk bannerette, which designated the "Mother Department."

Many of our members visited the World's Columbian Exposition, and the register at the Woman's Relief Corps Headquarters in the Woman's Building contained the names of numerous members who represented the " Mother Department " of the Woman's Relief Corps.

COMMITTEE TO VISIT INSANE ASYLUMS.

In compliance with Section 5 of National General Orders No. 4, referring to special work in behalf of veterans who are inmates of Insane Asylums, Mrs. Emily L. Clark, Department President, appointed in 1893 the following Committees to visit the Asylums named : —

McLean Asylum, Somerville . . .	Rose A. Knapp, Corps 21.
South Boston Asylum	Tryphena C. Berry, Corps 20.
Taunton Asylum	Harriet E. Howard, Corps 120.
Worcester Hospital or Asylum .	Anna H. Burbank, Corps 11.
Northampton Asylum	Sarah Bodman, Corps 18.
Danvers Hospital	Clara A. Pillsbury, Corps 12.
Tewksbury Hospital	Hallie E. Perry, Corps 33.
Westboro Asylum	Alice J. Forbush, Corps 80.
Winthrop Hospital	Samantha Sparhawk, Corps 126.

ANNUAL REUNIONS.

The first summer entertainment given by this Department was at Nantasket Beach, June 29, and was considered a social success. We were honored by the presence of Commander-in-Chief Weissert, Adjutant-General Gray of Milwaukee, Wis., Inspector-General Goodale, Department Commander Hall and many of his Staff, and a large number of comrades and Sons of Veterans, who united with us in a most enjoyable day. General Weissert gave an additional proof of his endorsement of our Order by taking the long journey to be with us and tell us in his own eloquent words his faith in woman's work in aid of the veterans. Ex-Gov. John D. Long also added much to our pleasure by his presence and encouraging, hopeful words. It was the desire of the committee having the affair in charge to combine pleasure and profit — that while we enjoyed a delightful, social day with the comrades and friends, we could also add something to our General Fund. In that we were not disappointed, as the net proceeds were $130.71, which were turned over to the Department President, and by her order placed in the General Fund. — From report of Mrs. Sarah E. Fuller, Department Treasurer, at the Fifteenth Annual Convention, Boston, Feb. 8, 1894.

(Arrangements for the first reunion were in charge of Sarah E. Fuller, Mary E. Elliot, Helen A. Brigham, Emilie L. W. Waterman and Sarah J. Williamson, Committee.)

The second Annual Reunion was held at Bass Point, Nahant, June 28. The day was all we could desire, and the attendance estimated at about fifteen hundred. We were honored by the presence of Commander-in-Chief John G. B. Adams, Adjt.-Gen. James F. Meech, Department Commander Wilfred A. Wetherbee, Asst. Adjt.-Gen. H. O. Moore, Past Commander-in-Chief Geo. S. Merrill, Past J. V. Commander-in-Chief John C. Linehan, Mrs. Julia K. Dyer, President of the Boston Charity Club, and other prominent comrades and ladies. Socially, it was pronounced a decided success. — From report of Mrs. Sarah E. Fuller, Department Treasurer, at the Sixteenth Annual Convention, Springfield, Feb. 13, 1895.

(A committee, consisting of Sarah E. Fuller, Clare H. Burleigh, Emilie L. W. Waterman and Lizzie F. Mudgett, had charge of the second annual reunion.)

The Third Annual Reunion of the Department of Massachusetts was held at Nantasket Beach, June 27, 1895, and was a very enjoyable occasion. Notwithstanding a heavy rain, several hundred people were present.

Addresses were made in the Arena by John E. Gilman, Department Inspector, G.A.R., Mrs. Eva T. Cook, Department President, Mrs. E. Florence Barker, Past National President, Mrs. L. A. Turner, Past National Senior Vice-President, J. G. B. Adams, Past Commander-in-Chief, Mrs. W. A. Bancroft, President Ladies' Aid Association, Soldiers' Home, and Fred Bolton, Division Commander Sons of Veterans.

Mrs. Mary E. Knowles, Chairman Department Committee on Patriotic Teaching, had charge of the Flag Salutes, given by pupils of the

Somerville High School. Mrs. Nellie Brown Mitchell sang the Star Spangled Banner, and Prescott Fuller, the little grandson of Mrs. Sarah E. Fuller who presided, waved the flag. Miss Adelaide J. Griggs, contralto soloist of the Park Street Church, Boston, rendered musical selections, and Mrs. Mary E. Knowles, Past National Chaplain, added to the pleasure of the entertainment by her readings.

The Committee of Arrangements consisted of Sarah E. Fuller, Mary L. Gilman, Etta A. Lockhart, Harriet A. Chamberlain, Dorcas H. Lyman, Mary E. Knowles and Mary F. White.

DISTRICT EXEMPLIFICATIONS.

It was the custom at the early Conventions to exemplify the ritualistic work of the Order at one of the sessions. In 1887, Corps 11 of Worcester was invited to exemplify the work, the Assistant Inspectors and Corps Presidents of the State being present.

For several years a series of District Exemplifications have been conducted in various parts of the State, and the gatherings which are held in May and June awaken great interest, not only by the Corps under whose auspices they are conducted, but by all who attend. They are under the supervision of the Department President and Department Inspector, who have charge of all the assignments, etc. The entire ritualistic work is performed, and the method of preparing and presenting reports and all business forms of the Order are thoroughly shown. Instruction is given when needed, the general work and plans of the Woman's Relief Corps discussed, and an interest aroused in all branches of the work.

The social features of the gatherings are pleasant, and a camp-fire, reception or social generally held in the evening when comrades of the Grand Army of the Republic are guests.

NATIONAL COUNCIL OF WOMEN FUND.

The sum of $163.00 has been forwarded to this fund from the Department of Massachusetts, the amount of contributions raised through the efforts of Mrs. Lue Stuart Wadsworth, a member of the National Committee.

WOMAN'S RELIEF CORPS.

From address of Wilfred A. Wetherbee, at the Twenty-eighth Annual Encampment of the Department of Massachusetts, G.A.R., held in Springfield Feb. 13, 1895.

This organization, composed not only of our mothers, wives and daughters, but of all loyal women, is entitled to our grateful thanks for the large sums expended for the relief of our needy comrades and their families, the support given to Posts by many deeds of kindness, and the enthusiasm manifested in carrying on their great work of charity and of spreading abroad all over our land lessons of loyalty and patriotism.

Through the efforts of this Order many weak Posts have been strengthened and given new life. I recommend that all Posts not so blessed (and there are but few) shall take immediate action, having for its object the establishing of a Corps.

From report of Mrs. Harriette A. Burrows (Delegate-at-Large to the National Convention at Pittsburgh, Pa., September, 1894), presented to the Department Convention of Massachusetts, Feb. 13, 1895: —

Massachusetts Headquarters were established at the Monongahela House, (Room 17), and there a meeting of the delegates was called at 10 A.M. Monday (September 11).

In the afternoon the visitors were taken to a drive about the city, and later in the day Mrs. George Westinghouse threw open the doors of her beautiful home and royal indeed was the welcome and entertainment extended to the visitors. During the evening Massachusetts was serenaded in Headquarters by the Lynn Band.

Tuesday was the day of the great parade, and every Massachusetts woman was invited to a seat upon the reviewing stand of the Commander-in-Chief, our own "Captain Jack." As we watched the "old boys" marching so proudly by, we realized that in a few short years at the most, we shall look upon the last one of these grand parades. Even now we miss many dear forms from the ranks: husbands and fathers, sons and brothers gone before; and we know that soon the last old soldier will be summoned home by the "great Commander of us all." Let each one of us so employ our time that when we are called to the great Headquarters above, there will be some there who will say, "She lived not for herself alone."

Tuesday evening was the time set apart for the reception to be given by the Department of Massachusetts Woman's Relief Corps, in their Headquarters at the Monongahela House, and from 8 to 10 the room was thronged with the visitors from nearly every State throughout the length and breadth of the land; all seeming happy to look into the faces and grasp the hands of the women from the " Mother Department." It was estimated that fully one thousand people attended the reception, including the Commander-in-Chief and National President, with their respective Staffs, Past Commander-in-Chiefs, Past National Presidents, Commanders and Presidents from many Departments, and the entire Massachusetts delegation of the Grand Army of the Republic. Many prominent residents of Pittsburgh also graced the occasion by their presence.

* * * * * * * *

In connection with the report of the National Chaplain, I would like to call attention to the statement that eighty-one Corps in the National organization sent contributions for Memorial Day *outside* their own Departments, and *fifty-nine* of these were Massachusetts Corps.

The report of the National Inspector shows Massachusetts still in advance in number of members, with $9,889.19 turned over to Posts.

* * * * * * * *

Previous to the National Convention, our honored Past Department President, Mrs. Mary G. Deane, was earnestly urged by many friends in Massachusetts, to allow the use of her name for the office of National President; for they felt that her personal worth as a woman, her valued services in her own Department, and her qualifications for the position would ensure a most successful administration in case of her election. Upon the assembling of Convention in Pittsburgh, this sentiment was also expressed by prominent friends in many other Departments. Mrs. Deane declined in a gracefully worded speech.

SALUTE TO THE FLAG.

Mrs. Lue Stuart Wadsworth, who served on Committee on Patriotic Teaching in 1894, reported that she received communications from one hundred and twelve Corps asking for information regarding a flag salute. Sixty-two Corps reported to her that the salute is already adopted; and forty-nine Corps reported progress, with indications of favorable results.

PATRIOTIC TEACHING.

Mrs. Mary E. Knowles, Committee on Patriotic Teaching, the present year (1895) has conducted a large correspondence with Corps, and distributed literature relating to patriotic teaching in public schools. She has addressed public flag meetings in various sections of the State, and visited Corps meetings in behalf of this educational patriotic work.

When journeying to the National Conventions at Denver, Minneapolis, San Francisco and other western cities, the members of the W.R.C. have enjoyed the beautiful scenery and noted places along the line of the Fitchburg Railroad and its connections.

Mr. J. R. Watson, General Passenger Agent of the Fitchburg R.R. (the Hoosac Tunnel route), has taken special interest in the plans of the W.R.C., and has for many years been regarded as a friend to the auxiliary of the G.A.R.

The excursions to Washington, D.C., in 1892, and Louisville, Ky., in 1895, were over the Baltimore & Ohio R.R., and the efforts of its New England Agent, Mr. A. J. Simmons, to make these trips to the battlefields of the South occasions of special interest, are appreciated.

In all the reports of Department Presidents, reference has been made to the valuable assistance rendered by Mr. E. B. Stillings, the official printer.

He has been a faithful friend from the first; his excellent judgment and advice and his thoughtful interest for the welfare of the Department, have been a great help to the officials and committees connected with the work at Headquarters.

Mr. Stillings is a member of E. W. Kinsley Post No. 113 of Boston, and is also the official printer of the G.A.R. of Massachusetts.

A systematic plan of reporting the work of Corps to Department Headquarters is one of the methods adopted by our Order, and numerous reports are filed at Headquarters, showing the condition of the work throughout the State. The following blank for reporting amounts expended for *special objects* has been issued by this Department for several years.

BLANK B.

FOR REPORT OF SPECIAL WORK.

Mrs... President Corps No......................

Madam:

This blank is to be filled out by the Corps Treasurer and forwarded with the reports for the fourth quarter to the Department Secretary.

Amount expended from Jan. 1, 18 , to Jan. 1, 18 , viz.:—

Turned over to Post	$................
For Department Relief Fund	$................
For Soldiers' Home	$.
For Soldiers or their relatives	$................
For National W.R.C. Home	$................
For Memorial Fund	$................
For Invalid Veterans' Fund (Department)	$................
For Memorial Day Work (in your town or city)	$................
For Memorial Day in the South	$................
For permanent Memorials (halls, monuments, urns, etc.)	$................
For patriotic work in Public Schools	$................

.....Corps President.

................................Corps Secretary.

NATIONAL RELIEF FUND.

Mrs. Sarah C. Mink, National President, in her annual address at Pittsburgh, Pa., September, 1894, said: —

I called upon Department Presidents for a small contribution from each Department Relief Fund, the aggregate of which would establish a National Relief Fund. I was deeply touched by the quick response to this request, for in a few days after sending the letter, Massachusetts responded with $25.00, which was immediately followed by donations from all other Departments that were financially able to do so.

Of the sum thus obtained, $50.00 were distributed by Mrs. Harriette L. Reed of Massachusetts, among the colored soldiers' families in Beaufort and Hilton Head, South Carolina, who were sufferers from the tidal wave which swept all of the earthly possessions of the inhabitants of these islands into the sea, and left a thousand dead on the sands.

Mrs. Turner, National President, 1895, has received contributions to the National Relief Fund from Corps in Massachusetts.

TRIBUTE TO THE MEMORY OF GENERAL LOGAN.

Presented by Mrs. Lucy M. James, Past President, William Logan Rodman Corps No. 53, New Bedford, at the Annual Convention, January, 1887.

Resolutions in memory of Gen. John A. Logan.

Resolved, That in the death of Gen. John A. Logan, the Woman's Relief Corps has lost a firm and true friend; the Grand Army of the Republic an earnest and faithful comrade; the disabled veteran an influential friend who never failed to advance the cause of "him who bore the battle, and his widow and orphans;" his country a senator as wise in counsel as he was brave in battle; the whole world an honest, upright man.

Resolved, That the love and sympathy of this Convention is hereby tendered to our sister member, Mrs. Mary A. Logan, whose loss is greater than all others, and that every tap of the gavel, muffled with the badge of mourning for her illustrious husband, brings us a loving thought of our beloved sister.

TRIBUTE TO THE MEMORY OF MRS. CARRIE SCOTT HARRISON.

We have extended to the President of the United States the heartfelt sympathy of the Woman's Relief Corps of Massachusetts, in the loss of his estimable wife, who was a member of our Order and interested in all the work for the Grand Army of the Republic.

While the nations of the world and the various organizations of our land are offering their tributes of honor, it is fitting that we place on record our expression of regard for her memory. We shall ever remember her as one of the noblest of American women. — From General Order issued by Mrs. Mary G. Deane, Department President, Nov. 1, 1892.

TRIBUTE TO THE MEMORY OF GENERAL BUTLER.

Another hero of the Civil War, whom the nation honors as one of its greatest soldiers, has passed away. The patriotic services of Major-General Benjamin F. Butler, his interest in the veterans and his comradeship in the Grand Army of the Republic, all entitle him to be gratefully remembered by the women of America. — From General Order issued by Mrs. Mary G. Deane, Department President, Jan. 10, 1893.

MARY E. ELLIOT

Fourth Department Secretary 1885—1895

APPENDIX C.

MESSAGES.

THESE messages indicate the pleasant relations existing between the Department of Massachusetts Woman's Relief Corps and its friends in this and other States. They are a few of the many fraternal greetings that have been extended to us in the past.

MESSAGE FROM MISS CLARA BARTON.

ALBANY, TEXAS. Feb. 3, 1887.

MARY E. ELLIOT,
Department Secretary, Woman's Relief Corps.

Dear Miss Elliot: It is very late to acknowledge your cordial invitation to the meetings of the 27th and 28th ult., but those days found me *en route* for Texas; the painful reports of suffering in that region enlisted the sympathies of the Red Cross, and claimed its attention the latter part of the month of January. Dr. Hubbell and myself left Washington for this point. I need not say how much I should have enjoyed being present at the meeting, nor need I say how appreciative I am of the thoughtful invitation. I am hearing always the best reports of the Relief Corps of our beloved old State, and knowing those engaged in it, I feel how well deserved they are.

Hoping at no distant day to meet you, and with great love to all, I remain,

Affectionately yours,

CLARA BARTON.

HOUSE OF REPRESENTATIVES,
WASHINGTON, D.C., Jan. 30, 1888.
MRS. S. AGNES PARKER,
President Woman's Relief Corps, Dept. of Mass.

Dear Madam: Your very kind invitation of the 27th inst. to attend a public reception under the auspices of your Department on the evening of February 9 next, is at hand, and for which please accept my heartfelt thanks.

Remembering how much I enjoyed a similar occasion a year ago, I should be more than glad to be present, but I feel that I can best show my interest in what your noble organization stands for by staying right here at my present post of duty; for it is here that the soldiers' cause needs most friends, voices and votes, and it is here that I can give it one of each.

In the little time allotted to me here, I hope I may never forget that such as you and your organization, that are so near to the people (the source of all power), are trying not to push us, but to lead us up to the realization of the fact that the most deserving of this Republic are its gallant, maimed and aging saviors. With my best wishes and thanks,

I am in F., C. and L.,
Yours very truly,
WILLIAM COGSWELL.

Message received at the Department Convention Feb. 13, 1889.

Mrs. President: Words fail me in attempting to convey to you, and through you to your noble co-workers in the Woman's Relief Corps of the Department of Massachusetts, the thanks of Mrs. Warner and myself for the beautiful basket of flowers this day sent us.

These roses may wither, but I beg to assure you that the grateful remembrance of this mark of your esteem will ever remain fresh in our memories.

Yours in F., C. and L.,
WM. WARREN,
Commander-in-Chief, G.A.R.

THE PENNSYLVANIA SOLDIERS' AND SAILORS' HOME,
ERIE, PENNSYLVANIA.
PHILADELPHIA, Feb. 3, 1890.

MRS. EMMA B. LOWD,
Department President, Woman's Relief Corps.

Dear Madam: It will be impossible for me to accept your kind invitation to the reception to the Grand Army on Thursday evening.

The organization of the Woman's Relief Corps has been a blessing to the Grand Army of the Republic in the continued practical assistance given in every phase of its relief work, and certainly every member in Massachusetts must rejoice in the grand record made in the past year and all other years of its history.

I am confident in the belief that you will not rest under the laurels of past victories, but go on in the good work as long as any old veteran or his family stand in need of your kind ministrations.

Very truly yours,
ROBT. B. BEATH,
Past Commander-in-Chief, G.A.R.

Messages received at the Twelfth Annual Convention, Boston, Feb. 11, 1891.

DENVER, COL., Feb. 7, 1891.

MARY E. KNOWLES,
President Department of Massachusetts, Woman's Relief Corps, and members of the Twelfth Annual Convention: —

Here from the foot of the Rocky Mountains we send fraternal greetings to our Eastern sisters, convened in Boston for the purpose of arranging plans for the work of love and charity — a work in which we are all so deeply interested.

We who shared your kind and generous hospitality during the late National Convention held in Boston, will ever feel grateful for the many courtesies extended us, and in behalf of the ladies of the Department of Colorado and Wyoming, who were recipients of your noble generosity, I take this opportunity of tendering our heartfelt gratitude, and sincerely trust that the mottoes of our Order — Fraternity, Charity and Loyalty — will be the ruling spirit of your Convention.

Yours in F., C. and L.,
AMERICA ANDERSON,
Department President.

OFFICE OF PRESIDENT,
BRODHEAD, WIS., Feb. 10, 1891.
MRS. MARY E. KNOWLES,
Department President,
Boston, Mass.

Dear Mrs. President : To you and the Woman's Relief Corps sisters in Department Convention assembled, the Woman's Relief Corps of Wisconsin sends cordial greeting.

The memories of Tremont Temple and the throng of intelligent women gathered there last summer are still fresh in our minds, and we recall with pleasure the faces of the Massachusetts sisters who gave us such kindly welcome.

That your deliberations at this time may result, not only in the increased prosperity of your own Department, but in the advancement of our fundamental principles in the hearts of all the people, is the earnest wish of

Yours in F., C. and L.,
HELEN HOLMES CHARLTON,
Department President.

COMMONWEALTH OF MASSACHUSETTS,
EXECUTIVE DEPARTMENT,
BOSTON, Jan. 25, 1893.
MRS. MARY G. DEANE,
President Department of Mass. W.R.C.,
Boston. Mass.

My Dear Madam : It is with greatest regret I find that an important engagement long since made for the evening of February 9 will deprive me of the pleasure of attending the reception of your Corps. It is a great disappointment to me not to be able to come, as I should enjoy extremely meeting the noble patriotic women who through your Corps have done such splendid work for the veterans.

Permit me in behalf of the Commonwealth, who has always taken a deep interest in everything that concerns the veterans, to express her thanks for these useful services of your Corps, and her earnest wish for its continued prosperity.

Thanking you most heartily for your kind invitation, and with sincere regret that I cannot accept it, I am

Very truly yours,
WM. E. RUSSELL.

Greetings from Past National President, Mrs. Kinne. Read at Annual Convention in Boston, 1894, viz.: —

SAN FRANCISCO, Jan. 31, 1894.

MRS. EMILY L. CLARK,
Department President, Mass. W.R.C.

Dear Madam: Your very kind invitation to attend your next Department Convention, to be held in Boston on February 7, received, and I assure you I know of nothing that would give me greater pleasure than to be present upon that occasion; but the weary waste of miles stretching between the Atlantic and Pacific shores will make it impossible.

The distance never seems so great except when the desire to be with my many friends in dear old Boston is greatest. I have never yet been weaned from my old home and friends, although I have lived in San Francisco twenty-seven years. I have watched with pride and interest the grand work accomplished by the army of the Woman's Relief Corps workers in the Old Bay State; and the record of your last quarter's work alone, as published in General Orders, you may well be proud of. The men of Massachusetts proved themselves an honor to their State and country during the great Civil War, and the women of Massachusetts have ably shown that they are well fitted to stand beside the noble heroes whom they love to honor.

Please present my congratulations to the Convention and my regrets that I cannot be present.

Trusting that your Convention may prove a pleasant and profitable occasion, and with loving remembrances,

Yours sincerely,
ELIZABETH D'ARCY KINNE,
National Counselor, W.R.C.

Message from Past National President, Mrs. Sherwood.

CANTON, OHIO, Feb. 3, 1894.

MRS. EMILY L. CLARK,
President Department Mass. W.R.C.

Dear Madam: To you and the Department of Massachusetts, W.R.C., and to your honored guests, Commander-in-Chief John G. B. Adams and National President Sarah C. Mink, I send my warmest greetings. A Massachusetts Relief Corps reception is the modern joust of chivalry, where all that is knightly and heroic in man honors all that is lovely and excellent in woman. My heart is with you, and, with thanks for the remembrance, I am very sincerely,

Yours in F., C. and L.,
KATE B. SHERWOOD,
Past National President.

From records of Department Convention, Feb. 7, 1894.

MESSAGE TO CORPORAL TANNER.

Mrs. Turner moved, That a telegram of sympathy be sent Corporal Tanner, who lies in a hospital at Brooklyn, N.Y.

Seconded by Mrs. Barker, who stated that she was preparing a message to forward Corporal Tanner. She referred to his eloquent plea for the recognition of the National Woman's Relief Corps at Denver, when he said to the National Encampment: "I shall not go out of this Encampment with the same pride that I entered it, if you refuse to recognize this organization of women." Mrs. Barker then alluded to Corporal Tanner's last address, which was delivered in the Opera House at Washington ten days ago, in behalf of a plan — conceived by him — in aid of poor veterans who are out of employment.

The motion to send a telegram was carried; and Mrs. Barker presented the following message, which was adopted: —

May the Great Commander of us all give you strength to continue the fight for life that is so precious to all your comrades and their auxiliary. Accept for yourself and for the noble woman who watches beside you our admiration and sincere sympathy.

The following reply was received February 8.

DEAR MRS. BARKER:

I am a couple of inches shorter than yesterday, and of course it is agonizing, but nerve is good yet.

Your sympathy is sweet to a suffering man.

Love to all,
JAMES TANNER.

APPENDIX D.

RECEPTIONS AND CAMP-FIRES.

EACH year since the Department of Massachusetts was formed, a reception, camp-fire or similar public gathering has been a feature of our Annual Conventions. These occasions have been attended by Department officers and other members of the G.A.R. of Massachusetts, and for the past ten years National officers of that organization have also participated.

On the evening of Jan. 28, 1886, Commander-in-Chief Samuel S. Burdette of Washington, D.C., Senior Vice-Commander-in-Chief Seldon Connor (ex-governor of Maine), and Past Commander-in-Chief Paul Van Der Voort of Nebraska were among the speakers. They were accompanied by Department Commander Richard F. Tobin, Past Department Commanders J. W. Hersey and George L. Goodale, Col. Thomas E. Barker, E. B. Stillings and other distinguished comrades.

Mrs. S. Agnes Parker, Department President, in referring to their presence at this reception, said : —

"I cannot find words to express my thanks to them for their kind counsel, the deep interest they manifested in our Order, and the eloquent words of tribute from all who spoke on that occasion."

The Convention of 1887 closed January 27 with a reception to Commander-in-Chief Lucius Fairchild (ex-Governor of Wisconsin) and the Grand Army of the Republic of Massachusetts. Horticultural Hall, Boston, was filled with an interested audience. Musical selections were rendered by the Grand Army Quartet of Chelsea and addresses were made by General Fairchild, Commander-in-Chief, Judge Advocate-General Henry Taintor of Connecticut, Aide-de-Camp S. B. Jones of Nebraska, Maj. George S. Merrill. Past Commander-in-Chief, and by Gen. William Cogswell, J. G. B. Adams, George S. Evans and John W. Hersey, Past Department Commanders.

This meeting resulted in several Corps being formed.

Judge John P. Rea of Minnesota, Commander-in-Chief G.A.R., was given a reception in Parker Memorial Hall, Boston, on the evening of Feb. 9, 1888, when an elaborate floral design was presented by Capt. B. Read Wales on behalf of the Department Encampment, G.A.R., and addresses were made by Department Commander Myron P. Walker, Past Department Commander Geo. S. Evans, Capt. Jack Crawford (the poet scout), General G. B. Abbott, Commander-in-Chief Sons of Veterans, and others.

A reception was tendered Commander-in-Chief William Warner and Staff, Department Commander Geo. L. Goodale and Staff, on the evening of Feb. 13, 1889, at Bromfield Street Church, Boston. Among other guests present were Colonel Upham, Division Commander Sons of Veterans, Capt. James F. Meech, Honorary member, Past Junior Vice-Commander-in-Chief, John C. Linehan and Past Department Commanders Adams, Creasey, Hersey and Walker.

Mrs. Warner, wife of the Commander-in-Chief, was present, under escort of Inspector-General Evans.

A public installation of officers and reception to the Grand Army of the Republic, was held in Tremont Temple, Boston, Feb. 6, 1890, and attended by over two thousand persons.

At eight o'clock P.M. the Reception Committee entered the Temple, accompanied by Commander-in-Chief Russell A. Alger,

Mrs. Alger, Mrs. Annie Wittenmyer, National President W.R.C., Department Commander George H. Innis, Department Senior Vice-Commander Arthur A. Smith, Assistant Adjutant-General A. C. Monroe, Past Department Commanders A. S. Cushman, George S. Merrill, J. G. B. Adams, George S. Evans, John W. Hersey, and George L. Goodale, James F. Meech, Honorary Member W.R.C., Silas A. Barton, Secretary Executive Committee for the National Encampment, and others.

On the evening of Feb. 12, 1891, a camp-fire was held in Tremont Temple, when Commander-in-Chief Wheelock G. Veazey and Mrs. Veazey, Adjutant-General L. S. Emery of Washington, D.C.; Governor Russell was represented by Col. Walter U. Cutting, a member of his Staff; Department Commander Arthur A. Smith and Staff, Past Department Commanders Adams, Evans and Innis, James Burrows (of Post 11, Charlestown), Col. Wm. Stevens, Division Commander Sons of Veterans, Mrs. Julia K. Dyer, President Ladies' Aid Association of the Soldiers' Home, and others participated. Tremont Temple was filled with Posts, Relief Corps and their friends.

A reception was given at the Meionaon on the evening of February 11, 1892, in honor of Commander-in-Chief John M. Palmer and Staff, and the Grand Army of the Republic of Massachusetts, which was a very pleasant social gathering.

The Grand Army of the Republic was also received at the Meionaon, Feb. 9, 1893, and invited guests, numbering a thousand, were present. Corporal Tanner, Department Commander Eli W. Hall and Staff were prominent participants. The installation of officers formed a part of the exercises.

On the evening of Feb. 8, 1894, a camp-fire was held in the Peoples Church, Boston, and attended by over three thousand persons.

Among the guests were His Excellency Governor Greenhalge and Staff, Commander-in-Chief Adams and Staff, Department Commander W. A. Wetherbee and Staff, Joseph B. Maccabe,

Commander-in-Chief Sons of Veterans, Capt. George W. Creasey, Superintendent Soldiers' Home, and many other friends.

By vote of the Department Council of the G.A.R., a Union camp-fire was held in the City Hall, Springfield, at the close of the Encampment and Convention, Feb. 14, 1895.

Mrs. Emma R. Wallace, National President, Mrs. Clare H. Burleigh, Past Department President, and Mrs. Eva T. Cook, Department President, represented the work of the Order.

Mrs. Lizabeth A. Turner having returned from the National Convention held at Louisville, Ky., in September, 1895, as National President, the following official circular was issued:—

HEADQUARTERS DEPARTMENT OF MASSACHUSETTS,
GRAND ARMY OF THE REPUBLIC,
AND
DEPARTMENT OF MASSACHUSETTS, WOMAN'S RELIEF CORPS.
BOSTON, Oct. 2, 1895.

To Post Commanders and Corps Presidents:—

Massachusetts has been honored by the Convention of the W.R.C., held at Louisville, Kentucky, in the election of Mrs. Lizabeth A. Turner to the exalted position of National President of that grand Order.

A reception to Mrs. Turner has been suggested and the undersigned, feeling assured that our comrades generally, also members of the Woman's Relief Corps, will be anxious to participate in such an event, we most respectfully request you to come or send a representative of your Post or Corps to Department Headquarters, State House, at 4 o'clock, Friday afternoon, October 4, when arrangements for said reception will be made.

Yours in F., C. and L.,
JOSEPH W. THAYER,
Commander Dept. Mass. G.A.R.

EVA T. COOK,
President Dept. Mass. W.R.C.

So great an interest was taken in the proposed reception that representatives of Posts and Corps filled Grand Army Headquarters on the afternoon designated.

A Committee of Arrangements was chosen, consisting of Joseph W. Thayer (Department Commander) as President, Mrs. Eva T. Cook (Department President) as Vice-President, E. B. Stillings of Post 113, Boston, as Secretary, and all Past Department Commanders and Past Department Presidents.

At the next meeting of the Committee, Hon. William M. Olin (Secretary of State) was elected Treasurer and Hubert O. Moore, Assistant Adjutant-General G.A.R., and the Department Secretary W.R.C. were chosen Assistant Treasurers.

Faneuil Hall, on the evening of October 24, was the scene of a brilliant gathering, when Posts in uniform, with their banners, and members of both organizations from every section of the State, gathered in honor of Mrs. Turner and to celebrate her election to the office of National President.

Decorations and patriotic designs added interest to this old historic hall, and music, songs and speeches were features of the evening's programme.

Contributions from Posts and Corps were so liberal that after all expenses of this reception were paid, a balance of two hundred dollars remained, which by vote of the Committee was presented to the Soldiers' Home in Massachusetts.

APPENDIX E.

SUMMARY OF THE NATIONAL WORK.

IT has been the aim of the committee to confine this history to a record of the work in Massachusetts, but a few statistics referring to the National Woman's Relief Corps are given in closing, to show the extent of the work that was begun in the *Old Bay State* in 1879.

Statistics from July, 1883 (date of the formation of the National W.R.C.), to July, 1895, viz. : —

Amount expended in relief (from Corps Funds)	$567,847 94
Turned over to Posts (from Corps Funds)	286,282 11
For Army Nurses (including National W.R.C. Home)	45,840 93
For relief of Johnstown sufferers	3,116 53
From National Headquarters Fund (special cases)	2,029 25
Total cash expenditures	$905,116 76
Value of relief *other than money*	251,270 00
Amount expended for Memorial Day	102,724 70
Total amount expended in relief, for Posts and Memorial Day	$1,259,111 46

Liberal sums have also been expended for other patriotic objects.

Mrs. Kate B. Sherwood, Past National President, one of the official delegates to the Triennial of the National Council of Women held in Washington, D.C., Feb. 17 to March 2 (1895), gave the following brief summary of the work accomplished: —

The Woman's Relief Corps has earned the confidence of the Grand Army of the Republic; it has proven its faith by its work. It has endowed and supports a National Relief Corps Home, for the wives and mothers of soldiers and dependent army nurses; it has led in the founding of homes in Michigan, Iowa, Wisconsin and California; it founded and supports the Memorial Home in Pennsylvania; it secured legislation for the founding of a home in New York; it secured the legislation that provides Government aid to the destitute army nurses, and that established industrial training for girls at the Ohio Orphans' Home; it has built memorial halls and monuments; it secured a united movement for patriotic teaching and a flag on every schoolhouse. They brought the work before the Council, as presented on Washington's Birthday, and expressed in the motto: "One country, one language, one flag."

In many public schools throughout the country a *salute to the flag* has been adopted through the efforts of Relief Corps Committees.

The flag meetings which are being held under the auspices of Corps in almost every State and Territory, are conducted with a spirit of enthusiasm, and although thirty years have passed since the close of the Civil War, the Woman's Relief Corps has a mission to perform in the great work of education, humanity and patriotism.

www.ingramcontent.com/pod-product-compliance
Lightning Source LLC
Chambersburg PA
CBHW020545300426
44111CB00008B/806